THE Union Generals Speak

THE Union Generals Speak

The Meade Hearings on the Battle of Gettysburg

EDITED BY BILL HYDE

LOUISIANA STATE UNIVERSITY PRESS
Baton Rouge

Manufactured in the United States of America
First printing
12 11 10 09 08 07 06 05 04 03
5 4 3 2 1

Designer: Laura Roubique Gleason
Typeface: Minion text, Birch display
Typesetter: Crane Composition, Inc.
Printer and binder: Thomson-Shore, Inc.

Library of Congress Cataloging-in-Publication Data:
The Union generals speak : the Meade hearings on the Battle of Gettysburg / edited by Bill Hyde.
p. cm.
Includes bibliographical references (p.) and index.
ISBN 0-8071-2581-4 (cloth : alk. paper)
1. Gettysburg, Battle of, Gettysburg, Pa., 1863—Personal narratives. 2. Meade, George Gordon, 1815–1872—Trials, litigation, etc. 3. Legislative hearings—United States. 4. Generals—United States—Interviews. 5. Witnesses—United States—Interviews. 6. United States. Congress. Joint Committee on the Conduct of the War. I. Hyde, Bill, 1945–
E475.53.U55 2003
973.7'349'0922—dc21

2002156014

The paper in this book meets the guidelines for permanence and durability of the Committee on Production Guidelines for Book Longevity of the Council on Library Resources. ♾

To my mother, Ida Mae Hyde.
Look, Ma, it's finally done.

Contents

Preface

THE CONGRESSIONAL HEARINGS ON Major General George Gordon Meade that were held in the winter of 1864 give us a unique view of the battle of Gettysburg as seen through the eyes of many of the Union officers present. The testimony not only offers eyewitness descriptions of the battle; it details the information upon which decisions affecting the outcome of the battle, and ultimately the war, were based. To the reader seeking more than a mere recitation of dates or facts, the hearings go a long way in providing answers to not just the "what," but more importantly the "why" in one of the most pivotal battles in American history.

It is difficult to pick up a modern history of the Civil War without finding some reference to the Joint Committee on the Conduct of the War. A few works, such as Bruce Tap's recent *Over Lincoln's Shoulder*, have covered the history of the committee, but the testimony itself has appeared only as verbatim copies of the transcripts, of little real value or interest except to scholars. By sifting through the often-conflicting testimony of the Union officers who actually participated in the events under investigation, the reader is given a rare firsthand view of Gettysburg. The confusion, uncertainty, and misinformation that plague even modern generals are brought into sharp focus by the words of the participants.[1]

We are not all scholars, however, and it is hoped that this edition will open up this important source document to everyone with an interest in the Civil War in general and the Gettysburg campaign in particular. The testimony of each witness is prefaced by a brief biographical account, as well as an effort to

1. Bruce Tap, *Over Lincoln's Shoulder: The Committee on the Conduct of the War* (Lawrence: University Press of Kansas, 1998).

contextualize the testimony in relation to Meade. Within the testimony itself, explanatory notes clarify obscure details and provide more in-depth explanations of events where required.

In exploring the testimony, certain things should be kept in mind. The actual field of view of a Civil War general was severely restricted, not only by the smoke of the battlefield but by his speed of movement and close involvement with his command. Though unusual, it was not unheard-of for army commanders to lead troops into the line of battle (as Meade himself did at Gettysburg). A general's perception of an event was often skewed by these limitations.

Obviously, the personal prejudices of the witnesses affected their testimony. The army was not a single-minded mass imbued with an "all for one and one for all" spirit. Instead, the antebellum army was subject to the same forces that were at work in the nation as a whole. Once war had broken out, the internal problems of the antebellum army were lessened with the resignations of officers going south. But almost immediately, there was the added complication of the influx of politically appointed officers. The army became, if anything, even more fractured as politics within the Union began to play among its ranks.

Two of the major cliques in the army, supporting or opposing General George B. McClellan, were at odds over the methods and goals of the war itself. This split over McClellan paralleled the political divisions in the Congress. McClellan, a Democrat and eventual presidential candidate, favored a reconciliation with the South. An able administrator, he assembled a high command composed of like-minded and loyal officers, who attributed an almost godlike status to their general. Like McClellan, many of these officers were graduates of West Point; the conservative nature of the academy at the time, and the fact that many officers and cadets came from the South, meant that there were large numbers of Democrats in the officer corps. Democrats and those who opposed the Lincoln administration represented a substantial minority of the population in the North and the army, but McClellan became the lightning rod for radical Republicans and the symbol of opposition and defeat to the members of the committee.

McClellan was not the only center of divisiveness within the army. Every commander of the Army of the Potomac had his adherents and detractors, and Meade was no different. The committee hearings on Meade's command of the Army of the Potomac reveal a strong after-the-fact anti-Meade sentiment among some of his officers. While there is no evidence that such feeling affected the battle of Gettysburg itself, these officers enthusiastically worked for Meade's removal from command after the battle.

The role of the Joint Committee on the Conduct of the War in bringing us this treasure trove of information adds an additional level of complexity to the testimony. The committee was decidedly political. Far from being a mere investigative body, the committee consisted of strong-willed, politically powerful men who, for good or bad, were determined to impose their wills on how the army, and the war, was to be run. By attempting—sometimes successfully—to impose their opinions upon Lincoln and his cabinet members, members of the committee played a significant role in the prosecution of the war.

The hearings on Meade, then, were not simply exercises in fact gathering. Far from it. For the most part, the committee aimed to justify a decision reached before the hearings even began: that Meade should be replaced by General Joseph "Fighting Joe" Hooker. The hearings were not intended to be, nor were they, a fair representation of the battle of Gettysburg; they were instead a device to point up the shortcomings and failures of Meade.

Despite the testimony's faults as history, and there are many, the hearings still have much to offer even the novice reader. For the vast majority of us their primary lesson is that generals are, after all, merely men. War, far from being a science governed by a set of rules, is in reality an art, influenced by the background, opinions, and even the moods of its practitioners. To understand a battle, we must first understand the men who fought the battle.

Acknowledgments

I NEVER INTENDED TO write this book. The book that I started to write, and in fact the one I first submitted, was a critique of the statements made by the witnesses called before the Joint Committee for the Conduct of the War. It was my first book, and I merrily sent in the manuscript with dreams of a Pulitzer Prize dancing in my head. I was wrong. In short order a scathing report came back from the scholarly reader at LSU Press, finding fault with nearly everything except the paper my book was written on. For this I owe him or her a great debt of gratitude. The criticism included a suggestion that I look more closely at the members of the committee itself, as well as the committee's history, and that is where this book really began. The anonymous reader has opened a whole new area to me, peopled with fascinating and complicated characters.

I wanted to thank the reader by name, but he or she declined. If he or she is a teacher, this is what teaching is all about. I will always remain a grateful student.

I also owe Sylvia Frank Rodrigue, acquisition editor at LSU Press, many thanks. Her kindness, patience, and guidance have helped me through a most difficult process. It is not an understatement to say that I could not have done this without her.

I owe a special debt to two ladies at the Freeman Memorial Library in Webster, Texas, Sue Davila and Linda Wong. Their tireless efforts in helping me find and obtain obscure reference material were invaluable. I would also like to thank the staffs of the libraries at the University of Houston at Clear Lake and at Rice University for their assistance in leading me through a maze of reference material. I must also thank Bruce Tap, a leading authority on the committee, for taking the time to give me his thoughts on Joseph Hooker.

I am also indebted to those who took the time to read and comment on my work. The brilliant prose of 4:00 A.M. is easily spotted as unintelligible babble by fresher eyes. I would like to thank Jim Shreve and Gary Hickey for help in this regard. I would especially like to thank John Karl, who spent many hours reading and rereading the same sections. His suggestions and encouragement are greatly appreciated.

I owe thanks also to numerous people who, in my eagerness or absent-mindedness, I forgot to include here. I apologize most sincerely for any omissions.

Although I am greatly indebted to many individuals for their help, the responsibility for the contents, conclusions, and any errors in these pages is mine alone.

Abbreviations

B&L Robert U. Johnson and Clarence C. Buel, eds. *Battles and Leaders of the Civil War.* 4 vols. 1884–89. Reprint, New York: Thomas Yoseloff, 1956.

CCW U.S. Congress. *Report of the Joint Committee on the Conduct of the War.* 38th Cong., 2nd sess. Washington, D.C.: Government Printing Office, 1865.

DAB Dumas Malone, ed. *Dictionary of American Biography.* 20 vols. New York: Charles Scribner's Sons, 1932.

GC Edwin Coddington. *The Gettysburg Campaign: A Study in Command.* New York: Charles Scribner's Sons, 1984.

LLM George Meade. *The Life and Letters of George Gordon Meade,* ed. George Gordon Meade. 2 vols. New York: Charles Scribner's Sons, 1913.

MG Freeman Cleaves. *Meade of Gettysburg.* Norman: University of Oklahoma Press, 1960.

OR U.S. War Department. *The War of Rebellion: A Compilation of the Official Records of the Union and Confederate Armies.* 128 vols. Washington, D.C.: Government Printing Office, 1880–1901.

THE Union Generals Speak

1 A Nation Divided

With the outbreak of the Civil War, both North and South sprang to arms with all the enthusiasm they could muster. In Washington, D.C., and throughout the country there were calls for action. Senator Zachariah Chandler called on Simon Cameron, the secretary of war, to "shove your troops directly into Virginia and quarter them there." Senator Edward Baker of Oregon declared, "I want, sudden, bold, forward, determined war." The gathering rebel army was not perceived as a great obstacle. Galusha Grow, Republican Speaker of the House, reported "[b]oasts that [the Union army] could march a drove of Durham cows into Virginia and capture the State without the loss of a calf."[1]

Yet Northern convictions proved ill-founded. On July 21, 1861, in the first major battle of the war, the Union army was routed at Bull Run. Among the many casualties both sides suffered that day was the illusion of a short, grand, and glorious war. The North was angry, indignant, and in a state of shock. A ragtag rabble of rebels had amply demonstrated that the South was not going to collapse at the mere appearance of Federal troops. The men of the Second Vermont, many of whom had never seen a Southerner, minced no words. "It was a disgraceful affair the whole of it," wrote Second Lieutenant Chester K. Leach. William Young Ripely felt "ashamed, at the causeless & senseless panic which seized our men." John Lothrop Motley, minister to Vienna, wrote to his wife, "A grim winter is before us. Gather you rosebuds while you may. The war is to be a long one." The enthusiasm and confidence with which the

1. Quoted in Maynard J. Brichford, "Congress at the Outbreak of the War," *Civil War History* 3, no. 1 (March 1957): 156; *Congressional Globe*, 37th Cong., 1st sess., July 10, 1861, p. 441 (hereafter *CG*); James T. DuBois and Gertrude S. Mathews, *Galusha A. Grow: Father of the Homestead Law* (New York: Houghton Mifflin, 1917), 250.

North had greeted the war had received a severe blow. There were more blows to come.[2]

On August 10 near Springfield, Missouri, at the battle of Wilson's Creek, Union forces under General Nathaniel Lyon were defeated, losing southwest Missouri to the Confederacy. Lyon, who had played an important and well-publicized role in defending Missouri, and who was recognized throughout the North as one of the early heroes of the war, was killed in the battle.

Disasters were not limited to the battlefield. Closely following the losses at Bull Run and Wilson's Creek came the controversy surrounding General John C. Frémont's command of the Western Department, which comprised Illinois and all land west of the Mississippi. Like many of the political generals, Frémont was the wrong man for the job. Opinionated, arrogant, and headstrong, he operated his department as a personal fiefdom. On August 30, 1861, Frémont issued a proclamation from his headquarters in St. Louis declaring martial law. While this in itself was not an unusual step, Frémont added a very unusual paragraph. "The property, real and personal, of all persons in the State of Missouri who shall take up arms against the United States, or who shall be directly proven to have taken an active part with their enemies in the field, I declare to be confiscated to the public use, and their slaves, if any they have, are hereby declared freemen." Frémont had issued his own emancipation proclamation.[3]

Frémont's proclamation was greeted by many in the North, especially among the radical Republicans in Congress, as encapsulating the true aim of the war. For President Abraham Lincoln, however, it was an immense complication. Lincoln had been at pains to make the point that the war was for the preservation of the Union, not the freeing of slaves. Beyond the fact that such a step far exceeded Frémont's authority, it threatened the precarious balance of neutrality in Kentucky, a slave state. If Kentucky went over to the Confederacy, so too might Missouri and Maryland—likewise states with numerous slaveholders—thus creating a nearly impossible strategic situation for the North. Asked by Lincoln to modify the proclamation, Frémont re-

2. Bruce Allardice, "West Points of the Confederacy: Southern Military Schools and the Confederate Army," *Civil War History* 43, no. 4 (December 1997): 330; Jeffrey D. Marshall, ed., *A War of the People: Vermont Civil War Letters,* foreword by Edwin C. Bearss (Hanover, N.H.: University Press of New England, 1999), 38, 40; quoted in Carl Sandburg, *Abraham Lincoln: The Prairie Years and the War Years* (1954; reprint, New York: Harcourt Brace, 1982), 257.

3. *OR,* vol. 3, pp. 366–7.

fused. Lincoln then revoked the proclamation himself, later removing Frémont from his command.

Bull Run, Wilson's Creek, and even Frémont's zealousness might have been only rough spots in the road if the administration could have gained a military success, but time ran out. As is often the case in history, something of little significance in itself created repercussions far beyond the event. By any measure the small skirmish at Ball's Bluff on October 21, 1861, would have faded into obscurity except for one of the forty-nine Union dead, Colonel Edward D. Baker, a sitting senator and old friend of Lincoln's. Baker was a popular man in the Senate, and his death proved to be the last straw. Military disasters, political misfires, and the Frémont debacle strained the patience of a none-too-patient Congress. A nation with three times the population of its opponent, larger and stronger in every way, was not only unable to defeat the enemy but was actually losing the war. A confused country and an angry Congress wanted to know how this could happen.[4]

THE COMMITTEE

The birth of the Joint Committee on the Conduct of the War was, like the committee itself, contentious. Bruce Tap, perhaps the foremost authority on the committee, attributes its beginnings to a resolution in the House on December 2, 1861, by Roscoe Conkling, Republican from New York. Conkling's resolution called on the secretary of war to divulge any information he might have on the Ball's Bluff disaster. There is nothing to suggest that Conkling considered the formation of an investigative committee. On December 5, however, Senator Zachariah Chandler of Michigan called for a committee to be appointed "to inquire into the disasters of Bull Run and Edward's Ferry [Ball's Bluff]."[5]

With Chandler's motion for an investigation, the floodgates opened. James Lane of Kansas wanted to include the battles of Wilson's Creek and Lexington. James Grimes of Iowa wanted to include not only the battles of Belmont and Big Bethel, but the causes of all military disasters. Oddly, Chandler objected.

4. Baker was only a colonel because he would have had to resign his seat in the U.S. Senate had he accepted a higher rank. At least twice Lincoln had offered to make him a brigadier general, but Baker had turned him down.

5. Tap, *Over Lincoln's Shoulder,* 223; *CG,* 37th Cong., 2nd sess., December 2, 1861, p. 6, and December 5, 1861, p. 16.

He hoped that the Senate "would not give the committee a roving commission to go all over the United States and see whether there have been other disasters, and to inquire into their cause." Considering the enthusiasm with which Chandler did this very thing, his objection is surprising.[6]

Chandler's attempt to limit the scope of the committee was to no avail. As Senator John Sherman of Ohio declared, "In my judgment, this ought to be a committee of inquiry into the general conduct of the war." Sherman's view prevailed. On December 9, by a vote of 33 to 3, the Senate passed the resolution creating the Joint Committee on the Conduct of the War. The committee consisted of three senators and four representatives who were charged with examining all aspects of the war, with power to send for persons and papers. The following day the House unanimously agreed to the resolution, and on December 20 the committee met for the first time in the basement of the Capitol building in the old Committee on Territories room.[7]

It will help in looking into the actions of the committee if two particular convictions of its principal members are understood. Those beliefs, certainly not unique to the committee's members, shaped and influenced their attitudes toward the war and the generals they would investigate.

The first of these was an almost pathological hatred for Democrats, from either the North or the South. For the radical Republicans of the Thirty-seventh Congress, Democrats were to blame not only for the disasters the North's armies had suffered, but for the war itself. As Representative George Julian, Republican from Indiana and member of the Committee on the Conduct of the War, declared in a speech to the House, "Sir, Democratic policy not only gave birth to the rebellion, but Democrats, and only Democrats, are in arms against their country. Democrats fired on its flag at Fort Sumter. Jefferson Davis is a Democrat, and so is every God-forsaken rebel at his heels."[8]

Closely related to the radical Republicans' animosity toward Democrats was their distrust of graduates of West Point. As if through some vast conspiracy on the part of Southern Democrats, the Union army was infested with disloyal officers. "If there had been no West Point Military Academy, there would have been no rebellion. . . . That was the hot-bed from which rebellion was hatched and from thence emanated your principal traitors and conspirators," proclaimed Ben Wade, chairman of the Committee on the Conduct of the

6. *CG*, 37th Cong., 2nd sess., December 9, 1861, p. 29.

7. Ibid., 37th Cong., 2nd sess., December 5, 1861, p. 16; December 9, 1861, pp. 29, 32.

8. Ibid., 37th Cong., 3rd sess., February 18, 1863, p. 1065.

War. He did not believe "there can be found an institution on the face of the earth, or in the history of the world, that has turned out so many false, ungrateful men as have emanated from this institution." James Lane, Republican of Kansas, declared, "West Point would be the death of this Government. . . . West Point officers have the command of our armies, and have no heart in the war, no desire to save the country at the expense of slavery." Zachariah Chandler, one of the most influential members of the Committee on the Conduct of the War, was "prepared to vote to abolish West Point Academy," calling on the Senate "in God's name [to] put no more West Point officers upon us at this time."[9]

What had provoked this venomous ranting? Neither Wade nor Chandler had said a word during the Thirty-sixth Congress, when the West Point appropriations bill for that session had passed easily. The same bill in the Thirty-seventh Congress brought forth spasms of anger approaching hysteria. The difference was, of course, the war. West Point officers offered an easily identifiable "enemy alien" upon which the radicals could vent their anger.[10]

Was West Point the hatching ground of traitors and conspirators? In his books *Generals in Blue* and *Generals in Gray,* Ezra Warner lists 1,009 men serving on both sides of the Civil War who obtained the rank of brigadier general or higher, 584 for the North, 425 for the South. Of that number a little more than a third, 38 percent, had attended the academy for one year or more. A significant percentage, 41 percent, of the men who had attended West Point joined the Confederacy. In actual fact, most Confederate field officers came from Southern military schools and programs, but the brains of the rebel army, its senior leadership, came from the academy.[11]

These two concepts—that the Democrats were solely responsible for the war, and that West Point was the breeding ground for their traitorous proclivities—would dominate the thinking of the radical Republicans in Congress and on the Committee for the Conduct of the War.

9. Ibid., 37th Cong., 2nd sess., December 23, 1861, pp. 162, 164–5; 3rd sess., January 15, 1863, pp. 324, 328.

10. The debate on the academy's 1860 appropriation can be found in *CG,* 36th Cong., 1st sess., March 1860.

11. Ezra Warner, *Generals in Blue: Lives of the Union Commanders* (Baton Rouge: Louisiana State University Press, 1964), xv; Ezra Warner, *Generals in Gray: Lives of the Confederate Commanders* (Baton Rouge: Louisiana State University Press, 1959), xx; Bruce Allardice, "West Points of the Confederacy," 331.

From the outset the majority of Republican members of the committee were strongly opposed to any effort from any source toward conciliation. Committed to defeating the rebellious South, they would not accept anything less than the same commitment from the army's generals. They agreed with John Sherman of Ohio when he called on the government to "do everything to strike at rebels; confiscate their land, their houses, their slaves." Owen Lovejoy in the House, an ordained minister, declared that his fellow representatives "need not make any appeals to us about peace; . . . 'There is no peace to the wicked, saith my God'; there is no peace to these rebels and traitors, who have raised their hands against the Government." According to Chandler, "A rebel has sacrificed all his rights. He has no right to life, liberty, property, or the pursuit of happiness. Everything you give him, even his life itself, is a boon which he has forfeited." This hard-nosed approach echoed the opinions of many Republicans, helping to reestablish the extreme partisan politics that had split the nation while dooming any hopes for conciliation.[12]

As the committee began its investigation, it quickly earned a sinister reputation. It was denounced by contemporaries, who characterized it as a "mischievous organization which assumed dictatorial powers." Critics pointed out that from the very beginning, "Witnesses were summoned and examined without order; there was no cross-examination; the accused was not confronted with the witnesses nor told their names, nor the charge upon which he had been already tried, condemned, and sentenced before he was even allowed to appear. . . . The secrets of a committee may not be divulged even to the authority from which its existence is derived."[13]

The committee's secrecy rule, however, quickly became an inconvenience for committee members; their investigations had produced too much politically useful information. On July 15, 1862, with only four members present, the committee accordingly modified the secrecy rule to allow committee members to use testimony before either house of Congress. Testimony would continue to remain secret, but only to the degree (and duration) that a member of the committee wanted it to. It was a modification that was quickly, and thereafter often, put to use.

The tenure of the committee as originally established expired thirty days after the adjournment of the Thirty-seventh Congress on March 4, 1863. With

12. *CG*, 37th Cong., 2nd sess., December 9, 1861, p. 32; 1st sess., July 11, 1861, p. 75; 3rd sess., February 27, 1863, p. 1338.

13. Richard B. Irwin, "Ball's Bluff and the Arrest of General Stone," *B&L*, 2:133.

the arrival of the Thirty-eighth Congress in December 1863, the committee was reestablished and given the power of subpoena, which it had not had initially. In January 1864 the Republican caucus broadened the committee's power to include examination of military contracts.[14]

14. Hans L. Trefousse, "The Joint Committee on the Conduct of the War: A Reassessment," *Civil War History* 10, no. 1 (March 1964): 17.

2 The Major Characters

MEMBERS OF THE COMMITTEE

THE ORIGINAL MEMBERSHIP OF the Joint Committee on the Conduct of the War was selected by Vice President Hannibal Hamlin, as president of the Senate, and Speaker of the House Galusha Grow. Seniority, while a consideration, was not the final arbiter. The personal likes and aims of both Hamlin and Grow played an equally important role in constituting the committee.

A former Democrat and early supporter of Lincoln, Hamlin's strong antislavery leanings had led him to the Republican Party in 1856. Hamlin was well acquainted with two of his choices for the committee, Benjamin Wade and Zachariah Chandler, having served with both men in the Senate. When a vacant seat arose on the committee in the Thirty-eighth Congress, the Republican caucus in the Senate chose Benjamin Franklin Harding to fill it. At the time of the Meade hearings in 1864, Wade, Chandler, and Harding comprised the committee members from the Senate.[1]

Benjamin Franklin Wade of Ohio was the committee's chairman, and he dominated committee proceedings from the beginning. The tenth of eleven children, Wade was born near Springfield, Massachusetts, in 1800. As was typical of most poor white farm children, North or South, Wade's formal schooling was limited; he spent most of his youth helping his family scratch a meager living from the rocky New England soil. It is not surprising that the prospect of being a farmer held no appeal for him, and in 1821 Wade joined his three older brothers in the frontier town of Andover, Ohio. Working at jobs ranging

1. McPherson, *Battle Cry of Freedom* (New York: Oxford University Press, 1988), 220; Stewart Sifakis, *Who Was Who in the Civil War* (New York: Facts on File Publications, 1988), 175.

from laborer to schoolteacher, his restless mind soon led him to the study of law, and after passing the bar he set up a practice in Jefferson, Ohio. It was here that Wade found his true calling. After serving as prosecuting attorney for Ashtabula County, Wade was elected to the Ohio state senate in 1837. Perhaps due to his New England background or the influence of his first law partner, Joshua R. Giddings, a vehement emancipationist, Wade aligned himself with the Whigs and the antislavery movement, fighting against the introduction of stiffer fugitive-slave laws in Ohio. Wade's early biographers argued that his opposition to slavery cost him reelection in 1839; more recent scholarship, however, suggests that his loss was due to a split in the Whig Party. Nonetheless, his political career was far from over. Wade was once again elected to the Ohio state senate in 1841 and served for six years, when he was appointed presiding judge of the Third Judicial Circuit Court. While this appointment was undoubtedly an honor, it proved to be a detour in Wade's career path, for his heart was in politics. His struggles in the party trenches bore fruit in 1851. With the Whig Party beginning to show signs of its ultimate collapse, he was elected to the U.S. Senate.[2]

Described by one contemporary as a "queer, rough, but intelligent-looking man . . . who does not care a pinch of snuff whether people like what he says or not," Wade quickly carved out a niche for himself in the Senate's small antislavery group, fighting against any effort to expand slavery beyond its current limits. His politically confrontational attitude was matched by a reputation for physical confrontation as well; he often went about Washington and even onto the Senate floor armed with a pistol. By 1860 his fiery speeches and aggressive attitude toward slavery had won him so much recognition that he was briefly considered for the Republican presidential nomination.[3]

Wade's personal courage was not the bluff and bluster of a bully; in one instance, he showed himself willing to take on an army. Like many civilians, Wade—accompanied by Zachariah Chandler and several other congressmen—journeyed across the Potomac to Manassas in order to view the first battle of the war, which many people on both sides believed would be the only one necessary. As the day wore on, the battle unfolded before the spectators' eyes. Multicolored columns of blue, red, green, and gray maneuvered in the

2. *DAB*, 10:303; Vernon L. Volpe, "Benjamin Wade's Strange Defeat," *Ohio History* 97 (summer–autumn 1988): 122–32.

3. Quoted in Hans L. Trefousse, *Benjamin Wade: Radical Republican from Ohio* (New York: Twayne, 1963), 131; *DAB*, 5:303–5; H. Draper Hunt, *Hannibal Hamlin of Maine: Lincoln's First Vice President* (Syracuse, N.Y.: Syracuse University Press, 1969), 114–5.

fields below, now visible, now enveloped in rolling clouds of smoke. Old Glory snapped in the breeze as the Union army surged forward here, ebbed there. Abruptly the flags grew closer, as groups of men began streaming back toward Washington, D.C. Soon the Union retreat became a rout, mingling soldier and civilian alike in a stampede for the safety offered by the forts of Washington. Although sixty-one years old, Ben Wade was not going to be panicked by fleeing Union soldiers or an advancing rebel army. Gathering his colleagues, he drove his buggy onto a road filled with terrified Federal troops. There Wade and his friends dismounted. Brandishing rifles and pistols, they corralled the fleeing men at gunpoint. Wade would probably have formed a line and fought any pursuing rebel troops, but the arrival of a New Jersey regiment moving to the front relieved him of the necessity.[4]

While Wade had never been shy about expressing his feelings, the outbreak of the Civil War let loose in him a new anger. Writing to Elisha Whittlesey, his former law teacher, Wade declared that the "South has got to be punished and traitors hung." He felt that the South, as the instigator of the war, had to be made to pay for it. "I will take their property, and I will relieve the loyal North, and the loyal men of the South, and indemnify them with the confiscated property; yea, to the last dollar of these scoundrels."[5]

Wade supported the radical element of the Republican Party. He opposed slavery, believing it the worst of human institutions, but he also felt that it would die its own death and that the advancing march of civilization had as surely doomed slavery as any legislation. He believed that the Civil War would speed up the process, since the South "could not escape this war without the emancipation of [the slaves]." While a passionate emancipationist, Wade's congressional speeches indicate that he was nonetheless a gradualist, closer to Lincoln's views than some of his more radical colleagues.[6]

The second committee member from the Senate was Zachariah Chandler of Michigan. Born in Bedford, New Hampshire, in 1813, Chandler hailed from a long New England lineage; his ancestors had first settled in America over two hundred years earlier. At the age of twenty Chandler moved West, settling in

4. This story is told in several sources, including Trefousse, *Benjamin Wade,* 150. My version is adapted from Carl Sandburg, *Abraham Lincoln: The War Years,* 4 vols. (New York: Harcourt, Brace, 1939), 1:389, and Walter Buell, *Zachariah Chandler: Part 3, Magazine of Western History* 4, no. 4 (August 1886): 434.

5. Wade to Whittlesey, April 30, 1861, quoted in Trefousse, *Benjamin Wade,* 148; *CG,* 37th Cong., 2nd sess., May 12, 1862, p. 1918.

6. See Wade's speech of May 2, 1862 in *CG,* 37th Cong., 2nd sess., p. 1919.

the frontier town of Detroit. The frugal teachings of his puritan background served him well, and over the next eighteen years he became one of the richest men in Michigan, with interests in commercial trade, banking, and land speculation. Like Wade, Chandler began his political life as a Whig, serving as mayor of Detroit for a year in 1851–52. His larger political dreams still exceeded his grasp, however; he failed in his first bid for higher office, that of the governorship of Michigan. The disintegration of the Whig Party led him actively to search for an alternative, and he joined the call for a meeting of the fledgling Republican Party in Jackson, Michigan, on July 6, 1854, which is generally credited with launching the party. The new party quickly gained adherents, and in 1857 Chandler was elected to the U.S. Senate, where he joined the rapidly growing antislavery wing of the Republicans. He sought immediate emancipation at any cost, even civil war. The idea of bloodshed did not faze him; in a postscript to a wire to Governor Austin Blair of Michigan, Chandler noted, "Without a little bloodletting, this Union will not, in my estimation, be worth a rush."[7]

When Chandler entered the Senate in 1858, the Republicans were still in the minority. It was thus to be expected that the Republicans would figuratively have to fight for their cause, but Chandler soon found that this was true literally as well. The decade of the 1850s saw extreme violence on the floor of the Senate. Challenges to duels were hurled across the aisle; brawls and physical assaults were not uncommon. In this charged atmosphere, it is perhaps unsurprising that Chandler soon came to the attention of Wade. The two men shared more than a similar political philosophy, forming a close personal bond as well. They would become the two most influential and powerful members of the Committee on the Conduct of the War, dominating it to a large degree by the force of their personalities.[8]

Since Chandler had proposed the creation of the committee, normal practice of the day would have made him its chairman. But on December 17, 1861, when Chandler made a motion for the appointment of Senate members to the committee, he declined the position of chairman before it could be offered. An early biographer of Chandler's has argued that he had already met with Hamlin and asked that Wade be appointed chairman, "saying it was important

7. *DAB,* 2:618; Chandler to Governor Blair, February 11, 1861, quoted in Buell, "Zachariah Chandler," *Magazine of Western History* 4 (May 1886): 352.

8. For Chandler's association with Wade, see Buell, "Zachariah Chandler: Part Two," *Magazine of Western History* 4, no. 3 (July 1886): 338–52, and "Zachariah Chandler: Part Three," 432–44.

that a lawyer should be given that place." Since Chandler was not shy of the limelight himself, the explanation rings true.[9]

The final member of the committee from the Senate was Benjamin Franklin Harding. Born in Pennsylvania in 1823, he abandoned a law practice in Illinois during the gold rush of 1848–49 to move to California. After only a brief stay he moved to Oregon in 1850. Here he seems to have hit his stride, entering territorial politics and rising quickly to become speaker of the territorial house of representatives, then territorial secretary. Upon the death of Oregon senator Edward Baker, Harding was appointed by the state legislature to complete Baker's term. Harding fell into the group of men known as "war Democrats." Critical of members of his own party who sought a peaceful compromise with the South, Harding strongly supported Republican war measures while remaining true to Democratic social programs. Yet he rarely attended meetings of the Committee on the Conduct of the War. He played no real role in the Meade hearings and retired from the Senate on March 3, 1865, before completing his term.[10]

In the House of Representatives, members of the committee were chosen by Speaker Galusha Grow of Pennsylvania. Entering the House as a Democrat the same year Ben Wade entered the Senate, Grow was firmly in the antislavery camp. Turning to the Republican Party during his third term, he rose to Republican whip and then gained the speakership. More moderate than many of his Republican colleagues, Grow served only one term as speaker before being defeated in the 1862 elections. He was an intimate friend of Wade's, and it is possible that Wade had some input in Grow's selection of committee members. Grow's choices ensured the radical Republicans a four-to-three majority on the committee.[11]

Among committee members from the House was Daniel Wheelwright Gooch of Massachusetts. Born in Wells, Maine, in 1820, Gooch was one of a relatively few college-educated lawyers at the time (Dartmouth class of 1843), most of whom studied law in law offices. After establishing a successful law practice in Boston, Gooch moved into politics, winning election to the Massachusetts house of representatives in 1852. In 1858, he was elected to the U.S. House of Representatives. Although Gooch was critical of the Lincoln ad-

9. *CG,* 37th Cong., 2nd sess., December 17, 1861, p. 110; Detroit Post and Tribune, *Zachariah Chandler: An Outline Sketch of His Life and Public Service* (Detroit: Post and Tribune, 1880), 216.

10. Sifakis, *Who Was Who in the Civil War,* 352.

11. DuBois and Mathews, *Galusha A. Grow,* 96, 234; Sifakis, *Who Was Who in the Civil War,* 168.

ministration as well as the military leadership, he was not consistent in backing the radicals. Gooch took an active part in the Meade hearings, missing only five sessions.[12]

Perhaps the most radical member of the committee was George Washington Julian. He was born in a log cabin in Indiana on May 5, 1817. His father died when he was six, and Julian was raised by his mother, a devout Quaker; his later zealous antislavery attitude stemmed from her early influence. Admitted to the bar in 1840, he won a seat in the Indiana legislature as a Whig in 1845. Julian's political career was varied; he belonged to six different political parties in his life. Defeated in 1847 in a run for the state senate, he switched allegiance to the Free-Soil Party and in 1848 was elected to the U.S. House of Representatives on the Free-Soil ticket. His antislavery crusade was too early for most people, and the fury of his attacks in speeches and articles moved him to the fringe of politics and society, losing him friends and even causing the dissolution of his law partnership with his brother. Defeated for reelection in 1850, he continued to work for the Free-Soil Party, earning the party's nomination for vice president in 1852. Despite an active campaign by Julian, the third-party ticket did not stand a real chance on the national level and he once again was defeated. In 1856 he again switched parties, helping to organize the fledgling Republican Party in Pennsylvania. By 1860 the times and temper of the nation had begun to catch up with Julian and he was again elected to House of Representatives, where he would stay for the next ten years.[13]

Julian strongly believed that the Civil War could be laid at the feet of the Democratic Party. Speaking about the war in early 1863, he remarked that "Democratic policy not only gave birth to the rebellion, but Democrats, and only Democrats, are in arms against their country."[14]

Moses Fowler Odell of New York was one of two House Democrats on the committee. Odell was born in Tarrytown, New York, in 1818; soon a natural talent for politics transformed him from a customhouse clerk in New York City to a power in state Democratic circles. He was elected to the House of Representatives in 1860. A war Democrat, Odell probably was appointed to the committee for two reasons. First, his support of the war gained him a certain degree of respect among the House Republican leadership. Second, since he

12. *Who Was Who in America: Historical Volume, 1607–1896* (New York: Marquis Who's Who, 1963), 208; Tap, *Over Lincoln's Shoulder,* 28–9.

13. *DAB,* 5:245–6, Sifakis, *Who Was Who in the Civil War,* 474; T. Harry Williams, *Lincoln and the Radicals* (Madison: University of Wisconsin Press, 1941), 70.

14. *CG,* 37th Cong., 3rd sess., February 18, 1863, p. 1065.

was only beginning his second term, he would not be likely to play a major role in the hearings. Although Democrats were needed on the committee to give it a semblance of broad representation, Gooch no doubt felt that Odell would be amenable to the committee majority. Odell, like all war Democrats, walked a fine line between white supremacy and states' rights; he twice voted in favor of the Thirteenth Amendment to abolish slavery. One of only seven war Democrats to survive the off-year elections of 1862, Odell also served on the Military Affairs Committee. After serving two terms, he failed to gain renomination in 1864.[15]

The newest member of the committee from the House was Missourian Benjamin Franklin Loan. Born in Hardinsburg, Kentucky, in 1819, he moved west to St. Joseph, Missouri, in 1838, where he was admitted to the practice of law in 1840. With the outbreak of war Loan played a key role in organizing pro-Union forces in Missouri; his efforts were rewarded by a commission as a brigadier general in the state militia in November 1861. A prewar Democrat, he was initially elected to the House of Representatives as an Unconditional Unionist in 1863, although he switched to the Republican Party for his second and third terms. His staunch opposition to slavery, in addition to his experience fighting Southern guerrillas in Missouri, helped to earn him a spot on the committee.[16]

Actual military experience was scarce on the committee. Neither Wade nor Chandler accepted the view that military command was a specialized, technical career which only those educated at West Point could understand. Wade believed that in only a few weeks the average American could learn all there was to know about the military and, untainted by the Southern leanings of West Point, would be the better for it. Such opinions were not limited to members of the committee, but were generally believed by members of Congress. During the debate over the creation of the Committee on the Conduct of the War, Owen Lovejoy commented that "men who have received a military education are more in the way of the success of our arms than anything else." The fallacy of this belief was amply demonstrated by the ineptitude of many of the political generals appointed by Congress, but it was not easily overcome. As late as 1864 an article in the widely read *Atlantic Monthly* proclaimed that the

15. Sifakis, *Who Was Who in the Civil War,* 474; Tap, *Over Lincoln's Shoulder,* 29–30. Despite strong support for the abolition of slavery, the Thirteenth Amendment did not pass Congress until January 31, 1865, being ratified by the states on December 6, 1865.

16. *Biographical Directory of the American Congress, 1774–1971* (Washington, D.C.: Government Printing Office, 1971), 1404.

average lawyer or businessman could "give an average army officer all the advantage of his special training, at the start, and yet beat him at his own trade in a year."[17]

GEORGE GORDON MEADE

Born of American parents in Cadiz, Spain, on December 31, 1815, Meade was the ninth of eleven children. Meade's father, Richard Wortham Meade, was a well-to-do merchant and part-time envoy to the Spanish royal court. Unable to collect on lines of credit and loans to the monarchy after the overthrow of the Spanish crown by Napoleon, Richard Meade was financially ruined when the restored royals refused to repay him. In 1816 his demands for payment irritated the authorities enough that he was thrown in jail and his wife and children returned to America. Eventually released and allowed to return to the United States, Meade's father would spend the remainder of his life in pursuit of the debt owed him.[18]

While hardly destitute in America, the Meades could no longer afford the lifestyle to which they had become accustomed, cutting expenses wherever they could. Although the young George Meade was educated at some of the better private schools in and around Philadelphia, the cost of his college education would have put a severe strain on the family's finances. Meade's appointment to West Point provided a suitable solution, and he entered the academy in 1831. His tenure there, however, was hardly distinguished. Graduating nineteenth out of fifty-six in the class of 1835, his disregard for details of dress and disinterest in drill resulted in his accumulating 168 demerits, only thirty-two short of mandatory dismissal.[19]

Following graduation Meade completed the then-required one year of service before resigning his commission to pursue a career as a civil engineer. Meeting with only limited financial success and wanting a more stable income so that he could marry, he rejoined the army in 1842. He was appointed second lieutenant in the elite Topographical Bureau of the Corps of Engineers and given survey work. Although he had served in Florida during the Seminole

17. Williams, *Lincoln and the Radicals,* 72; *CG,* 37th Cong., 2nd sess., January 6, 1862, p. 194; Thomas Wentworth Higginson, "Regular and Volunteer Officers," *Atlantic Monthly* 14 (September 1864): 349.

18. *MG,* 3–9.

19. Ibid., 9; *Register of the Officers and Cadets of the U.S. Military Academy, 1832–1835* (West Point, N.Y.: U.S. Military Academy, 1832–35), 6, 7, 13, 18, 20.

War, his first real taste of combat came during the Mexican War. He spent much of his time surveying or on scouting missions, but he also took part in several skirmishes and was on the fringe of a couple of major battles. Upon his return from the war, Meade resumed his career in building lighthouses and breakwaters and in coastal survey work.[20]

Promotion came slowly in the army. At the beginning of the Civil War, nineteen years after reentering the service, Meade had only risen to the rank of captain. As units began to fill up following Lincoln's call for volunteers, Meade was made a brigadier general of volunteers and was given command of one of the three Pennsylvania brigades then organizing in the state. The shortage of experienced officers was acute; very few men had ever commanded anything larger than a company. But Meade also had some help in getting this important assignment. His wife, Margaretta Sergeant, called simply Margaret, was from a prominent Philadelphia family; her father, John Sergeant, had served eight terms in the U.S. House of Representatives. Though the elder Sergeant had died in 1852, the family still maintained many important political contacts, including the governor of Pennsylvania, Andrew Curtin. The Meade family was also well known to Curtin.[21]

Fighting with his brigade on the Peninsula, Meade participated in actions at Mechanicsville, Gaines's Mill, and Glendale during the Seven Days battles, being twice severely wounded at Glendale. He had not fully recovered from his wounds when he returned to command his brigade at Second Bull Run. At South Mountain and at Sharpsburg he commanded a division in Hooker's First Corps. At the disaster of Fredericksburg, Meade led the Third Division in Franklin's "Left Grand Division," successfully penetrating Confederate lines on the rebel right. Within a few days of that battle, Meade replaced Major General Daniel Butterfield in command of the Army of the Potomac's Fifth Corps, leading it at the battle of Chancellorsville. On June 28, 1863, Meade replaced Hooker in command of the Army of the Potomac and led it until the end of the war.[22]

Physically Meade was a tall, thin, very plain man; his most prominent facial features were a large roman nose and baggy-lidded, bulging eyes, which were accentuated when he wore his glasses. His full beard was in marked con-

20. James Lunsford Morrison Jr., "The United States Military Academy, 1833–1866: Years of Progress and Turmoil" (Ph.D. diss., Columbia University, 1970), 12–3; *MG*, 13–4.

21. *Congressional Directory*, 1667; *MG*, 72.

22. This brief sketch of Meade's career is based on *MG*, 3–9, and Warner, *Generals in Blue*, 315–7.

trast to his receding hairline, both of which were liberally sprinkled with gray. His lack of attention to detail in his personal appearance had not improved since his academy days; as one of his officers wrote, "His habitual personal appearance is quite careless, and it would be rather difficult to make him look well dressed."[23]

The moral code instilled in Meade at West Point continued to hold sway throughout his life. For him honor and duty were not abstract thoughts but a way of life. He possessed the strength of character to accept the responsibility and consequences of his actions even when they were wrong, a trait not always found among general officers in the Army of the Potomac. An imperfect man, he strove for perfection, showing little patience with those who did not do so as well, regardless of their rank. Meade was intolerant of stupidity, bungling, or halfhearted measures, an attitude which came from his hard-earned appreciation for the horrors of war. Deeply concerned over the welfare of his men, he had watched helplessly as Burnside and Hooker had needlessly wasted lives in hopeless situations or to no good end. He did not allow such behavior in his subordinates, nor did he permit his superiors to force him to act against his own judgment. As his aide and close friend Theodore Lyman noted, "woe to those, no matter who they are, who do not do it right!" Indeed, Meade's most commented-on trait was his volatile temper. Ulysses S. Grant recalled that Meade had a "temper that could rise beyond his control." Lyman described Meade's temper as "like a firework, always going bang at someone, and nobody ever knows who is going to catch it next, but all stand in a semi-terrified state."[24]

Yet while Meade handled the stress and pressure of army command poorly at times, on those infrequent occasions when he could escape his heavy responsibilities he was a different man. A shy man, interacting with his subordinates was difficult for him, and he was uncomfortable engaging in idle conversation or storytelling with his staff or aides. The fact that he was quick to condemn but slow to praise, however, did not mean he was unaware of the contributions of others to his success. After the war, a gold medal in commemoration of his success at Gettysburg was awarded to Meade by the Union League of Philadelphia. He gave one of the bronze copies of the medal to

23. Frank L. Byrne and Andrew T. Weaver, eds., *Haskell of Gettysburg: His Life and Civil War Papers* (Kent, Ohio: Kent State University Press, 1989), 132.

24. Theodore Lyman and George R. Agassiz, eds., *With Grant and Meade from the Wilderness to Appomattox,* introduction by Brooks D. Simpson (Lincoln: University of Nebraska Press, 1994), 25, 73; quoted in Harry W. Pfanz, *Gettysburg: The Second Day* (Chapel Hill: University of North Carolina Press, 1987), 3; *GC,* 211–2.

Brigadier General Alexander S. Webb for his "distinguished personal gallantry on that ever memorable field." Perhaps more revealing was his comment to Webb thanking him for his "cordial, warm, & generous sympathy and support so grateful for a commanding General to receive from his Subordinates." If during the war Meade had been as lavish with his praise as he was stingy with the lives of his men, history might have remembered him differently.[25]

Meade was neither flashy nor a self-promoting braggart, although in the politically charged atmosphere that surrounded the Army of the Potomac both traits had previously been almost a prerequisite for command. He had no great interest in politics, which was considered by many as a bar to higher command, but in fact this indifference served him well by keeping him from the morass of political intrigue, which appealed to Lincoln. Politically naïve, Meade was often surprised to find he had friends in powerful positions. He was helped at various times by Lincoln, Stanton, army commander-in-chief Major General Henry W. Halleck, and committee member Moses Odell. Much of this support was due to Meade's honesty and self-effacing character.

It is a matter of speculation why Meade was chosen by Lincoln and Stanton to command the Army of the Potomac. At the time there were three corps commanders in the Army of the Potomac who ranked Meade based on seniority—Henry Slocum, John Sedgwick, and John Reynolds—but none of them were offered the position. Slocum had vehemently denounced Hooker to Lincoln, which may have left a bad impression on the president. Possibly more important was the fact that Slocum was a Democrat. This would not have influenced Lincoln, but Stanton, as well as members of Congress, were more partisan. John Sedgwick was next on the list, but the rout of his corps at Chancellorsville, though no fault of his own, had reflected badly on him. Reynolds had refused the job; and both Slocum and Sedgwick had already indicated a willingness to serve under Meade. Yet Meade was not chosen only on a "what's left" basis, as is sometimes claimed. He was a good tactician, handled troops well, was physically courageous, and enjoyed the confidence of his peers. In short, he was not a bad choice at all.

BACKGROUND TO THE HEARINGS

By 1864 the Joint Committee on the Conduct of the War had clearly established itself as a major player in the administration of the war. Involved in a

25. Quoted in *GC*, 212–3.

wide range of investigations covering the entire war effort, the committee's hearings revealed broad corruption in the administration of government and army contracts. In addition, its inflammatory, one-sided reports on such events as the Fort Pillow massacre and the Confederate treatment of Union prisoners aroused Northern passions against the South. Throughout its duration, however, the main focus of the committee was the Union army and its generals. Members of the committee were determined to use any means available to rid the army of what they considered conservative and disloyal generals.

Investigative committees have historically been the source of legislation to correct the problems uncovered in their hearings, but members of the Committee on the Conduct of the War did not see their role in this way. As Wade stated in his report on the hearings, committee members viewed their purpose as "endeavoring to obtain such information in respect to the conduct of the war as would best enable them to advise what mistakes had been made in the past and the proper course to be pursued in the future; . . . and to lay before them [the president and his cabinet] with such recommendations and suggestions as seemed to be most imperatively demanded." In other words, rather than a subunit of the Congress, the committee believed itself to be a fourth arm of the government, with the special province of advising Lincoln on how to run the war.[26]

While the committee investigated a variety of people and events, ranging from ice contracts (used to comfort the wounded) to commanding generals, it is best known for its series of investigations into the commanders of the Army of the Potomac. Every officer who held this position was called before the committee and investigated. There were several reasons for this sharp focus on the Army of the Potomac. First, the army's primary responsibility was the defense of Washington and Baltimore, which necessarily made it the closest army to the committee. Though members of the committee would at times travel widely, difficulties of transportation made the Army of the Potomac, often within one day's travel time, a favorite destination.[27]

But ease of accessibility, it should be noted, proved to be a two-way street. The appointment of men to the rank of brigadier general and above whose only qualifications were political connections or influence had created a group

26. Quoted in W. W. Pierson, "The Committee on the Conduct of the War of the Civil War," *American Historical Review* 23 (October 1917–July 1918): 560.

27. Many authors add "with the exception of Grant." Grant commanded all the Union armies, and though he traveled with the Army of the Potomac, command of the army was vested in Meade.

of officers not only knowledgeable in the art of political leverage, but willing to use it to their advantage. The road to Washington was heavily traveled by these officers, often without proper leave, where they imparted information and opinions, many times incorrectly, about events or people in the army.

The Army of the Potomac also suffered from its proximity to the major media centers of the time, such as Washington, New York, Baltimore, and Philadelphia. War events were big news. Anything, real or imagined, which affected the army nearest those cities would ultimately bear on the safety of the cities themselves, and that was even bigger news. As the army closest to Richmond, the Army of the Potomac was widely expected to capture the enemy capital. From early in the war Lincoln had recognized the proper aim of the army as the destruction of rebel forces, not the capture of cities, but for the media and the public at large Richmond was the golden prize. No other army would be graced—or plagued, depending on the point of view—with as many reporters and illustrators wanting to be in on the greatest event of the war.

In addition, the Army of the Potomac was the army that faced the vaunted Robert E. Lee and his Army of Northern Virginia. By 1863, Lee and his rugged veterans had gained an almost mythical reputation of invincibility. Until Lee and his army were destroyed there could be no peace, and the Army of the Potomac's record against them was not good.

Any one of these factors could and did serve to bring a steady stream of congressmen to the headquarters of the Army of the Potomac. All combined, they almost guaranteed the army's continual scrutiny by the Committee on the Conduct of the War.

The story of the Meade hearings actually begins in the waning days of Joseph Hooker's command of the army. For the duration of the Meade hearings the lives of these two men would be inexorably entwined in a political battle for their military careers and for command of the Army of the Potomac. Hooker, a favorite of the committee members, held what the committee considered as "correct" views of the war, favoring emancipation, confiscation of property, and harsh reconstruction. Though Hooker's removal from command of the Army of the Potomac was not publicly protested, it was not a popular move with many in the administration or on the committee.

A graduate of West Point with a brilliant service record during the Mexican War, Hooker had been out of the army for nearly ten years at the outbreak of the Civil War. Early on, he had been a Democrat and anti-abolitionist, both of which were often viewed in the North as suspect. Politically astute, outspoken, and ambitious, he was a supreme egotist and had an unsavory personal reputation that included gambling, drinking, and associating with women of fallen virtue (he is often credited as the source for the term "hooker" in referring to prostitutes). All these traits would seem to have made Hooker an odd choice for the committee to support. Yet over time Hooker had come around to agreeing with the views of the committee. In short, his convictions were slave to his ambition. In late 1862, prior to Hooker's assuming command of the army, Meade noted, "Hooker is a Democrat and anti-abolitionist—that is to say, he was. What he will be, when the command of the Army is held out to him, is more than anyone can tell."[28]

Above all, Hooker was a schemer and intriguer, not above sabotaging the efforts of his superiors or pinning the blame on his subordinates to gain his own ends or protect his reputation. He was a man who, according to his contemporary John Gibbon, had "sacrificed his soldierly principles whenever such sacrifice could gain him political influence to further his own ends." Appointing Hooker to command of the army, Lincoln himself noted, "You are ambitious, which, within reasonable bounds, does good rather than harm; but I think that during [Major] General [Ambrose] Burnside's command of the army, you have taken counsel of your ambition, and thwarted him as much as you could."[29]

Hooker talked a good fight, which endeared him to many in Washington, including the committee members. Even after losing his only major battle at Chancellorsville, where he admittedly lost his nerve, he still retained strong backing. In Lincoln's cabinet, Secretary of the Treasury Salmon Chase was a noted Hooker booster. Charles F. Benjamin, a War Department commentator, wrote, "The friends of Mr. Chase considered that the fortunes of their leader were too much bound up with Hooker to permit of the latter's ignominious removal . . . the Treasury faction had grown so powerful that Lincoln could not consent to a rupture with it, and a temporizing policy was adopted all around." Zachariah Chandler also supported Hooker, maintaining that Hooker would have succeeded at Chancellorsville if the Eleventh Corps had held its ground. In a masterpiece of understatement, Chandler noted, "This deranged his plan of battle and discouraged him a little." As news of the extent of the defeat at Chancellorsville and rumors of Hooker being drunk during the battle seeped back to the capital (despite Hooker's efforts to censor them), his sup-

28. Warner, *Generals in Blue,* 233–5; Meade to his wife, October 12, 1862, in *LLM,* 1:318–9.

29. Quoted in David M. Jordan, *Winfield Scott Hancock: A Soldier's Life* (Bloomington: Indiana University Press, 1988), 67; quoted in Sandburg, *Abraham Lincoln: The Prairie Years and the War Years,* 357.

port in Congress and on the committee continued to hold firm. Meanwhile, his support in the army was anything but universal. Three of his corps commanders talked openly of requesting Hooker's removal; one, Major General Darius N. Couch, commander of the Second Corps and senior corps commander in the Army of the Potomac, was so disgusted that he refused to serve under Hooker any longer.[30]

Lincoln was not yet prepared to act, saying that "he was not disposed to throw away a gun because it missed fire once, that he would pick the lock and try it again." Meade, in a letter to his wife, thought that the reasons for Lincoln's hesitation were "(1) the difficulty of finding a successor and (2) the ridiculous appearance we present of changing generals after each battle." Despite strong opposition to Hooker in the army, he would not be replaced right away.[31]

As May slipped into June, Hooker's position, though shaken, seemed secure. On June 3, 1863, Lee began his second invasion of the North, moving along the Rappahannock. Swinging west of the Blue Ridge Mountains and controlling the passes, Lee effectively screened his movements from Hooker, causing confusion and uncertainty about his whereabouts and aims. As it became clear that the Army of Northern Virginia was on the move northward, Hooker set the army into motion towards the Potomac.

Meanwhile, Lincoln's confidence in Hooker had taken a downturn. His previous decision to keep Hooker in command had been influenced by Hooker's aggressive talk, but as time passed after Chancellorsville it became apparent that Hooker was all talk and no action. For nearly two months Hooker and his army had not moved against the opposing Confederate force. Now, as Lee moved north, Lincoln urged Hooker to attack Lee and cut his army in half. "If the head of Lee's army is at Martinsburg and the tail of it on the plank road between Fredericksburg and Chancellorsville, the animal must be very slim somewhere. Could you not break him?"[32]

Hooker realized that Lee would be able to cross the Rappahannock before he could get into position with his whole army. On June 5, he proposed to break the "tail of the animal" by attacking Confederate general A. P. Hill's fifteen thousand men at Fredericksburg, threatening both Lee's line of communication and Richmond. By doing so, Hooker believed that Lee would be forced to cancel his invasion plans and would turn back to fight on ground of Hooker's choosing. Both Lincoln and Halleck disapproved of the plan, and

30. Quoted in Sandburg, *Lincoln,* 2:101; Tap, *Over Lincoln's Shoulder,* 170; *MG,* 118.

31. Quoted in Sandburg, *Lincoln,* 2:100; *LLM,* 1:379.

32. Quoted in Sandburg, *Lincoln,* 2:99.

Hooker was quickly informed of their disapproval. Hill's men were far from the easy pickings envisioned by Hooker. Lincoln, who had become a good amateur strategist over the last two years, correctly pointed out that Hill's men were well fortified along Marye's Heights across the Rappahannock. This was the same position the Confederates had held during the battle of Fredericksburg the previous December, only now they had had six more months to dig in. Hill's fortifications would easily negate any numerical advantage of Hooker's army, which would face the very great risk of being "entangled upon the river, like an ox jumped half over a fence and liable to be torn by dogs front and rear, without a fair chance to gore one way or kick the other." Lincoln's analysis was correct and Hooker, certainly not a fool, should have seen it.[33]

In fact, Lee had anticipated just such a move and on June 5 he had issued instructions to Hill in the event of an attack. If Hill was unable to hold his line, he was to fall back along the railroad and call on Pickett's division and Pettigrew's brigade—around 9,500 men—for reinforcements. If Hooker withdrew from the Rappahannock, Hill was to attack his rear. With Hooker thus occupied Lee would have the option of returning to attack Hooker's right or continuing toward the Potomac and Washington with his main body of troops. But in any event, with his plan rejected by Lincoln and Halleck, Hooker had little choice but to follow after Lee.[34]

As the two armies moved north Hooker formed and discarded plan after plan, all the while constantly calling for reinforcements. In Lincoln's opinion, Hooker had become infected with the same problems that had afflicted McClellan, balking at orders and begging for reinforcements. Some reports state that Hooker also began to drink heavily again. Whether through liquid courage or otherwise, Hooker finally crossed the Potomac and began to stalk Lee. As had every other general who had commanded the Army of the Potomac, Hooker overestimated the size of the enemy opposing him. Searching for more troops, Hooker's eye fell upon the garrison at Harpers Ferry, some eleven thousand men under the command of General William H. French, an old friend of Halleck.[35]

33. Quoted in *GC*, 52–3.

34. *OR*, vol. 27, pt. 3, pp. 859–60; *GC*, 53.

35. *MG*, 121–2. As Meade's biographer, Cleaves was not a Hooker fan, but the statement on drinking has a ring of truth to it. Cleaves also asserted that Hooker had requested the garrison at Harpers Ferry during a visit to Washington on June 23, but that does not seem to correspond with other records. Correspondence in *OR*, vol. 27, pt. 1, pp. 57–8, indicates that he was not in Washington on that date.

Hooker became obsessed with the Harpers Ferry garrison. On June 26 he asked for the troops, stating that he faced a superior enemy and needed every man available. The next morning Halleck refused the request, citing the importance of the post as well as the cost and labor spent in fortifying it. Later that afternoon Hooker once again requested the garrison, correctly pointing out that in its present position it served little purpose and asking that the request be forwarded to the secretary of war and the president. Within five minutes of sending this telegram, Hooker sent a second wire: with the forces at his disposal he would be unable to comply with his instructions, and he requested to be relieved. Before midnight an officer was on the way with orders relieving Hooker and appointing Meade to command the army.[36]

The battle of Gettysburg followed a few days later, from July 1 to July 3, 1863. Since the events of the battle are so well known, only a brief outline needs to be given here. On July 1, Union cavalry under Brigadier General John Buford made contact with the troops of Major General Henry Heth's Confederate division west of the small Pennsylvania town of Gettysburg. As both sides poured troops into the battle, the Union army formed a line to the west and north of the town. That afternoon the men of Confederate lieutenant general Richard Ewell's Second Corps arrived from the north and northeast, flanking the Union position and driving the Federals back through the town onto the heights of Cemetery Hill.

On July 2, Lee, after much delay, attacked on the southern end of the Federal line in the area of Little Round Top and the Peach Orchard, using the men of Longstreet's First Corps. To the north, in an uncoordinated effort, Ewell's men attacked Culp's Hill. Both attacks met with limited success. Meade's line was bent but not broken. These attacks represented the last real chance Lee had of winning the battle.

July 3 was the climactic day of the battle, with the famous Pickett's charge occurring that afternoon. After their repulse, Lee's troops rallied along Seminary Ridge and awaited the expected follow-up attack of the Army of the Potomac. They waited throughout July 4. When no Union attack materialized, the rebel army slipped away that night under cover of a heavy rain.

News of the victory at Gettysburg, combined with Grant's capture of Vicksburg on July 4, caused an outburst of celebrations and optimism throughout the North. With the Confederacy now cut in half along the Mississippi and Lee's army defeated and in retreat, victory was near at hand. All that remained

36. *OR*, vol. 27, pt. 1, pp. 58–60.

was for Meade to pin Lee along the flood-swollen Potomac and crush him. But Meade's pursuit was slow, and Lee escaped.

The public, Congress, and the army itself were devastated. For the Lincoln administration, Lee's escape was more than a disappointment; it was a catastrophe. Lincoln told Gideon Welles, his secretary of the navy, "There is bad faith somewhere. Meade has been pressed and urged, but only one of his generals was for an immediate attack, was ready to pounce on Lee; the rest held back." On July 14, Halleck wired Meade of the president's great dissatisfaction over Lee's escape, writing that "it will require an active and energetic pursuit on your part to remove the impression that it has not been sufficiently active heretofore."[37]

Meade correctly viewed the message as a reprimand. As he saw it, a wrong move could easily have lost all they had gained at Gettysburg. Lee had been defeated in battle, but his army was a long way from being destroyed. The Union army had been badly battered and its men were exhausted; under such circumstances, the pursuit had been more than adequate. Meade's temper flashed; a deskbound general and politicians were telling him how to fight the war. Within an hour and a half, about the time it took for Halleck's message to reach him, Meade shot back, "Having performed my duty conscientiously and to the best of my ability, the censure of the President conveyed in your dispatch of 1 P.M. this day, is, in my judgment, so undeserved that I feel compelled most respectfully to ask to be immediately relieved from the command of this army." Halleck's reply was not long in arriving. The president's "dissatisfaction" now became "disappointment." The telegram was not meant as a censure, but merely as a "stimulus to an active pursuit." Meade's resignation was not accepted.[38]

That evening Lincoln sat at his desk and wrote a personal letter to Meade.

> Executive Mansion,
>
> Washington, July 14, 1863.
>
> Major General Meade,
>
> I have just seen your despatch to Gen. Halleck, asking to be relieved of your command, because of a supposed censure of mine. I am very—very—grateful to you for the magnificent success you gave the cause of the country at Gettysburg; and I am sorry now to be the author of the slightest pain to you, but I was

37. Quoted in Tap, *Over Lincoln's Shoulder,* 174; *OR,* vol. 27, pt. 1, p. 92.

38. *OR,* vol. 27, pt. 1, pp. 93–4.

in such deep distress myself that I could not restrain some expression of it. I have been oppressed nearly ever since the battles at Gettysburg by what appeared to be evidences that yourself, and Gen. Couch, and Gen. Smith, were not seeking a collision with the enemy, but were trying to get him across the river without another battle. What these evidences are, if you please, I hope to tell you at some time, when we shall both feel better. The case, summarily stated is this. You fought and beat the enemy at Gettysburg; and, of course, to say the least, his loss was as great as yours. He retreated; and you did not, as it seemed to me, pressingly pursue him; but a flood in the river detained him, till, by slow degrees, you were again upon him. You had at least twenty thousand veteran troops directly with you, and as many more raw ones within supporting distance, all in addition to those who fought with you at Gettysburg; while it is not possible that he had received a single recruit; and yet you stood and let the flood run down, bridges be built, and the enemy move away at his leisure, without attacking. And Couch and Smith! the latter left Carlisle in time, upon all ordinary calculation, to have aided you in the last battle at Gettysburg; but he did not arrive. At the end of more than ten days, I believe twelve, under constant urging, he reached Hagerstown from Carlisle, which is not an inch over fifty-five miles, if so much. And Couch's movement was very little different.

Again, my dear general, I do not believe you appreciate the magnitude of the misfortune involved in Lee's escape. He was within your easy grasp, and to have closed upon him would, in connection with our other late successes, have ended the war. As it is, the war will be prolonged indefinitely. If you could not safely attack Lee last Monday, how can you possibly do so South of the river, when you can take with you very few more than two thirds of the force you then had in hand? It would be unreasonable to expect, and I do not expect you can now effect much. Your golden opportunity is gone, and I am distressed immeasurably because of it.

I beg you will not consider this a prosecution, or persecution of yourself. As you had learned that I was dissatisfied, I have thought it best to kindly tell you why.[39]

Lincoln never sent the letter, quietly filing it away in a desk drawer. Nonetheless, it expressed not only his feelings, but those of many others—including members of the committee—as well.

What the committee members saw as Meade's lack of military success was only one of several objections they had to his continued command of the Army

39. Quoted in Roy P. Basler, ed., *The Collected Works of Abraham Lincoln*, 9 vols. (New Brunswick, N.J.: Rutgers University Press, 1953), 6:27–8.

of the Potomac. The fact that Meade was a West Point graduate was cause enough for suspicion to the academy-hating Wade and Chandler. Strangely, they also distrusted Meade's lack of interest in partisan politics, thinking such indifference showed a "lukewarm patriotism."[40]

The hearings were not in any legal sense a trial; yet when they opened there were four major accusations against Meade. First, Meade had not wanted to fight at Gettysburg and once there had wanted to retreat. Second, Meade had failed to pursue promptly the rebel army after its defeat at Gettysburg. Third, Meade had failed to attack and destroy Lee and his army when they were trapped against the Potomac. Fourth, due to Meade's timidity and military failures he was not fit to command the Army of the Potomac. Interlaced with these charges was a host of side issues, which, while diverting the time and energy of Meade and his defenders, also served to support one or more of the accusations.

These charges are even now cited as proof of Meade's poor generalship. Unlike the public in 1864, we have access to literally reams of documents, histories, and the full transcripts of the hearings, which enable us to make a more informed judgment.

A NOTE ON THE TRANSCRIPT

The transcript is reproduced as it was originally printed. Original page numbers are included in brackets. Spelling has been unchanged, with a few minor exceptions for clarity. The ranks of officers used in the notes are their ranks at the time of Gettysburg. My comments, when interspersed with the transcript, are in italics.

40. Tap, *Over Lincoln's Shoulder,* 177.

3 Major General Daniel Edgar Sickles

PROBABLY THE MOST interesting, and certainly the most controversial, character to testify before the committee was its first witness, Major General Daniel Edgar Sickles. Born into a wealthy New York family, Sickles matured (the term "grew up" is not quite accurate) into an overindulged playboy. Used to the presence of money, Sickles never learned to manage it effectively, suffering through one financial crisis after another throughout his life. Despite a poor personal reputation among his peers, Sickles was a good attorney and, perhaps not so surprisingly, a good politician. A Tammany Hall Democrat, he served two terms in Congress before the Civil War. Sickles's promising political career was cut short in 1859 when he murdered Philip Barton Key, son of composer Francis Scott Key. Philip Key had been having an affair with Sickles's wife, who was some twenty years his junior, and Sickles shot the unarmed man down in the streets of Washington. Acquitted through the efforts of a defense team that included Edwin Stanton, Sickles was ostracized by Washington politicos and society. His close friend and mentor President James Buchanan felt that Sickles's public life would end with his congressional term in 1861. Even Sickles seemed to believe so at the time, not running for reelection.

In the months before the secession crisis Sickles toed the party line, joining the rising chorus of Southern Democrats who declared that it was only an "illusion . . . that this Union can be preserved by force." It was the right of each state, said Sickles, to secede and "seek safety in a separate existence." As with many of his fellow Democrats in the North, the key to Sickles's feelings on secession lay in the peaceful withdrawal of a state. To him the right of secession was simply a matter of law. The Constitution did not expressly forbid it, and therefore it was permitted. But the attack on Fort Sumter changed everything. By resorting to violence against the government, the South had given up on what Sickles viewed as possible legal alternatives. Here Sickles drew the line. The events in Charleston Harbor were nothing but "naked, unmitigated war." With all the fervor of a born-again evangelist, Sickles took up the cause of preserving the Union.[1]

Filled with a newfound energy and enthusiasm, Sickles returned to New York, where he helped to raise first a regiment and then a full brigade of over three thousand men, which was christened the Excelsior Brigade. According to custom, the rank of a volunteer officer was based on the number of men he brought into the army. A regiment made one a colonel; a brigade gained one the star of a brigadier general. Sickles's provisional rank of brigadier general was precarious, because it needed approval from Congress once the brigade entered Federal service. His notorious past, along with his strong Democratic credentials, cast a dark pall over his chances.

With the brigade formed and moved from New York to Washington, Sickles set about improving those chances, calling on old friends and making new ones, most notably Mary Todd Lincoln. Through Mrs. Lincoln—who was disliked, distrusted, and nearly friendless in the capital—Sickles became a frequent visitor at the White House. His other friends included Edwin Stanton, who was soon to replace Secretary of War Simon Cameron. Sickles's campaign for his star was initially unsuccessful, but finally was confirmed in the Senate by the narrow margin of 19–18.

For a person with little military experience, Sickles proved to be a good officer. He led a brigade in the Peninsula campaign; at Antietam, he commanded a full division. By November 1862, he was a major general of volunteers. The following month, Joseph Hooker was given command of the army in the wake of Major General Ambrose Burnside's debacle at Fredericksburg. Hooker quickly scrapped Burnside's grand division organization (established at the suggestion of members of the Joint Committee on the Conduct of the War) and returned to a corps structure. Among the new corps commanders, and one of only two non–West Pointers, was Hooker's friend Daniel Sickles. Once again Sickles's promotion—now to major general—was subject to Senate approval. Once again the first nomination was refused. But on March 9, 1863, after Lincoln had presented his name for a second time, Sickles got his second star and his corps.

1. W. A. Swanberg, *Sickles the Incredible* (1956; reprint, Gettysburg, Pa.: Stan Clark Military Books, 1991), 109, 111. This brief account of Sickles's life is based upon Swanberg's book.

The new army commander chose Daniel Butterfield as his chief of staff, bringing together the triumvirate that would play a major role in the Meade hearings. In light of future events it is not without irony that Meade, then commander of the Fifth Corps, wrote to his wife, "I believe Hooker is a good soldier; the danger he runs is of subjecting himself to bad influences, such as Dan Butterfield and Dan Sickles, who, being intellectually more clever than Hooker, and leading him to believe they are very influential, will obtain an injurious ascendancy over him and insensibly affect his conduct." Clearly, Meade did not hold either Sickles or Butterfield in high regard.[2]

A lover of parties and social gatherings, Sickles saw no reason for the war to interfere unduly with his social activities. The winter of 1862–63 proved to be a particularly enjoyable time. With the army camped only a day's ride from Washington and his wife banished to New York, Sickles found many opportunities to enjoy life. The camp's proximity to Washington also brought almost daily visits from various senators, governors, and cabinet members, which in turn called for numerous reviews and nearly nightly entertainment. Daniel Sickles "was the most confirmed party-giver . . . that winter."[3]

Yet the gaiety of that winter's scene was not without criticism. As Charles Francis Adams Jr., grandson of President John Quincy Adams and a cavalry captain, remembered some fifty years later, "that was a period in its history when, so far as character was concerned, the Army of the Potomac sank to its lowest point. It was commanded by a trio, each of whom the least said the better. It consisted of 'Joe' Hooker, 'Dan' Sickles and 'Dan' Butterfield. All three were men of blemished character. During the winter . . . when Hooker was in command, I can say from personal knowledge and experience that the headquarters of the Army of the Potomac was a place to which no self-respecting man liked to go, and no decent woman would go. It was a combination of barroom and brothel."[4]

Adams's comment contained more than a drop of truth, but Sickles also had his share of admirers. Colonel P. Regis de Trobriand, commander of Sickles's Third Brigade, said of his superior, "He has a quick perception, an energetic will, prompt and supple intelligence, an active temperament. Naturally ambitious, he brings to the service of his ambitions a clear view, a practical judgment and a deep knowledge of political tactics. When he has determined

2. *LLM*, January 26, 1863, 1:351.

3. Swanberg, *Sickles the Incredible*, 171.

4. Ibid., 173–4. It should be noted that Adams was of conservative Bostonian stock and something of a prude.

on anything, he prepares the way, assembles his forces, and marches directly to the assault. Obstacles do not discourage him."[5]

Sickles's motives in testifying against Meade were multiple. To a large extent, he was driven by sheer ego. Sickles's unauthorized advance at Gettysburg on July 2 had brought on a near disaster and had resulted in the loss of much of his beloved Third Corps. As a man of great ambition who had risen from the ashes of political disaster, Sickles could not accept responsibility for what was viewed by many critics as a blunder of great magnitude. To be blamed for the events at the Peach Orchard would have opened up the very real possibility of losing his command, along with the recognition, honor, and glory that came with a military career. For Sickles there could have been no worse fate.

Having climbed to the rarified ranks of corps commander, there remained only one man who could have been guilty of the omissions that had caused Sickles's actions—George Gordon Meade. If Sickles was to remain blameless, then Meade must be guilty. Once committed to the course of damning Meade to save himself, Sickles had no choice but to continue. Moreover, Sickles's access to influential members of Congress, the administration, and the press gave him a platform to present his version of events to the public, and he was not shy about exploiting his connections. His future depended upon Meade's destruction, and for the remainder of his long life (he died in 1914) Sickles asserted his version of events at Gettysburg to anyone who would listen.

Sickles doubtless saw his appearance before the committee as an unparalleled opportunity. Not only was the committee sympathetic to his views, but it was in a position to take action. Acting alone, Sickles could sully Meade's reputation among both the general public and government officials, but he could not get Meade removed from command. With the assistance and backing of the committee, however, Sickles hoped that enough political pressure could be brought to bear on Lincoln that he would be forced to act against Meade.

In addition to his obvious animosity toward Meade, Sickles had other qualities that recommended him highly to the committee. He had been wounded at Gettysburg, and to some—including himself—he was the real hero of the battle. As an ex-congressman, Sickles still had important and influential friends in Washington and New York in both the government and the press, friends that might prove helpful to the committee. Also, Sickles was not a West Pointer and therefore not tainted by exposure to what members of the committee considered the nearly traitorous influences of that institution.

5. Ibid., 174.

Sickles, who had been recuperating from his wound in Washington and New York, formally began the hearings on Meade on February 26, 1864. Though five of the committee's members were present—Wade, Chandler, Gooch, Julian, and Loan—the only one to ask questions was Wade.

[295] Testimony of Major General Daniel E. Sickles.

Washington, February 26, 1864.
Major General Daniel E. Sickles sworn and examined.

By the chairman:
Question. I believe we reached yesterday that point in your testimony where General Meade assumed command of the army of the Potomac. Please resume your narrative from that point, and proceed with it in your own way.

Sickles had been testifying in the hearings on his close friend Joseph Hooker. The committee ran multiple hearings and investigations at the same time.

Answer. I joined the army at Frederick, Maryland, and reported to General Hooker on Sunday, the 28th day of June.

Coincidentally, Sickles had ridden the train from Washington to Frederick with Colonel James A. Hardie, who had delivered the order making Meade the new commander of the Army of the Potomac.[6]

He informed me that he had been relieved from command, and the General Meade was assigned to the command. I then reported to General Meade, who had just reached headquarters to assume command. Immediately thereafter I joined my corps, which was then moving by the way of Frederick towards Taneytown. My corps moved to Taneytown, and from there I was ordered to Emmitsburg. I reached Emmitsburg on the night of the 30th of June, and encamped near there, taking position somewhat in front and to the left of Emmitsburg, on the morning of the 1st of July. On that morning I received a circular from General Meade's headquarters having reference to the occupation of a new line. The army was to fall back, and not to follow up the enemy any further; the general regarding the objects of the campaign to have

6. *GC*, 664 n. 30.

been accomplished, and considering Washington, Baltimore, and Pennsylvania to have been relieved. The circular indicated a line of retreat, the new position to which we were to fall back being substantially the line of what was known as Pipe creek.

Question. How many days was that before the battle of Gettysburg commenced?

Answer. It was the day the battle commenced; the day Reynolds fell; that is, it was the day which is popularly understood to be the day that the battle commenced. We in the army do not regard the operations of the two corps under General Reynolds as properly the battle of Gettysburg. We regard the operations of Thursday and Friday, when the whole army was concentrated, as the battle of Gettysburg.[7]

Throughout his testimony, Sickles spoke as though he was a professional soldier. His comment that Thursday and Friday—and not Wednesday—comprised the battle of Gettysburg was no doubt motivated by the fact that he did not participate in Wednesday's fighting.

Question. Was this contemplated retreat before or after General Reynolds had fallen?

Answer. It was coincident with it, on the very same morning; but I suppose it was before General Meade had heard that General Reynolds was [296] seriously engaged. I do not know, but I presume it undoubtedly was before he heard it. I have that order among my papers here, and I will read an extract from it, so as to show that I have stated it correctly:

Headquarters, Army of the Potomac
July 1, 1863
[Circular.]

"From information received, the commanding general is satisfied that the object of the movement of the army in this direction has been accomplished, viz., the relief of Harrisburg, and the prevention of the enemy's intended invasion of Pennsylvania, &c., beyond the Susquehanna. It is no longer his intention to assume the offensive, until the enemy's movement or position renders such an operation certain of success. If the enemy assume the offensive and at-

7. For a brief description of persons named in the testimony but not testifying, see the appendix.

tack, it is his intention, after holding them in check long enough to withdraw the trains and other *impedimenta,* to withdraw the army from its present position and form a line of battle with the left resting in the neighborhood of Middleburg, and the right at Manchester, the general direction being at Pipe creek."

[The rest of the order indicates the method in which that is to be done, so far as my corps is concerned.]

"For this purpose, General Reynolds, in command of the left wing, will withdraw the force at present at Gettysburg, two corps, by the road to Taneytown and Westminster, and after crossing Pipe creek, deploy towards Middleburg. The corps at Emmitsburg (my corps) will be withdrawn *via* Mechanicsville to Middleburg."

That is sufficient of the order to cover the operation of my corps.

The Pipe Creek circular was the keystone to Sickles's charge that Meade had not wanted to fight Lee. Even a cursory reading of the order, however, reveals that it was intended not as a peremptory order to retreat, but as a "general plan . . . for receiving attack if made in strong force upon any portion of our present position" *(emphasis added). Even Sickles's own excerpt states that the order was to be executed only if the enemy attacked. In no less than eight different places the circular makes clear that the order was only a contingency one, and that "[d]evelopments may cause the commanding general to assume the offensive from his present positions." None of this was noted by Sickles.*

Question. What was the distance to which they intended to retreat, from where the battle actually took place?

Answer. I suppose in a straight line.

Question. I mean by the way you would have to go.

Answer. I suppose it was about fourteen miles, as near as I can tell without looking at the map. I proceeded to make such preparations as would enable me to execute my part of that movement. I soon ascertained that the principal part of my train had been already ordered to the rear by a staff officer from headquarters.

Sickles's statement about his supply train was apparently meant to bolster his testimony that the Pipe Creek circular was an order to retreat. There is nothing other than Sickles's testimony to support his claim.

I was giving my troops a little repose during that morning. They had been very severely marched for many days, and a great many of them were barefooted. I had expected shoes and clothing to be issued for them that morning. Between two and three o'clock in the afternoon I got a dispatch from General Howard, at Gettysburg, informing me that the first and eleventh corps had been engaged during the day with a superior force of the enemy, and that General Reynolds had fallen; that he (Howard) was in command, and was very hard pressed, and urging me in the most earnest terms to come to his relief with what force I could. I, of course, considered the question very anxiously. My preliminary orders in going to Gettysburg were to go there and hold that position with my corps, as it was regarded as a very important flanking position, to cover our rear and line of communication. Then on the other hand was this order of General Meade which I had received that morning, contemplating another and entirely different line of operations. Then there was this new fact which I assumed was not known to General Meade, who was ten miles or so distant. I therefore determined to take the principal part of my corps and move as promptly as possible to Gettysburg.

Most modern writers give credit to Sickles for moving "to the sound of the guns" without orders, but Sickles's testimony that he agonized over conflicting instructions was pure theater. A careful examination of the record indicates that there was far less reason for confusion than Sickles would have had the committee believe. Sickles's Third Corps, as part of the left wing, was under the command of Reynolds. On the morning of July 1, Sickles had sent an aide to Reynolds for any orders for the day. If Sickles had orders from the army commander to fall back, with specific marching instructions, it was hardly necessary to send to Reynolds for more instructions. Nor would he have been concerned with holding Emmitsburg, since he was to withdraw from that area.[8]

Howard's appeals for help might have made for some tough decisions for Sickles. His first orders from the army commander were to hold the Emmitsburg area; yet those orders were over twenty-four hours old. Under such rapidly changing circumstances, it would not be unreasonable to expect a corps commander to act on his own. What is often overlooked, however, is Major Henry Tremain's return from his early morning visit to Gettysburg with a message

8. Swanberg, *Sickles the Incredible,* 202. Swanberg quotes Tremain's book, *Two Days of War: A Gettysburg Narrative and Other Experiences,* published in 1905.

from Reynolds that said, "Tell General Sickles I think he had better come up." This was an order from Sickles's immediate superior to move the Third Corps to Gettysburg. It did not, of course, negate Meade's previous order; but given the fluid situation and Reynolds's more intimate knowledge of Meade's intentions, Sickles's decision to move should not have created much of a dilemma for him. Leaving a small force at Emmitsburg and marching "to the sound of the guns" was the correct thing to do. To have sat idly by would have been by far the greater sin. It is only in comparison to the failures of others during the Civil War—failures recognized and condemned at the time—that Sickles can be praised for his actions.

I took all except two brigades and two batteries,[9] which I left to protect [297] Emmitsburg and that line. I regarded that force as ample, because careful reconnaissance made in the vicinity of Emmitsburg disclosed the presence of no enemy there, and the information which I received from General Howard, in connection with other circumstances, convinced me that the main body of the enemy was in his front. I therefore moved to Gettysburg on my own responsibility. I made a forced march, and arrived there about the time that General Howard had taken position on Cemetery hill. I found his troops well posted in a secure position on the ridge. The enemy in the mean while had not made any serious attack upon him during my march. The arrival of my force seemed to reassure General Howard in the security of his position.

It is easy to imagine that the arrival of any force would have cheered Howard, as his position was precarious, but Sickles's description of his arrival was designed more to inflate his own reputation than to provide factual information. The force that Sickles brought to Gettysburg initially consisted of two brigades of Birney's First Division, some 3,700 men. They arrived between 5:30 and 7:00 P.M., well after Howard and Hancock had established the Cemetery Hill position and the fighting was over for the day. Humphreys's Second Division had taken a different route and did not arrive until much later.[10]

9. These were: 3d Brigade, First Division, Third Corps, under Col. P. Regis de Trobriand; 3d Brigade, Second Division, Third Corps, under Col. George C. Burling; 1st New York Light Artillery, Battery D, Capt. George B. Winslow; and New York Light Artillery, 4th Battery, under Capt. James E. Smith.

10. *OR*, vol. 27, pt. 1, pp. 16, 115, 482.

Soon after my arrival I met there General Hancock and General Slocum. In the evening General Slocum, being the senior officer present, assumed command, although there were no troops of his corps or of General Hancock's corps there; but he assumed command by virtue of his seniority of rank. By his orders my troops were massed on the left of Cemetery ridge. Early in the night, about nine o'clock or so, there was a consultation. The question was whether we should remain in that position, or whether we should fall back. There was a difference of opinion on that point. I wrote to General Meade, either directly or through his adjutant general or chief of staff; I am not positive to whom I addressed the letter; the usual official way would have been to have addressed it either to General Williams or General Butterfield, and I presume I adopted that course; at all events, I addressed a written communication to General Meade, begging him by all means to concentrate his army there and fight a battle, stating that in my judgment it was a good place to fight; that the position of General Howard was an admirably chosen one, and that the enemy would undoubtedly mass there in great force, and that in my judgment it would be most destructive to the *morale* of the army to fall back, as was apparently contemplated in his order of that morning.

No such message now exists. The closest thing to such a dispatch bears no resemblance to Sickles's testimony. That dispatch notified Meade of the movement of the Third Corps to Gettysburg and informed him that troops had been left to guard Emmitsburg. The bulk of the dispatch was concerned with Sickles's defense of his movement, ending with a request for approval of his actions or instructions. Almost as an afterthought, the last sentence of the dispatch said, "This is a good battle-field." There were no references to concentrating the army at Gettysburg. (Indeed, such a request on the part of a corps commander who was not the senior officer on the field would have been extremely presumptuous, although Sickles's claim generated no questions from any committee member.) There was no reference to Howard choosing the battlefield. There was no reference to the enemy massing in great force, even though the lowliest private in the First or Eleventh Corps could have testified to that point. Finally, there was no reference to the morale of the army suffering should they fall back. In short, Sickles's testimony on this point has no foundation in fact.[11]

11. Swanberg, *Sickles the Incredible,* 205; *OR,* vol. 27, pt. 1, p. 469.

The soldiers were eager to fight a battle there, and so were a great number of the officers. I sent that communication by an officer; I do not remember his name now, but he was an officer from General Meade's headquarters, who had been sent by him to Gettysburg. Late in the night I understood that it was determined to concentrate there, and that the army was moving up to Gettysburg as rapidly as possible, and during the night considerable bodies of troops arrived. At a very early hour on Thursday morning I received a notification that General Meade's headquarters had been established at Gettysburg, and I was directed by him to relieve a division of the 12th corps, (General Geary's division, I think) which was massed a little to my left, and which had taken position there during the night. I did so, reporting, however, to General Meade that that division was not in position, but was merely massed in my vicinity; the tenor of his order seemed to indicate a supposition on his part that the division was in position.

This is the opening of Sickles's justification for advancing his corps to the Emmitsburg Road on July 2.

I also received a notification from General Meade that he approved of my course in moving up to Gettysburg. Of course, as soon as I had determined to do that, I addressed a communication to General Meade from Emmitsburg, informing him of what I had done, and expressing my anxiety to have his sanction of it. I received a communication from him informing me that he approved of my course, and that the two brigades and two batteries which I had left at Emmitsburg would be relieved and ordered to join me. I brought them up during the night, under General [Brigadier General Charles K.] Graham, and they arrived in the neighborhood of daybreak.

Meade had issued the order for these units to move up at 7:30 P.M. on July 1. For some reason they did not follow specific march instructions and did not begin until around 4:00 A.M. on July 2. Far from arriving in the neighborhood of daybreak, they did not reach Gettysburg until between 9:00 and 10:00 A.M. on July 2.[12]

Not having received any orders in reference to my position, and observing, from the enemy's movements on our left, what I thought to be conclusive in-

12. *GC*, 335–6.

dications of a design on their part to attack there, and that seeming to me to be our most assailable point, I went in person to headquarters and reported the facts and circumstances which led me to believe that an attack would be made there, and asked for orders. I did not receive [298] any orders, and I found that my impression as to the intention of the enemy to attack in that direction was not concurred in at headquarters; and I was satisfied, from information which I received, that it was intended to retreat from Gettysburg.

In these two sentences can be found the basis of the Meade-Sickles controversy, which the committee eagerly exploited for its own purposes. The desire of many committee members to replace Meade with Hooker would have had little chance of success against the hero of Gettysburg, even with the negative publicity of the later Bristoe and Mine Run campaigns. But Sickles's public denunciation of Meade as a timid, inept general who practically had to be forced to fight at Gettysburg provided the committee with a counterbalance to Meade's victory.

Sickles made two points in his testimony. First, he had received no orders and had acted on his own initiative; second, the army was going to retreat from Gettysburg. Yet there is ample evidence that Sickles did receive orders about his position. Meade himself later testified before the committee to such effect. While no written order survives, logic alone would dictate that Sickles had received some orders.[13]

The writings of Meade's son, an aide on Meade's staff, also suggest as much. According to then-Captain Meade, around 8:00 or 9:00 A.M. on July 2 Meade had sent him to ask about the position of Sickles's troops. Arriving at the headquarters of the Third Corps, Captain Meade was met by Captain George E. Randolph, chief of Third Corps Artillery. Randolph took the message to Sickles, who was sleeping in his tent, having been up much of the night. Returning to Captain Meade, Randolph said that the Third Corps was not in position because Sickles was in "some doubt as to where he should go." Randolph's reply suggests that there had been some instructions for Sickles to be in doubt about.[14]

Further evidence can be found in the battle report of Major General David B. Birney, commander of Sickles's First Division. As he wrote, "At 7 A.M., under orders from Major-General Sickles, I relieved Geary's division, and formed a line, resting its left on Sugar Loaf Mountain and the right thrown in a direct

13. *CCW*, 331.
14. *LLM*, 2:66.

line toward the cemetery, connecting on the right with the Second Division of this corps." Birney's report thus contains a significant part of the orders Meade said he had issued and Sickles said he had not gotten. Birney's movement would have occurred an hour or more before Captain Meade's first visit to Third Corps. It should be noted, however, that Geary's division had withdrawn from its position around 5:00 A.M.[15]

Sickles's statement is further undermined by Brigadier General John W. Geary, whose Second Division, Twelfth Corps Sickles was to relieve. After the war, Geary wrote Meade that he had offered the services of one of his aides to guide Sickles or someone from his staff to where the Second Division had been during the night. According to Geary, Sickles replied that he would "attend to it in due time," but never did.[16]

Captain Meade's report to his father resulted in another trip to Third Corps to repeat the instructions given earlier. A short time after Captain Meade delivered this message, Sickles finally went to headquarters himself. As we have seen, Sickles's testimony about this meeting was that he went on his own account, since he had received no orders and was concerned about enemy movements on his left. He went to warn Meade of an impending attack and to ask for orders. According to Sickles, Meade did not believe an attack was pending and intended to retreat from Gettysburg. For the committee, this was a crucial allegation.[17]

Based upon the time of Captain Meade's visit to Third Corps, Sickles's visit to headquarters occurred between 10:00 and 11:00 A.M. At that time, across the valley on the Confederate side of the lines, there was not much happening in Sickles's area. The pop and crackle of scattered gunfire as pickets exchanged occasional shots was the only tangible evidence of the rebel presence. The only large command near Sickles at the time was Perry's Florida Brigade (under Colonel David Lang) of Major General Richard H. Anderson's division, Confederate Third Corps. It was not until sometime after noon that Brigadier General Cadmus M. Wilcox's Alabama Brigade would move onto Lang's right and make contact with advance elements of the Third Corps. Sickles's testimony

15. *OR*, vol. 27, pt. 1, p. 482.

16. Richard Meade Bache, *Life of General George Gordon Meade: Commander of the Army of the Potomac* (Philadelphia: Henry T. Coates, 1897), 321. See also Meade to G. G. Benedict, March 16, 1870, *LLM*, Appendix W, 351–4.

17. For an excellent discussion of the question of orders and the Meade-Sickles controversy, see Richard A. Sauers, *A Caspian Sea of Ink: The Meade-Sickles Controversy* (Baltimore: Butternut and Blue Press, 1989), 109–20.

about a pending attack would thus appear to be the result of a case of nerves or, more likely, hindsight.

By far the most damaging part of Sickles's testimony was his statement about a retreat from Gettysburg; yet he gave no evidence to support his assertion. It is possible that during his visit to headquarters Sickles spoke to his friend Major General Daniel Butterfield, who at the time was working on, or had just completed, Meade's contingency plan for a withdrawal. Giving this the most charitable view possible, Sickles may have, in a hurried conversation and under stressful conditions, understood the plan Butterfield was working on to be an order to retreat.

I asked General Meade to go over the ground on the left and examine it. He said his engagements did not permit him to do that. I then asked him to send General Warren with me, or by himself; but General Warren's engagements were such as to make it inconvenient for him to go. I then asked him to send General Hunt, his chief of artillery, and that was done. General Hunt accompanied me upon a careful reconnaissance of the whole position on the left, in reference to its topography and the best line for us to occupy, and also with reference to the movements of the enemy.

Both Hunt and Meade generally agreed with Sickles on this point, with two subtle but important differences. Sickles testified that he and Hunt examined the entire area, searching for the "best line for us to occupy, and also with reference to the movements of the enemy." No such reference to enemy movements was ever made by either Meade or Hunt, and it seems to be just another attempt by Sickles to justify his actions.

In regard to the line, Meade testified that Sickles had sought assistance in posting his artillery, which was why Hunt was sent to the Third Corps. Hunt testified that Meade had wished him to examine Sickles's line, "or the line that he wanted to occupy," and that "General Sickles had no good position for his artillery." Hunt later wrote that according to Meade, Sickles wanted him to examine a new line, "as he [Sickles] thought that assigned to him was not a good one, especially that he could not use his artillery there." On leaving headquarters, Hunt wrote, "I accompanied Sickles direct to the Peach Orchard, where he pointed out . . . his proposed line."[18]

18. *CCW*, 331, 449; *B&L*, 3:301.

I pointed out to General Hunt the line that on a subsequent part of the day, when the battle opened, I actually occupied; that is, a line from Round Top on the left, perpendicular to the Emmitsburg road, but somewhat *en echelon,* with the line of battle established on Cemetery ridge. I asked for General Hunt's sanction, in the name of General Meade, for the occupation of that line. He declined to give it, although he said it met with the approval of his own judgment; but he said that I would undoubtedly receive such orders as soon as he reported to General Meade. Before making my dispositions on that line, I waited for some time for orders, but received none. The enemy's demonstrations became more and more decided.

Neither Hunt's testimony nor his later writings mention any orders that approved the proposed line. Since Sickles insisted he had received no orders from Meade, his testimony on this point was added "evidence."[19]

I had strengthened and supported my outposts in order to give me timely notice of the attack, which I knew was very imminent. Buford's cavalry, which had been on the left, had been withdrawn. I remonstrated against that, and expressed the hope that the cavalry, or some portion of it, at all events, might be allowed to remain there. I was informed that it was not the intention to remove the whole of the cavalry, and that a portion of it would be returned. It did not return, however.

Sickles was quite right in complaining about the removal of Buford's cavalry. Meade seems to have presumed that Pleasonton would not leave the area undefended, but Pleasonton did not try to replace Buford until it was too late.

My outposts became engaged, and were being driven back from their supports. I determined to wait no longer the absence of orders, and proceeded to make my dispositions on the advanced line, as it is called. I took up that position, which is described in the report of General Halleck as a line from half to three-quarters of a mile in advance, as he says, and which, in his report, he very pointedly disapproves of, and which he further says I took up through a misinterpretation of orders. It was not through any misinterpretation of orders. It was either a good line or a bad one, and, whichever it was, I took it on my own responsibility, except so far as I have already stated, that it was ap-

19. *CCW,* 450; *B&L,* 3:202.

proved of in general terms by General Hunt, of General Meade's staff, who accompanied me in the examination of it. I took up that line because it enabled me to hold commanding ground, which, if the enemy had been allowed to take—as they would have taken it if I had not occupied it in force—would have rendered our position on the left untenable; and, in my judgment, would have turned the fortunes of the day hopelessly against us. I think that any general who would look at the topography of the country there would naturally come to the same conclusion.

Sickles's almost boastful testimony about his advanced line reflects his skills as an attorney. He was attempting to turn a negative into a positive. The idea that his movement was based upon a mistake was totally reprehensible to Sickles; he was neither stupid nor foolish and would not be seen as such. His only option therefore was to show that his advance was necessary to save the army from an attack on its poorly placed line and, by forcing a battle, to compel Meade to fight at Gettysburg.

While Sickles would spend the next fifty years defending his advance, he was quite succinct in his testimony. His advance enabled the Third Corps to hold "commanding ground," which would have been disastrous for the Union left if the enemy had been allowed to take it. The fallacy of this argument is obvious. Sickles did not hold his advanced position, but was pushed back. The line that was finally established was where he had been told to form in the first place.

By advancing without orders, Sickles had placed the entire Federal position at risk. The length of his advanced line left Little Round Top unoccupied, which was one of the keys to the entire Union line; in addition, his line left both of his flanks uncovered. Moreover, he did not bother to tell anyone, including Meade, what he was doing. As Civil War historian Edwin Coddington has accurately noted, "When he moved his forces without reference to the others, even if the position were the best in the world, Sickles put the safety of the whole army in jeopardy. Whether his judgment was better than Meade's was not the point. For better or worse, Meade was commander of the Army of the Potomac, and it was his responsibility to coordinate its various parts to gain victory. Unless he could get them to mesh properly, the best-laid plans would be ruined and with them the army." This apparently never occurred to Sickles.[20]

One of the many imponderables of Gettysburg is the question of why Sickles

20. *GC*, 348.

advanced. When he had first pointed out the advanced line to Hunt, there had been nothing to indicate an imminent or even planned attack on his position. Longstreet's corps was nowhere near the area; in fact, even Lang's brigade, which had the first major skirmish with Sickles's troops and formed the extreme right of the Confederate line until Longstreet's arrival, was not yet fully in position.

There is some truth to Sickles's contention that the advanced line dominated his previous position. The Third Corps occupied ground that was between thirty and forty feet higher than the lower half of Cemetery Ridge. If possession of high ground had been the sole consideration and determining factor for victory, Sickles's line was a better position. It obviously was not, as subsequent events showed.

While I was making my disposition on this line I received a communication from headquarters to attend a consultation of corps commanders. I sent word verbally by the officer who brought me the communication, begging, if possible, to be excused, stating that the enemy were in great force in my front, and intimating that I would very soon be engaged, and that I was making my dispositions to meet the attack. I hastened forward the movements of my troops as rapidly as possible, and had got my batteries in position, when I received another and peremptory order to report at once in person at headquarters, to meet the corps commanders. I turned over the command temporarily to General Birney in my absence, feeling assured that before I could return the engagement would open. I hastened to headquarters with all speed, but before I got [299] there the sound of the cannon announced that the battle had opened. However, I was quite near headquarters at the time and pushed on, but found that the consultation had been broken up by the opening of the battle. General Meade met me just outside of his headquarters and excused me from dismounting. He remarked that he observed, from the sound of the cannon, that my troops were engaged with the enemy. He said that I should return at once, and that he would follow me very soon.

On my way I found that the enemy were moving up to the attack in great force, in two lines of battle, supported by three columns. Fortunately, my left had succeeded in getting into position on Round Top and along the commanding ridge to which I have referred; and those positions were firmly held by the 3d corps.

Sickles's comment that his left had occupied Round Top is simply a lie. Sickles's troops did not occupy either of the Round Tops at any time during the battle.

General Meade soon afterwards arrived on the field and made a rapid examination of the dispositions which I had made, and of the situation. He remarked to me that my line was too extended, and expressed his doubts as to my being able to hold so extended a line; in which I coincided in the main—that is to say, I replied that I could not, with one corps, hold so extended a line against the rebel army; but that, if supported, the line could be held; and, in my judgment, it was a strong line, and the best one.

If Sickles knew he could not hold the line with one corps and had had no orders to advance or no known prospects for support, what was he doing out there? No one on the committee bothered to ask.

I stated, however, that if he disapproved of it was not yet too late to take any position he might indicate. He said "No"; that it would be better to hold that line, and he would send up the 5th corps to support me. I expressed my belief in my ability to hold that line until supports could arrive. He said he would send up the 5th corps on my left, and that on my right I could look to General Hancock for support on my right flank. I added that I should want considerable artillery; that the enemy were developing a strong force of artillery. He authorized me to send to General Hunt who commanded the reserve of the artillery, for as much artillery as I wanted. I then assured him of my entire confidence in my ability to hold the position; which I did. The 5th corps came up, somewhat tardily, to be sure. It was three-quarters of an hour, or an hour, I suppose, before it got into position. My request to General Hancock for supports was promptly met; and I feel myself under obligations principally to General Hancock and the troops of his command for the effective support which enabled me, in connection with my own corps and the artillery which I received from the reserve, to hold the position during that very desperate encounter of Thursday, where the principal operations of Thursday occurred. The position was held and the attacks of the enemy, which were made in great force and with great obstinacy and determination, were successfully repulsed, with terrific loss to them and a very heavy loss on our side, until I was wounded and carried from the field. The command of the 3d corps then devolved on Major General Birney, and, of course, I only know about the subsequent operations from the perusal of his report.

Sickles neatly shifted the blame for the loss of the position to Birney, who took over the corps after Sickles was wounded. Given the situation, it is highly ques-

tionable if Sickles could have done much better. He also testified that the Fifth and Second Corps came to his support. Actually those two corps, along with portions of the Twelfth Corps, replaced the battered Third Corps as it fell back.

Question. You were not with the army, then after that, up to the time when the enemy recrossed the Potomac?

Answer. No, sir; I was carried to the rear. Major General Birney was with the army, and continued in command of the corps.

Question. It was the second day of the fight that you were wounded?

Answer. The second day of fighting; but, as we in the army consider it, the first day of the battle. When I speak of the general engagement I mean that engagement which occurred after we had concentrated at Gettysburg. The fighting of Wednesday, although important and sanguinary, was an engagement in which only two corps of our forces took part.

Question. If I have understood you all through, it was not contemplated by the commander of that army to fight a battle at that place?

Answer. I think not, on Sunday. I suppose that on Wednesday night he undoubtedly intended to fight there, else he would not have concentrated there; but I have reason to know that his plan of operations was changed again on [300] Thursday, and that he resumed, in substance, the plan that he had on Wednesday morning, which was to fall back to Pipe creek, or to some place in that neighborhood.

This is the second time Sickles claimed that Meade intended to retreat from Gettysburg on July 2. Again Sickles offered no explanation or evidence for this belief, and the committee did not pursue the issue.

Question. In your opinion, as a military man, what do you think of the propriety of again encountering the enemy at the river before he recrossed?

Answer. He should have been followed up closely, and vigorously attacked before he had an opportunity to recross the river.

Question. Under the circumstances, as you understand them, could there have been any great hazard to our army in venturing an engagement there?

Answer. No, sir. If we could whip them at Gettysburg, as we did, we could much more easily whip a running and demoralized army, seeking a retreat which was cut off by a swollen river; and if they could march after being whipped, we certainly could march after winning a battle.

As a corps commander Sickles was entitled to his opinion, but this testimony reveals second guessing on a grand scale. Sickles could have had no knowledge of troop condition, terrain, or Lee's defenses at Williamsport.

Question. Do you know any reason why none of the forces here at Washington were moved up the river to prevent the enemy's recrossing there? Was there anything to prevent that?

Answer. If there were available forces here, as I have understood—

Question. General Heintzelman's corps was here, was it not?

Answer. I presume he had some troops here. I think the main body of his cavalry had been previously ordered to join General Hooker. I have no information of what force of infantry he had here.

In fact, in addition to cavalry, some ten thousand troops from Washington's defenses had been sent to General John Dix on the Peninsula. What remained was well below the strength actually needed to defend the capital.[21]

Question. Did you understand that any of the troops stationed at Baltimore, under General Schenck, were brought into that engagement at Gettysburg?

Answer. No, sir; I do not think any troops were engaged there except those of the army of the Potomac proper. They may have been employed in guarding the line of communication, but I heard of no troops participating in the battle of Gettysburg except those that belonged to the army of the Potomac.

What follows is a pair of masterfully phrased questions by Wade about other troops.

Question. Suppose there had been ten thousand troops in Baltimore, was there any difficulty in bringing them into the fight?

Answer. No, sir; communication was open with Baltimore, with occasionally slight interruptions; but the best way to protect Baltimore was to win that battle.

Question. And would you not say the same about Washington?

Answer. Certainly; the only way to save Washington was to win that battle.

21. Ibid., 99.

Wade implied that there were ten thousand troops at Baltimore that were not used, which was not the case. On June 28, Hooker had sent his chief of staff, Butterfield, to Washington and Baltimore to obtain all available men. After being told by both Halleck and Lincoln that no more troops could be drawn from Washington, Butterfield had gone to Baltimore. There, after examining the actual troop returns, he found that there were not 36,000 men as reported, but only a few thousand. Taking Brigadier General Henry H. Lockwood's brigade of some 2,500 men, Butterfield reported to Hooker that he had taken all available men. The phrasing of Wade's question indicates that he knew there were no troops available in Baltimore.[22]

Question. In your judgment now, should not all the troops disposable about Washington, Baltimore, and Maryland heights have been brought together and concentrated to assist in the fighting of that battle?

Answer. Yes, sir, except those required to guard the line of communication—the railroad. I should say most clearly that all the disposable forces should have been concentrated; and all posts not absolutely essential to be held were secondary and of minor importance compared with strengthening that army for the battle.

Question. Were there any reasons why the troops from the Peninsula, say at Suffolk, could not as well have been brought up before the battle as afterwards?

Answer. None at all; they could have been, unless employed in a co-operative movement on the Peninsula, if an attack on Richmond should have been contemplated.

Such a move was exactly what was planned; in the event, it turned into a pathetic failure. Wade knew this, if only by hindsight.

Question. Do you know what was the reason why General Halleck would not allow the withdrawal of the troops at Harpers Ferry?

One of Wade's aims was to show that Hooker had been treated unfairly, and the garrison at Harper's Ferry provided an excellent example. In hindsight there did not exist a sound reason for denying these troops to Hooker, as their subsequent release to Meade clearly shows. It should be noted, however, that Hal-

22. *OR*, vol. 27, pt. 1, pp. 354–8.

leck's original reply to Meade's request allowed him to "increase or diminish" the garrison as he saw fit, but did not give him permission to abandon Harper's Ferry. It was only after Meade carefully explained his reasons for doing so—something that Hooker had never bothered to do—that permission was granted. In contrast, Hooker's request had been a peremptory demand coupled with the threat of his resignation.[23]

Answer. The reason assigned was, that that post was necessary for the protection of the Baltimore and Ohio railroad; that is, there was an important bridge there, which had been put up at considerable cost, and it would otherwise be destroyed by the enemy.

Question. Are you certain that that bridge was there then—that there was anything more there, at the time the battle was fought, than a pontoon bridge?

Answer. I do not speak of the time the battle was fought; I speak of the time that General Hooker wanted to withdraw the force there, some eight or [301] ten thousand men, and add them to his army. The difference of opinion between General Halleck and General Hooker on that point was the immediate cause of General Hooker's being relieved from command. The reason assigned by General Halleck for not permitting General Hooker to withdraw that force was the one I have stated—that it was necessary to retain it there for the protection of that bridge and the public property that was there.

Question. Was not the true way to protect that bridge to destroy the army of the enemy?

Answer. The destruction of that army was of far more importance than the bridge, or even the railroad itself. That was the great aim and object of our army and of the country at that time, upon which everything appeared to depend.

Question. Do you know whether General Hooker requested these disposable troops to be concentrated with his army for the purpose of fighting that battle?

Answer. He did.

Question. Now, as a military man, and one of a great deal of experience, in your opinion was there any difficulty, under all the circumstances, after the battle of Gettysburg, in destroying Lee's army? If so, will you state from what circumstances that difficulty arose?

Answer. In my judgment as a military man, from all the light I have been

23. Ibid., 63, 66–7.

able to gather upon the subject, from a careful examination of the subject, and from information that I have obtained from officers of the army who followed up Lee's army, I do not think there was any military difficulty to prevent a decisive attack upon General Lee, which must have resulted in the destruction of his army. I think the *morale* of our own troops was never better. I think they would have endured any amount of hardship, marching, and exposure. They were enthusiastic in their wish to attack, as I have reason to know.

Sickles's comments are representative of contemporary feelings among the general public, the administration, Congress, and not a few in the army itself. Meade's failure to bring Lee to battle before he recrossed the Potomac was a great disappointment to everyone, including Meade.

I believe the enemy were substantially out of ammunition, and were in no condition to fight a battle. I have information to that effect from an intelligent officer of my command, [Brigadier] General [Charles K.] Graham, who was wounded and taken prisoner at Gettysburg, and who accompanied General Lee's army on its retreat. Our prisoners expected that we would follow up our success, and so did the enemy. The enemy had no hope of escaping the consequences of another attack, if made. That is to say, that was the statement made by many intelligent officers of the army who conversed with General Graham. If you desire information on that subject, you could probably get it from General Graham more fully and satisfactorily than I could be able to give it to you.

Graham was a brigade commander in Birney's division of Sickles's corps who had been wounded and captured at the Peach Orchard on July 2; he was exchanged a few months later. A close friend of Sickles, he served as a pallbearer at Sickles's wife's funeral in 1867. Sickles was too good a lawyer not to know and be able to count on what a close friend would say before the committee.

Question. But that would be judging of the matter after the battle, and from information that our officers could not be in possession of at the time.

Answer. Those were the facts, and we had reason to suppose that to be the case, because General Lee had to bring all his ammunition with him; he was far away from his base; he had no means of supplying himself in Pennsylvania with any more ammunition than he had brought with him in his column; and every military man knows that three days of fighting will exhaust not only the supplies that men carry with them, but also exhaust the ammunition train, such as is practicable for an army invading an enemy's country to take with it. And that presumption, which would naturally suggest itself to any military mind, was in accordance with the facts.

Question. I was about to ask you whether, after three day's fighting so far from the base of supplies, a military man would not have reason to suspect that the ammunition of the enemy's army was very low?

Answer. Yes, sir; he would be entitled to assume that.

Question. Then I must ask you this question: you have already stated that after that battle, as you understand it, our troops were in good condition and eager to renew the fight?

Answer. Yes, sir.

Question. And that the enemy were on the bank of the river, so that it is a [302] very plain case to you, as you have stated, that they should have been vigorously attacked?

Answer. Yes, sir. I think so.

Question. How, then, do you account for the fact that, under these circumstances, a council of war, by a two-thirds vote, should say that the attack should not be made?

Answer. I cannot account for it in any other way than by the supposition that the immediate purpose of the enemy having been defeated by the result of the battle of Gettysburg, it was not deemed prudent to incur the chances of another fight; that they seemed to be satisfied with what they had done, and did not think it necessary to follow up the advantage.

This testimony played to another of the committee's theories, since the corps commanders (excepting Sickles) were all West Point men.

Question. Do you suppose that that want of harmony and unity of action, to which you have already alluded in your former deposition, had anything to do with the result of that council?

Wade was referring to Sickles's testimony in the Hooker hearings, in which Sickles blamed the lack of support from the corps commanders for many of Hooker's problems.

Answer. I could only say that I have understood that that cause had some influence; but I cannot state any facts of my own knowledge that would indicate that, not having attended any council. I did not attend any council that was held under General Meade. There were several councils held, as I understood. There was a council held on Thursday morning, before the battle opened. There was another one held on Thursday night, and I understood that there were those who voted on Thursday night to retreat. And I have understood that there was another council held on Friday night, the night after the battle, and that there was a pretty strong disposition then to retreat; and, as I have understood from reliable authority, the reason why the enemy was not followed up was on account of differences of opinion whether or no we should ourselves retreat or follow up the enemy.

Question. After the final battle?

Answer. Yes, sir. It was by no means clear in the judgment of the corps commanders, or of the general in command, whether we had won or not. I was not present at the council, and cannot state that of my own knowledge; I have understood that to be the fact. What I am now stating is the result of inquiries which I made in order to find some solution of the query why the enemy was not followed up. As an officer of the army, I expected to hear of nothing else but that the enemy would be followed up. I therefore sought such information as I could get, and that is the result of my inquiries.

After admitting he had not attended any of the councils, Sickles did not hesitate to testify about what he had heard about what had occurred in these councils. Yet Sickles's unnamed sources are incorrect. The only negative comments at the July 2 council came from Major General John Newton, then commanding the First Corps, who was concerned about the actual placement of the line but did not contemplate a retreat. Even Sickles's friend Butterfield could provide no names to the committee of any officer who believed that a retreat was in order. The decision to stay and fight was unanimous.[24]

Question. What did you understand the real meaning of General Meade to be when, in that circular to which you have referred, he stated that the object of the movement had been already accomplished, inasmuch as Washington and Baltimore were covered, and the enemy prevented from crossing the Susquehanna, or something like that?

24. John Gibbon, "The Council of War on the Second Day," *B&L*, 3:313–4. This article contains a copy of Butterfield's minutes of the meeting, with detailed notes on the votes of each of the participants. Also see *LLM*, 2:95–6; *CCW*, 407, 425, 442, 460.

Answer. I understood by that that General Meade considered that General Couch had force enough at Harrisburg to prevent the enemy's crossing the Susquehanna, and that he himself was in sufficient force between General Lee and Washington to cover Washington and Baltimore, and that therefore he need not attack, but might fall back towards Washington, take up a defensive line, and wait until he was attacked in his works.

Given yet another opportunity, Sickles reiterated that Meade did not want to fight at Gettysburg.

Question. Will you state whether, in your opinion as a military man, it was not a very rash and hazardous movement to displace the commanding officer of the army while in the vicinity of the enemy and on the eve of a battle, as was the case when General Hooker was relieved?

Answer. At the time I considered it a misfortune to the army, and apprehended that disaster might result from it.

Question. Was not its tendency to weaken the confidence of the army in their leader?

Answer. Yes, sir. I think the rank and file had entire confidence in General [303] Hooker. I should always regard it as a most hazardous expedient to change the commander of an army in such exigencies as then existed.

Sickles's claim that the rank and file had confidence in Hooker may well have been his real opinion. But officers of the Army of the Potomac were generally dissatisfied with Hooker. According to one officer, there was "no confidence in either his honesty or ability."[25]

Question. Can you give any satisfactory reason why the troops at Harper's Ferry should have been refused to General Hooker, and immediately awarded to General Meade?

Answer. The only solution I can give of it is that General Meade had the confidence and friendship of General Halleck, while General Hooker had not, and that General Halleck would accede to suggestions made by General Meade, while he would not accede to suggestions made by General Hooker.

Question. The request was the same in both cases?

25. Byrne and Weaver, eds., *Haskell of Gettysburg*, 91.

Answer. It is for that very reason that I must say I can see no military reason that could have altered the circumstances, and therefore I must look for it in personal reasons. I suppose the personal relations which existed between General Halleck and General Hooker disinclined him to accede to General Hooker's request. The personal relations being altered, that obstacle did not exist.

Question. Was it not eminently hazardous to withhold ten thousand men from such a battle, when our numbers were not superior to those of the enemy?

Answer. It was sacrificing a great end for a minor consideration; it was periling our success in a general battle, upon which everything depended, to enable us to hold a subordinate post, of no importance whatever if we lost the battle and which could not be held by the enemy if he lost the battle.

Question. Can you really find anything else in this than a willingness in the general-in-chief to jeopard the army to personal considerations—can you place it upon any other ground?

Answer. I cannot conceive of any military reason which explains that extraordinary inconsistency. That is all that, as a solider, I can judge of.

Both Wade and Sickles insulted Halleck's professional conduct by saying he allowed personal feelings to influence a military decision. Neither man had much use for Halleck, but such a personal attack was not warranted.

The remainder of Sickles's testimony covered the ensuing Bristoe and Mine Run campaigns.

Sickles's letter of July 1, 1863.

HEADQUARTERS THIRD ARMY CORPS, July 1, 1863—9.30 P.M.
Major-General BUTTERFIELD,
Chief of Staff:

GENERAL: Before the receipt of your dispatch (dated 4.45 P.M.), four brigades and three batteries of my corps had advanced to the support of General Howard, and reached Gettysburg. I left two brigades and two batteries at Emmitsburg, assuming that the approaches through Emmitsburg toward our left and rear must not be uncovered. General Hancock is not in command—General Howard commands. My impression is, if I may be allowed to make a suggestion, that our left and rear are not sufficiently guarded. Nothing less than the earnest and frequent appeals of General Howard, and his supposed danger, could have induced me to move from the position assigned to me in general orders; but I believe the emergency justified my movement. Shall I return to my position at Emmitsburg, or shall I remain and report to Howard? If my corps is to remain in position here, I hope my brigades at Emmitsburg (and batteries) may be relieved and ordered to join me. This is a good battle-field. Very respectfully,

D. E. SICKLES,
Major-General, Commanding.[26]

Sickles had certainly started off the hearings with a bang. His testimony accused Meade of planning to retreat to the Pipe Creek line before the battle and of favoring a general retreat during the battle. Unnamed corps commanders were also accused of wanting to retreat during and after the battle. It was only through Sickles's advance on July 2 that the army, and the country, had been saved from defeat and destruction.

In Sickles's opinion there was no reason that Meade should not have attacked and destroyed Lee's army before it had crossed the Potomac. Some of the corps commanders were also at fault for Meade's failure to do so.

From the standpoint of military history Sickles's testimony is so full of misstatements and outright lies as to be of little value. Yet it cannot be disregarded by the serious student of the Civil War or the battle of Gettysburg. Its worth lies in what it represents. Sickles's vendetta against Meade shows the degree and intensity of divisions among members of the officer corps in the Army of the Potomac. These divisions had contributed to the removal of both Burnside and Hooker and were no doubt counted on by Sickles and the committee to help remove Meade.

Indeed, Sickles's testimony demonstrates the extent to which the committee was willing to go in its efforts to oust Meade. Most, if not all, of Sickles's testimony was known to the committee prior to his appearance through newspaper articles and general gossip in Washington. It would have been a simple matter for committee members to ascertain the validity of Sickles's claims prior to his testimony. Equally telling is the lack of follow-up questions to some of Sickles's

26. *OR*, vol. 27. pt. 3, p. 468.

more curious statements. No committee member asked, for example, what information Sickles had received and from whom he had received it that satisfied him Meade intended to retreat on July 2 prior to Longstreet's attack. The fact that the committee failed to ask this (as well as other pertinent questions) is indicative of its attitude.

4 Major General Abner Doubleday

Major General Abner Doubleday was the second witness to testify before the committee. At Gettysburg Doubleday was commander of the Third Division, First Corps, and for a short time commander of the First Corps itself. Appearing three days after Sickles, Doubleday did not draw even a majority of the committee; only Wade, Chandler, and Julian are recorded as being present for his testimony. Called to support Sickles's contention that Meade had never wanted to fight at Gettysburg, Doubleday managed to come up with some spectacular revelations of his own.

Abner Doubleday is remembered today as the creator of modern baseball, but in the nineteenth century he was known primarily for his military exploits. The grandson of a Revolutionary War soldier and the son of a newspaper editor and two-term Democratic congressman, Doubleday was born in Ballston Spa, New York, in 1819. He graduated from West Point in 1842 and was commissioned into the artillery. Following service in the Mexican and Seminole Wars, he was posted to various garrisons along the Atlantic coast. In 1861 Doubleday was stationed in Charleston Harbor, where on April 12 he awoke to find himself in the middle of a shooting war.[1]

Appointed a brigadier general of volunteers in February 1862, he commanded a brigade at Second Bull Run and South Mountain. At South Mountain he took over command of his division after the wounding of his commander. Normally a division was led by a major general, but Doubleday led his division as a brigadier general at both Antietam and Fredericksburg before being appointed as a major general in November 1862. At Chancellorsville

1. *DAB*, 3:191.

his division was in reserve and not engaged, a fate of nearly two-thirds of the army there.[2]

During the Gettysburg campaign, Doubleday was the senior division commander in Major General John Reynolds's First Corps. When Meade replaced Hooker, Meade put Reynolds in charge of the left wing of the army, consisting of the First Corps (Reynolds), the Third Corps (Sickles), and the Eleventh Corps (O. O. Howard). With Reynolds's elevation to wing commander, Doubleday, as senior division commander, assumed command of the First Corps. It was as commander of the First Corps that Doubleday fought the first day at Gettysburg.

On July 1, against heavy pressure, John Buford's First Cavalry Division delayed the advancing corps of Lee's army for much of the morning. The arrival of Reynolds with the First Corps gave Buford's men much-needed support, enabling the Federal forces to hold the Confederates at bay for some time. Yet Reynolds's untimely death created some confusion about who was in overall command of the field. The question was solved, at least momentarily, by the arrival of Major General O. O. Howard and the Eleventh Corps. As the senior officer on the field, Howard assumed command of the battle.

Seniority was important not only to the officers, but to the smooth functioning of the army itself. The system of seniority was based on an officer's date of promotion; it created a chain of command that allowed for the rapid replacement of commanders who were killed or disabled in battle. With the death of Reynolds, Doubleday not only continued in command of the First Corps, but—as the senior division commander—expected that the permanent command of the corps would now be his.

Unfortunately for Doubleday, the drawbacks of a system based strictly on seniority were being recognized by army officials and the Lincoln administration. The reward of command was no longer reserved for those who had served the longest. More than a year before Gettysburg, Congress had attempted to solve the problems associated with seniority by authorizing Lincoln to assign command "without regard to seniority of rank." While well intentioned, the resolution was flawed, since it referred to officers in the same field or department. A conservative interpretation of the resolution, and the one placed on it by many in the army, was that it did not apply to the basic structure of the army itself. In other words, the officer corps believed that while seniority might be ignored in a case involving two cavalry officers in a

2. Ibid.

cavalry regiment, an artillery officer could not replace a senior infantry officer in an infantry regiment. Conservatives in the army also believed that an officer from outside the unit, regiment, division, or corps should not be brought in and placed over available officers within the unit. Both Lincoln and Stanton, however, interpreted the congressional resolution as allowing for appointments to command regardless of seniority, branch of service, or unit. General Halleck followed this more liberal interpretation when he wrote Meade a letter, along with his orders to assume command of the Army of the Potomac, saying, "You are authorized to remove from command, and to send from the army, any officer or other person you may deem proper, and to appoint to command as you may deem expedient."[3]

With Reynolds dead, Meade exercised this prerogative when he sent for Major General John Newton, commander of the Third Division, Sixth Corps, to take over the First Corps. For Doubleday, this was the equivalent of a slap in the face. To be supplanted by another officer called into question his ability to command. Adding insult to injury, Newton—a classmate of Doubleday's at West Point—was Doubleday's junior in rank.[4]

Another problem for Doubleday was that upon hearing of Reynolds's death, Meade sent Major General Winfield Scott Hancock, commander of the Second Corps, to assume command of the left wing and to determine if Gettysburg was a good place to fight. After surveying the situation, Hancock notified Meade that the "ground appears not unfavorable," but adding, "Howard says that Doubleday's command gave way." If Meade already had concerns about Doubleday, Hancock's negative report sealed Doubleday's fate.[5]

After the battle Doubleday asked Meade to either restore him to command of the First Corps or give him permission to leave the army. When Meade refused to reinstate him to command, Doubleday left the army on July 7 and returned to Washington, where he remained in various posts for the remainder of the war. Perhaps justifiably, Doubleday felt embittered and humiliated about being relieved by his junior. He had fought the First Corps about as well as could have been expected under the circumstances. Howard's comment to Hancock about Doubleday's troops could well have been intended to deflect questions about what appeared to be the second (Chancellorsville being the first) dismal showing of the Eleventh Corps. Though Doubleday was not

3. General Order No. 37, April 8, 1862; *OR*, vol. 27, pt. 1, p. 61.

4. Warner, *Generals in Blue*, 345; *MG*, 143.

5. *OR*, vol. 27, pt. 1, p. 366.

alone in being superseded by a junior (Hancock was Howard's junior), he bore ill feelings toward both Meade and Howard for the rest of his life.[6]

[305] Testimony of Major General Abner Doubleday.

Washington, March 1, 1864.
Major General Abner Doubleday sworn and examined.

By the chairman:

Question. You were with the army of the Potomac when the battle of Gettysburg was fought?

Answer. Yes, sir.

Question. Give the committee an account of that battle in your own way.

Answer. When we marched to Marsh creek there was a rebel force on our left flank at Fairfield. When General Meade assumed the command of the army he gave General Reynolds the command of the right wing of the army, consisting of the 1st, 3d, and 11th corps. General Reynolds told me that his duties frequently required him to absent himself from the 1st corps—his own corps—and that I must assume command of it, which I did.

After we got to Marsh creek it was found that the force of the enemy which had been at Fairfield had left—had gone north—so that we had then no enemy directly to the west of us. General Buford's cavalry had gone to Gettysburg, and were engaged in feeling the enemy on the roads leading from that town. They reported that the enemy were in heavy force at Cashtown and Mummasburg, places to the northwest of Gettysburg. Cashtown is on the great road from Chambersburg.

On the 30th of June General Meade sent a circular to the effect that the enemy were apparently marching in heavy force on Gettysburg, stating that we should remain as we were until the enemy developed his intentions. This was very much like saying that he would give us orders after the battle was fought, for he had already stated the intention of the enemy to be to take Gettysburg.

Actually, the circular was what one would expect of an army commander feeling his way toward battle. Meade stated that he would basically hold his current position until the "plans of the enemy shall have been more fully developed,"

6. Abner Doubleday, *Chancellorsville and Gettysburg* (1882; reprint, with a introduction by Gary W. Gallagher, New York: Da Capo Press, 1994), x; *DAB*, 3:392.

and said that the corps commanders were to be ready to move against the enemy at a moment's notice. The circular was conservative, but—given Lee's reputation and ability—prudent. It was hardly as tentative as Doubleday described.[7]

That place was a point of very great importance. It is like the hub of a wheel, having seven great roads and a railroad leading out of it, namely, the roads to Hagerstown, Chambersburg, Carlisle, Harrisburg, York, Frederick, and Taneytown, all of which places may be considered as on the circumference of the wheel. With our troops in possession of Gettysburg we could check the enemy on any one of these roads, as we could hold the center. The enemy in possession of that point would have gained a great advantage, in my opinion; shortening and strengthening his line to Williamsport, from which place his supplies of ammunition, &c., were supposed to come, and being in a condition to strike in any direction.

General Reynolds, believing that it was the best policy to fight the enemy as soon as he could meet him, and prevent his sending off those immense quantities of supplies from Pennsylvania, and finding on the morning of the 1st of July that Buford's cavalry were hard pressed, directed me to put the 1st corps in motion to go to the assistance of Buford.

Doubleday's description of Reynolds's aggressive tendencies offers a narrow but illuminating window into Meade's thinking. On the morning of June 30, Meade moved his headquarters from Middleburg to Taneytown, about fifteen miles southeast of Gettysburg and north of the proposed Pipe Creek line. It was a position, he told Reynolds, "given more with a view to an advance on Gettysburg than a defensive point." If Meade's only plan was to stand at Pipe Creek, why did he send to Gettysburg an officer likely to pick a fight? If Reynolds found only a portion of Lee's army at Gettysburg, the rest of Meade's forces could concentrate quickly with an opportunity to defeat Lee in detail. If Lee was at Gettysburg in overwhelming force, Reynolds could fall back to the Pipe Creek line. While hardly indicative of a plan to attack Lee's army, this demonstrates that Meade was not thinking purely defensively.[8]

He told me that he had already ordered [Brigadier General James] Wadsworth's division to go forward, and that it was already underway. I think this

7. *OR*, vol. 27, pt. 3, pp. 416–7.
8. *OR*, vol. 27, pt. 1, p. 144; *MG*, 133.

was about half past seven o'clock in the morning. General Reynolds read his telegrams to me, showing where our troops were, and what they were doing. He then sprang on his horse and rode forward to join Wadsworth's division, which had started, directing me to bring up the balance of the corps and the batteries. Wadsworth's division had but one battery with it, Hall's Maine battery.

The rest of the corps consisted of Brigadier General John C. Robinson's Second Division and Doubleday's Third Division under Brigadier General Thomas A. Rowley. Four batteries traveled with these two divisions.

I waited until I had drawn in my pickets, and put the other two divisions and the batteries of the 1st corps in motion; I then heard rapid cannon firing, showing that the cavalry were briskly engaged. I say "cavalry," for there had not been time for Wadsworth's division of infantry to reach there. Hearing [306] this cannon firing I put spurs to my horse, and with my staff galloped in advance of the last two divisions of infantry, and reached the ground just as the head of Wadsworth's division was going into action. I had previously sent my adjutant general and an aid[e] to General Reynolds for orders. There are two roads leading into Gettysburg from the westward, the one from the northwest, and the other from the southwest. It was on the road from the northwest that the main force of the enemy were approaching.

To the west of Gettysburg is an eminence that we called Seminary ridge, because there is a seminary situated on it, between the two roads referred to. This ridge runs north and south, and is about a quarter of a mile to the west of Gettysburg. About four hundred yards to the west of the first ridge there is another [McPherson's Ridge], also running north and south. Nearly parallel to the road from the northwest there is a railroad grading, part of it embankment and part of it deep cut, passing through these ridges. General Reynolds simply said to me, "I will defend this Cashtown road," or rather, "I will hold on to this road, and you will hold on to the other." These were the orders he sent to me. He established a brigade and a battery to hold the road which came from Cashtown, placing his men under shelter of the most westerly of the ridges. Wadsworth's division now going into action consisted of two brigades—one under General Cutler, and the other, usually called the Iron brigade, under General Meredith—and one battery, called Hall's battery.

Cutler's brigade consisted of the 7th Indiana, 76th New York, 84th New York (also known as the 14th Brooklyn), 95th New York, 147th New York, and the

56th Pennsylvania. In all, it had approximately 2,000 men. The Iron Brigade consisted of the 19th Indiana, 24th Michigan, 2nd Wisconsin, 6th Wisconsin, and 7th Wisconsin, totaling approximately 1,800 men. At Gettysburg the Iron Brigade lost 61 percent of its men.

Hall's battery was Captain James A. Hall's 2nd (B) Battery, Maine Light Artillery, with six 3-inch rifles.

General Reynolds took Cutler's brigade and Hall's battery to hold his part of the line, and directed the other brigade to be placed on a line with the first in a piece of woods which lay between the two roads. These woods were already occupied by the enemy, who opened fire upon us, killing General Reynolds almost at the first volley.

The Confederate brigade involved was Archer's Third Brigade of Heth's division.

The Iron brigade charged with great gallantry; rushed into the woods, and on the left and somewhat on the right of the woods, and drove the enemy before them into a little ravine called Willoughby's run; there they captured a large number of prisoners, with general officers.[9] They formed on the high ground on the other side of the run. This was being accomplished as I rode up. I sent word to them that this movement had carried them too far to the front, and they must fall back on a line with Cutler's brigade. They had got several hundred yards beyond that. I think some one else gave a similar order—whether General Meredith or General Wadsworth I do not know. They returned and took up a position in the woods and on the left of the woods. In the mean time Cutler's brigade had been ordered back by General Wadsworth. Its right flank had been turned and the battery attacked, and it was ordered back to Seminary ridge, as I have stated, leaving the battery and two regiments standing on the left of the battery. The right of the battery was now uncovered. The enemy charged up the railroad grading and attacked the right of the battery, killing, I think, all the horses and wounding all the men at one piece—doing a great deal of damage. The battery was directed by General Wadsworth to take up a new position, and finally was withdrawn by way of the railroad grading—the captain of the battery said, by an aid[e] of General Wadsworth. He complained of this route, inasmuch as once on the grading there was no

9. Brig. Gen. James J. Archer was the first general officer captured since Lee had assumed command of the Army of Northern Virginia.

getting off it for a long distance, and the enemy had guns planted to enfilade it. He states that he finally reached Seminary ridge and took shelter behind it, and was again ordered to the front by another aid[e] of General Wadsworth; that he advanced towards the position indicated until he found that the enemy held the ground he had been ordered to take, and that if he went any further he would lose his battery; he then returned. That gives the history of the battery so far.

Cutler's brigade, as I have stated, fell back, with the exception of two regiments—the 14th Brooklyn and the 95th New York. When this condition of affairs attracted my attention, I found the enemy massing themselves in front of Cutler. I had kept one regiment, the 6th Wisconsin, as a reserve. I ordered [307] that regiment to attack on the flank of the enemy as he formed, if he formed in front of Cutler. That regiment, under Lieutenant Colonel Dawes, together with the 14th Brooklyn, under Colonel Fowler, and the 95th New York, under Colonel Biddle, made a most gallant charge, and surrounded the enemy, who had rushed into the railroad cut, and after a short but desperate conflict we captured two rebel regiments, with their battle flags. The remainder of the enemy retreated to their first position. I ordered the line of battle to be resumed as it was originally. The enemy, to all appearance, were repulsed, and we were perfectly successful at this stage, having captured Brigadier General Archer and a large number of prisoners from his brigade, two regiments, with their battle flags, from [Brigadier General Joseph] Davis's rebel brigade, and driven the enemy back so that their attack had become comparatively a feeble one. Shortly after this the remaining divisions of the 1st corps, with the batteries, came up. One of these divisions (Robinson's) I kept in reserve behind the Seminary. I placed one brigade of the other division on the right, and one on the left, of the woods; and General Howard arrived at Gettysburg about the same time with the 11th corps. The most prominent successes of the day occurred before he assumed command of the field.

This account suggests that Doubleday prepared extensively for his appearance before the committee. It is unlikely that his highly detailed description of the actions of Captain James A. Hall's Second Maine Battery—a small unit on a very busy battlefield—had not been rehearsed earlier. Doubleday's posting in Washington would have given him the opportunity to talk to both Sickles and members of the committee prior to his testimony.

I now received information from General Buford, in person, that the troops of the enemy with which we had been contending were A. P. Hill's corps, numbering altogether, I suppose, some 30,000 or 35,000 men; opposing them we had the 1st corps, numbering about 8,200 men. General Buford now reported to me that the rebel General Ewell, with his whole corps, was coming down from York, on my right flank, making another 30,000.

Doubleday's estimate of A. P. Hill's and Ewell's strength is interesting, though inaccurate; their actual combined strength was closer to forty thousand, some twenty to twenty-five thousand less than his estimate. It was common for both sides to overestimate opposing forces by as much as 50 percent, and Doubleday doubtless felt that it would do no harm to his reputation to show that he had fought against overwhelming odds.

I sent word to General Howard, and requested him to keep Ewell off of my flank, as I had as much as I could do to attend to A. P. Hill. About the same time I received an order from General Howard to this effect: "Tell Doubleday to fight on the left, and I will fight on the right." About the same time he sent word to me that if forced back I must try and hold on to the Seminary. These were all the orders I received from him during the day that I remember.

Over the years Doubleday twice changed his story about his orders. In an 1875 letter to S. P. Bates, he wrote that Howard had told him to retreat to Cemetery Hill if necessary. In his 1882 book Chancellorsville and Gettysburg, *he wrote that he thought he had been given only one order: if forced to retreat, he was to fall back to Cemetery Hill. In his book he also recounted that he had sent an aide, Lieutenant Slagel, to ask for reinforcements for Steinwher's division of the Eleventh Corps, which Howard refused. Doubleday wrote that he then had sent his adjutant general, Halstead, to ask again for reinforcements or to obtain an order for retreat. Both requests had been denied.*[10]

He also sent me word of Ewell's approach about the same time that I informed him of it, and formed the 11th corps to keep Ewell off. Ewell now made a junction with A. P. Hill's corps, so that Ewell's line was northwest and east of me, and A. P. Hill's was nearly west. The men on our side were in very fine spirits, and were elated to the highest degree. One division that I had was composed almost entirely of Pennsylvanians.[11] I made short speeches to each regiment as it passed and went into action, and the men were full of enthusiasm.

10. *GC*, 706 n. 125; Doubleday, *Chancellorsville and Gettysburg*, 141, 146.

11. This was Doubleday's Third Division, First Corps, where 60 percent of the regiments were from Pennsylvania.

I had assigned one brigade, under Colonel Stone, to quite an open position, where they were shelled pretty severely. Colonel Stone remarked, as he took the position, "*We have come to stay.*" This went quickly through his brigade, the men adopting it as a watchword; they all said, "*We have come to stay.*" And a very large portion of them never left that ground.

My attention was called to a wide and dangerous gap between the 11th and 1st corps, and I sent two regiments of Baxter's brigade, Robinson's division, to fill it and keep the enemy out. After a short time I found that that force was inadequate, and I then sent the remainder of the brigade. This left me but one brigade in reserve. But I found that even that force was inadequate, and with the greatest reluctance was compelled to send General Robinson and the last brigade of my reserve to assist in holding the position, which was on our extreme right. They held it successfully, capturing a large number of prisoners, estimated as high as a thousand, and taking several battle flags from the enemy. But the division of the 11th corps on our right fell back about half past 2 o'clock.[12] The time is given by General Wadsworth in his report. I did not look at the time myself. One of my generals—General Baxter—said that [308] division fell back before the enemy's line of skirmishers. General Wadsworth, in his report, says they "partially" engaged the enemy.[13]

The Eleventh Corps became a favorite whipping boy for the Army of the Potomac and was eventually broken up in April 1864. The corps contained a high percentage of men of German birth in its ranks, and more than one of its officers was unable to speak English. While anti-Irish sentiments in the North are now well known, there also existed strong anti-German feelings among Northerners and in the army. It is ironic that a nation that declared it fought for the freedom of blacks should at the same time harbor such resentment for so many other minorities.

The enemy entered into this interval and folded their lines right around my right flank. I did not think I ought to retreat until General Howard gave the order, as he was then the ranking officer on the field, and I held on until a quarter before 4 o'clock, when the whole country was filled with the advancing lines of the enemy, double lines, in some cases treble lines, with reserves of

12. This was the Third Division, Eleventh Corps, under the temporary command of Brig. Gen. Alexander Schimmelfennig. The division's commander, Maj. Gen. Carl Schurz, commanded the corps while Howard commanded the field.

13. *OR*, vol. 27, pt. 1, p. 266.

battalions in mass. Our forces had fought with desperation, a portion of them for nearly six hours. Regiments were reduced to mere squads. They had made repeatedly the most heroic bayonet charges against overwhelming masses and driven them back. It was not possible to remain a moment longer. I had given orders in the morning to throw up a little rough rail intrenchment, a feeble pile of rails, around the seminary, and behind this the remnants of my line rallied. They fought by the seminary until the artillery, ambulances, and everything had retired in safety. When they were overpowered and fell back, I wanted to gain a little longer time, and I threw my personal guard of forty men around and into the building, and then fought a whole brigade for twenty minutes. In the onslaught upon us at this point, our artillery gained an enfilading fire on the front line of the enemy and swept it away. But the other rebel lines came up and outflanked us on all sides, and when we fell back we did so in fact between two lines of the enemy. I remained at the seminary myself until I thought everything had been got off, and was among the last to leave. I then rode through the streets of the town and rejoined my command.

I think the retreat would have been a very successful one, if it had not been unfortunately the case that a portion of the 11th corps, which had held out very well on the extreme right, had been surrounded and had fallen back at the same time that my right flank fell back. These two bodies of men became entangled in the streets of the town, and quite a number were captured. I lost but one gun and two or three caisson bodies. The men behaved in the most heroic manner in falling back. They would retreat a hundred or a hundred and fifty yards and then turn around and face the enemy again, fire upon them and keep them off for a time; then fall back another hundred yards, turn around and make a further stand. They passed through the town quietly and calmly; I saw no running, no undue haste. We re-formed our lines about a mile and a half from our first position, on an eminence called Cemetery hill, where the battle of the next day was fought.

During this time General Meade was at Taneytown, some ten or twelve miles off, engaged in laying out a very long line of battle—I should judge ten miles long at least—from Taneytown to Manchester, along Pipe creek. He seemed to have determined that the battle should take place there. It is inexplicable to me that he could hear the thunder of that battle all day without riding up to see something in relation to it, as he could have come up in an hour. Had he done so, there were two corps in our vicinity which he could have ordered to our assistance. General Sickles did start for that purpose without orders, though too late to be of service. There was no enemy in front of either of those two corps, but Slocum refused to leave without orders from General Meade, and I suppose he was right on strict military principles.

Doubleday had at last gotten to what the committee wanted to hear. Meade had seemed to want to fight at Pipe Creek. Moreover, he had not responded to the sounds of battle, although Sickles had done so without orders.

Doubleday implied that if Meade had ordered two corps to the scene, Union forces would have been victorious. Yet his testimony did not tell the whole story. Howard's Eleventh Corps was already on the field, Sickles's Third Corps was on the way, and Slocum's Twelfth Corps was only five miles from Gettysburg an hour or so before noon. Meade's orders had anticipated the possible events at Gettysburg, and by afternoon he had ordered all corps commanders to hurry their troops forward. Slocum's tarrying was due to his own indecisiveness, not a lack of instructions.[14]

At the close of the day an order arrived from General Meade displacing both Howard and myself, placing me under the command of a junior officer, General Newton; and placing General Howard under General Hancock, who was his junior officer also. I thought this was done as a token of disapprobation at our fighting at all that day. When General Meade issued the order he was absent from the field and knew but little of the battle. He never asked me a single question in relation to the operations of that day.

This is the heart of Doubleday's grievance against Meade. He had been displaced from a position he thought he had earned, commander of the First Corps, by an officer junior in rank. Howard had not been replaced as a corps commander but was temporarily placed under the command of his junior, Hancock, who was Meade's representative. Even this had greatly upset Howard. Unlike Doubleday, however, Howard had not lost command of a corps.[15]

Question. Had you received any orders from General Meade before this battle commenced, with regard to what you should do?

[309] Answer. If any orders were received they are buried with General Reynolds; his staff know of none. When we went into this battle we supposed, as General Reynolds was very high in General Meade's confidence, that it was

14. *GC*, 310, 313.
15. Ibid., 666; *MG*, 143.

understood that the remainder of the army would come to our assistance. I think everything was left at loose ends, and there were no orders at all. I do not believe that our forces actually engaged, belonging to the two corps, amounted to over 14,000 men. There was a reserve of 3,000 or 4,000 of the 11th corps which did not join actively in the fight. It fired some shots from Cemetery hill, but the most of them fell short into our own front line. Now, 14,000 men were wholly inadequate to contend against two immense corps of the enemy, amounting to 60,000 men. I do not mean that 60,000 of the enemy were in the front line opposed to us, but that there were 60,000 including the reserves of the two rebel corps, enabling them to bring up fresh troops continually to attack us while our men were worn out.

The long, feeble line of battle on Pipe creek, laid out by General Meade, seemed to be chosen for defensive purposes, to cover Washington and Baltimore. It appears to me that the results of occupying that line would have been that the enemy would simply have let us severely alone, and either have taken Harrisburg or gone on *ad infinitum* plundering the State of Pennsylvania.

Doubleday was intimating that Meade had been caught unprepared and had reacted poorly to the situation. His only plan had been the Pipe Creek line, which was strictly defensive in nature and easily turned. While this was more of what the committee wanted to hear, it was not the case.

Doubleday's comments on the ease of flanking the Pipe Creek line generally agree with Confederate general James Longstreet's ideas. In a controversy still with us today, Longstreet had wanted to turn the Union right at Gettysburg. Had Meade fallen back to Pipe Creek or elsewhere, Longstreet would have found suitable ground and awaited Meade's attack. Longstreet believed, probably correctly, that public, congressional, and administration pressure would have forced Meade to attack, greatly increasing the Army of Northern Virginia's chances of success.[16]

Question. You have described the first day of the fight?

Answer. Yes, sir. According to the reports rendered to me, we entered the fight with 8,200 men in the 1st corps, and came out with 2,450.

Question. Go on and describe the fight of the second day.

16. James Longstreet, "Lee in Pennsylvania," in *Annals of the War,* ed. Alexander K. McClure (1879; reprint, Edison, N.J.: Blue & Gray Press, 1996), 414.

Answer. On the second day I was in command of a division[17] stationed behind Cemetery hill. Nothing remarkable occurred in which I was engaged until towards sundown, when Sickles, who was pretty far advanced to the front, was driven in, and a part of Hancock's force sent to help him was also thrown back. I had been joined the night before by a Vermont brigade under General Stannard, increasing my force to about 2,500 men.

I received orders on the evening of that day to bring up this force with all haste to Hancock's assistance, who was suffering severely and being driven back. My division was formed in several lines, I think five lines in all. Having arrived at the place, a charge was ordered. This was about dusk. General Newton issued orders that that charge should be stopped. My front line, however, kept on at the request of General Hancock, who happened to be near them. He told them he had lost four guns, and asked them to try and retake them, as the enemy were retiring. This front line continued on their charge and did not halt, but went in and regained Hancock's four guns which he had lost, and captured two guns from the enemy, and brought in quite a number of prisoners. They apologized to me for not halting, and I accepted the apology. We remained in that position for the remainder of the battle.

Doubleday's testimony here is self-promoting bombast, as is much of the rest of his testimony. The intimation that he led his troops to the front is not supported by other witnesses, or even by his own writings. In his battle report Doubleday said that he arrived at the scene after the enemy had retired. The charge by Doubleday's troops was made by the Thirteenth Vermont under Colonel Francis V. Randall and was ordered by General Hancock before Doubleday reached the area. Doubleday's account of the troops apologizing for their enthusiasm also does not appear elsewhere, even in his own book.

More serious is Doubleday's assertion that General Newton, his junior and replacement, had tried to stop the successful charge of the Thirteenth Vermont. This charge is also not supported by the evidence and is not repeated in his book.[18]

About 2 o'clock in the afternoon on the third day of the battle a tremendous cannonade was opened on us from at least 125 guns. They had our exact range, and the destruction was fearful. Horses were killed in every direction; I

17. This was Doubleday's own Third Division, First Corps.

18. *OR*, vol. 27, pt. 1, p. 258; Pfanz, *Gettysburg: The Second Day,* 421–3; Doubleday, *Chancellorsville and Gettysburg,* 176–7. See also *GC,* 424, and Jordan, *Winfield Scott Hancock,* 93.

lost two horses myself, and almost every officer lost one or more, and quite a large number of caissons were blown up.

The lack of an effective preparatory bombardment is often cited as a contributing factor in the failure of the Confederate assault. At least as far as Doubleday was concerned, the fire was effective.

I knew this was the prelude to a grand infantry charge, as artillery is generally massed in this way, to disorganize the opposing command, for the infantry to charge in the interval. I told my men to shelter themselves in every way behind the rocks, or little elevations of ground, while the artillery firing took place, and to spring to their feet and hold their ground as soon as the charge came.

When the enemy finally charged, they came on in three lines, with additional lines called, in military language, wings, the object of the wings being to prevent the main force from being flanked. This charge was first directed towards my lines, but seeing that they were quite strong, five lines deep, and well strengthened [310] with rails, stones, and behind which the men lay, the enemy changed his mind, and concluded to make the attack on the division of 2d corps, on my right, where there were but two lines.[19] He marched by his right flank, and then marched to his front. In doing this, the wing apparently did not understand the movement, but kept straight on. The consequence was, that there was a wide gap between the wing and the main charging force, which enabled my men on the right, the brigade of General Stannard, to form immediately on the flank of the charging column, while the enemy were subjected to an awful fire of artillery in front. It is said some few of them laid their hands on our guns. The prisoners state that what ruined them was Stannard's brigade on their flank, as they found it impossible to contend with it in that position; and they drew off all in a huddle to get away from it. I sent two regiments to charge them in front at the same time. While this was going on the enemy were subjected to a terrific artillery fire at short range, and the result was that they retreated with frightful loss.

Some five minutes after the charge was broken up and they began to retreat, a large number of batteries and regiments of infantry reported to me, as I sat on horseback, for orders to repulse the attack. I posted them, with the ap-

19. The change of direction was a preplanned move to bring the focus of the attack on the famous "Copse of Trees."

proval of the corps commander, though they were a little too late to be of essential service.

I would state that the wing of the enemy which got astray was also met by part of Stannard's brigade, which also formed on its flank and it also retreated. Thus the day was won, and the country saved.

Question. That was the last day of the battle?

Answer. Yes, sir.

By Mr. Chandler:

Question. In your judgment, which army suffered the most in those three days' battle?

Answer. I think the enemy suffered far more than we did. We suffered heavily the first day, on account of the overpowering army brought against us. But the other days we were partially sheltered by stone barricades, &c., which protected our men from musketry fire, while the enemy advanced through the open fields.

By the chairman:

Question. How far was General Meade from where the battle of the last day was fought?

Answer. The battle-field was very contracted, and he could not have been very far from it.

Question. If I have understood you, from what you could learn, the plan and intention of General Meade was not to fight the battle where it was fought?

Answer. It would seem not; and yet the enemy was in General Reynolds's immediate front. They were three or four miles from Gettysburg on one side, and we were three or four miles on the other. Under those circumstances it was almost impossible to prevent a collision, unless one party or the other withdrew.

Question. Do you know whether there were any orders from General Meade to retreat before this battle of the first day?

Answer. I do not think there were when General Reynolds commenced the fight. About the close of that day's fight I have no doubt such orders were issued. I have alluded to a circular informing us that the enemy was marching in heavy force on Gettysburg. It was of vital importance to know whether we were to defend the place or give it up. But we got no orders, although the enemy were marching on the town, and something had to be done immediately.

Doubleday's answer may have caught Wade by surprise. It was Sickles's contention that the Pipe Creek circular was an order to retreat.

Wade did find good material in the first part of Doubleday's answer, in which he said that he had no doubt that a retreat order was issued on the first day. Like Sickles, Doubleday offered no evidence or support for his assertion. In his 1882 book, however, his story changed completely. In a lengthy footnote Doubleday actually defended the prudence of issuing the Pipe Creek circular and did not mention any order to retreat on the first day. In fact, he did not mention any order to retreat at all; he merely asserted his opinion that Meade "did desire" to retreat during the council on the second day but was dissuaded by the vote of his corps commanders.[20]

Question. Did you know that General Reynolds and General Sickles had an order to retreat just before that battle commenced?

[311] Answer. I do not know that General Reynolds had such an order. He was a man who always obeyed orders literally.

Question. You do not know whether General Sickles had such an order?

Answer. I do not.

This exchange about the Pipe Creek circular must have been a disappointment for Wade. His first question, in which he presumed that a retreat order had been issued and asked for confirmation, was answered in the negative. Of course, a division commander did not always know a corps commander's orders, but Doubleday added that if Reynolds had received a retreat order he would have obeyed it.

Doubleday's assertion that he did not know if Sickles had received a retreat order was a little surprising. Having been in Washington for some time, Doubleday must have been aware of Sickles's very public denouncements of Meade. It is also likely that Doubleday met with Sickles during this time.

Question. Which army outnumbered the other?

Answer. He thought the enemy had 90,000 men, while we had but 70,000. That is the best information I could gather.

Question. Did you have to assist you in that battle the troops stationed in and around Baltimore under General Schenck?

Answer. Not to my knowledge.

20. Doubleday, *Chancellorsville and Gettysburg*, 185.

Question. Can you tell why, after that fight, General Howard and yourself were removed from your command?

Answer. I was removed from the command of the 1st corps. General Howard was not removed from command of his corps, but directed to obey General Hancock, who was his junior, after the first day of the fight.

Question. Why was that?

Answer. I think General Meade thought a couple of scapegoats were necessary; in case the next day's battle turned out unfavorably, he wished to mark his disapprobation of the first day's fight. General Meade is in the habit of violating the organic law of the army to place his personal friends in power. There has always been a great deal of favoritism in the army of the Potomac. No man who is an anti-slavery man or an anti-McClellan man can expect decent treatment in that army as at present constituted.

This was exactly the type of testimony the committee wanted. Meade had been looking to shift the blame if things went badly, and he played favorites in putting his personal friends in power. More importantly, he did not look with favor on men who were either antislavery or anti-McClellan. For a committee whose majority felt strongly on both issues, here was cause enough for Meade's removal. But what should have concerned the committee was whether the charges had merit. In particular, what were Meade's feelings on McClellan and slavery?

Meade's letters during the period of McClellan's command of the army reveal admiration for "Little Mac." Despite his faults, McClellan was without a doubt the most beloved commander of the Army of the Potomac. Yet Meade's opinion of McClellan was not without criticism. He believed that Little Mac was too biased by personal influences and lacked the "nerve to run . . . risks." Meade was thus not one of the small clique of officers and politicians who sought the return of McClellan to command at almost any cost, which was something the committee bitterly opposed.[21]

Meade's position on slavery is somewhat more difficult to pin down. One of the few insights into his views on the issue comes from a published account of a dinner party. When one of his fellow diners joked that Meade would be assigned to command a corps of black soldiers, Meade responded that if the black soldiers "were going into the field and really could be brought heartily to fight, I was ready to command them and should prefer such duty to others that might be assigned me." Members of the committee were not concerned with the truth of the

21. *LLM*, November 28, 1861, 1:232; January 2, 1863, 1:345.

matter, however. They simply wanted to use Doubleday's testimony to bolster their own agenda, which they did in their final report.[22]

By 1883, eleven years after Meade's death, Doubleday had completely changed his mind on the antislavery and anti-McClellan charges he had leveled at Meade. Writing to the New York Times *on April 1, 1883, he explained his remarks before the committee: "The fact is, that just before the battle of Gettysburg I was applied to by an officer of high rank, a confidential friend of Gen. Meade, to give him a list of such officers of my division as had made strong demonstrations when Gen. McClellan was removed from command. The object of the inquiry was to promote these men over the heads of others equally deserving. . . . Believing Gen. Meade to be a party to this arrangement, I thought he intended to carry out this policy, and testified accordingly. I afterward ascertained that I was mistaken in this respect; . . . When I understood the circumstances I did not blame him for his action toward me at Gettysburg."*[23]

Question. Has that, in your judgment, led to great disasters, from time to time, in the army of the Potomac?

Answer. Yes, I think it has.

Question. You speak of political favoritism. Explain what you mean by that.

Answer. I think there have been pro-slavery cliques controlling that army, composed of men who, in my opinion, would not have been unwilling to make a compromise in favor of slavery, and who desired to have nobody put in authority except those who agreed with them on that subject.

This was more confirmation of the committee's belief that West Point men favored slavery and were willing to compromise on the issue.

Question. Do you believe that this feeling of rivalry and jealousy, that seems to have actuated the high corps commanders of that army, has been detrimental to the public service, and led to checks and defeats?

Answer. Undoubtedly. I cannot but think that there has been an indifference, to say the least, on the part of certain officers, to the success of our army. I do not believe that General Pope received all the co-operation he was entitled to; and I do not believe that General Burnside received it.

22. Ibid., February 27, 1863, 1:356.

23. Ibid., 2: Appendix.

Doubleday was probably as close to saying there were traitors in the army as he could get without saying it. His implication, or at least the one the committee would draw, was that Meade numbered among those officers who showed an "indifference" to the success of the army.

Doubleday's comment on Burnside verged on dangerous ground. The most prominent officer who had failed to support Burnside was Hooker.

Question. Can you give any reason why, after you had whipped the enemy, and they finally retreated, they were not followed up vigorously?

Answer. I have no idea why they were not pursued. I believe the 6th corps had not been very actively engaged—at least not so much as the other corps. They were comparatively fresh, and could have been thrown upon the enemy.

By Mr. Chandler:

Question. After the repulse of the enemy, were our troops so much exhausted by the three days' fighting, that it was impossible for them to follow up the enemy vigorously?

Answer. I think not; our troops for two days had been lying down a great deal in a defensive position.

By the chairman:

Question. Could our troops have been as much fatigued after the fight as the troops of the enemy?

Answer. No, sir; I think the enemy must have been the most fatigued, as they made the attack.

[312] Question. Were you down at Williamsport, or near there, where the enemy effected a recrossing of the Potomac?

Answer. I was not. I left the army on the 7th of July.

Question. You have heard that a council of war was held down there?

Answer. Yes, sir.

Question. And you know how they voted?

Answer. I have heard partially how the vote was. I am not sure as to the vote of every member.

Question. Can you give any reason, satisfactory to yourself, why that council came to the conclusion that it was not best to attack the enemy before they recrossed the river?

Answer. I can give no reason; it is perfectly absurd to suppose that the enemy would choose a position on the bank of a deep river for the purpose of fighting us. You would as soon expect a man to place his back to a precipice, and then engage in a life and death struggle with another.

Question. Have you any doubt that, after the enemy got to the river, and were unable to cross on account of the water being so high, it was in the power of our army to have conquered them?

Answer. I have no doubt; not a particle.

This is reminiscent of Sickles's testimony. Doubleday had not been at the council and had no firsthand knowledge of the condition or supply situation of the army after July 7. He was unfamiliar with the terrain, unaware of the strength or condition of the enemy, and knew nothing about any fortifications the enemy may have built. Yet Doubleday had "not a particle" of doubt about a Union victory.

Question. You know the march General Lee had been compelled to make; the distance he was from his base of supplies, and the amount of ammunition he must have spent in such a battle as you had witnessed there?

Answer. I think he must have almost completely exhausted his ammunition.

Question. I was going to ask whether, as a military man, you would not come to the conclusion that, after the battle, the enemy must have been very destitute of ammunition?

Answer. I certainly should.

Question. You left the army on the 7th of July?

Answer. Yes, sir.

Question. Where were you then?

Answer. I was on the battle-field of Gettysburg.

Question. So that you know nothing personally of what occurred after that?

Answer. I do not.

Doubleday's testimony gave the committee additional leverage in its goal to oust Meade. While he had not supported Sickles's claim that Meade intended to retreat from Gettysburg, he had added a new indictment: that there was a controlling clique in the Army of the Potomac, including Meade, of men willing to compromise in favor of slavery. These men denied positions in the army to anyone who disagreed with them. This, Doubleday believed, was why he had lost command of the First Corps.

Doubleday also made three minor points that reinforced the committee's belief that Meade was not fit to command. First, Doubleday and Howard had been replaced by their juniors not because of the way they had fought on July 1 but because they had fought at all. This shored up the committee's contention that Meade had not wanted to fight at Gettysburg. Second, Meade had been caught unprepared by Lee's maneuvers. His only plan had been the Pipe Creek line, which was weak and strictly defensive in nature. Third, Doubleday had been removed from command in part because Meade had wanted a scapegoat if things went badly and in part because Meade habitually placed his personal friends in power. To the committee, this must have been reminiscent of McClellan's rampant favoritism.

5 Brigadier General Albion P. Howe

THE THIRD WITNESS TO appear before the committee was Brigadier General Albion P. Howe, commander of the Second Division, Sixth Corps at Gettysburg. Howe would not be the only witness who had commanded nothing larger than a division during the battle—three others also fit into this category—but his appearance reveals the committee's desire to call anti-Meade witnesses early in the hearings. Although Howe saw little, if any, action at Gettysburg, he provided the committee with the first real testimony about the pursuit of Lee's army.[1]

A graduate of West Point and an experienced professional soldier, Howe fought in the Mexican War and in most of the major engagements of the Civil War. His bravery was rewarded by three brevets, the last for his conduct at Rappahannock Station. Howe would largely be forgotten today (like most Civil War brigadier generals) but for two footnotes to his career. One was his assignment to the honor guard that stood watch over Lincoln's corpse. The second, and more controversial, was his membership on the commission that tried the Lincoln conspirators. Both responsibilities indicate that, at least by 1865, Howe had developed strong political connections among Republican power brokers. In the frenzied days immediately following Lincoln's assassination, Howe's selection to the tribunal for the Lincoln conspirators also indicates that the Republican leadership felt he could be trusted.

Like Sickles and Doubleday, Howe had his own reasons for disliking Meade. On February 29, 1864, two days prior to his appearance before the committee, Howe was removed from infantry command and transferred to the Light Artillery Depot, where he was placed in charge of the Office of the Inspector

1. *OR*, vol. 27, pt. 1, pp. 675–6.

of Artillery in Washington. He held no further field commands during the war. While this move may have been orchestrated by Grant or Sedgwick, Meade had played a role in Howe's transfer. Howe's new position was a result of the impending reorganization of the Army of the Potomac, a project Meade had been working on for some time. Though the order for his transfer had come from the secretary of war, Howe knew that it had to have been approved—or at least not opposed—by Meade.[2]

Howe testified for two days. The first day of his questioning, only Senators Wade and Chandler were present. Following that day's testimony, Wade and Chandler went to see Lincoln and Secretary of War Stanton "on behalf of the army and the country." The following day Chandler had the stenographer of the committee enter a statement concerning their meeting into the official record. As this statement reflects the attitude of the committee's two most powerful members, it is presented in its entirety:

> The chairman directed the stenographer to enter upon the journal that, having become impressed with the exceeding importance of the testimony taken by the committee in relation to the army of the Potomac, more especially in relation to the incompetency of the general in command of the army, he and Mr. Chandler had believed it to be their duty to call upon the President and the Secretary of War, and lay before them the substance of the testimony taken by them, and, in behalf of the army and of the country, demand the removal of General Meade, and the appointment of some one more competent to command. They accordingly did so yesterday afternoon; and being asked to name what general they could recommend for the command of the army of the Potomac, they said that for themselves they would be content with General Hooker, believing him to be competent; but not being advocates of any particular general, they would say that if there was any general whom the President considered more competent for the command, then let him be appointed. They stated that Congress had appointed the committee to watch the conduct of the war; and unless this state of things should soon changed [*sic*] it would become their duty to make the testimony public which they had taken, with such comments as the circumstances of the case seemed to require.[3]

Given the aims of some members of the committee, such a meeting was perhaps inevitable. The timing of the meeting, however, was highly question-

2. Warner describes the transfer as an "obvious move by U. S. Grant and/or Sedgwick to remove him from infantry command." Warner, *Generals in Blue,* 239.

3. *CCW,* xix.

able. At this point the committee had only heard from three witnesses, Howe had not even completed his testimony, and Meade had yet to tell his side of the story. The two witnesses who had completed their testimony—Sickles and Doubleday—were openly hostile to Meade, a fact that was well known to both Lincoln and Stanton. Both Sickles's and Doubleday's testimony, though supposedly confidential, was being openly discussed in Washington and the press.[4]

Why would Wade and Chandler have been in such a hurry? A probable explanation is found in a bill passed by Congress on February 26, 1864, reviving the rank of lieutenant general. Lincoln sent Ulysses S. Grant's name to the Senate on March 1 and Grant was confirmed as lieutenant general the next day. Wade, realizing that his influence with the administration was slipping, adroitly maneuvered for Grant's favor. When the bill creating the new rank had first come up in the Senate, Wade had voted for an amendment that would have appointed Grant by name to the post. The amendment had failed, but Wade had gone on record as supporting Grant.[5]

As the situation stood, there would soon be a new general in chief who would have full authority to name army commanders, just as Meade could name officers in his command. Wade and Chandler thus moved quickly, going to Lincoln the day after Grant's confirmation to demand Meade's removal. Grant was still in the West, and the senators must have reasoned that if they could succeed in having Meade removed before Grant arrived, they might be able to compel Lincoln to return Hooker (or some other general of their liking) to command the Army of the Potomac. Should that fail, Wade was still on record as supporting Grant and hopefully would be able to influence him. But Lincoln would not remove Meade, and the hearings continued.

[312] Testimony of General A. P. Howe.

Washington, March 3, 1864.
General A. P. Howe sworn and examined.

By the chairman:

Question. General Meade succeeded General Hooker in command of the army of the Potomac.

4. *OR*, vol. 27, pt. 1, p. 122; *LLM*, March 6, 1864, 2:169.

5. Ulysses S. Grant, *Personal Memoirs of U. S. Grant* (1885; reprint, New York: Konecky & Konecky, 1992), 403; Trefousse, *Wade*, 208.

Answer. Yes, sir.

Question. Go on and state the operations of the army under his command, particularly the battle at Gettysburg; how it was brought on, and all about it, so far as you know.

Answer. We continued our movement until the 6th corps reached Manchester. We reached there the last day of June, I think. We remained there one night, and the next evening about 8 o'clock, I think, we received orders to move on Gettysburg. The other corps had been moving on our left and rear as we reached Manchester. From my own knowledge, I cannot tell what positions the other corps had, only as given in the reports. The evening that we received [313] orders to move on Gettysburg, news came that General Reynolds, who commanded the 1st corps, had met the rebels in considerable force, had had a fight with them, and been killed. General Newton was sent for by General Meade to take command of the 1st corps, because it was said the officer left in command was wounded, or was not satisfactory, or something of that kind.

We moved on Gettysburg, my division in the rear of the 6th corps. I left Manchester between 12 and 1 o'clock on the morning of the 2d of July, and reached Gettysburg about 4 o'clock P.M., on the 2d of July. We were then being threatened with an attack, as I understood, and with but a short halt the 6th corps was ordered up to support the 5th corps. We moved up and found not a heavy fight going on, but pretty spirited.

After the fight was over, it soon was dark. The 6th corps had stood upon the ground. I do not think they fired a shot; there was no occasion for them to do so, for the position was a strong one, and the troops that were there had not given way at all that we could see. The 6th corps, of course, was pretty well jaded, for it had made a long march. Night was coming on, and it was very evident that there would be no more fighting that day. I said to General Sedgwick, "We ought to let our men have the best chance to rest that they can get right off; we are not likely to be called on to fight to-night; let us give the men a chance to get some coffee, and rest all they can, for there will be something done to-morrow undoubtedly." He remarked to me, "It is a little early yet; they are discussing whether we shall stay here, or move back to Westminster." That is twenty-one or twenty-two miles. I said, "It is some distance back there." Said he, "Can we move back?" I replied, "Yes, if it is necessary; we have just come over the road, and we know it. The men are worn; but if it is necessary, the 6th corps can go back, after resting two or three hours." General Sedgwick gave me to understand that our army would probably move back to Westminster.

While exactly the type of testimony the committee was seeking, Howe's account has several flaws. First, Howe placed the time of his conversation with Sedgwick around sunset, but the council took place well after dark. At 8:00 P.M. Meade had sent a telegram to Halleck, saying in part that he would have more to report after he had met with his corps commanders. This shows that the council had not yet taken place. In Meade of Gettysburg, *Freeman Cleaves placed the time of the telegram as three hours later, or 11:00 P.M. Either time calls Howe's statement into question.*[6]

Moreover, Howe testified that Sedgwick had indicated that the council was discussing whether to stay or move back. While Howe did not say who was discussing a withdrawal, he left the distinct impression that it was the corps commanders in the council who were doing so. Yet Sedgwick was present at the council, and it is hard to see how he could have been in two places at the same time. If Howe was suggesting that Meade and his staff discussed a withdrawal after the council, he was on equally shaky ground; by then, the question had already been decided.

Indeed, Sedgwick's own testimony before the committee, which followed five weeks later, flatly contradicted Howe's account. Sedgwick testified that the council voted to stay and receive Lee's attack the next day. It is inconceivable that Sedgwick would have perjured himself over such a matter. It is perhaps just as telling that the committee failed to ask Sedgwick about Howe's story.

Question. This was the night after General Sickles was wounded?

Answer. Yes, sir, this was the second day of the fight, the 2d of July.

Question. Who was in that council discussing the question of retreating?

Answer. I do not know. What I heard I had from General Sedgwick. He said, "I think we are going to move back." The impression he gave me was, that General Meade had the question under consideration. General Sedgwick said, "The question of falling back was then being considered." And the impression given to me was that we should move back to Westminster. Soon after, however, it seemed to be decided that we were to remain there.

Question. Go on and state all about the fight there, so far as you know.

Answer. As I have said, the 6th corps got up the latter part of the second day of the fight. The next day all the troops of our army were there. Nothing

6. *OR,* vol. 27, pt. 1, p. 72; *MG,* 157 n. 6. For a colorful description of the members of the council see Haskell's account in Byrne and Haskell, eds., *Haskell of Gettysburg,* 131–5, though Haskell errs in stating Pleasonton was at the meeting.

was done until the beginning of the afternoon, when the enemy opened with artillery, and we replied. The first fire was heavy all around, and was of such a character that I took out my watch and looked at it to see what time it was, and how long the fire would continue. I believed, at the time, that the position we were in was so strong that there was no possibility of the enemy dislodging us from it. This artillery fire, as I timed it, was kept up for a little over an hour and forty-five minutes; and I never heard a more furious cannonading, nor one where there was a greater expenditure of ammunition on both sides. The result of the day was that the enemy met with no success. They did not drive us from the position.

Howe did not actually see Pickett's charge, being approximately one and a half miles away from it, but his comments on the length of the preparatory bombardment are notable.[7]

Question. After the artillery ceased, did the enemy make an infantry charge?

Answer. Yes, sir; there was an attack with infantry, but it was repulsed. The enemy gained no success in advancing, and, of course, lost heavily in their attack. The attack was characteristic of rebel attacks. I have always found that their best fight is at first; and if any change is made which requires [314] a change in their order of attack after it is commenced, they go down in efficiency 50 per cent, at once. My experience has been that they are easily demoralized if any new state of affairs arises after their first attack. This attack was of the same character. They opened with the best they had at first, and kept up this violent cannonading for a long time, and then made their infantry attack, but did not succeed. It appeared to me that they were staking largely upon gaining their point, and that if they failed they would be correspondingly depressed and dispirited. I inferred that from the impression I had of their way of fighting, and when, on the 3d, they gave up the contest, I considered them badly whipped, because they had tried in an unusually spirited manner to succeed, and had failed.

Howe's comment concerning a 50-percent decrease in Confederate fighting efficiency after a change in the order of attack seems to be based on an erroneous

7. John D. Bachelder, *Map—Position of Troops—Third Day* (Boston: John D. Bachelder, 1876), Q-27–S-28.

view of the converging movement used in the charge. Though a planned move, it apparently appeared to those on the Federal line to have been forced (which Doubleday took credit for in his testimony).

But I did not consider that the fighting on our side was such as taxed us to the utmost, because our position was naturally a very strong one; and, as it seemed to me, a large portion of the strength of our army was not brought to bear. Our position mainly did the work for us. The enemy worked at great disadvantage. I was under the impression at the time, and have been ever since, that General Lee made a mistake there, for he evidently thought he could carry the place very much easier than the result proved; and after the fight of the 3d of July, I considered that our army had plenty of fight in it, if I may so express myself. Our army was not badly cut up; we had had quite a number of disabled men, to be sure, but it was an orderly fight. We were in a position where there was no straggling and demoralization; we had some pretty sharp cuts from that cannonading, but it was the most orderly fight I have ever been in, growing out of the position. In a military point of view it was not much of a battle; it was a very ordinary affair as a battle. In its results it was immensely important, for it checked the rebel advance upon vital points; but as a military operation on our side, no particular credit can attach to it. There was no great generalship displayed; there was no maneuvering, no combinations.

This is an extraordinary statement. From his position across the Taneytown Road, behind Big Round Top, Howe claimed to be able to determine that the entire Union position was a naturally strong one, that a large portion of the army was not used, and that it was a very ordinary battle. While it is possible that he may have left his position for a time and ridden around the area, it is unlikely that he could have covered even half of the length of the line, since he did not arrive at Gettysburg until late in the day on July 2. It is therefore hard to see how his claims could be anything but hindsight.[8]

Howe erroneously stated that a large portion of the army was not involved at Gettysburg. From Howe's perspective at the time of the battle, this would have appeared to be true. The Sixth Corps was used only as a central reserve, supplying men where needed; the corps suffered relatively few casualties, and Howe was little more than a bystander. Actually, Gettysburg represented the first major battle in which the entire Army of the Potomac was available and

8. Howe's report gives his arrival time at 5:00 P.M. *OR,* vol. 27, pt. 1, p. 675.

used. Though individual men may not have seen much or any fighting, all seven infantry corps were engaged to some extent. By the time Howe testified, some eight months after the battle, he could not have failed to know this.[9]

Howe's assertion that "no great generalship was displayed" at Gettysburg was what the committee wanted to hear. Compared to Napoleon's sweeping grand strategies at Marengo or Austerlitz, Gettysburg was a poor second. Compared to Fredericksburg, it was a masterpiece. The truth is somewhere in the middle. Though Meade's moves were mostly reactive instead of proactive, he handled the battle as well as anyone in the army at the time could have done, and considerably better than most.

Question. Such a fight was not calculated to fatigue our men like some other fights?

Answer. No, sir; it was an orderly, economical fight on our side, although we lost pretty heavily. In other words, when the fight was over our troops were by no means exhausted, but they were comparatively fresh.

Question. Can you, as a military man, tell us why, when the enemy had retreated, dispirited as you say they were, our army did not follow them up vigorously? You say that our troops were not jaded; that a large portion of our forces had not been engaged at all. Then why were not the enemy followed up vigorously?

Answer. I cannot answer that question. It is like a great many other questions that have been asked me, which I cannot answer. I can see no reason why we did not follow them more vigorously than was done. This action was on the 3d of July. On the 4th of July it seemed evident enough that the enemy were retreating. How far they were gone we could not see from the front. We could see but a comparatively small force from the position where I was.

While the Confederate retreat may have been evident to Howe from his position on the edge of the battlefield behind Big Round Top, it was not evident to either Meade or his corps commanders. On the morning of July 4, reports showed that the enemy had withdrawn from the extreme right of Meade's line but was still in position on the left and left center. At 5 A.M. Gettysburg had been reoccupied by Federal forces. Brigadier General Francis Barlow, commander of the First Division, First Corps, who had been wounded and left in town, sent word to Meade that he believed the Confederate withdrawal was only a feint. By 10:20

9. *GC*, 480–1.

A.M. Meade was fairly certain Lee was awaiting an attack on Seminary Ridge; he telegraphed General French that the "enemy may have retired to take a new position and await an attack from us." By noon he had telegraphed Halleck, "The enemy apparently has thrown back his left, and placed guns and troops in position in rear of Gettysburg."[10]

Howe did not say why it was evident that Lee was retreating, but he was wrong. On July 4, the "Confederate positions along the ridges [at Gettysburg] bristled defiantly with thousands of muskets and hundreds of guns" waiting for Meade to cross the valley. It was not until the night of July 4, when pursuit would have been impossible, that Lee actually left his positions at Gettysburg with his main force.[11]

On Sunday the 5th and 6th corps moved in pursuit. As we moved, a small rear guard of the enemy retreated. We followed them, with this small rear guard of the enemy before us, up to Fairfield, in a gorge of the mountains. There we again waited for them to go on. There seemed to be no disposition to push this rear guard when we got up to Fairfield. A lieutenant from the enemy came into our lines and gave himself up. He was a northern Union man, in service in one of the Georgia regiments, and, without being asked, he unhesitatingly told me, when I met him as he was being brought in, that he belonged to the artillery of the rear guard of the enemy, and that they had but two rounds of ammunition with the rear guard. But we waited there without receiving [315] any orders to attack. It was a place where, as I informed General Sedgwick, we could easily attack the enemy with advantage. But no movement was made by us until the enemy went away.

Howe's story about the artillery lieutenant is impossible to confirm. The Twenty-sixth Georgia Regiment of Gordon's Brigade was in the Fairfield Gap, but the only Georgia artillery with Ewell's corps was the Georgia Battery of Captain John Milledge Jr., and it was well west of Fairfield Gap at the time. The importance of the story to the committee, however, was to reaffirm the weakness of the defense at Fairfield Gap and Sedgwick's failure to push on through, despite Howe's assurances that it could be easily done. Howe intimated that Sedgwick, and thus Meade, did not want to bring the enemy to battle.

There is no reason to expect that Howe would have been privy to the plans

10. *LLM,* 2:113–4, 116.
11. *GC,* 538, 540.

or desires of the army commander or his corps commander, and his testimony does not paint a true picture of the events. In addition to having the largest corps in the army, Sedgwick could call upon the men of the badly depleted First and Third Corps which had been placed under his marching orders, giving him nearly a third of the army for a reconnaissance. Meade's orders to Sedgwick on July 4 had been to prepare for a reconnaissance, the object being to "find out the position and movements of the enemy." Again on July 5, Sedgwick was told, "The orders for the reconnaissance were with a view to ascertaining the position and movement of the enemy, not for a battle." Yet again on July 6, Sedgwick was told to push his reconnaissance "in case I should determine to advance on that line." It seems clear, therefore, that Meade desired a reconnaissance by Sedgwick and at the time of the Sixth Corps' arrival at Fairfield Gap had yet to determine the best course for his pursuit to follow.[12]

In his classic work The Gettysburg Campaign: A Study in Command, *Edwin Coddington has suggested that Butterfield, Meade's chief of staff, had misinterpreted Meade's July 5 message to Sedgwick to mean that Meade did not want to bring on a fight. Coddington argued that the use of an entire corps for reconnaissance was absurd and that Meade had wanted Sedgwick to advance aggressively and come to grips with the enemy, causing the rear guard to turn and fight. The message of July 5 is certainly the most aggressive one that Sedgwick received, but it is the only one of this tone. Nor does Coddington's interpretation of the message reflect its wording. Sedgwick was told that Sykes's Fifth Corps was available to cover his withdrawal if necessary, thus indicating Meade's desire not to bring on a major battle. Moreover, the message to Sedgwick in the early morning hours of July 6 was virtually an order not to attack, saying that he was to ascertain, if practicable, how far the enemy had retreated, the character of Fairfield Gap, and the feasibility of carrying it* if *Meade should decide to advance on that line.*[13]

Then one brigade of my division with some cavalry was sent to follow on after them, while the remainder of the 6th corps moved to the left. We moved on through Boonsboro, and passed up on the pike road leading to Hagerstown. After passing Boonsboro it became my turn to lead the 6th corps. That day, before we started, General Sedgwick ordered me to move on and take up the best position I could over a little stream on the Frederick side of Funkstown.

12. *OR*, vol. 27, pt. 3, pp. 517, 530–1, 554.

13. *GC*, 551.

As I moved on it was suggested to me by him to move carefully, "Don't come into contact with the enemy; we don't want to bring on a general engagement." It seemed to be the general impression that it was not desired to bring on a general engagement. I moved on until we came near Funkstown. General Buford was along that way with his cavalry. I had passed over the stream referred to and found a strong position, which I concluded to take and wait for the 6th corps to come up. In the mean time General Buford, who was in front, came back to me and said, "I am pretty hardly engaged here; I have used a great deal of my ammunition; it is a strong place in front; it is an excellent position." It was a little further out than I was—nearer Funkstown. He said, "I have used a great deal of my ammunition, and I ought to go to the right; suppose you move up there, or send up a brigade, or even a part of one, and hold that position." Said I, "I will do so at once if I can just communicate with General Sedgwick; I am ordered to take up a position over here and hold it, and the intimation conveyed to me was that they did not want to get into a general engagement; I will send for General Sedgwick and ask permission to hold that position and relieve you." I accordingly sent a staff officer to General Sedgwick with a request that I might go up at once and assist General Buford, stating that he had a strong position but his ammunition was giving out. General Buford remained with me until I should get an answer. The answer was, "No, we do not want to bring on a general engagement." "Well," said I, "Buford, what can I do?" He said, "They expect me to go further to the right; my ammunition is pretty much out. That position is a strong one, and we ought not to let it go." I sent down again to General Sedgwick, stating the condition of General Buford, and that he would have to leave unless he could get some assistance; that his position was not far in front, and that it seemed to me that we should hold it, and I should like to send some force up to picket it at least. After a time I got a reply that if General Buford left I might occupy the position. General Buford was still with me, and I said to him, "If you go away from there, I will have to hold it." "That's all right," said he, "I will go away." He did so, and I moved right up. It was a pretty good position, where you could cover your troops. Soon after relieving Buford we saw some rebel infantry advancing. I do not know whether they brought them from Hagerstown, or from some other place. They made three dashes, not in heavy force, upon our line to drive us back. The troops that happened to be there on our line were what we considered in the army of the Potomac unusually good ones. They quietly repulsed the rebels twice, and the third time they came up they sent them flying into Funkstown.

Yet there was no permission to move on and follow up the enemy. We remained there some time, until we had orders to move on and take a position a mile or more nearer Hagerstown. As we moved up we saw the rebels had thrown up some light field-works, hurriedly thrown up, apparently to cover themselves while they recrossed the river. I think we remained there three days, and the third night, I think, after we got up into that position, it was said the rebels recrossed the river.

Question. From your experience as a military man, had you not reason to believe, after that terrible cannonading at Gettysburg, and the fight there, and [316] considering also the distance Lee's army was from its base of supplies, and the great distance they had to carry their ammunition, that they must have very nearly exhausted their supply of ammunition?

Answer. There can be no question about it; I think that it was. I said to some officers, "I am more surprised than I have been at any time during this war, that this force does not attack the enemy, or make some attempt to attack him. We are morally certain that their ammunition is about out; we ought to know that from the cannonading at Gettysburg." I told them that I had timed them at Gettysburg; that I knew from the rate and duration of artillery firing, and from the transportation they had, they must have very nearly exhausted their artillery ammunition, and the artillery officer we had captured from their rear guard, who I believe spoke truthfully, stated that there were only two rounds of artillery ammunition left for the rear guard.

For Howe and his fellow officers to think Lee may have been short or out of ammunition was reasonable, but they were not correct. Following Pickett's charge, Colonel Edward Porter Alexander, Longstreet's de facto artillery chief, recalled, "An anxious inventory of ammunition left on hand was made." It was with a great sense of relief, he noted, that there was "enough for one day's fight." Despite the swollen river at his back, Lee was not idle. Badly needed supplies of rifle and artillery ammunition, though in small quantities, began to cross the Potomac as early as July 5, and on July 6 two wagon loads of artillery ammunition were ferried across.[14]

Question. Can you give us the course of reasoning that brought General Meade and a majority of his corps commanders to the conclusion that, under these circumstances, it was not best to attack the enemy?

14. Edward Porter Alexander, *Military Memoirs of a Confederate: A Critical Narrative* (1907; reprint, New York: Da Capo Press, 1993), 435; Jennings Cropper Wise, *The Long Arm of Lee*, 2 vols. (1915; reprint, Lincoln: University of Nebraska Press, 1991), 2:699–700.

Answer. I was not in the council, and I could not presume to give you the logic by which they arrived at that conclusion.

Question. Can you give any reason, satisfactory to yourself as a military man, why you did not attack the enemy there?

Answer. No, sir, I cannot; the reasons were all the other way, as it seemed to me. Our forces had not been demoralized or dispirited by the orderly fight at Gettysburg; they had had plenty to eat; they had ammunition; they had not been hard marched from Gettysburg up there. In fact, I looked upon our army at that time as in good fighting condition. We had lost some; but the rebel army had lost much more than we had, and were, besides, demoralized and dispirited by the retrograde movement they had made. General Neil, who was in command of a brigade of my division that followed the retreat of the rebels from Fairfield, when he came back and rejoined us, before we got up to Hagerstown, stated to me that "the mountains," to use his expression, "were full of rebels who had fallen out and were going in every direction." Said he, "They were so plenty [*sic*] that we would not stop and pick them up," showing the demoralizing, dispiriting effect upon the rebels of that retrograde movement. I expressed my astonishment that we should remain there without attacking, with the river so high that the rebel army could not cross it, and were almost without ammunition, while our men were in good fighting trim, and the rebels dispirited and demoralized.

Question. Can you have any doubt, under these circumstances, that a vigorous assault by our army would have been fatal to that under Lee?

Answer. That is only a matter of opinion.

Question. I know that; but it is your opinion, as a military man, that we want.

Answer. It is my opinion that, with a comparatively small fight, the rebels would have been thrown into utter disorder, and could not have got across the river.

Question. And must have surrendered?

Answer. They must have been captured or killed. I have never had any doubt that if our force had attacked, it did not matter much how or in what order, the morale was so much in our favor; the supply of ammunition was so full with us and so nearly exhausted with them, we should have overcome them easily, if we had made anything like a formidable attack upon them. It is my belief they would have caved right in; that was my impression. It was replied to me by an officer, "Suppose they whip us here; wouldn't they go to Washington?" I replied to him, "This is as safe a place to fight as we could desire; if they whip us, as is possible in the course of human events, we have only to move back to South mountain, and this whole force of rebels cannot drive out [317] of those passes one-fourth of the force we have; after they whipped us, what is left of them will be able to do but little mischief in Washington." But I can see no reason why we should have been whipped there, when, as far as I could judge, everything was in our favor.

Question. If you were whipped anywhere it would endanger Washington, I suppose. But was not that the best place to have a fight?

Answer. I thought so. I thought it was one of those opportunities that occur but once in a long time.

This was valuable testimony for the committee. Yet if it truly reflected Howe's opinion, it speaks poorly of his abilities as a general and perhaps explains why he did not rise to corps command despite his lengthy experience.

By July 11, Lee had taken up a line in defense of his bridgehead which ran along high ground, with the right resting on the river and the left near Hagerstown. This line was covered by earthworks, including a parapet six feet wide along the top and numerous gun emplacements. One eyewitness account by a Federal sympathizer described the Confederate defenses as "two ranges of hills . . . [with] a marsh and open fields [between] . . . an obvious trap for any attacking force."[15]

Without reconnaissance, how was Meade (or Howe) to know this? Meade knew that Lee would certainly not lay down and surrender. If he was unable to get across the river, as it then appeared, Lee would probably choose a strong defensive position and wait. This was one reason why Meade probed cautiously. The nature of the ground near Williamsport and Falling Waters had been described to Meade by Couch in a message on July 7. "There is high ground on the right bank of the Conococheague Creek, that overlooks Williamsport ford. The country around Falling Waters is very strong for defense." A division commander might not have been privy to this information, but Howe already knew the area; Couch's message continued, "General Howe is well acquainted all about there." Given Howe's knowledge of the ground and his experience with the defensive tenacity of the rebels, it is difficult to understand how he could have believed that a small effort would have ensured a Union victory and the destruction of Lee's army.[16]

Question. Can you have great confidence in the ability of officers who counsel to forego such an opportunity?

15. *GC,* 565–6; *MG,* 182.
16. *OR,* vol. 27, pt. 3, p. 588.

Answer. As an officer, I must say, as you ask me, that I lost my respect for the judgment of the council which it is said voted not to attack.

Question. Was not such overcaution well calculated to weaken the confidence of the army in the ability and resolution of their officers?

Answer. I am decidedly of the opinion that it was.

Question. You remained there until the enemy had recrossed the river, and for some time afterwards. How long was it before you started to follow them up?

Answer. They crossed in the night. We found it out the next day, in the morning; and that afternoon, if I remember rightly, the 6th corps moved back on the pike towards South mountain and encamped. Then we crossed the old crossing place at Berlin, I think it is. There we crossed with the army, and moved along slowly until we reached different points. The 6th corps moved up towards Manassas gap—not up to it, but towards it, as if going there. When at a point some miles distant from the gap—I do not remember the name of the place—we were ordered to move up towards Gaines's Crossroads, which was a pretty long march. We started in the afternoon, and got up there quite late at night. My impression was that we were not in the way to strike the enemy, for they were on the other side of the mountains and well out of our reach, except a rear guard. We remained there for a little time, when a rumor was circulated abroad in the army from headquarters that the rebels had ingloriously fled from their camp and gone off, declining to give battle. Then we moved down on to the Rappahannock again, near Warrenton.

[The portion of Howe's testimony relating to the Bristoe and Mine Run campaigns has been deleted.]

Washington, March 4, 1864.

General A. P. Howe. Examination resumed.

By the chairman:

Question. Tell me, if you can, whether, after all you have stated here, the officers of that army with whom you are well acquainted retain confidence in the ability of General Meade as the commander of that army?

[327] Answer. I cannot answer that question without going somewhat into matters which do not lie right on the surface.

Question. You can give your general impression from all you know. I ask the question because it seems to me that these constant mortifications of missing opportunities to do something would lead them to think that there was some want of ability in the head of the army.

Answer. I do not know exactly how to answer that question. I may say that I think there are some officers of high rank in the army of the Potomac who, if you asked them that question would express themselves as having full confidence in General Meade as the commander of that army.

Question. Is that class of officers composed of those whose hearts are really in the vigorous prosecution of this war?

Answer. It seems to me that those officers have a sympathy with the policy that has been heretofore pursued in the command of the army of the Potomac while under General McClellan. I look upon our army upon the Peninsula as having been unfortunate in the character and state of mind of its commander at that time, and that policy has been transferred in a great degree to its present commander, perhaps, as I am led to believe, from the connexion the present commander had with that one. There are certain sympathies, feelings, and considerations of action which seem to govern now as they did then. And from my experience of the army, the disposition of its commanding general, and the view which he takes of the general state of things, has a very marked effect upon some of those who are immediately associated with him; and hence I say that if some of those officers I speak of were asked the question they would say that the present commander of the army of the Potomac is fully competent for his position.

Question. Do you speak now of the corps commanders principally?

Answer. Yes, sir, of those who affect the movements of the army, whose views are taken when a council of war is called, which seem to be given as the sentiment of the army.

Question. Take the other officers, commanders of division, brigades, and the colonels and the other officers, do they retain full confidence in the ability of the commanding general?

Answer. I do not think they have full confidence in the ability or state of mind of General Meade. What I mean by that is the animus that directs the movements of the army. They do not think there is that heart, and energy, and earnestness of purpose in the war to make every use of the means at his command to injure the enemy and carry on the war successfully. I do not think they have, I will not say confidence, but faith in him. They do not expect from him what the crisis seems to call for. They believe that if he is attacked he will do all he can to defend his position. But that he will act with zeal and energy, or that his whole heart and soul are in the bringing all the means successfully to bear to break down the enemy, as far as I can judge, they do not look for that; they do not expect it. As far as I can judge, a great many officers think he can do very well in a defensive fight. If he was called upon to guard the Potomac or Washington, he will make good marches to stop the enemy; but that he will be active, zealous, energetic, in using his means to strike successful offensive blows against the enemy, not at all; he is not the man for that, at least that is my impression.

This was telling testimony for the committee. In reply to what seems to have been a well-choreographed series of questions by Wade, Howe had made damaging replies. Although Howe stated that some high-ranking officers still had full confidence in Meade as commander of the army, he also asserted that the views of the officers who backed Meade were identical to those who served under McClellan. Howe charged that Meade had infected his subordinates with his views and feelings, and that a lack of confidence extended to the corps commanders. Howe did not say how Meade was able to "infect" his subordinates with such opinions in less than three weeks, nor did any committee member pursue the issue.

Question. The same observation you apply to General Meade will apply to the corps commanders you refer to, will it not?

Answer. I think so. I do not know as it would be proper for me to state here the terms we use in the army. However, we say there is too much copperheadism in it. This is so for different reasons; with some there is a desire to raise up General McClellan; with others there is a dislike to some of the measures of the government; they do not like the way the negro question is handled. And, [328] again, the impression is made upon my mind that there are some who have no faith in this war, who have no heart in it; they will not do anything to commit themselves; but there is a wide difference between doing your duty so as not to commit yourself, and doing all that might reasonably be expected of you at these times. I do not know as I can express myself better than saying that there is copperheadism at the root of the matter.

After dancing around the point for awhile Howe summed up his criticism of Meade in one word, "copperheadism," a term applied to Northern Democrats opposed to the Union's war policy and favoring a negotiated peace.

Question. Do you mean that many of the high officers sympathize with those politicians of the north who are called "peace men?"

Answer. I am fully of that opinion. If I was asked to state the acts and sayings of those officers, to any one who has not been connected with military matters, and who has not caught the real meaning of expressions and manners and all those little things, I might not, perhaps, be able to satisfy him of what I mean, but I must say that it is my opinion that there is too much sympathy with men and measures in opposition to the principal measures of the government, and those who are in control of the government.

Howe's characterization of Union officers would have just as well fit Jefferson Davis.

Question. You think that politics are mixed up with military movements?

Answer. Yes, sir; I think there are outside considerations which qualify the efficiency and energy which we have a right to expect from officers in command. That is my opinion now, and it has been for some time.

Question. You have been under General Meade all the time he has been in command. Do you know of any aggressive movement he has led against the enemy at any time?

Answer. An independent movement?

Question. Yes, sir; where he planned an expedition against the enemy and undertaken to carry it out.

Answer. No, sir; I do not. The only time I have ever known General Meade to be actively engaged was at Fredericksburg.

Question. That was when General Burnside was in command. I mean since General Meade has been in command of the army of the Potomac.

Answer. No, sir; I do not, unless you consider the cutting the enemy's line of march at Gettysburg was an aggressive movement.

Question. If I have understood it, the battle of Gettysburg was not a premeditated movement of General Meade; but it was brought on by the fact that some of our corps were attacked there, and it was not until quite late in the fight that it was really determined to fight a decisive battle there.

Answer. No, sir; I do not think that can be given as a direct answer to your inquiry. That battle grew out of the necessity of the hour. The army of the Potomac was moving to stop the march of the rebels. Our advance struck them there, and the position being a good one our forces were brought up and we accepted battle there.

Question. I want to ask you whether the rank and file of this army are not more than ordinarily intelligent for private soldiers? I mean in their ability to comprehend and understand things that are going on.

Answer. Before answering that question directly, I will say that I have been 22 years in the army; I graduated in 1841. I was in what was known as Twigg's division in the war with Mexico, on General Scott's line, and before we left Puebla to go into the valley of Mexico there was a great deal of pride and emulation between that division and another regular division commanded by General Worth, as to which should become the most efficient, and I refer to the condition of things at Puebla as showing perhaps the highest degree of efficiency in any large division that we have had since I have been in the service.

And when I come to compare the personnel of this army, or that portion of it with which I am familiar, the degree of efficiency which it is capable of rapidly attaining, with anything I have before seen, I may say that I do not think the old army can compare with this one. As I have said to several old officers whom I have met here, there is a degree of military efficiency and discipline in the [329] division of the 6th corps which I have commanded, there is a skill and ability to perform evolutions as a division, which has been rapidly acquired, that I have never seen equaled at all in the best showing I have ever seen in the old army. The character and intelligence of the men is markedly superior; they are men of far more intelligence, and more readily acquire efficiency in military matters.

Question. Do not this intelligent rank and file of the army of the Potomac appreciate somewhat the want of resolution in their officers in leading them to attack? In other words, do not they appreciate the advantages of a position such as you had on the left of the enemy at Mine run, and are they not disappointed when they find themselves called upon suddenly to retreat from such a position?

Answer. I think they do appreciate them most unquestionably, and I think the effect of those retrograde or abortive movements must be marked. And except for the high character of the rank and file as men of intelligence and ability to understand, I cannot account for the good morale of our army as it stands at this day, in the face of the failures and disappointments and mortifications with which they have met.

Howe was a strong witness for the anti-Meade faction on the committee. He had confirmed the testimony of Sickles and Doubleday about Meade's desire to withdraw from Gettysburg without a fight. In the pursuit of Lee's army, Meade had been seemingly content to allow the rebels to escape over the Potomac. Sickles had been making this claim for months, but he had not been there; Howe, on the other hand, had actually participated in the pursuit. Howe's testimony about Williamsport was valuable for the same reason. Neither Sickles nor Doubleday had been there, and their testimony could accordingly be criticized as hearsay or speculation; but not Howe's.

What Sickles and Doubleday had merely hinted at, Howe came out and said: the army was infested with "copperheads" and the source of the infection was Meade. Additionally, some of the corps commanders (and Meade himself) sought the return of McClellan to command, while others did not like the way the slavery question was handled and were not truly committed to the war. Howe had damned the entire upper echelon of the Army of the Potomac as traitors or men in sympathy with the rebel cause.

6 Major General George Gordon Meade (First Appearance)

Meade was finally called before the committee on March 5. His appearance may have been at the recommendation of Lincoln, though there is no direct evidence to corroborate this point. In any event, Meade's first appearance seems to have been the result of chance timing. He was in Washington on March 4 for meetings about the upcoming reorganization of the army when he first became aware that the committee was investigating the Gettysburg campaign. Upon his arrival in town he was surprised to find everyone talking about "certain grave charges" Sickles and Doubleday had made before the committee.[1]

When Meade arrived to testify, the only member of the committee present was Benjamin Wade, who greeted him very civilly and denied that there were any charges against him. Wade told Meade that the committee was merely taking evidence to write a "sort of history of the war." Later that same day, however, Meade learned from Secretary of War Edwin Stanton that there was a move to return Hooker to command of the Army of the Potomac. Although Stanton assured Meade that he would not be removed from command, Meade nonetheless feared that his reputation would be damaged by the effort to oust him. In a letter to his wife, he bemoaned the fact that "persons like Sickles and Doubleday can, by distorting and twisting facts, and giving a false coloring, induce the press and public for a time, and almost immediately, to take away the character of a man who up to that time had stood high in their estimation."[2]

Stanton had supported the committee's efforts from its inception, and his

1. Tap, *Over Lincoln's Shoulder,* 183; *LLM,* March 6, 1864, 2:169–72.

2. *LLM,* March 6, 1864, 2:169–72; Meade's letter states that only Wade was present to ask him questions. The committee's journal, however, shows that Chandler was also present. *CCW,* xix.

conversation with Meade might seem surprising. Based on his previous experience with McClellan, Stanton believed that West Pointers—such as Meade—were too lenient about the issue of slavery and too cavalier toward their civilian superiors. Following Democratic victories at the polls in the aftermath of Fredericksburg, radical Republicans had begun a new campaign to remove Democratic generals, and Stanton had joined the campaign with a vengeance. He had even provided secret information from War Department files to help Republican senators in their attacks against West Point graduates.[3]

Although Stanton had been keenly disappointed by Meade's performance after Gettysburg, he had written a friend on July 22, "As long as General Meade remains in command he will receive the cordial support of the department, but since the world began no man ever lost so great an opportunity of serving his country as was lost by his neglecting to strike his adversary at Williamsport." Yet Stanton's continued support for Meade was not the result of some vacillating or unreasoned policy. Stanton believed that only proven, victorious generals had the right to express themselves on policy matters. Army officers who "indulge in the sport [of politics] must risk being gored. They can not, having exposed themselves, claim the procedural protection and immunities of the military profession." Meade met Stanton's criteria of a victorious, obedient officer and thus merited his protection.[4]

Despite Meade's private whining to his wife, Stanton was not his only political friend in Washington. Maryland Democrat Reverdy Johnson had risen to Meade's defense in the Senate. Meade even had support in the joint committee itself. Moses Odell had become "most indignant at the course pursued" by the committee and had told Meade that he would "see justice done." Odell was as good as his word. Having missed the first seven sessions entirely, he missed only three of the remaining thirteen committee meetings.[5]

In assessing the members of the committee in mid-March 1864, Meade identified Odell, Benjamin Harding, and Daniel Gooch as his "warm friends." Yet Harding attended none of the sessions before Meade testified and only seven sessions after Meade's first appearance; nor did he ask any questions of any witness. Why Meade would classify him as a warm friend is a mystery. Odell and Gooch were different matters. Odell, a war Democrat, asked nu-

3. Benjamin P. Thomas and Harold M. Hyman, *Stanton: The Life and Times of Lincoln's Secretary of War* (New York: Alfred A. Knopf, 1962), 259–61, 311.

4. Charles C. Gorham, *Life and Public Service of Edwin M. Stanton*, 2 vols. (New York: Houghton Mifflin, 1899), 2:100, 262.

5. *CG*, 38th Cong., 1st sess., March 2, 1864, 896–8; *LLM*, March 15, 1864, 2:179.

merous questions that supported Meade's defense. Gooch was even more active on behalf of Meade. The freethinking conservative Republican attended every meeting of the committee after March 9, and his questions to witnesses often tried to elicit a more favorable or balanced version of events. Gooch held the floor during the testimony of both Hunt and Sedgwick, asking most of the questions despite the presence of both Wade and Chandler. Meade completely misread Benjamin Wade, feeling that he was rather friendly. Whether this was due to Wade's duplicitous nature or Meade's naïveté is unknown, but Meade plainly erred in his assessment of the committee chairman.[6]

Nonetheless, Meade had reason for a certain amount of confidence. Benjamin Loan played only a small part in the hearings and may also have supported Meade. If so, Meade had a four to three majority vote on the committee. The split ran along party lines, with maverick Daniel Gooch as the swing vote.

[329] Testimony of Major General George G. Meade.

Washington, March 5, 1863 [*sic*].
Major General George G. Meade sworn and examined.

By the chairman:
Question. What is your rank and position in the service?

Answer. I am a major general of volunteers, commanding the army of the Potomac.

Question. When were you invested with the command of that army?

Answer. I think it was the 28th of June, 1863.

Question. Where was the army at that time?

Answer. It was lying around and near Frederick, Maryland.

Question. You superseded General Hooker?

Answer. I relieved General Hooker.

Question. Will you give a statement, in your own way, of the battle of Gettysburg, and the disposition of your troops there?

Answer. When I assumed the command of the army of the Potomac, on the morning of the 28th of June, it was mostly around Frederick, Maryland; some portions of it, I think, were at that time at Middletown; one or two corps were the other side of a range of mountains between Frederick and Middletown. I had no information concerning the enemy beyond the fact that a large

6. *LLM,* March 14, 1864, 177–8.

force under General Lee, estimated at about 110,000 men, had passed through Hagerstown, and had marched upon the Cumberland valley; and through information derived from the public journals.

Newspapers were a common source of information on troop movements and circulated readily through both lines. Then as now, editors had little hesitation in publishing whatever they knew (or thought they knew) about troop movements or plans. While obviously valuable to both sides, such information had to be checked closely for accuracy.

I had reason to believe that one corps of the rebel army, under General Ewell, was occupying York and Carlisle, and threatening the Susquehanna at Harrisburg and Columbia.

My predecessor, General Hooker, left the camp in a very few hours after I relieved him. I received from him no intimation of any plan, or any views that he may have had up to that moment. And I am not aware that he had any, but was waiting for the exigencies of the occasion to govern him, just as I had to subsequently.

Meade's testimony implied that there was little conversation, and none of substance, between himself and Hooker after Meade took command. There is ample evidence to the contrary, however. Charles F. Benjamin, who "occupied responsible and confidential positions at the headquarters of the Army of the Potomac and in the War Department," later wrote that Meade, Hooker, Butterfield, and Hardie (who had brought the orders changing the command) set to work transferring the command and discussing the position of the army. Some of the details of Benjamin's account are questionable; however, the length of time he claimed that Hardie remained at Meade's headquarters would indicate some detailed discussions. Indeed, Hardie's own communication with General Halleck concerning the transfer of command reveals a conference between Meade and Hooker of nearly eight hours. In correspondence after the battle of Gettysburg, both Butterfield and Meade recalled discussing the situation at Harper's Ferry. (Butterfield would later include this correspondence in his testimony before the committee.) Meade's modern biographer Freeman Cleaves also has written that Meade and Hooker fully discussed the situation and Lee's likely movements.[7]

7. Charles F. Benjamin, "Hooker's Appointment and Removal," *B&L*, 3:243; *CCW*, 430–1; *OR*, vol. 27, pt. 3, pp. 373–4; *MG*, 125–6. Meade's reply to Butterfield's letter is dated February 4, 1864.

Under this existing state of affairs I determined, and so notified the general-in-chief, that I should move my army as promptly as possible on the main line from Frederick to Harrisburg, extending my wings on both sides of that line [330] as far as I could consistently with the safety and the rapid concentration of that army, and should continue that movement until I either encountered the enemy, or had reason to believe that the enemy was about to advance upon me; my object being at all hazards to compel him to loose his hold on the Susquehanna and meet me in battle at some point. It was my firm determination, never for an instant deviated from, to give battle wherever and as soon as I could possibly find the enemy, modified, of course, by such general considerations as govern every general officer—that when I came into his immediate neighborhood some maneuvers might be made by me with a view to secure advantages on my side in that battle, and not allow them to be secured by him.

On the morning of the 29th of June the army was put in motion. On the night of the 30th, after the army had made two days' marches, I had become satisfied, from information which I had received from different sources, that the enemy was apprised of my movement; that he had relinquished his hold on the Susquehanna; that he was concentrating his forces, and that I might expect to come in contact with him in a very short time; when and where, I could not at that moment tell. Under those circumstances I instructed my engineers, with such information as we had in our possession, from maps and from such knowledge of the country as we could obtain from individuals, to look about and select some general ground, having a general reference to the existing position of the army, by which, in case the enemy should advance on me across the South mountain, I might be able, by rapid movement of concentration, to occupy this position and be prepared to give him battle upon my own terms. With this view the general line of Pipe-clay creek, I think, was selected; and a preliminary order, notifying the corps commanders that such line might possibly be adopted, and directing them, in the event of my finding it in my power to take such a position, how they might move their corps and what their positions should be along this line. This order was issued, I think, on the night of the 30th of June, possibly on the morning of the 1st of July, certainly before any positive information had reached me that the enemy had crossed the mountain and were in conflict with any portion of my force.

Meade was no doubt aware of the widespread popular criticism of the Pipe Creek circular. He may have been unaware of its importance to the committee;

more probably, he did not have his facts gathered, since he had not been able to prepare for his appearance before the committee. A more complete defense of the circular is made during his second appearance.

On the 1st of July, my headquarters being at Taneytown, and having directed the advance of two corps the previous day to Gettysburg, with the intention of occupying that place, about 1 or 2 o'clock in the day, I should think, I received information that the advance of my army, under Major General Reynolds, of the 1st corps, on their reaching Gettysburg, had encountered the enemy in force, and that the 1st and 11th corps were at that time engaged in a contest with such portions of the enemy as were there. The moment I received this information I directed Major General Hancock, who was with me at the time, to proceed without delay to the scene of the contest; and, having in view this preliminary order which I had issued to him, as well as to other corps commanders, I directed him to make an examination of the ground in the neighborhood of Gettysburg and to report to me, without loss of time, the facilities and advantages or disadvantages of that ground for receiving battle. I furthermore instructed him that in case, upon his arrival at Gettysburg—a place which I had never seen in my life, and had no more knowledge of than you have now—he should find the position unsuitable and the advantages on the side of the enemy, he should examine the ground critically as he went out there and report to me the nearest position in the immediate neighborhood of Gettysburg where a concentration of the army would be more advantageous than at Gettysburg.

Meade was confused about the sequence of events. Around noon on July 1, he received word that Reynolds was at Gettysburg in the path of two corps of Lee's army. Turning to Hancock, who was with him at the time, Meade ordered him to take his corps on the direct road to Gettysburg. If Reynolds was holding that road, Hancock was to withdraw to Frizellburg, implementing the Pipe Creek circular. This order was issued at 12:30 P.M. Returning to his headquarters, Hancock was joined by Meade and Butterfield before he had a chance to move. News that the First and Eleventh Corps were engaged with Lee's forces, and that Reynolds had been killed, caused a change in plans. A new order was issued at 1:10 P.M., ordering Hancock to proceed to Gettysburg and take command of the First, Eleventh, and Third Corps. In consultation with General Warren, who had already been sent to Gettysburg, Hancock was to decide if the army should fight there.[8]

8. *OR*, vol. 27, pt. 3, p. 461; Jordan, *Winfield Scott Hancock*, 81.

Early in the evening of July 1, I should suppose about 6 or 7 o'clock, I received a report from General Hancock, I think in person, giving me such an account of a position in the neighborhood of Gettysburg, which could be occupied by my army, as caused me at once to determine to fight a battle at that point; having reason to believe, from the account given to me of the operations of [331] July 1, that the enemy were concentrating there. Therefore, without any reference to but entirely ignoring the preliminary order, which was a mere contingent one, and intended only to be executed under certain circumstances which had not occurred, and therefore the order fell to the ground—the army was ordered immediately to concentrate, and that night did concentrate, on the field of Gettysburg, where the battle was eventually fought out.

Meade's testimony again contains minor errors of detail. Hancock had sent messages by two aides, Major William G. Mitchell and Captain I. B. Parker. Mitchell's message, sent about 4 P.M.*, explained the situation and said that Hancock would hold his ground until dark to give Meade time to make a decision. Parker's message, timed 5:25, gave a detailed account of the situation, as well as the position's advantages and disadvantages. Having sent these messages, it was not until about dark that Hancock left for Meade's headquarters, arriving after Meade had already left for Gettysburg.*[9]

It seems fairly clear that Meade had determined to fight at Gettysburg before receiving Hancock's messages. During the afternoon of July 1 he had received convincing reports that Lee intended to concentrate his army at Gettysburg. In his official battle report Meade stated that due to favorable reports from Hancock and Howard, "I determined to give battle at this point." These messages had been received around or after 6:00, but Meade had sent a message at 6:00 (oddly, addressed to Hancock and Doubleday and not to Howard, who commanded the field) that "we have so concentrated that a battle at Gettysburg is now forced on us." The timing of this message shows that Meade had reached his conclusion before reading the reports from Hancock and Howard.

I dwell particularly upon the point of this order, in consequence of its having been reported on the floor of the Senate that an order to retreat had been given by me.

Meade was referring to a speech made before the Senate on March 3, 1864, by Morton S. Wilkinson, a radical Republican from Minnesota, who compared

9. *LLM*, July 1, 1863, 2:38–9; *B&L*, 3:287; *GC*, 324; *CCW*, 405.

Meade unfavorably with Grant. In his speech Morton said, "I am told, and I believe it can be proven, that before the fight commenced at Gettysburg, . . . the order went forth from the commander of that army to retreat; and but for the single fact that one of the corps commanders had got into a fight before the dispatch reached him, the whole army would undoubtedly have been retreating."[10]

Wilkinson was a friend and traveling companion of Chandler's. In July 1864, after the hearings on Meade ended, he went with Chandler to visit the Army of the Potomac and again sought the removal of Meade. Chandler also called upon Wilkinson in October 1864 for help in a tough reelection campaign. This connection would serve to explain Wilkinson's thinly veiled allusion to the Pipe Creek circular in his speech.[11]

No order to retreat was at any time given by me. But, as I have already stated, a preliminary order, a copy of which is herewith furnished, [see copy appended to this deposition] was issued by me before I was aware that the enemy had crossed the mountain, and that there was any collision between the two forces. That preliminary order was intended as an order of maneuver, based upon contingencies which did not occur, and therefore the order was not executed. Such an order was given, as I have already acknowledged.

On the next day, July 2, the army was got into position at Gettysburg. Early in the morning it had been my intention, as soon as the 6th corps arrived on the ground—it having a distance of nearly thirty-two miles to march—and a preliminary order had been issued, to make a vigorous attack from our extreme right upon the enemy's left, the command of which was to be given to Major General Slocum, who commanded the 12th corps on the right. The attacking column was to be composed of the 12th, 5th, and 6th corps. Major General Slocum, however, reported that the character of the ground in front was unfavorable to making an attack; and the 6th corps, having so long a distance to march, and leaving at nine o'clock at night, did not reach the scene until about two o'clock in the afternoon. Under these circumstances I abandoned my intention to make an attack from my right, and, as soon as the 6th corps arrived, I directed the 5th corps, then in reserve on the right, to move over and be in reserve on the left.

10. *CG*, 38th Cong., 1st sess., March 2, 1864, pp. 896–900.

11. *MG*, 272–3; Sister Mary Karl George, *Zachariah Chandler: A Political Biography* (East Lansing: Michigan State University Press, 1969), 93.

Here Meade established that he had not planned to retreat from Gettysburg in the morning of July 2 at least, but had planned to attack Lee's army with three corps.

About three or half past three o'clock in the afternoon—it having been reported to me about two o'clock that the 6th corps had arrived—I proceeded from my headquarters, which were about the centre of the line, and in rear of the cemetery, to the extreme left, in order to see as to the posting of the 5th corps, and also to inspect the position of the 3d corps, about which I was in doubt.

I had sent instructions in the morning to General Sickles, commanding the 3d corps, directing him to form his corps in line of battle on the left of the 2d corps, commanded by General Hancock, and I had indicated to him in general terms, that his right was to rest upon General Hancock's left; and his left was to extend to the Round Top mountain, plainly visible, if it was practicable to occupy it. During the morning I sent a staff officer to inquire of General Sickles whether he was in position. The reply was returned to me that General Sickles said there was no position there. I then sent back to him my general instructions which had been previously given. A short time afterwards General Sickles came to my headquarters, and I told him what my general views were, and intimated that he was to occupy the position that I understood General Hancock had put General Geary in the night previous. General Sickles replied that General Geary had no position, as far as he could understand. He then said to me that there was in the neighborhood of where his corps was some very good ground for artillery, and that he should like to have some staff officer of mine go out there and see as to the posting of artillery. He also asked me whether he was not authorized to post his corps in such manner as, in his judgment, he should deem the most suitable. I answered General Sickles, "Certainly, within the limits of the general instructions I have given you; any ground within those limits you choose to occupy I leave to you." And I directed Brigadier General Hunt, my chief of artillery, to accompany General [332] Sickles and examine and inspect such positions as General Sickles thought good for artillery, and to give General Sickles the benefit of his judgment.

In consequence of these several messages to General Sickles, and this conversation with him, as soon as I heard that the 6th corps had arrived, and that the 5th corps was moving over to the left, I went out to the left for the purpose of inspecting General Sickles's position, and to see about the posting of the 5th corps. When I arrived upon the ground, which I did a few minutes before 4 o'clock in the afternoon, I found that General Sickles had taken up a position very much in advance of what it had been my intention that he should take; that he had thrown forward his right flank, instead of connecting with the left of General Hancock, something like a half or three-quarters of a mile in front of General Hancock, thus leaving a large gap between his right and General Hancock's left, and that his left, instead of being near the Round Top mountain, was in advance of the Round Top, and that his line, instead of being a prolongation of General Hancock's line, as I expected it would be, made an angle of about 45 degrees with General Hancock's line. As soon as I got upon the ground I sent for General Sickles and asked him to indicate to me his general position. When he had done so I told him it was not the position I had expected him to take; that he had advanced his line beyond the support of my army, and that I was very fearful he would be attacked and would lose the artillery, which he had put so far in front, before I could support it, or that if I undertook to support it I would have to abandon all the rest of the line which I had adopted—that is, that I would have to fight the battle out there where he was. General Sickles expressed regret that he should have occupied a position which did not meet with my approval, and he very promptly said that he would withdraw his forces to the line which I had intended him to take. You could see the ridge by turning around which I had indicated to him. But I told him I was fearful that the enemy would not permit him to withdraw, and that there was no time for any farther change or movement. And before I had finished that remark, or that sentence, the enemy's batteries opened upon him and the action commenced.

Question. Before General Sickles had time to retire his corps?

Answer. Yes, sir; while I was speaking to him. And the subsequent events of that battle fully confirmed my judgment upon this occasion. The enemy threw immense masses upon General Sickles's corps, which, advanced and isolated in this way, it was not in my power to support promptly. At the same time that they threw these immense masses against General Sickles a heavy column was thrown upon the Round Top mountain, which was the key-point of my whole position. If they had succeeded in occupying that, it would have prevented me from holding any of the ground which I subsequently held to the last. Immediately upon the batteries opening I sent several staff officers to hurry up the column under Major General Sykes, of the 5th corps, then on its way, and which I had expected would have reached there by that time. This column advanced, reached the ground in a short time, and, fortunately, General Sykes was enabled, by throwing a strong force upon Round Top mountain, where a most desperate and bloody struggle ensued, to drive the enemy from it and secure our foothold upon that important position. In the mean time re-enforcements were rapidly thrown from all parts of the line, so that by the time that General Sickles's corps, notwithstanding their gallantry and their stubborn resistance, was shattered and broken and driven into our lines, a reformation and a new line were made by the supports, and the enemy were repulsed and driven back to their former position.

I also make these remarks *in extenso* in consequence of my position and views in reference to the position occupied by General Sickles not being fully comprehended by the public, and not being expatiated on in my report. It is not my intention in these remarks to cast any censure upon General Sickles. I am of [333] the opinion that General Sickles did what he thought was for the best; but I differed with him in judgment. And I maintain that subsequent events proved that my judgment was correct, and his judgment was wrong.

This terminated the contest of the second day. The enemy was repulsed, and the line which I had intended originally General Sickles should form on was finally occupied by our troops and held to the last of the battle.

Unsurprisingly, Meade's version of the events surrounding Sickles's advanced line differed from Sickles's own explanation. Yet Meade made at least one omission in his testimony. He did not mention that he had called a council of his corps commanders to convene just as Longstreet began his attack on the Third Corps. The timing of the council was inopportune, but with the army finally assembled a planning session was probably needed.

Meade's failure to mention the council might have been intentional. He had been criticized by Halleck, among others, for calling councils. Aware of the charges of timidity laid upon him by Sickles and Doubleday, Meade may have decided not to add to his troubles by mentioning the council to the committee. It is also possible, though unlikely, that since Longstreet's bombardment interrupted the council and it never actually met, Meade simply forgot that he had called it.[12]

Meade's defense of Sickles's actions might seem surprising. Almost apologetically, Meade explained that the public did not understand the situation and that he had not fully explained his attitude towards Sickles. A far different man from the politically savvy Sickles, Meade was uncomfortable and somewhat naïve in the glare of public and political scrutiny. His testimony indicates a man

12. *OR*, vol. 27, pt. 1, p. 92.

going out of his way to avoid controversy. Colonel Theodore Lyman, an aide on Meade's staff, later wrote that Meade "was a man who did not strive for cheap popularity but actually would go out of his way to frown it down." For the remaining eight years of his life, Meade took the moral high ground, rarely responding to Sickles's attacks and leaving his son George with the task of defending his reputation after his death.[13]

During these operations upon the left flank, a division and two brigades of the 12th corps, which held the right wing, were ordered over for the purpose of re-enforcing the left. Only one brigade, however, arrived in time to take any part in the action, the enemy having been repulsed before the rest of the force came up. The absence of this large proportion of the 12th corps caused my extreme right flank to be held by one single brigade of the 12th corps, commanded by General Greene. The enemy perceiving this, made a vigorous attack upon General Greene, but were held at bay by him for some time, until he was re-enforced by portions of the 1st and 11th corps, which were adjacent to him, when he succeeded in repulsing them.

During the night that portion of the 12th corps which had been sent to the left was returned to its former position. On returning, however, they found that the enemy had advanced and were occupying a portion of the line of breastworks which the 12th corps had constructed before they left. The next morning at early daylight, the enemy having been re-enforced during the night, a spirited contest commenced, and was continued until 10 or 11 o'clock in the morning, in which nearly the whole of the 12th corps were engaged. It resulted in their finally driving the enemy from the position he had occupied and securing the line of the right flank as it was designed it should be.

Meade's short account did not do justice to just how near to disaster the right flank was, but the successful defense on the right was not in contention before the committee.

About one o'clock in the day, as near as I can remember, the enemy opened upon our lines, with, I should judge, about 125 guns, a severe cannonade which they kept up between one and two hours, and which was directed at my left and left centre; principally at my left centre. The object of this was to demoralize my command by the severe fire, the enemy hoping that they would

13. *MG*, 351.

be enabled to drive us back from our lines, and to injure my artillery; and then intending, as they subsequently did, to make a grand assault, which should secure them the victory. This assault was made about 3 o'clock in the afternoon, and was directed principally against that portion of the line commanded by Major General Hancock, on the left centre. After I became fully satisfied of the object of the enemy's fire, I directed my artillery to cease firing in order to save their ammunition, and also with the view of making the enemy believe that they had silenced our guns, and thus bring on their assault the sooner. It resulted as I desired. As soon as we ceased our firing they ceased firing, and shortly afterwards they made their assault. This assault, which was made in three lines of battle, which were apparently over a mile and a half in extent in front, was entirely and successfully repulsed, although the enemy bravely and gallantly advanced until they came within the guns of our line of battle; one of their generals, General Armistead, being wounded and captured inside of my batteries. This assault was repulsed, and the enemy retired about five o'clock.

As soon as the assault was repulsed, I went immediately to the extreme left of my line, with the determination of advancing the left and making an assault upon the enemy's lines. So soon as I arrived at the left I gave the necessary orders for the pickets and skirmishers in front to be thrown forward to feel the enemy, and for all preparations to be made for the assault. The great length of the line, and the time required to carry these orders out to the front, and the movement subsequently made, before the report given to me of the condition of the forces in the front and left, caused it to be so late in the evening as to induce me to abandon the assault which I had contemplated.

No less than ten of the witnesses were questioned by the committee on this point, and Meade should have given a fuller explanation. It is obvious from the brevity of Meade's remarks that he was unaware of Doubleday's and Howe's negative comments on this non-event, and the failure of members of the committee to question him further must have indicated to Meade their satisfaction with his explanation.

The next day, which was the 4th of July, it was reported to me from the [334] extreme right that the enemy had disappeared from our front, but that he still maintained his appearance on the left and the left centre. I immediately directed General Slocum, in command of the right, to advance his corps and his skirmishers, and ascertain the position of the enemy. I likewise directed General Howard, in the centre, to push into Gettysburg, to see whether the enemy still occupied that town. I found, from the reports of those officers, that the enemy had retired from the circular position which they had occupied around us, and had assumed a position about parallel to my left and left centre. It rained very violently during portions of this day, so violently as to interrupt any very active operations if I had designed making them.

During the night of the 4th, the enemy, as I ascertained on the 5th, retired through the Cashtown and Fairfield passes. So soon as I was positively satisfied, from the reports of my officers, that the enemy had actually retired, I directed General Sedgwick, in command of the 6th corps, which corps had been comparatively unengaged during the battle, and was in full force and strength, to advance on the Fairfield road and pursue the enemy vigorously. At the same time I despatched a cavalry force to follow the retreating column on the Cashtown road, believing that the enemy was retiring into the Cumberland valley, and not satisfied what his further movements would be, not being satisfied that he was in full retreat for the Potomac, and not aware of what injury I had done him in the battle of Gettysburg, although satisfied that I had punished him very severely.

It is possible that Meade, speaking offhand, simply confused or forgot the sequence of events. Yet it is more likely that, aware of the rampant criticisms of his pursuit of Lee's army, he was putting as good a face on events as he could. In order to refute charges of timidity and suspicions of sympathy with the rebels, Meade had to convince the committee that he had pursued Lee closely following his withdrawal from Gettysburg.

Nonetheless, Meade's account was not accurate. After the discovery of Ewell's withdrawal to Seminary Ridge on Lee's left on July 4, Meade sent seven of his eight available cavalry brigades to gain the rear of the Confederates. Colonel J. Irvin Gregg's Third Brigade of Brigadier General David M. Gregg's Second Cavalry Division was sent on a roundabout route toward Cashtown, with the rest of the brigades scattered in a southerly direction.[14]

On July 4, Meade also issued General Order 68 thanking the army on "behalf of the country" for the "glorious result of the recent operations." This was a common method used by Civil War generals to maintain the morale of their troops. In this instance, however, Meade chose his words poorly. Reminding the troops that their job was not complete, Meade called for "greater efforts to drive from our soil every vestige of the presence of the invader." But Meade's rhetoric

14. *OR*, vol. 27, pt. 1, p. 916.

caused Lincoln great distress. On first reading the order, Lincoln is said to have exclaimed in anguish, "Drive the invaders from our soil! My God! Is that all?" Ten days later Lincoln was still upset, saying, "Will our generals never get that idea out of their heads? The whole country is our soil."[15]

Lincoln felt that Meade intended to cover Baltimore and Washington, as his orders directed, while getting the enemy across the Potomac without fighting him again. The president had long believed, without any foundation in fact, that once the rebel army was north of the Potomac it would be trapped and defeated. Lee's defeat at Gettysburg served to reinforce this belief. Meade's General Order 68, combined with his caution in following up the Union victory, made a bad impression on Lincoln. The president had shared his views about Meade with Halleck by telegram, and so they were doubtless known to Stanton, who as secretary of war would have seen telegrams to Halleck. Lincoln's views were probably known at least in substance to Wade and Chandler.[16]

Contrary to Lincoln's belief, however, Meade expected and preferred a fight before Lee crossed the Potomac. Writing to his wife on July 8 he said, "For my part, as I have to follow him to fight him, I would rather do it at once and in Maryland than to follow into Virginia." On July 10 he wrote, "I expect in a few days, if not sooner, again to hazard the fortune of war." Had Lincoln known of these letters he might have felt better about Meade's intentions.[17]

From information which I had previously received of the character of the passes at Fairfield and Cashtown, having been informed that they had been fortified by the enemy, and that a small force could hold a large body in check for a considerable time, I made up my mind that a more rapid movement of my army could be made by the flank through the Boonsboro Pass, than to attempt to follow the enemy on the road which he himself had taken. I therefore directed that orders should be prepared, but not issued, for the movement of the various corps by way of Middletown and South mountain towards Hagerstown. This was, I think, the 6th of July. The 5th of July, I think, was occupied, after the retreat of the enemy, in burying our dead and attending to the wounded, of which we had a large number.

During this day, the 6th, I received reports from General Sedgwick that he was following the enemy's rear guard as rapidly as he could, but that he had

15. Ibid., pt. 3, p. 519; Gabor S. Boritt, "Unfinished Work: Lincoln, Meade, and Gettysburg," in *Lincoln's Generals,* ed. Gabor S. Boritt (New York: Oxford University Press, 1994), 89.

16. *OR,* vol. 27, pt. 3, p. 567.

17. *LLM,* July 8, 1863, 2:132; July 10, 1863, 2:133.

reason to believe, from reports of prisoners, or from other information (which I do not recollect) that the main body of the enemy was around and in the vicinity of Fairfield Pass, and that it was not impossible that another engagement might be had with the enemy in those mountains. Under those circumstances, as a matter of security, and also willing to meet such a movement on the part of the enemy, I directed that two corps, I think the 3d and 5th—I am not positive about that—should be immediately moved in the direction of General Sedgwick, so as to be near him to assist him if he were attacked, or to re-enforce him if he himself required re-enforcement. When I had given this order I found that the other order, for the movement of the whole army, had been issued by my chief of staff, General Butterfield, without my authority. I so informed General Butterfield; and at the same time sent officers and arrested the progress of the 3d and 1st corps, which had not moved very far, and detained them to sustain General Sedgwick in case it was necessary. The other corps moved on.

This was not the first time Butterfield had issued preliminary orders without authority and Meade had reached the limit of his patience. Butterfield, who had been slightly wounded at Gettysburg, was relieved and Humphreys was asked to take his place. It was three days before Humphreys decided to accept the position and a promotion to major general. In the interim the duties of chief of staff were divided between Pleasonton and Warren.[18]

During that day, towards evening or at night, I received a report from General Sedgwick that he had pushed the enemy's rear guard as far as Fairfield Pass; that the Fairfield Pass was a very strong position; that a very small force could hold him in check for a considerable time, though he could finally take it; and that, in his judgment, it would involve delay and waste of time to endeavor to push the enemy any further on that road. Upon receiving this [335] information I directed the whole army to move down towards Middletown; and directed General Sedgwick to move from Fairfield pass in the direction of Emmitsburg, leaving a force of cavalry and infantry to harass the rear of the enemy.

I have been thus particular in speaking of these movements because a report has also reached me that I lost a day by having stopped these two corps to sustain and re-enforce General Sedgwick, in case he should require it.

After reaching Middletown, it having been reported to me by my corps

18. *MG*, 175.

commanders that there were many necessary articles of clothing and other supplies that the army were very much in want of, and having myself, as I rode along, seen I may say hundreds of men walking over these broken turnpikes barefooted on these long marches, I deemed it my duty to remain at Middletown one day in order to obtain the necessary supplies, and put my army in condition, and give them some rest. I may say that it was not until the end of that day that the whole army had come up, for, in consequence of the heavy rains which, as I have already stated, visited us on the 4th of July, the roads over which we had moved, notwithstanding they were the best roads in Pennsylvania, had been so cut up by the passage of my trains and artillery, that a considerable portion of the trains were in the rear, and the army did not get up and in hand until the close of the day which I remained for the purpose of obtaining supplies. As soon as the army was in condition we moved from Middletown through the South mountain.

I ought to have stated before, that in advancing from Frederick, upon assuming command of the army, I had directed a portion of the garrison at Harpers Ferry, under General French—which was placed under my command by the general-in-chief—7,000 of that garrison, to move up from Harpers Ferry to Frederick, to hold Frederick and the line of the Baltimore and Ohio railroad, not knowing but that my communication would be dependent upon that road. The balance of that garrison, consisting of 4,000 men, I at first ordered to remain and hold Maryland heights. I did this, not because I considered the occupation of Harpers Ferry an important matter so far as the crossing of the Potomac river was concerned, for I did not, any more than any other where the river could be crossed. But I did consider it important to hold that point as a *debouche* into the Cumberland valley, so that, if upon my return I should have found the enemy occupying the other passes, so long as I held Harpers Ferry I could always enter. Having been informed, however, that the supplies at Harpers Ferry were limited, and that in consequence of the railroad and the canal being right alongside the river and exposed to fire from the other side, the enemy with a small force could cut off communication with Harpers Ferry and prevent them from being supplied, and not knowing how long a time the campaign I was entering on might last, I yielded to the suggestions made to me to evacuate Harpers Ferry entirely; and late on the night of the 28th of June I ordered the 4,000 men previously ordered to remain there to garrison the place, to collect all the canal-boats that they could, load them with the public property at Harpers Ferry, so that nothing should be destroyed, and proceed with them down to Washington, where, in case of any disaster to me, they could act as part of the defense of Washington; or in the event of my being successful, they could be returned to my army. Those orders I believe were executed; General French occupied Frederick and threw a force into South Mountain pass.

In his testimony before the committee, Daniel Butterfield would later take credit for convincing Meade to take this course of action.

As soon as it became evident that the enemy were retiring, information was sent to General French, and he was directed to immediately seize and hold South Mountain pass, and also reoccupy Harpers Ferry, bringing up the force from Washington for that purpose. All of which orders were not only executed, but General French, in advance of any instructions to that effect, had sent a cavalry force in his command across the mountain during the battle, which had penetrated as far as Williamsport, where they partially destroyed or rendered [336] ineffective a pontoon bridge of the enemy, capturing the greater portion of the small guard left there to defend it.

Having crossed the South mountain, I moved my army forward, by way of Boonsboro, until about the 12th of July I got into position in front of the enemy, whom I found on a line extending from Hagerstown towards a place called Downiesville, I think. So soon as my troops were in line, or as soon as my army was in hand and ready for offensive operations, although I had had no opportunity of examining critically and closely the enemy's position, still knowing the importance of not permitting the enemy to recross the river without a further action, it was my desire to attack him in that position. Having, however, been in command of the army not more than twelve or fourteen days, and in view of the important and tremendous issues involved in the result, knowing that if I were defeated the whole question would be reversed, the road to Washington and to the north open, and all the fruits of my victory at Gettysburg dissipated, I did not feel that I would be right in assuming the responsibility of blindly attacking the enemy without any knowledge of his position. I therefore called a council of my corps commanders, who were the officers to execute this duty, if it was determined upon, and laid before them the precise condition of affairs.

Question. Will you, as you pass along, give us the names of those corps commanders in that council?

Answer. The 1st corps was represented by General Wadsworth; General

Newton, who commanded the corps, being sick at the time. The 2d corps was commanded, I think, by General William Hays; the 3d by General French; the 5th by General Sykes; the 6th by General Sedgwick; the 11th by General Howard; and the 12th by General Slocum.

I represented to those generals, so far as I knew it, the situation of affairs. I told them that I had reason to believe, from all I could ascertain, that General Lee's position was a very strong one, and that he was prepared to give battle and defend it if attacked; that it was not in my power, from a want of knowledge of the ground, and from not having had time to make reconnaissances, to indicate any precise mode of attack or any precise point of attack; that, nevertheless, I was in favor of moving forward and attacking the enemy and taking the consequences; but that I left it to their judgment, and would not do it unless it met with their approval. The opinion of that council was very largely opposed to any attack without further examination. I cannot state positively what each individual vote was without referring to my papers. But I am now under the impression that there were but two officers decidedly in favor of attacking; I think that General Wadsworth and General Howard were the only two in favor of attacking, while all the rest were opposed to it.

In view of this opinion of my subordinate officers I yielded, or abstained from ordering an assault, but gave the necessary directions for such an examination of the enemy's position as would enable us to form some judgment as to where he might be attacked with some degree and probability of success.

Meade's controversial use of councils to decide his actions met with much justifiable criticism. On July 12 he had wired Halleck that he intended to attack on the following day unless something occurred to change his mind. Meade said that the July 13 council convinced him not to attack. There is reason to question this statement, however. It was five o'clock in the afternoon on July 12 when he sent his message to Halleck informing him of the decision of his corps commanders and the postponement of the attack. Had the corps commanders voted in favor of attacking, the lateness of the hour would have hindered the development of any assault.[19]

Halleck, no doubt in great frustration, telegraphed back, "You are strong enough to attack and defeat the enemy before he can effect a crossing. Act upon your own judgement and make your generals execute your orders. Call no coun-

19. *OR*, vol. 27, pt. 1, p. 91.

cil of war. It is proverbial that councils of war never fight. . . . Do not let the enemy escape." But his telegram was a classic case of closing the barn door after the horse had escaped.[20]

It is interesting to note that Halleck's telegram was timed at 9:30 P.M., nearly three hours after the receipt of Meade's telegram. This suggests that Halleck may have had time to discuss his response with others.[21]

The 13th of July, which was the day spent in this examination, was very rainy and misty, and not much information was obtained; nevertheless, on the night of the 13th I directed that the next morning at daylight the whole army should move forward with a view to attacking the enemy. This order was duly executed, but during the night of the 13th the enemy had retired across the river.

It is proper I should say that an examination of the enemy's lines, and of the defences which he had made—of which I now have a map from an accurate survey, which can be laid before your committee—brings me clearly to the opinion that an attack, under the circumstances in which I had proposed to make it, would have resulted disastrously to our arms.

Question. Will you give us the reasons for that opinion?

[337] Answer. It is founded upon the strength of their position. I will say that if I had attacked the enemy in the position which he then occupied—he having the advantage of position and being on the defensive, his artillery in position and his infantry behind parapets and rifle-pits—the very same reasons and causes which produced my success at Gettysburg would have operated in his favor there, and be likely to produce success on his part.

Question. Have you any reason to suppose that after that terrible artillery fire at Gettysburg his ammunition was nearly exhausted?

Answer. No, sir; from all the information I could obtain—which I acknowledge, however, was quite scanty—I had reason to believe that ammunition trains had been brought from Winchester and crossed on the ferry at Williamsport for the supply of General Lee's army; and from the character of the battle at Gettysburg, which consisted in a series of offensive operations on his part, mostly subjected to artillery fire, I had no reason to believe that the expenditure of ammunition by him had been such as to reduce him to a low point.

20. Ibid., 92.
21. Ibid.

Question. You are now speaking of small-arms ammunition.

Answer. Yes, sir; and all the information which I obtained led to the belief that his army had been supplied with ammunition from Winchester, for I had positive information that ammunition trains had been ferried across at Williamsport; and my opinion is now that General Lee evacuated that position, not from any want of ammunition, or the fear that he would be dislodged from it by any active operations on my part, but that he was fearful that a force would be sent by Harpers Ferry to cut off his communications, which I had intended to do, having brought up a bridge from Washington and sent the cavalry down there, and that he could not have maintained that position probably a day if his communications had been cut. That was what caused him to retire.

Question. Did you discover, after the battle of Gettysburg, any symptoms of demoralization in Lee's army, such as excessive straggling, or anything of the kind?

Answer. No, sir; I saw nothing of that kind. I have no doubt his army was somewhat demoralized, for every army is, in some measure, demoralized after a defeat. But I doubt whether it was any more demoralized than we were when we fell back to Washington in 1862, after the second battle of Groveton, under General Pope. Then in forty-eight hours afterwards, when we got over on this side and got into the presence of the enemy, our morale was just as good as ever it was. I do not think that a great many stragglers or deserters from General Lee's army were picked up.

Question. I will ask you, in this connexion, about the comparative strength of the two armies at the battle of Gettysburg. What was your opinion about that?

Answer. My opinion about that was that General Lee was, as far as I could tell, about 10,000 or 15,000 my superior.

Question. What was your strength upon that battle-field?

Answer. Including all arms of the service, my strength was a little under 100,000 men—about 95,000. I think General Lee had about 90,000 infantry, from 4,000 to 5,000 artillery, and about 10,000 cavalry.

Question. There were other troops of ours at that time under General Schenck?

Answer. Yes, sir; and I had command of everybody. I had command of General Schenck, of General Couch, and of general [*sic*] everybody else.

Question. You did not bring General Schenck's forces into the field?

Answer. I never had any return from him; I did not know what force he had.

Question. What was the strength of the force about Washington?

Answer. I do not know what the strength about Washington was; but I understood that Washington was quite stripped.

Question. Did not General Heintzelman have a corps here?

[338] Answer. I do not know. The very next day after I took command of the army I had no telegraphic communication with General Halleck. I think the returns showed me, when I took command of the army, amounted to about 105,000 men; included in those were 11,000 of General French, which I did not bring up, which would reduce it down to about 94,000. Of that 94,000 I was compelled to leave a certain portion in the rear to guard my baggage trains.

Question. You say that the enemy had 125 pieces of artillery that he brought to bear upon you on the third day of the fight?

Answer. That is my estimate; their own estimate is 115 pieces.

Question. Was that not a heavier artillery fire on both sides than was ever before in a battle?

Answer. I must have had on the field at Gettysburg but little short of 300 guns; and I think the report of my chief of artillery was that there were not more than two batteries that were not in service during that battle.

Question. Was not that a greater proportion of artillery than is generally used in battles?

Answer. I think it was. I know I had then, and have now, more artillery with me than is usual. The artillery I have now is the artillery which General McClellan had when he led an army of 150,000, and he got a little more artillery even than was necessary for that army, because it was thought at that time that artillery would be the turning point; and I have kept all the artillery while my infantry has been reduced. I think I had some 325 or 330 guns last summer; but I had some heavy siege guns which I had sent to the rear. I think there were about twenty-five guns with my trains at Westminster. I only had field guns on the field.

In reference to the re-enforcements, I desire to say that after moving from Gettysburg, the forces under General French, which I had left at Frederick, amounting to about 8,000 men, were added to my army. That was the only addition to my army until I had arrived in the presence of General Lee's army. Subsequent to my crossing the mountains, but before the day that I advanced to attack the enemy at Williamsport, I received notice of troops arriving both at Frederick and at Harpers Ferry. But in connexion with that notice came information that those troops were mostly nine-months men from North Carolina and the Peninsula, who had but one or two days longer to serve and who were from that fact in a very unsuitable moral condition to bring to the front; and so little reliance did I place upon them that I brought none of them any further to the front than Frederick, South mountain, and Harpers Ferry, to cover my communications in case anything happened to me.

And about the 12th of July, I should think, in connexion with a brigade of infantry, and some cavalry which I had left to follow the retreat of the enemy through Fairfield pass, and who joined me about that time, I also received under General William F. Smith a portion of General Couch's command, charged with the defences of the Susquehanna, and which General Couch had sent forward after the enemy evacuated Carlisle. General Smith arrived at Boonsboro with a force of from 4,000 to 5,000 men; but he reported to me that those men were entirely new and totally undisciplined, and when I offered to attach him as a division to one of my corps, and put him in the front, he advised so strongly against it that I left him in the rear at Boonsboro. The foregoing are all the re-enforcements which I can now remember of receiving, unless there may have been one or two regiments under General Gordon, which were old and efficient regiments, and which arrived about the 12th or 13th of July. So that I may say, notwithstanding I am aware that every exertion was made to send forward to me all the available troops that could be obtained from everywhere, that really and practically, with the exception of General French's command which was attached to the army when I took command of it, I was in front of the enemy at Williamsport with very much the same army that I moved from Gettysburg.

[339] Question. The enemy recrossed the river at Williamsport?

Answer. Yes, sir.

[There followed a lengthy discussion of the Bristoe and Mine Run campaigns, which is omitted.]

Question. Is there anything further that you desire to say?

Answer. I would probably have a great deal to say if I knew what other people have said.

Question. I have briefly called your attention to the points upon which I have heard criticisms. Are you heartily sustained by your corps commanders under all circumstances, so far as you believe?

Answer. I believe I have been; I have no complaint to make of want of assistance from all my corps commanders, except what is stated in my evidence in reference to Mine run.

In a letter to his wife, Meade acknowledged that his movement at Mine Run had been a failure, but asserted that the "causes were not in my plans, but in the want of support and co-operation of the part of subordinates."[22]

The witness then said:

The following is the rough draught of the original preliminary order before the battle of Gettysburg. The whole jist of the thing is contained in the first part of it.

(General Meade subsequently appeared before the committee and withdrew this rough draught of the preliminary order, and substituted in place of it a series of orders, &c., which will be found at the close of his testimony.)

Many writers consider the following testimony as a separate appearance by Meade, bringing the total of his depositions to three. Since no other witnesses were called in the interim, however, I have chosen to consider this testimony as a continuation of Meade's first appearance.

March 11, 1864.

Major General George G. Meade appeared before the committee, and said:

I desire to substitute, in lieu of the rough draught of the preliminary order which I left here when I gave my testimony, a series of orders and circulars issued by me on the 30th of June and the 1st day of July, a careful perusal of which, I am sure, will satisfy every member of this committee that there was no intention on my part to withdraw my army from the position at Gettysburg the very moment that I ascertained that they were there in force, that the ground was favorable for a battle, and that I could fight one there. I will not read all of these orders—only enough to substantiate the point I have here made.

Meade then presented a series of thirteen orders to support his testimony. These orders can be found in the Official Records, *volume 27, The Gettysburg Campaign. For the reader's convenience the corresponding part and page number follow each exhibit. Due to its importance, exhibit E, the Pipe Creek circular, is printed in its entirety at the end of Meade's testimony.*

The papers herewith submitted, marked A [3:415], B [3:416], and C [1:923], are the orders issued on the 30th of June, together with the information from

22. *LLM,* December 7, 1863, 2:160.

General Buford, in command of the cavalry. The information from General Buford, C, was not received, however, until pretty late on the morning of the 1st of July. Letter D [3:416] contains the orders for the movement of troops on July 1, under which two corps were moved up to Gettysburg. Letter E is the circular, of which I left a rough draught when here before, issued to corps commanders on the morning of July 1, before the information from General Buford had been received, and before I had any positive information that the enemy were moving on the Cashtown road. To show that this circular did not contemplate, under all circumstances or emergencies, a withdrawal or retreat of the army, I would call the attention of the committee to the paper marked F [3:460–1], which are the instructions [348] issued to the commanding officer of the 1st corps, Major General Reynolds, who was ordered up to Gettysburg. Those instructions were sent to him about the time that the circular marked E was sent to him. The paper marked F I will now read. (See appendix to this disposition.)

I desire to say, in connexion with this despatch, that at the time I wrote it I simply knew of the concentration of the enemy, without having any accurate knowledge of the point at which he would strike; and it would be evident to any one perusing it, it having been sent simultaneously with the circular, that I was calling upon my corps commanders to give me information which would justify me in fighting at Emmitsburg, Gettysburg, or any other point where the enemy might suitably be met.

The next despatch I propose to read was a despatch to the commanding officer of the 6th corps, who was to my right and rear, at Manchester. Between the despatch marked F, just read, and the one I now propose to read, marked G [3:462], I had received a despatch from General Buford which indicated a strong concentration of the enemy at Gettysburg. Hence this order to the commander of the 6th corps, the most remote from me, to move up to Gettysburg, should such be decided upon as the most commanding position to be adopted. (The paper marked G was then read.) This despatch was to notify General Sedgwick that there was every probability that a battle might be fought at Gettysburg, and that he should hold his corps in readiness to move up there; and that it was also within contingencies that General Reynolds might find himself in the presence of a superior force, and might be compelled to fall back, in which case it would be essential that the line should be concentrated on his rear, and in that event the circular order should be enforced.

About 1 o'clock on the 1st of July I received the sad intelligence of the fall of General Reynolds and the actual engagement of my troops at Gettysburg. Previous to receiving this intelligence I had had a long conversation with Major General Hancock, and explained to him fully my views as to my determination to fight in front if practicable; if not, then to the rear, or to the right or the left, as circumstances might require. Without any further reflection than the fact that General Reynolds was the officer upon whom I had relied under my instructions, and anxious to have some one in front who understood and could carry out my views, I directed General Hancock to proceed to Gettysburg and take command of the troops there, and particularly to advise me of the condition of affairs there, and the practicability of fighting a battle there. The paper marked H [3:461] contains my instructions to General Hancock. (The paper was then read.) General Hancock immediately proceeded upon this duty. But from information received from the field, from officers returning, I became satisfied that the enemy were in such force there that it was evident that General Lee was about to concentrate his army there. I therefore did not wait for the report from General Hancock, as I can prove from staff officers who took my orders, but immediately commenced to move my troops to the front, being determined to fight a battle there.

This account is different from Meade's testimony on March 5. Initially Meade testified that he received a report from Hancock on the position at Gettysburg which caused him to decide to fight the battle there. Now he claimed that he did not wait for Hancock's report before ordering up the rest of the army. Meade's first account—given without notes or preparation—is incorrect. At six o'clock on July 1 Meade sent a telegram to Halleck referring to his concentration near Gettysburg and the possibility of attacking Lee the next day.

Meade temporarily skipped Exhibit I (1:924–5), which was a message from Buford to Pleasonton reporting the battle and the death of Reynolds. Note that there is no Exhibit J.

I will, however, read General Hancock's first report, marked K [1:366], and dated 5.25, from Gettysburg, and received by me, I should suppose, about 7 o'clock. (The paper was then read.) As I have already stated, before this despatch was received I ordered up the troops immediately in my neighborhood, the 12th and 5th corps, to the scene of action. Afterwards I sent written instructions to both the 6th and 5th corps to move up. The instructions to the 6th corps, marked M [3:467–8], I will read. (The paper was then read.)

Meade skipped exhibit L [3:467], which was an order directing the Fifth Corps to move at once to Gettysburg.

I trust that a careful perusal of these orders, with the explanations I have made here as to the time at which they were written or received, will satisfy the committee that my only doubt about fighting at Gettysburg was caused by, first, the unknown position of the enemy; and secondly, the character of the ground. That the moment those points were made clear to my mind, there was [349] no hesitation on my part to order my troops up there and fight the battle out at that place.

I will call the attention of the committee to another despatch received by me from General Buford, marked I, and dated 20 minutes past 3 o'clock, and which must have been received by me after General Hancock had gone to the front. I read it to show that my sending General Hancock there was in a measure justified by the opinion of that distinguished officer, General Buford, now deceased. (Paper marked I was then read.)

That is all I have to say about the report which has been prevalent in the public press, that the battle at Gettysburg was never intended by me to have been fought there, and that if my plans had been carried out as I intended them to be carried out the battle would not have been fought out there. In connexion with these papers I have appended a map, which will show the position of the army and the line proposed to be taken, and its reference to these different points.

This map is not in the records.

There are two other points upon which I would like to speak.

The chairman. Certainly; I desire you to state whatever you may think necessary or proper—anything you may desire to state.

Answer. I have understood that an idea has prevailed that I intended an order should be issued on the morning of the 2d of July requiring the withdrawal of the army or the retreat of the army from Gettysburg, which order was not issued, owing simply to the attack of the enemy having prevented it.

In reply to that, I have only to say that I have no recollection of ever having directed such an order to be issued, or ever having contemplated the issuing of such an order; and that it does seem to me that to any intelligent mind who is made acquainted with the great exertions I made to mass my army at Gettysburg on the night of July the 1st, it must appear entirely incomprehensible that I should order it to retreat, after collecting all my army there, before the enemy had done anything to require me to make a movement of any kind.

On the morning of the 2d of July I directed an order to be issued to Major General Slocum, commanding the 12th corps, and at that time commanding the 5th corps also, to examine the ground in front of his position, and to hold himself in readiness to make an assault upon the enemy's line so soon as the 6th corps, then on their way, should arrive on the ground. Whether that order was issued verbally or in writing I cannot say; I think it must have been a verbal order, because I cannot find any record whatever of it on my books. However, at that time a great many orders and directions were written on little slips of paper, and no copies kept of them. Before the 6th corps arrived, which was late in the afternoon, it having to march thirty-two miles in a night and day, Major General Slocum reported to me that the character of the ground in his front was not favorable to an assault, and the idea of an assault from the right was abandoned by me.

So soon as the 5th corps arrived, the 5th corps was ordered over to the left, as stated in my previous testimony; and I went to the left with the view of ascertaining as far as I could the position of my own troops and the troops of the enemy, and with the intention of ordering an attack from there, if the enemy did not themselves attack. The enemy, however, attacked and were repulsed.

I beg leave to say, in connexion with this subject of attacking or receiving an attack, that I do not hesitate to say that it was my policy and intention to act upon the defensive, and receive the attack of the enemy, if practicable, knowing that the enemy would be compelled either to attack me or retire from his position; that it was not within his power to wait any length of time in my front and maneuver, and that the chances of victory on my side were greater if I acted on the defensive than they would be if I assumed the offensive.

Having thus denied any recollection of having issued, or directed to be issued, any order on the morning of the 2d of July for the retreat of my army be-
[350] fore any attack from the enemy, I now desire to refer to a consultation of my corps commanders held on that evening, which, it has occurred to me, may possibly be the groundwork for this report that I had directed an order to retreat.

On the evening of the 2d of July, after the battle of that day had ceased, and darkness had set in, being aware of the very heavy losses of the 1st and 11th corps on the 1st of July, and knowing how severely the 3d corps, the 5th corps, and other portions of the army had suffered in the battle of the 2d of July—in fact, as subsequently ascertained, out of the 24,000 men killed, wounded, and missing, which was the amount of my losses and casualties at Gettysburg, over 20,000 of them had been put *hors du combat* before the night of the 2d of July; and taking into consideration the number of stragglers, and weakening of my army from the two days' battle, my ignorance of the condition of the corps, and the morale condition of the troops, caused me to send for my corps commanders to obtain from them the exact condition of affairs in their separate commands, and to consult and advise with them as to what, if anything, should be done on the morrow. The strong attack of the enemy that day upon my left flank, and their persistent efforts to obtain possession of what is called Round Top mountain, induced the supposition that possibly, on the next day, a very persistent attack might be made, or that a movement, upon their part, to my left and rear might be made to occupy the lines of communication I then held with the Taneytown road and the Baltimore pike.

The questions discussed by this council were, first, whether it was necessary for us to assume any different position from what we then held; and secondly, whether, if we continued to maintain the position we then held, our operations the next day should be offensive or defensive. The opinion of the council was unanimous, which agreed fully with my own views, that we should maintain our lines as they were then held, and that we should wait the movements of the enemy and see whether he made any further attack before we assumed the offensive. I felt satisfied that the enemy would attack again, as subsequently proved to be the case, for he made a vigorous assault upon my right flank, which lasted from daylight in the morning until 10 o'clock. He then made one of his heaviest assaults upon my left and left centre, which lasted from one o'clock until six in the evening.

I have been specific in giving the details of this council, because it has occurred to me as possible that some erroneous report of what took place there may have given rise to the idea that I desired to withdraw my army and retreat, and that I called my corps commanders together to know if they were in favor of retreating.

I should like to have the committee, and I trust they will do so, call upon all the principal officers I had upon that field—the corps commanders and division commanders; that their attention should be called to all the points to which I have alluded here; and that they should be specifically questioned as to their recollection and views upon those points.

Question. The council to which you have referred is one held on the evening of the 2d of July?

Answer. Yes, sir.

Question. I believe one of the witnesses we have examined states that a council was held on the night of the 3d of July also. Was there such a council held?

Answer. I do not remember any council held on the night of the 3rd of July. I had one on the night of the 4th of July, as to a plan of action in reference to pursuing the enemy. I do not remember any council on the 3d of July; if there was one, it was a council with my corps commanders, and they are all as well able to state what transpired there as myself; but I do not remember calling any council at that time. It is possible there was a consultation. I never called [351] those meetings councils; they were consultations, and they were probably more numerous and more constant in my case, from the fact that I had just assumed command of the army, and felt that it was due to myself to have the opinions of high officers before I took action on matters which involved such momentous issues.

[CIRCULAR.]

HEADQUARTERS ARMY OF THE POTOMAC, Taneytown, July 1, 1863.

From information received, the commanding general is satisfied that the object of the movement of the army in this direction has been accomplished, viz., the relief of Harrisburg, and the prevention of the enemy's intended invasion of Philadelphia, &c., beyond the Susquehanna.

It is no longer his intention to assume the offensive until the enemy's movements or position should render such an operation certain of success. If the enemy assume the offensive, and attack, it is his intention, after holding them in check sufficiently long, to withdraw the trains and other impedimenta; to withdraw the army from its present position, and form line of battle with the left resting in the neighborhood of Middleburg, and the right at Manchester, the general direction being that of Pipe Creek.

For this purpose, General Reynolds, in command of the left, will withdraw the force at present at Gettysburg, two corps by the road to Taneytown and Westminster, and, after crossing Pipe Creek, deploy toward Middleburg. The corps at Emmitsburg will be withdrawn, via Mechanicsville, to Middleburg, or, if a more direct route can be found leaving Taneytown to their left, to withdraw direct to Middleburg.

General Slocum will assume command of the two corps at Hanover and

Two Taverns, and withdraw them, via Union Mills, deploying one to the right and one to the left, after crossing Pipe Creek, connecting on the left with General Reynolds, and communicating his right to General Sedgwick at Manchester, who will connect with him and form the right.

The time for falling back can only be developed by circumstances. Whenever such circumstances arise as would seem to indicate the necessity for falling back and assuming this general line indicated, notice of such movement will be at once communicated to these headquarters and to all adjoining corps commanders.

The 2d Corps now at Taneytown will be held in reserve in the vicinity of Uniontown and Frizellburg, to be thrown to the point of strongest attack, should the enemy make it. In the event of these movements being necessary, the trains and impedimenta will all be sent to the rear of Westminster.

Corps commanders, with their officers commanding artillery and the divisions, should make themselves thoroughly familiar with the country indicated, all the roads and positions, so that no possible confusion can ensue, and that the movement, if made, be done with good order, precision, and care, without loss or any detriment to the morale of the troops.

The commanders of corps are requested to communicate at once the nature of their present positions, and their ability to hold them in case of any sudden attack at any point by the enemy.

This order is communicated, that a general plan, perfectly understood by all, may be had for receiving attack, if made in strong force, upon any portion of our present position. Developments may cause the commanding general to assume the offensive from his present positions.

The Artillery Reserve will, in the event of the general movement indicated, move to the rear of Frizellburg, and be placed in position, or sent to corps, as circumstances may require, under the general supervision of the chief of artillery.

The chief quartermaster will, in case of the general movement indicated, give directions for the orderly and proper position of the trains in rear of Westminster. All the trains will keep well to the right of the road in moving, and, in case of any accident requiring a halt, the team must be hauled out of the line, and not delay the movements.

The trains ordered to Union Bridge in these events will be sent to Westminster. General headquarters will be, in case of this movement, at Frizellburg.

General Slocum as near Union Mills as the line will render best for him.

General Reynolds at or near the road from Taneytown to Frizellburg.

The chief of artillery will examine the line, and select positions for artillery. The cavalry will be held on the right and left flanks after the movement is completed. Previous to its completion, it will, as now directed, cover the front and exterior lines, well out.

The commands must be prepared for a movement, and, in the event of the enemy attacking us on the ground indicated herein, to follow up any repulse.

The chief signal officer will examine the line thoroughly, and at once, upon the commencement of this movement, extend telegraphic communication from each of the following points to general headquarters near Frizellburg, viz., Manchester, Union Mills, Middleburg, and the Taneytown road.

All true Union people should be advised to harass and annoy the enemy in every way, to send in information, and taught how to do it; giving regiments by number of colors, number of guns, generals' names, &c. All their supplies brought to us will be paid for, and not fall into the enemy's hands.

Roads and ways to move to the right or left of the general line should be studied and thoroughly understood. All movements of troops should be concealed, and our dispositions kept from the enemy. Their knowledge of these dispositions would be fatal to our success, and the greatest care must be taken to prevent such an occurrence.

By command of Major-General Meade:

S. WILLIAMS,
Assistant Adjutant-General.

With virtually no preparation, Meade had managed to give a succinct and decent, if not always accurate, defense of his actions. He asserted at some length that the Pipe Creek circular was a preliminary order concerning a line he "might possibly adopt," and stated emphatically that "no order to retreat was at any time given by me." He had a "firm determination" to give battle wherever and whenever he could. In support of this contention, he detailed his planned attack for the morning of July 2, which he had had to abandon.

The council held at Williamsport was a more sticky point for Meade. He gave three reasons why he would not attack without the approval of his corps commanders: 1) he had been in command only two weeks; 2) if the Union army had been defeated Washington and Baltimore would have been open and the Gettysburg victory would have been wasted; 3) he did not feel it was right to assume the responsibility of attacking without a more through knowledge of the enemy's position.

But Meade was wrong on all counts. His first mistake had been in calling the council, as Halleck had pointed out a little too late. Meade's short time in command was simply an excuse. He had been chosen for command precisely to make the difficult decisions. He had maneuvered and fought the army in its greatest campaign to date, but now he hesitated because he had not been in command very long. Meade's claim that Washington and Baltimore would have been vulnerable if Union forces had lost a follow-up attack was also mistaken. As later witnesses would testify before the committee, there were ample positions to fall back on if necessary. Additionally, the defenses of Washington offered a secure shelter and would have placed the Union army on Lee's flank should he have moved toward Baltimore. The only defensible reason that Meade cited to justify himself—a lack of knowledge of the enemy's position—was shaky. In attempting a reconnaissance on July 14, Meade had discovered that he was a day late, which was his own fault. His cautious pursuit of Lee's army over the course of ten days offered many opportunities to make up twenty-four hours, placing him at Williamsport in time to make a reconnaissance in force and develop an attack before Lee escaped.

In hindsight Meade believed that his attack "would have resulted disastrously to our arms." Perhaps he was right, but that was hardly the point. Lincoln, Congress, the army, and the country at large, including Lee, had expected Meade to attack and he had not done so.

There is a very blurred line between explanations and excuses. Meade's testimony has been seen as both by his contemporaries and Civil War historians alike; and both, at different points, are correct interpretations. In the case of Williamsport, however, Meade made excuses even as he thought he was offering explanations.

7 Major General Alfred Pleasonton

WITH THE POSSIBLE EXCEPTION of Daniel Sickles, there was no greater self-promoter to appear before the committee than Major General Alfred Pleasonton, commander of the Cavalry Corps of the Army of the Potomac at Gettysburg. A graduate of West Point, Pleasonton saw active service in the Mexican War; thereafter most of his duty was as an adjutant officer rather than in the field. At the outbreak of the Civil War he was still a captain after seventeen years of service.

Pleasonton's war did not begin until the spring of 1862, when—at last a major—he attracted McClellan's attention during the Peninsula campaign. As a result, Pleasonton was given his first star and command of a brigade. In the battle of Antietam he gained some success against Stuart's cavalry but failed to break through the Confederate cavalry screen, which was a key role for the horsemen. It was at Antietam that Pleasonton revealed a major flaw in his abilities as a cavalry officer, sending McClellan a mixed collection of rumors, guesses, and just plain wrong information.[1]

During the Antietam campaign, Pleasonton showed a characteristic which, while hardly admirable, would serve him well in the future. During the battle his division seized and held a bridge opposite the Confederate center. Although this success was only a minor sideshow in the theater of battle, Pleasonton's subsequent report and his conversations with newspaper reporters turned it into a major military success. Pleasonton's self-aggrandizement reached new heights as he grabbed credit for the exploit, even though he had sat comfortably in the rear while his men had carried out the attack.[2]

1. Edward G. Longacre, "Alfred Pleasonton: Knight of Romance," *Civil War Times Illustrated* 13 (1973), 12–23.

2. *OR*, vol. 19, pt. 1, pp. 211–2.

In October 1862 Pleasonton missed an opportunity to enhance his media reputation by failing to stop Stuart's rebel horsemen after their second ride around McClellan. Having arrived at a position to cut Stuart off from his crossing point at White Ford, Pleasonton refused to launch an attack. Whitewashing this failure in his battle report, Pleasonton blamed Brigadier General George Stoneman, then commanding the Cavalry Corps, for failing to occupy the ford. In a sharp retort, Stoneman called Pleasonton's statement ridiculous and asked for a court of inquiry. For whatever reason, the inquiry never took place.[3]

Ironically, his feud with Stoneman gave Pleasonton yet another chance for unwarranted glory. During Hooker's Chancellorsville campaign, Pleasonton had been left behind with the main army while Stoneman led a raid against rebel communications between Fredericksburg and Richmond. The raid itself accomplished little, but Pleasonton's banishment to a seemingly backwater position turned out to be a blessing in disguise for him. On the evening of May 2, shortly after Stonewall Jackson had turned Hooker's right near Hazel Grove, a small Confederate force attacked the part of the line guarded by Pleasonton's brigade. The attack spread panic along much of the line, for Hooker and many others at the time believed it to be Jackson's entire corps. Hurrying to the threatened area, Pleasonton ordered a charge of the Eighth Pennsylvania Cavalry and then rode off to collect some twenty-two cannons to scatter the small band of perhaps two hundred Confederates.[4]

Pleasonton's dramatic battle report convinced Hooker that he had beaten back a major attack by Jackson aimed at blocking the Federal retreat. Later Pleasonton would claim that he had singlehandedly saved the army from suffering an even greater disaster at Chancellorsville. When Lincoln visited the army a few days after that battle, Hooker introduced Pleasonton to him with the explanation, "Mr. President, this is General Pleasonton, who saved the Army of the Potomac the other night." Pleasonton's second star was assured and command of the Cavalry Corps soon followed.[5]

Like Hooker, Pleasonton was a man of vast ambition and massive ego—traits which antagonized many of his officers. A cavalry surgeon sneered that Pleasonton "is about as fit for it [command] as any 2d Leutentant [*sic*] in the command." A captain in the First Massachusetts noted that "Pleasonton . . . is

3. Longacre, "Alfred Pleasonton," 15; *OR*, vol. 19, pt. 2, pp. 44–5.

4. John Bigelow Jr., *Chancellorsville* (New York: Konecky & Konecky, 1995), 309–10.

5. Edward G. Longacre, *The Cavalry at Gettysburg* (Lincoln: University of Nebraska Press, 1986), 47; Alfred Pleasonton, "The Successes and Failures of Chancellorsville," *B&L*, 3:180–1.

pure and simple a newspaper humbug. . . . He does nothing save with a view to a newspaper paragraph."[6]

Pleasonton blatantly used his friends and exploited his connections in order to further his personal advancement. On June 23, 1863, wanting to add the cavalry of Julius Stahel's division to his command, Pleasonton wrote to an old friend, ex-congressman John Farnsworth of Illinois, who had served with Pleasonton earlier in the war. Farnsworth's nephew Elon Farnsworth was, by a happy coincidence, a captain on Pleasonton's staff. In his letter Pleasonton claimed Stahel had neither the good sense nor the energy required of a cavalry commander, and, moreover, that Stahel was a foreigner. (Pleasonton's dislike and distrust of foreigners was not unusual, but unlike many people, he was in a position to act on his xenophobic beliefs.) Pleasonton enclosed a short note from Farnsworth's nephew, which said that the "Genl. speaks of recommending me for Brig[adier General]. I do not know that I ought to mention it for fear that you will call me an aspiring youth. I am satisfied to serve through this war in the line. . . . But if I can do any good anywhere else of course 'small favors &c.' Now try and talk this into the President and you can do an immense good." Five days later Stahel was relieved of his command and his division was added to Pleasonton's corps. On the same day the twenty-six-year-old Elon Farnsworth went from captain and company commander to brigadier general and brigade commander. Within a week he would die in a fruitless charge at Gettysburg.[7]

Pleasonton's integrity and courage were also questioned. Charles Russell Lowell, a Massachusetts cavalry officer, wrote that "it is the universal opinion that Pleasonton's own reputation, and Pleasonton's late promotions are bolstered up by systematic lying." To those "who had served under him and seen him under fire," Pleasonton's personal courage was notable for its absence.[8]

Pleasonton served under two different army commanders during the Gettysburg campaign, under markedly different circumstances. Hooker gave Pleasonton considerable latitude in his operations and viewed him as one of his corps commanders rather than as a staff officer. While the Army of the Potomac waited for Lee to reveal his intentions, Hooker sent the cavalry to patrol likely invasion routes across the Rappahannock. Pleasonton, feeling that his troopers needed rest and refitting, but also wanting to stay close to Stuart's horsemen near Brandy Station, took it upon himself to obey only part of his orders.

6. Quoted in Longacre, *Cavalry,* 48–9.

7. Ibid., 161–2.

8. Quoted in ibid., 48–9.

Extending his line barely some ten miles above Beverly Ford, he sent messages to Hooker that gave the impression his scouts were covering an area three times larger than they were. On June 12 Pleasonton unabashedly lied to Hooker, telling him that he had placed pickets as far west as Chester Gap in the Blue Ridge Mountains. Had that been true, Pleasonton would have been able to report the movement of Confederate troops through the gap that very day. Examples abound of Pleasonton's disservice to Hooker and the army. In short, his information could not be trusted, and for all practical purposes he was of no use in his position. Unfortunately for the army, most of Pleasonton's failures were unknown beyond his own command.

When Meade gained command of the Army of the Potomac, Pleasonton's situation changed dramatically. Meade saw the position of cavalry commander as a staff position rather than a field command. Historian Edward Longacre has argued that Meade was considering Pleasonton as an eventual replacement for Dan Butterfield as chief of staff, a position that Pleasonton would in fact share temporarily with Warren after the battle. But if Meade somehow remained unaware of Pleasonton's shortcomings, he had already indicated a preference for either Humphreys (division commander in the Third Corps) or Seth Williams (assistant adjutant general) as his chief of staff. In any case, Pleasonton found himself tied to headquarters, where glory was hard to come by.[9]

Pleasonton's position at headquarters gave him more access to information about the army's movements, disposition, and plans than he had had as a corps commander. This should have enabled him to coordinate more effectively the movements of his cavalry with the army, but it did not. He made more than his share of mistakes. At Gettysburg he failed to replace Buford's cavalry division in a timely fashion when it was relieved on the army's left flank. Without cavalry to perform the vital role of reconnaissance, Sickles's almost paranoid conviction that he was being flanked early in the day was compounded. During Lee's retreat Pleasonton spread his three divisions over such a wide area that they were unable to bring their full weight to bear on the retreating Confederates before they recrossed the Potomac. Such inept handling of the cavalry prompted one cavalry officer to say, "We have done our work decently, but Pleasonton is, next to Hooker, the greatest humbug of the war."[10]

9. Ibid., 168; *MG,* 130.

10. J. Cutler Andrews, *The North Reports the Civil War* (Pittsburgh: University of Pittsburgh Press, 1955), 435. The man quoted in a letter dated July 12, 1863, was Charles Francis Adams, brother of John Quincy Adams, ambassador to England.

Pleasonton's motives for testifying against Meade were not as straightforward as those of Sickles and Doubleday. Far from having injured Pleasonton, Meade had actually protected him from being removed from command, and he was shocked to learn of Pleasonton's testimony. Writing to his wife on March 9, 1864, Meade described Pleasonton's betrayal as the "meanest and blackest ingratitude; for I can prove, but for my intercession he would have been relieved long since." Such a statement reveals Meade's complete lack of understanding of Pleasonton's character.[11]

Pleasonton was probably sincere in his belief that Meade had let decisive victory slip from his grasp after Gettysburg, yet his attack on Meade before the committee went well beyond that criticism. His unbridled ambition seems to have reared its head again. As a new major general in command of a corps, Pleasonton impatiently schemed to ascend the military ladder and gain army command. His swaggering ego, bolstered by an article in the *New York Herald* speculating that he would be offered command of the Army of the Potomac, blinded him to the fact that he had no chance for such a command. Nonetheless, Pleasonton's aspirations led him to the same conclusion that the committee had already reached: Meade had to go.[12]

Pleasonton was also a close friend of both Hooker and Sickles. These friendships do not appear to have affected his professional relationship with Meade, but they may have played a role in his attacks on Meade before the committee.[13]

[359] Testimony of Major General Alfred Pleasonton.

Washington, March 7, 1864.
Major General Alfred Pleasonton sworn and examined.

By the chairman:
Question. General Meade assumed command of the army of the Potomac upon General Hooker being relieved?

11. Meade did not reveal his proof, but it appears that Stanton was the main mover in getting rid of Pleasonton. On March 24, 1864, less than three weeks after taking command, Grant wrote to Stanton asking that the order sending Pleasonton to the Department of the Missouri be made at once. This indicates that Grant had discussed the matter with Stanton previously. *OR*, vol. 33, pt. 1, p. 727; *LLM*, March 9, 1864, 2:176.

12. *MG*, 215.

13. Walter H. Hebert, *Fighting Joe Hooker* (Indianapolis, Ind.: Bobbs-Merrill, 1944), 229; Swanberg, *Sickles*, 194.

Answer. Yes, sir.

Question. Go on with your narrative from that point.

Answer. When General Meade assumed the command, he adopted the decision of General Hooker to place General Stahl's [*sic*] division of cavalry in the cavalry corps under my command, and I assigned General Kilpatrick to the command of it; and I also recommended Captains Farnsworth and Custer as brigadier generals and they were appointed, and that division fought Stuart's cavalry and defeated it on the 1st day of July, two days after, at Hanover Junction, Pennsylvania. I may say here that I had studied that whole country the year before very carefully indeed, all its roads and topographical features, and was probably about as well posted in regard to it as any officer in the army.

Pleasonton began his testimony with a distortion of the truth, as well as a remarkable instance of second sight. He may have studied maps of the country around Gettysburg, though they were in short supply and hardly thorough, but there is no indication that he had ever actually been in the area, either before or after Antietam. In 1876 he wrote Hooker, "I was thoroughly acquainted with all of that country & had occupied it the year before, the year of Antietam," but Hooker vehemently denied Pleasonton's claim.[14]

And in the distribution of the cavalry force I sent the strongest division on the left flank of our army, that is, nearest the enemy, to cover and occupy Gettysburg till our army could move in that direction. That division was General Buford's division. It moved on the 29th of June from near Middleburg, and arrived in front of Gettysburg that evening or early the next morning. The 1st division was on the left; Kilpatrick's took the front, and Gregg's division took the right. When Stuart made his raid between our army and Washington, General Meade was very anxious for me to send some cavalry after him. But I have always opposed movements of that sort, because it is very difficult, if not impossible, for one mounted command to catch another with a day's or even a half a day's start. And I urged that if Stuart encumbered himself with plunder, we would head him off as he proceeded up into Pennsylvania, and he would become a much easier victim than he would of prepared to fight without plunder. My views were confirmed by the result of Kilpatrick's fight with Stuart at Hanover, for Stuart's cavalry gave us very little annoyance after that event. I then turned my attention to the infantry and securing the flanks of the army. I was satisfied from my general knowledge of the country—and so men-

14. *GC*, 128, 633 n. 96.

tioned to General Meade several times—that there was but one position in which for us to have a fight, and that was at Gettysburg; and I had given orders to General Buford to hold that point to the last extremity until we could get there.

Pleasonton's claim to have ordered Buford to Gettysburg with orders to "hold that point to the last extremity" is without foundation. He had indeed sent Buford to Gettysburg, but not for the reasons he gave the committee. In his orders for the army to march towards Pennsylvania, Meade had instructed the cavalry to guard the flanks and rear of the army. It was in compliance with Meade's instructions that Pleasonton had sent Kilpatrick's division to the right and Buford's to the left, which included Gettysburg. Pleasonton's Special Order Number 99, dated June 29, indicates no urgency or even the possibility of contact with the enemy. Moreover, Pleasonton directed only two of the First Division's brigades to Gettysburg, holding one at Mechanicstown. Such action hardly demonstrates the importance of the position as he claimed to have perceived it. But as far as the committee was concerned, Pleasonton's testimony helped to prove that Meade did not choose the battlefield and that he relied upon his corps commanders to direct the army.[15]

The enemy attacked General Buford at Gettysburg on the 1st of July; and the first mistake they committed was in permitting him to keep them in check until the 1st and 11th corps, under General Reynolds, came up and held that position. On the 2d of July, Buford's division, having been so severely handled the day before, was sent by me back to Westminster, our depot, to protect it, and also to recruit. General Gregg's division was placed on our right to prevent the enemy from turning our flank; Merritt's brigade of the 1st division being at Emmitsburg, and Farnsworth's brigade of Kilpatrick's division having been sent to the left.

Pleasonton's obvious intent here was to cover a tactical blunder on his part. Buford's division had begun its withdrawal as early as 9:00 A.M. on July 2. Merritt's brigade was still in Maryland at the time, while Farnsworth's brigade, as a part of Kilpatrick's division, was miles away to the northeast. It was not until 1:45 P.M. that Pleasonton issued orders to Gregg, on the army's right, to cover the left. The other units did not arrive until late in the day. In fact, Kilpatrick's division (including Farnsworth's brigade) had moved to the area of

15. *OR*, vol. 27, pt. 3, pp. 400–1.

Two Taverns and was not in a position to assist Sickles's corps on the right even if it had arrived in time.[16]

On the 3d of July Merritt's brigade was ordered up from Emmitsburg to take the enemy in rear at Gettysburg, and join with Farnsworth's brigade in preventing them turning our flank on the left. Both of those divisions had very heavy fighting, and I have always been of the opinion that the demonstration of cavalry on our left materially checked the attack of the enemy on the 3d of July; for General Hood, the rebel general, was attempting to [360] turn our flank when he met there two brigades of cavalry, and the officers reported to me that at least two divisions of the rebel infantry and a number of batteries were held back, expecting an attack from us on that flank.

This testimony is typical of Pleasonton: it served to inflate his importance but was somewhat short on truth. Hood had been wounded on July 2 and was not in command of his division or anything else on July 3. Hood's division (under the command of Brigadier General Evander M. Law) and Lafayette McLaws's division had been kept back partly because of the heavy losses they had suffered in attacking the Third Corps on July 2, but also to guard against the possibility of an attack by Federal cavalry on that flank. In what Edwin Coddington described as a "poorly conceived and badly conducted assault," Pleasonton had ordered Kilpatrick's division and Merritt's brigade to attack the enemy's right and rear that morning, well before any Confederate attack was made. It was in that botched attack that young Brigadier General Elon Farnsworth was killed.[17]

The rebel army was finally repulsed on the 3d of July. Immediately after that repulse, I rode out with General Meade on the field, and up to the top of the mountain, and I urged him to order a general advance of his whole army in pursuit of the enemy, for I was satisfied that the rebel army was not only demoralized, but that they must be nearly, if not quite, out of ammunition; and that our army, being in fine spirits with this last repulse, could have easily defeated and routed the enemy.

This was the type of testimony the committee wanted to hear. In the late 1870s Pleasonton elaborated on this story, saying that he had told Meade, "General, I

16. *GC*, 351–2; *OR*, vol. 27, pt. 3, pp. 489–90.
17. *GC*, 523–5.

will give you half an hour to show yourself a great general. Order the army to advance, while I will take the cavalry, get in Lee's rear, and we will finish the campaign in a week." However, there is no confirmation of Pleasonton's claim to have urged an attack.[18]

But General Meade ordered me to send my cavalry to the rear of the rebels, to find out whether they were really falling back. This took some time. The cavalry rode all night. The first officer who reported was General Gregg. He reported, 22 miles on the Chambersburg road by the next morning at 8 o'clock, that the road was strewn with wounded and stragglers, ambulances and caissons, and that there was great demoralization and confusion.

By Mr. Chandler:

Question. Was this reported to General Meade?

Answer. It was reported to General Meade immediately. And, in fact, General Gregg had captured a large number of prisoners; I cannot mention the number now, but it showed that the rebel army had suffered terribly. He captured their wounded, left in the hospitals, and other prisoners, showing that they were greatly demoralized.

By the chairman:

Question. Were many stragglers found?

Answer. Yes, sir, a great many. Kilpatrick's command was ordered to the left to get in rear of them and destroy their trains as they were passing over the mountains, while Buford was ordered by the way of Frederick city to go to Williamsport and destroy what trains he could there. Both of these commands traveled day and night and succeeded in inflicting a great deal of damage upon the enemy.

A cursory reading of this series of questions and answers would indicate that the events Pleasonton described took place on July 4, which would support the contention that Meade had failed to seize his opportunity to crush a beaten enemy. While Pleasonton may have wanted to leave such an impression, his implications were not correct. It was not until July 4 that most of the cavalry began to scatter about the countryside in pursuit of Lee's supply columns. It was not until July 5 that one lone brigade, under General David Gregg, began the actual pur-

18. Alfred Pleasonton, "The Campaign of Gettysburg," in *Annals of the War,* ed. McClure, 455.

suit of Lee's army. The reports that Pleasonton cited in his testimony probably did not arrive before July 6.

Question. You advised an immediate advance of the whole army?

Answer. Yes, sir.

Question. What reasons did General Meade give against ordering it?

Answer. General Meade said he was not sure they might not make another attack on him. And to satisfy himself, he wanted to know first that they were in retreat; and for that reason was to send the cavalry out to ascertain.

Question. You ascertained that they were in retreat?

Answer. Yes, sir; the other commands, besides General Gregg's, found out that the whole rebel army was retreating to Williamsport or Falling Waters, and they inflicted upon the enemy a great deal of damage in proportion to their power.

Question. With what expedition did our army advance after you had ascertained the enemy were retreating?

Answer. We were one or two days at Gettysburg after we received the information from General Gregg that the enemy were in retreat. The bulk of the army marched by the way of Frederick city to Middleburg, to a position on the Antietam river, the right resting about Hagerstown.

Though generally correct, Pleasonton's assessment was hardly a fair one. Again Pleasonton left the impression that he had notified Meade as early as July 4 that the rebels were in retreat, and that despite the reports Meade had delayed for one or two days before advancing. The army did begin to move on July 5, but not as a result of Pleasonton's reports. Meade decided to move based on reports from various signal stations, along with reports from Howard, Birney, and others. Messages from the Cavalry Corps are conspicuously absent from the Official Records.[19]

By Mr. Chandler:

Question. Were you in that council of war that was held in relation to attacking the enemy at Williamsport?

Answer. Yes, sir, I was in the council.

Here Chandler set a pattern that would recur in future sessions, in which he opened up a new line of inquiry, only to turn the follow-up questions over to

19. *OR*, vol. 27, pt. 3, pp. 532–7.

Wade. Chandler was the only nonlawyer on the committee and perhaps felt that Wade did a better job of questioning the witnesses.

[361] By the chairman:

Question. I want to know of you, as a military man of a great deal of experience, what your opinion was that our army ought to have done under the circumstances?

Answer. It was my opinion that our army should have attacked the rebel army then at Falling Waters. Every position that our army occupied on the Antietam had been won by the cavalry. It satisfied me that the enemy were not very strong. On the day of the council, the brigade that was in front of General Slocum's command, under Colonel Henry,[20] of the Pennsylvania cavalry, near St. James's college, or St. James's church, I think they call it, drove in the enemy, and reported to me that he could have carried that position, but that General Slocum had ordered him to halt for fear of bringing on a general engagement. The enemy afterwards brought a strong force there to hold that point. A second reason for this opinion for attacking the enemy was, that I was satisfied their army was short of ammunition; that they had not a sufficient supply to last for more than a three or four hours fight; while our army was well supplied. The third reason was that they had a river at their back, which was swimming, and also one on their flank; and from the disappointment of their hopes in the battle of Gettysburg, and the discomforts that they had met with during the march to Falling Waters, and the buoyant feeling in our army, I believed that we should have captured—if not captured, at least dispersed—three-fourths of that army, at least taken all their artillery, and the sequel, proving that the enemy were also of that opinion, was the fact that they themselves moved off.

Question. What reasons were given by those who voted for not attacking the enemy? What was their idea about it?

Answer. There were various reasons given. The council was late at night. It was wet weather, and it struck me, when the question was asked of them, that most of the party did not attach that importance to the matter that I did. I knew several of those generals, who, from all I had seen of them in action, would much sooner fight a battle than run after the enemy. That was what we all wanted, to fight. There was one general, General French, I think, who re-

20. I am unable to find Col. Henry with the Pennsylvania Cavalry in the Army of the Potomac. There is a Col. Pennock Huey of the Eighth Pennsylvania Cavalry, Second Brigade, Second Division of the Cavalry Corps.

marked, after General Meade declared that he would not order an attack against the vote of the council, "Why, it does not make any difference what our opinions are; if you give the order to attack, we will fight just as well under it as if our opinions were not against it." I mention that to show that the generals did not attach that importance to the matter that I did.

Either because of the questions asked by Wade or because he did not want to give any credit to Meade, Pleasonton did not mention that Meade initially favored an attack. Pleasonton's reasons in favor of an attack were widely held by other senior officers. But his conclusions about the possible results of such an attack were "thunderous humbug," to use a term in vogue at the time.

[The questions concerning the Bristoe and Mine Run campaigns have been omitted.]

Question. Since the battle of Gettysburg the army has done little else but retreat?

Answer. No, sir; it has not fought as an army since then.

Question. I want to know of you whether the commanding general retains the confidence of his officers and men after all these retreats?

Answer. Well, sir, as far as my own corps is concerned, I do not think General Meade has their confidence. There has been a great deal of dissatisfaction for some time past among the cavalry in consequence of the manner in which they have been used. I have mentioned that to General Meade more than once. They find that they are throwing a great deal of hard work away to no purpose; that they have lost a great many men and yet no beneficial results are obtained.

A little surprisingly, Pleasonton did not try to speak for the entire army. His comment about Meade's use of the cavalry implied that Meade should not command the army if he could not use all its units effectively; yet the same criticism applied to all previous commanders of the Army of the Potomac. The cavalry was an underappreciated arm of the army, confined to limited roles by its commander, the army commander, or both. Meade's attitude that the cavalry was "fit for little more than guard and picket duty" did not change until the arrival of Sheridan from the West.[21]

21. Gordon C. Rhea, *The Battle of the Wilderness, May 5–6, 1864* (Baton Rouge: Louisiana State University Press, 1994), 40.

Question. As a military man, do you think it possible for us ever to conquer the rebellion by defensive operation alone?

Answer. No, sir; it must be done by offensive operations.

Question. What effect is produced upon the men by this constant shrinking from an engagement with the enemy, when we have reason to suppose that our force is equal to or superior to theirs?

Answer. It discourages them very much. I think our army was very much discouraged in coming away from Mine run without a fight. At least that is my impression. I may be mistaken. I am only giving you my impression about it.

Question. In your judgement, is there cordial co-operation of these commanders of army corps in these enterprises? Do the leading generals co-operate and act with one mind to effect the general result? It is a pretty searching question, I know, but we want to get inside of these matters if we can.

Answer. I do not know any profession in which the character of the leaders tells more upon those under them than the military profession. I have been a long time a soldier, and I do not know any people who have to be more of actors than military men who understand their profession. I know that the men do look to their officers, their leaders. I have frequently seen men, when under great excitement and trepidation, calmed down by a quiet, jocular, or encouraging remark from their commander, turning the whole tenor of their minds, so that the thing they looked upon before as dangerous they would go right into without hesitation. I have seen men when they have been hesitating or excited, and some gallant, dashing man would come up, and you would see the men brighten up at once. You could see an immediate change to a different state of feeling. In fact, I do not know any profession in which the character of one man stamps itself more indelibly upon masses of men than in the military profession.

Question. And the spirit of the commanding general usually diffuses itself through the whole army?

Answer. Yes, sir.

Question. You have said that in your corps you think that after all these occurrences, General Meade does not retain the entire confidence of the officers and men?

Answer. That is my impression.

[366] Question. I do not know that I have any further questions to ask you. If there is anything further you wish to say you may go on and say it.

Answer. I do not now think of anything. I may not have made my statements here as connectedly as I might have done if I had thought the matter over; but I have given you just as the matters impressed me at the time.

With Pleasonton's testimony, the committee continued to build its case against Meade. Indirectly supporting the charge that Meade had not wanted to fight at Gettysburg, Pleasonton claimed that he himself had picked the battlefield before the army had made contact with Lee's forces. Once the battle was joined, Meade had failed to follow up his advantage after the repulse of Pickett's charge, despite Pleasonton's urging. At Williamsport, Meade did not attack even though the enemy was weak, short on ammunition, demoralized, and had a flooding river at its back. According to Pleasonton, Meade's constant failure to attack had taken the fight out of the army.

By claiming that Meade could not use cavalry effectively, Pleasonton also bolstered the contention that Meade was an unfit commander.

8 Major General David Bell Birney

On the same day that Pleasonton testified, the committee heard from Major General David Bell Birney. Born in Huntsville, Alabama, Birney was the son of the internationally known abolitionist James G. Birney, a Kentuckian who had once owned slaves. The elder Birney ran for president twice on the Liberty Party ticket, and was executive secretary of the American Anti-Slavery Society. Not surprisingly, the family left Alabama for Cincinnati when David was thirteen.

Birney, like many of his better-educated contemporaries, studied law after trying his hand at business. A short stay in Michigan convinced Birney that frontier life was not for him, and in 1848 he moved to Philadelphia, where he practiced law until the outbreak of the war. In Philadelphia Birney belonged to the City Troop militia, where he acquired a knowledge of military matters which was more extensive than that of most civilians. With the outbreak of the Civil War he served as lieutenant colonel of the Twenty-third Pennsylvania, one of the many three-month service regiments organized at the time. When the Twenty-third was reorganized into a three-year regiment, Birney became its colonel.

Within six months Birney was a brigadier general of volunteers, commanding a brigade in Brigadier General Philip Kearny's division during the Peninsula campaign. On the Peninsula Birney was tried and acquitted for disobedience of orders and cowardice. Upon his return to the army, he was given Kearny's division after that general's death at Chantilly in 1862. Birney led the division at Fredericksburg, after which he once again faced charges—this time for dereliction of duty—and was again acquitted. As senior division commander of the Third Corps at Gettysburg, Birney assumed temporary command of the corps following Sickles's injury on July 2. On July 9, Birney returned to his division.[1]

Theodore Lyman, a member of Meade's staff, described Birney as "one who had many enemies, but, in my belief, we had few officers who could command 10,000 men as well as he. He was a pale, Puritanical figure, with a demeanor of unmovable coldness; only he would smile politely when you spoke to him. . . . He was a man, too, who looked out for his own interest sharply and knew the mainspring of military advancement. His unpopularity among some persons arose partly from his own promotion, which, however, he deserved; and partly from his cold covert manner." Similarly, in 1876 General Gouverneur K. Warren recalled that Birney "had no hesitation at times to tell lies."[2]

Yet Birney was also a capable man and one of great pride, which played an important role in his conflict with Meade. When Meade took over the army, Sickles was away on leave and Birney was temporarily in command of the Third Corps. He made the most of it. As Colonel Charles Wainwright wryly described the Third Corps' march with Birney at its head, "First was a line of orderlies with drawn sabers to clear the way; then a band of music, and in due time Major General Birney with all his staff riding in order behind him. He certainly means to have all the 'pomp and circumstances of war' he can get."[3]

The animosity between Birney and Meade predated the battle of Gettysburg. At Fredericksburg, Meade had accused Birney of not supporting him. Although Meade had quickly forgotten the incident, Birney continued to harbor ill feelings for what he believed to be the unfounded charges leveled at him. When Meade assumed command of the Army of the Potomac, an officer in Sickles's Third Corps wrote that "Meade was not liked in the Third Corps

1. This short sketch of Birney's life is based upon Pfanz, *Gettysburg: The Second Day,* 83; *DAB,* 2:290; Warner, *Generals in Blue,* 34; *MG,* 177. Warner omits the charge of cowardice, which Sam Wilkeson, saying that it was well merited, reported in a story in the *New York Tribune* on June 5, 1862. The statement involved Wilkeson in a bitter controversy with Birney for years. J. Cutler Andrews, *The North Reports the Civil War* (Pittsburgh: University of Pittsburgh Press, 1955), 207, 688; *OR,* vol. 27, pt. 1, p. 489.

2. Quoted in Pfanz, *Gettysburg: The Second Day,* 84–5; quoted in Sauers, *A Caspian Sea of Ink,* 142.

3. Charles S. Wainwright, *A Diary of Battle: The Personal Journals of Colonel Charles S. Wainwright, 1861–1865,* ed. Allan Nevins (Gettysburg, Pa.: Stan Clark Military Books, 1962), 228.

and especially not by Maj. Gen. David B. Birney." After the Gettysburg campaign Birney would have other reasons for disliking Meade.[4]

At Gettysburg, shortly after Sickles was wounded, Meade sent General Winfield Scott Hancock to the left with reinforcements. Hancock was to direct the overall actions of both his Second Corps and the Third Corps, much like the three-corps wing Reynolds had commanded earlier. Under this arrangement Birney still retained command of the Third Corps. Yet even though Birney's new command had been shattered and driven from much of the field, he did not appreciate the arrangement. That evening, following the officer's consultation, Birney complained to Meade about it. Meade answered curtly, "Gen. Hancock is your superior and I claim the right to issue the order." What should have been a tempest in a teapot became much more serious on July 9, when Meade placed Major General William H. French in command of the Third Corps and sent Birney back to his division. French, a friend of Major General Halleck, also ranked Birney. Nonetheless, this was twice in seven days that Birney felt his command had been usurped at the direct instructions of Meade.[5]

Birney's testimony against Meade would later backfire somewhat. Birney initially believed that Sickles had the winning side in the hearings; in his own appearance before the committee, he supported Sickles's testimony. Within six weeks, however, Birney began to have second thoughts. Given his ambition and character, it is also possible that he wanted to play both ends against the middle. On April 11, 1864, Meade wrote his wife, "There is no doubt General Birney is scared at the turn things have taken . . . for I received a note from Hancock . . . saying Birney had been to see him, disclaiming being a partisan of Sickles, and saying he would like to come and see me to explain matters." On April 18 Meade wrote, "I had an interview with General Birney to-day, who disclaimed ever having entertained unfriendly feelings toward me, or being a partisan of Sickles, and expressed the hope he would be permitted to serve under me." Birney remained with the Army of the Potomac, but he knew he walked a fine line and there would be no second chances.[6]

4. Pfanz, *Gettysburg: The Second Day,* 3; *OR,* vol. 27, pt. 1, pp. 128, 363.

5. Pfanz, *Gettysburg: The Second Day,* 376; Jordan, *Winfield Scott Hancock,* 92–3; John Gibbon, *Personal Recollections of the Civil War* (1928; reprint, Dayton, Ohio: Press of Morningside Bookshop, 1988), 144; *OR,* vol. 27, pt. 1, p. 489; *MG,* 177.

6. *LLM,* April 11, 1864, 2:189; April 18, 1864, 2:190.

[366] Testimony of Major General David B. Birney.

Washington, March 7, 1864.
Major General David B. Birney sworn and examined.

By the chairman:

Question. How many days before the battle of Gettysburg did General Meade assume command of the army of the Potomac?

Answer. He took command at Frederick city, Maryland, on the 28th of June, 1863, and on the 1st of July the fight at Gettysburg was commenced by General Reynolds.

Question. Was it not most extraordinary to change commanders where two great armies were approaching each other so near a battle?

Answer. I think it was very extraordinary.

This was a sentiment expressed by almost everyone and probably felt by Meade himself.

Question. Will you give us your observations in regard to the battle, how it came on, how it was fought, &c., so far as you may think it material?

Answer. I reached Emmitsburg, with my division of the 3d corps, on the 30th of June. I had been relieved at Frederick city of the command of the corps by General Sickles, who had returned to the army and assumed command of the corps, and I resumed the command of my division. As I said, I reached Emmitsburg on the 30th of June. On the 1st of July I was ordered beyond Emmitsburg to take position and cover the road that came from a gap in the mountains. About 2 o'clock in the afternoon a staff officer from General Sickles rode up to me with an order to proceed immediately to Gettysburg and report to General Howard, who had succeeded to the command there when General Reynolds was killed; to move with all dispatch with my division. It was about ten miles from Emmitsburg to Gettysburg. We reached there about 5 o'clock in the afternoon, and formed upon the left of the 1st corps, on Cemetery ridge, as it is called there. We bivouacked in that position for the night.

There are some problems with Birney's testimony. In his battle report he wrote that the roads were made "almost impassable by mud and the passage over it of the First and Eleventh Corps through the rain." Yet in an era when two miles an hour over good dry roads was considered fast, Birney claimed to have traveled about three miles an hour. Secondly, Birney could not have received an order to advance from Sickles at 2:00 P.M. because Sickles did not issue such an order before 3:15 P.M. Finally, Birney arrived at Gettysburg not around 5:00 P.M. but near dark, at approximately 7:30, according to most of his brigade and regimental commanders.[7]

Upon the 2d of July I was ordered to relieve Geary's division of the 12th corps, that during the night had bivouacked on my left. I took position with my left at and on Round Top about 9 o'clock in the morning, and threw out skirmishers along the Emmitsburg road to cover the left.

While this testimony supported what Sickles had said earlier before the committee, it is at odds with Birney's battle report. There Birney had written, "At 7 A.M., under orders from Major-General Sickles, I relieved Geary's division, and formed a line, resting its left on the Sugar Loaf Mountain." Speaking before the committee, however, Birney asserted that his line was "on Round Top," which was not the case. He also omitted any mention of receiving orders from Sickles, which would have undermined Sickles's claim that he had received no orders about where he was to go.

About 11 o'clock, the firing with my skirmishers being very sharp, and seeming to increase, I asked permission of Major General Sickles to send a regiment and a battalion of sharpshooters to make a reconnaissance and see what the enemy were doing.

Birney claimed to have discovered Confederate preparations for an attack on the left. This is the same reconnaissance that, in his testimony, Hunt claimed to have suggested. Birney's intimation that the reconnaissance was his idea is not supported by the evidence or by any other testimony.[8]

I received from General Sickles permission to do so. The reconnaissance showed that the enemy were moving in three columns, under cover of the woods, to our left.

7. *OR*, vol. 27, pt. 1, pp. 482–8.
8. *CCW*, 449; Pfanz, *Gettysburg: The Second Day*, 995–7.

The reconnaissance, led by Colonel Hiram Berdan, found units of Anderson's division, A. P. Hill's Third Corps. Longstreet's corps, which later made the attack against the Third Corps, was not in sight from Berdan's position in the woods.

I reported this immediately to General Sickles, and he ordered me at once to prepare to meet the attack. About half past two o'clock in the afternoon the columns of the enemy could be plainly seen from the left of my position, and at three o'clock I ordered Clark's[9] rifled battery to open upon them, as they were within fair range. At that time General Meade rode down to the line, accompanied by General Sickles, and asked what the firing was for. General Sickles and myself explained to him the position and movements of the enemy; that they were moving in order to turn our left, and we had opened upon them.

In their testimony, neither Sickles nor Meade mentioned Birney's presence at their meeting near the Peach Orchard. Modern scholars also make no mention of his presence. Once again, Birney seems to have been simply enlarging his role in the battle. Such embellishments were not unusual.[10]

[367] At that time General Sickles told me that General Sykes would, at my request, send me a division to support me upon my left; and that I could also call upon General Hancock, of the 2d corps, for another division upon my right, if it was necessary; that they had been ordered by General Meade to support us with those two divisions. I sent a staff officer to General Sykes asking him to send up at once the division that had been ordered from his corps to support me; that an attack by the enemy was imminent, and that I thought it would be made at once. The staff officer saw him, and he returned for answer that he would come up in time; that his men were making coffee and were tired, but that he would come up in time. He came up with one of his divisions in about an hour from that time, and formed upon my left upon Round Top, and placed Barnes's division massed behind my centre. I held with my division from Round Top to the Emmitsburg road.

This account differs markedly from Birney's battle report of seven months earlier, which stated that Sykes had "reached my left opportunely, and pro-

9. Captain A. Judson Clark, 1st New Jersey Artillery, 2nd Battery.
10. *MG*, 148; Pfanz, *Gettysburg: The Second Day*, 42–3.

tected that flank." Despite evidence that Sykes had moved quickly once he had received Meade's orders, Birney's accusation would follow him in postwar reviews.[11]

I present here a map of the battle-field of Gettysburg, which gives, with accuracy, the position of the 3d corps during the battle on Thursday. I wish it received as a part of my testimony, to explain it.[12]

The attack was commenced by the enemy about half past 3 o'clock, their force being formed in three lines. It was resisted by us, but my line was so long and thin that I was forced to send to General Sickles, asking for more support, as I had no troops in reserve. My line was almost a single one, and as the enemy, in the fight, attacked any particular point, I had to take regiments from other points to meet their attack. General Sickles sent me a brigade from the 2d corps, with one of his staff officers, which was placed by me in position in the centre of the line held by me.

About 5 1/2 o'clock P.M. I received word from one of his staff that General Sickles had been wounded, and that he would like to see me. I rode to him and saw him, and at his request took command of the corps. The fight with our corps lasted until about 7 o'clock, we receiving support from brigades of the 2d corps and from brigades of the 5th corps. At about 7 o'clock I withdrew my corps from the front line, and massed it some half a mile to the rear of the line which I had held during the day.

Birney's division and the rest of the Third Corps had been smashed by Longstreet's attacks at the Peach Orchard and the Wheatfield. The word "withdrawal" is hardly accurate. But for the timely arrival of reinforcements and the judicious shifting of troops by Meade, the Union line would have been breached.

Birney's brevity in describing such important events may have been due to the fact that he stayed with the Third Corps troops as they retreated. He also erroneously implied that the Third Corps was supported by other units rather than relieved. Another influence on his testimony may have been his mood following the fight on July 2. Colonel de Trobriand met Birney around dusk as his division reformed east of the Taneytown Road. Birney was dejected and felt that the Confederates had won the day. According to de Trobriand, Birney remarked to him that his horse had been killed and he wished that he had been too.

11. *OR*, vol. 27, pt. 1, pp. 483, 592; *GC*, 400, 747–8.
12. The map is not included in the committee papers.

Though this seems to have been only a momentary bout of depression, Birney must have felt that his brief tenure as a corps commander had been a failure.[13]

After this the enemy made no attack during the night. On the 3d of July we supported the 1st and 2d corps, but were not seriously engaged, and met with very small loss.

Question. Was there any council of war held the night after General Sickles was wounded? If so, state what you know about it.

Answer. There was a council of the corps commanders held at General Meade's headquarters that night, of which I was one present. It was there determined to remain and fight the next day; to make no attack the next day, but to receive one should the enemy make it.

General Meade said that his orders were to cover Baltimore and Washington, and he seemed indisposed to hazard a battle except on the most favorable terms. On Saturday night there was another council held, as to whether we should remain there or retire. The enemy had manifested no disposition to attack, but had drawn back his left flank, maintaining his position in front of our left.

This is the first testimony to support Meade's claim that the enemy was not in retreat during the day of July 4.

Question. That was after the enemy had been finally repulsed on the third day of the fight?

Answer. Yes, sir.

Question. What could have been the object of that council at that time?

Answer. It was suggested that the enemy were making a flank movement, and would probably try to interpose between us and Washington. At this council, on Saturday night, it was decided to remain twenty-four hours longer in our position, and that General Sedgwick, who had come up with fresh troops, whose troops had not been in the fight, should be sent with his corps to find out as to the enemy's right, and as to their position upon our extreme left, to see whether they were still in position there.

In the council on July 4, Birney voted to remain in their lines rather than to assume the offensive and pursue Lee if he was falling back on his direct line of retreat. His vagueness about the council is therefore understandable.

13. *OR*, vol. 27, pt. 1, p. 371; Pfanz, *Gettysburg: The Second Day*, 429.

I was also ordered to send out a reconnaissance at daylight to ascertain the position of the enemy. I did so [368] early Sunday morning, and reported that the enemy were in full retreat. I also sent back for permission to open upon the enemy with my rifled batteries as they were crossing a point very near me, upon the turnpike going towards Hagerstown, and the staff officer brought me permission to do so. I had commenced the movement to attack, when another staff officer arrived from General Meade with a written order from him to make no attack, which was done.

My skirmishers advanced and took possession of their hospitals, with a large number of their wounded. I had sent some twenty orderlies with a staff officer, who had led the reconnaissance, and I reported these facts constantly to General Meade; but this peremptory order from him not to open fire at all prevented any pursuit of the enemy.

Birney's story of wanting to fire on the retreating Confederates does not appear to have any basis in fact. None of the Second Division Artillery battle reports mention it. More telling are the brigade and regimental commanders' reports. Only one regiment, the Third Maine, Second Brigade, was on a picket line on July 5, and it was positioned along the Emmitsburg road. The Hagerstown Pike would not have been visible from that position. All the other regimental reports show Birney's division moving back to the woods behind Cemetery Ridge, which it had occupied on the morning of July 2. From this position it is over two miles to the Hagerstown Pike, and Birney would have had to have seen through both Cemetery and Seminary Ridges to have spotted the rebels. There is no copy of an order to Birney not to fire on the retreating rebels.[14]

The Third Corps, along with the First, was being held to support the Sixth Corps' reconnaissance and pursuit which began that day. Both corps began to move on July 5 but were halted due to Butterfield's error in sending the wrong orders.[15]

Question. This was after the final repulse of the enemy?

Answer. Yes, sir. The council was held on Saturday night for retiring to another position.

Question. I would like to know who could have been of the opinion that a beaten and repulsed army could have endangered Washington by any movement they could have made?

14. *OR*, vol. 27, pt. 1, pp. 497, 503, 506, 509, 512, 514, 527.
15. *MG*, 175.

Answer. There were several, I think, voted on Saturday night for retiring to another position.

Question. Who were they?

Answer. I forget now exactly who they were. It was a matter of some doubt in the council on Saturday night whether we should remain or retire; but it was finally decided to remain there twenty-four hours longer before we made any retrograde movement. It was decided not to make an aggressive movement, but simply to wait developments.

Question. Do you remember how the vote stood in that council?

Answer. My impression is that it was three to five.

Question. Do you remember the names of those who voted to retire?

Answer. I cannot give the exact vote. I know that in both councils General Howard, General Sedgwick, General Pleasonton and myself were for fighting. The first council was also divided.

Birney was trying to mask his position in the July 4 council, in which Meade had asked the corps commanders whether the army should remain at Gettysburg. Before the committee, Birney implied that three officers—Newton, Pleasonton, and Slocum—wanted to retire to another position, when in fact they favored aggressive action in assuming the offensive. Birney was among the five who voted to remain at Gettysburg until Lee's movements could be ascertained. He also voted not to assume the offensive or to follow Lee if he fell back on his direct line of retreat. Birney would have been well aware that members of the committee would not view his votes favorably. It is also notable that Pleasonton was not at the council on July 2, contrary to Birney's testimony.[16]

Question. On Thursday night?

Answer. Yes, sir.

Question. Whether you should retire?

Answer. Yes, sir, I think so. I know that several of the corps commanders objected to the position; said that our left was weak.

Question. Do you recollect how General Meade stood on that question?

Answer. General Meade stated that his orders were positively to cover Washington and Baltimore, and that he did not wish to hazard a battle without he was certain of victory; that was his statement to the council. He said that he intended to be guided by the opinions of his corps commanders.

16. Details of the council vote can be found in Butterfield's testimony, *CCW*, 426–7.

Question. The council might have understood him to be rather of the opinion that it was safest to retire, might they not?

Answer. I could only state my own impression. I have given his language as I remember it.

Birney's testimony is incorrect and misleading. There was no division in the council, but rather a surprising accord in wanting to stay and await Lee's attack.

The statement Birney attributed to Meade again branded him as timid and wanting to avoid a fight at Gettysburg. No other evidence exists to suggest that Meade ever made such a statement.[17]

Question. What was the condition of our army after the fight was over?

Answer. I have never seen the army so confident of success, in most admirable spirits, and so anxious for a fight.

Question. Were they not less jaded and fatigued by the battle than were the enemy?

Answer. Much less; the enemy had made longer marches and had attacked, and we had received it and repulsed them. Our men were somewhat jaded from their long march from Falmouth; but the army was never in a better condition physically than it was then, and very buoyant over their success.

Question. Suppose that the first council, where you think they divided [369] equally, had determined to retire, and you had done so, what, in your judgment as a military man, would have been the effect?

This is an interestingly phrased question. Birney had not testified that the council was equally divided on July 2. If Birney had told Wade the corps commanders were equally divided, it would have had to have been prior to his appearance before the committee.

Answer. It would have been very demoralizing to the army. They had marched with great spirit and animation to meet the enemy, and to have retreated at that time, while the enemy were in our own loyal State of Pennsylvania, in my opinion, would have been almost fatal to the command, if not to the country.

Question. How long did you remain at Gettysburg, after the enemy were finally repulsed, before you commenced the pursuit in force?

17. *B&L*, 3:313–4.

Answer. The enemy retreated Saturday night. We remained there Saturday, Sunday, and Monday. General French, with General Milroy's troops from Harpers Ferry, 10,000 men, was assigned to the corps, which had suffered heavily in the battle. He ranked me, and consequently assumed command of the corps on the 9th day of July, and I resumed command of my division.[18]

Question. Do you know why those 10,000 troops were not brought up earlier, so as to have participated in the battle?

Answer. I do not.

Question. Do you know why the troops at Baltimore, under General Schenck, were not brought into that battle?

Answer. I do not.

Question. Those troops joined the army after the battle was over?

Answer. Yes, sir; and there were a large number of militia from New York, and other troops that were in Frederick, which would have swollen the army; and I have understood that troops from General Foster's command, in North Carolina, were sent up.

Question. What number of troops do you understand came from there?

Answer. I understood that the accession of good troops to the army amounted to 20,000 or 25,000 men.

Question. I cannot forbear asking this question: Do you know any reason why those troops from all these different points could not have been brought up to participate in the battle from its commencement, as well as they could have been brought up after its close?

Answer. I do not know any reason.

Question. Was it not a great military blunder not to have concentrated them there?

Answer. I think so.

The idea of concentrating these troops at Gettysburg was delusionary. French's troops were to block the Susquehanna, Schenck's command had already been stripped bare, the New York troops at Frederick were either raw or had very little time left in their enlistments, and Foster's troops could not possibly have reached Gettysburg in time. Nonetheless, Birney agreed with Wade that Meade's failure to have concentrated his forces was a "great military blunder."

18. "On grounds of seniority, Meade gave the Third Corps to Halleck's friend General French and relegated Birney, who was hardly pleased, to the First Division, his former command." *MG*, 177.

Birney also inaccurately estimated that the army had been joined by some 20,000 to 25,000 "good troops." While significant numbers of troops did join the Army of the Potomac after Gettysburg, at the same time many units whose enlistment had expired left the army. Additionally, many of the troops that joined the army after Gettysburg had less than ten days remaining on their enlistment. The North Carolina troops of Foster's Eighteenth Corps, mentioned by Birney, were actually on their way home to be mustered out. By July 14, the Army of the Potomac had gained only between 7,500 and 8,500 reliable men—less than half of Meade's losses at Gettysburg.

Question. The enemy retreated, and you finally followed them?

Answer. Yes, sir. At Middleburg General French, with those 10,000 troops from Harpers Ferry, joined the army, and took command of the 3d corps. I left the army and did not rejoin it again until it reached Warrenton, when I resumed command of my division.

Question. Nevertheless, you understand the condition of affairs when the enemy reached Williamsport and Falling Waters?

Answer. From hearsay; yes, sir.

Question. Although you were superseded by General French, and did not participate in the movements of the army until they reached Warrenton, I will ask you, as a military man, what would probably have been the effect of a vigorous assault upon the enemy at Williamsport before they recrossed the river?

Answer. The utter defeat of the rebel army, I think.

Question. What re-enforcements had our army received between the time of the final battle at Gettysburg and the recrossing of the Potomac by the enemy?

Answer. I can only give an estimate, for I have no official knowledge. I should judge that of good troops there was an addition of 25,000 men, and I understood that of the militia in Pennsylvania there were 30,000 more.

Birney added 30,000 militia in Pennsylvania to the total number of troops available but not called upon. The militia, under Major General Couch, actually numbered around 25,000 and were mostly emergency troops, hastily recruited and with almost no training. Simon Cameron, once Lincoln's secretary of war, referred to these troops as a "fine army," and many in Washington (including Birney) blindly accepted this opinion. It was not an opinion shared by professional military men, however, or even by the commanders of the troops in question. General William "Baldy" Smith, who commanded nearly a third of those troops, described them as "quite helpless" and as an "incoherent mass" which could not be maneuvered. On his arrival at Hagerstown on July 12, Smith's troops were without supplies or any way of getting them, since he had not brought any wagons or quartermasters. Couch himself worried that some of his men would refuse to leave Pennsylvania or might "break on the field." Such reinforcements were more a burden on the army than a help to it.[19]

Question. Would not those militia have been very useful against a retreating army?

[370] Answer. Very useful. I have found that new regiments, when they are inspirited by a confidence of success, will fight nearly as well as old troops, especially if they are sustained by old troops. I have had regiments the first time they have been under fire fight as gallantly and handsomely as my old regiments, and they perhaps stood greater loss, because they were not used to retreating.

Question. Is it not your experience that the great difference between old well disciplined troops and raw troops is, that you can maneuver the old troops better, especially in retreating, though the raw troops may fight right ahead about as well as the old ones?

Answer. The new troops are better, perhaps, to attack; but they will not do as well in retreating as the army of the Potomac, because they do not understand it so well; they are more easily demoralized.

Question. Do you know of any military reason that should have justified a general in permitting that army of the enemy to recross the Potomac at that time without a general assault on them?

Answer. I know of none.

Question. You were relieved by General French from the command of the 3d corps?

Answer. Yes, sir.

Question. When did you again rejoin the army?

Answer. I rejoined it at Warrenton, on the 26th of July; the army was then lying at Warrenton.

[The following segment involved the Bristoe and Mine Run campaigns and is omitted.]

[374] Question. Do the officers and men of the army, so far as you know, retain confidence in their commander after all these retreats?

19. *OR*, vol. 27, pt. 1, pp. 611, 651, 700.

Answer. There is no enthusiasm for him. I think he is rather liked by them; but, so far as I know, they have very little confidence in him as a military leader, or as a decided, resolute general.

Question. Why do they not retain their confidence in his ability and resolution?

Answer. The general opinion is that he lacks decision of character, and will not take responsibility at the proper time; and responsibility naturally devolves upon him as the commanding general.

[375] Question. You have been a long time in the army. I want to know if there is anything like politics operating among the corps commanders in that army; and do they, under all circumstances, support each other with that enthusiasm that is necessary to the unity and efficiency of the army?

Answer. I do not know that there is anything like politics. There are several who are very strong admirers of General McClellan, and who feel that he is the only general that should command that army; but I think they support each other, in obedience to orders. I have never known an instance when they have not carried out the orders which they have received.

Question. Do they carry them out always with that alacrity which is necessary to success? There is a great difference whether you do a thing so as merely to escape censure, or whether you do it with zeal.

Answer. That is rather a hard question for me to answer.

Question. Well, I will waive that question. You spoke of their [sic] being admirers of General McClellan in the army. Are they not generally in opposition to that part of the army that do not so particularly believe in General McClellan? Is there not, to some extent, an antagonism between these admirers of General McClellan and the other portion of the army?

Answer. I think that was somewhat more the case before General McClellan's letter about the election of Judge Woodward, of Pennsylvania, than it has been since. I have heard very little said about him, since he has become an acknowledged politician in the army. But my own position has always been so well known that I would be likely to hear very little of these matters. There was quite an excitement at the time of the McClellan testimonial—quite a feeling throughout the army.

The affair of the Judge Woodward letter has become relatively obscure, yet at the time it caused quite a stir. Briefly the letter reiterated McClellan's support for Democrat George W. Woodward, a state supreme court justice in Pennsylvania who was running for governor against incumbent Republican Andrew Curtin, a strong supporter of Lincoln and the Union. In the letter, written on October 12, 1863, McClellan listed his points of agreement with Woodward, which included the destruction of the military power of the South, respect for the rights of citizens and property, and restoration of the Union as the only objective of the war. Such opinions were contrary to almost everything that the committee and the radical Republicans in Congress hoped to accomplish.[20]

Question. Have the rank and file now that enthusiasm for General McClellan that they are said sometimes to have, so that they will not fight under any other leader?

Answer. I do not think there is anything of that, except in those corps where the commanders are the strong personal friends of General McClellan, and make that a point. I know that in my corps there is not a single subscriber to that testimonial. I was approached by a general to know why I had prohibited it within my division, and refused to allow a staff officer to act upon it at that time. I answered that I had not prohibited it, but there was no one in the 3d corps that I knew of who would subscribe. If there was, they were at perfect liberty to do so. But there was no feeling that way in the corps at all; therefore I think the rank and file reflect, to a certain extent, the opinion and belief of their leader. I think that if the commander of an army is active and enthusiastic, the men would reflect the same feelings. I think the army is now in a good condition, and will obey any one willingly and promptly, although it is, to a certain extent, disheartened.

Question. And if the army was not composed of the best material in the world it would not be worth anything to-day?

Answer. No, sir; I think there has been enough to dispirit it. Its history, since the battle of Gettysburg, has been a succession of useless advances and rapid retreats. The summer and fall were wasted, and our army has, in every instance, after seeking it, avoided a general engagement. In my opinion, the rebel army could have been defeated at Williamsport; badly worsted on their retreat at Manassas gap; badly defeated October 11, 1863, in its attempt to turn our right flank, and during our rapid retreat to Centreville. I also believe that

20. Stephen W. Sears, ed., *The Civil War Papers of George B. McClellan* (New York: Da Capo Press, 1992), 558–9. Woodward lost the election and in 1872 Curtin became a Democrat, serving three terms in Congress. Mark Mayo Boatner III, *The Civil War Dictionary* (New York: Vintage, 1987), 214.

after crossing Kelly's ford, November 9, 1863, a rapid movement by way of Stevensburg would have cut off a considerable portion of their army, and that on Friday, November 27, 1863, a vigorous, determined attack by the 3d and 6th corps, supported by the 2d corps, on the enemy would have resulted in a victory, and in preventing the enemy from occupying their subsequent position [376] at Mine run. All these opportunities being lost, or not taken advantage of, has dispirited the army, with good cause.

Birney would be the last witness supporting the committee's case for awhile, but he did a good job. He had backed Sickles's claim of receiving no orders about his position on July 2. He had also agreed that Meade had not wanted to fight at Gettysburg.

Birney's testimony about the councils on July 2 and 4 reflected poorly on Meade's leadership. Birney characterized Meade as wanting to avoid taking responsibility for an attack. This, Birney charged, was one of the reasons the army had little confidence in Meade.

Birney also confirmed the committee's belief that there were still McClellan supporters in the army. Indeed, he said that some men believed McClellan was still the only one fit to command the army. For the committee, Birney's testimony on this point had a double benefit: it showed that some corps commanders lacked confidence in Meade and that support for McClellan remained strong among those officers.

9 Major General Gouverneur Kemble Warren

THE OFFICERS WHO DEFENDED Meade before the committee were at times a mixed blessing. Confident, powerful men, they were often at odds with Meade over details or opinions about what should have been done at Gettysburg. Some of Meade's defenders, with the best of intentions, caused much grief for him on the political front. Nonetheless, they all saw Meade as a competent—if fallible—officer who accepted the heavy responsibilities inherent in the command of the Army of the Potomac. Mistakes had been made, but the army had won a signal victory under Meade, and these officers realized the difficulties attendant in the destruction of Lee's army.

Gouverneur Kemble Warren was born in New York and graduated from West Point, finishing second in the class of 1850. His prewar service was, like Meade's, in the topographical engineers, and he taught mathematics at West Point. When the Civil War began Warren was appointed lieutenant colonel of the Fifth New York. Soon promoted to colonel, he led a regiment on the Peninsula, where he was wounded. At Second Bull Run and Sharpsburg Warren commanded a brigade, rising through the ranks to become a major general in May 1862. By June 1863, he was chief engineer of the Army of the Potomac. His place in history was secured by his fortuitous discovery of Hood's attack on Little Round Top. Though not exercising a line command at the time, he rushed troops to the defense of the hill. Had Hood's attack not been spotted by Warren, the rebels would have swept to the top of Little Round Top, turning the Union flank while making the Cemetery Hill line indefensible.[1]

Unlike many of the upper-level officers during the war, Warren seems to have taken almost no interest in politics, even though he was named for his

1. Warner, *Generals in Blue,* 541; Boatner, *Civil War Dictionary,* 891.

father's close friend Gouverneur Kemble, a former member of Congress from New York and a power in the Democratic Party. When Warren was stationed in Louisiana during the 1850s, not one of the letters he wrote from the South made a reference to politics. Rather, Warren appeared "serenely indifferent to the feverish changes and movements of the nation's political life." On the eve of the crucial 1857 election, Warren wrote, "The presidential contest interests me not at all; but we are closely watching the proceedings of Congress in reference to the [engineer corps] appropriations."[2]

Warren's lack of interest in politics did not blind him totally to the world outside the army. Hostilities focused in him a simple yet overwhelming patriotism. Warren went to war not out of duty or because of his feelings on slavery, states' rights, or sectionalism. He went to war to save the Union. Writing to his lifelong friend Henry L. Abbot, Warren revealed a startling anger: "The condition to which unscrupulous and ambitious men have brought our country fills me with alternate sorrow for its state and rage against the disturbers of public peace and tranquillity. . . . I [do not] feel that it is fraternal blood that is to be shed, if it is. It is the blood of the brother that would slay the mother that bore us. I admit there was cause for complaint by the South; but they had redress in the Union, and I would have done all in my power to secure it for them, but I will not have sympathy for those who have tried to insult the flag of the most glorious republic that time has ever produced."[3]

In spite of his noninterest in political affairs, Warren occasionally had to involve himself in the political world. As the Civil War neared, Warren's name was put forward as a volunteer officer for a then-forming New York regiment. To accept an appointment in the New York regiment—a state militia regiment—he had to get leave from the regular army. Warren therefore traveled to Washington and presented the War Department with several letters of endorsement, including one from New York governor Edwin Denison Morgan. Morgan had turned to the Republican Party in a disagreement over the Whig Party's abolitionist methods and had served as the new party's national chairman. It is not known whether his endorsement of Warren reflected politics or simply parochialism. Given the tenor of Warren's writings, it was more likely the latter.[4]

Warren's testimony was spread over two days and followed a string of anti-

2. Emerson Gifford Taylor, *Gouverneur Kemble Warren: The Life and Letters of an American Soldier, 1830–1882* (New York: Houghton Mifflin, 1932), 16–7.

3. Ibid., 50; Wainwright, *A Diary of Battle,* ed. Nevins, 509.

4. Taylor, *Gouverneur Kemble Warren,* 47–8.

Meade witnesses previously broken only by Meade's first appearance. On the second day of Warren's testimony, all the committee members were present for the first time since the hearings on Meade began. It was one of only three occasions the entire committee would be present.

[376] Testimony of Major General G. K. Warren.

Washington, March 9, 1864.
Major General G. K. Warren sworn and examined.

By the chairman:
Question. You were present at Gettysburg after General Meade assumed command of the army of the Potomac?
Answer. Yes, sir.
Question. In what capacity did you act there?
Answer. I continued right along in the same capacity as under General Hooker, chief of engineers of the army of the Potomac. When General Meade assumed command, he changed hardly any of General Hooker's staff. He deliberated about it, I think; but after a while continued them the same as before. He assumed command on Sunday morning, and the troops continued to move on just the same as if the command had not been changed.

Warren probably meant this as a compliment, meaning that the transition of command had been smooth. From the committee's point of view his remark suggested that Meade had not changed any of Hooker's plans but merely adopted them as his own.

Question. Will you go on and give us your views of that campaign?
Answer. To go back a little; when the army with General Hooker was at Fairfax, we had a great difficulty and uncertainty about where General Lee's army was. If we crossed the river too soon we might be thrown out of position; if we stayed where we were too long we might be thrown too far behind. It was exceedingly difficult to get reliable information, even though the enemy was in our own country. Therefore General Hooker waited until he felt assured that the enemy were going into Maryland. Finding that General Lee had gone over there and was gathering forage and supplies, and preparing evidently to stay there, General Hooker determined to strike him wherever he could find him. And when General Meade took command he continued that

same idea right along, moving forward as rapidly as possible, for the purpose of hitting Lee's army with something, no matter what it was, so as to bring him into line and bring on a battle. The army moved, as we generally move, in three columns. When we got into the neighborhood of Taneytown, we began to get pretty definite information of where Lee was; but it was still quite uncertain whether the main strength of his army was off over on our right, towards York, or on our left, towards Chambersburg. We could not tell exactly where the mass of his army was, though his forces were lying off on both sides of us. If he could get off on our right, he could go down to Baltimore; if to the left, he might escape us and go to Washington.

Our route of march took us into Carroll county, Maryland, and about that county we had very little information. It was the only county in all the operations of the campaign that we had no decent map of.

At the beginning of the war, useful military maps of the interior of the country were almost nonexistent. Throughout the conflict, one of the main jobs of the engineers was to map an area as the army passed through it. Many officers used commercial maps, which were often inaccurate, outdated, and lacking topographical features.

The cavalry on our left, that portion under General Buford, was very far in advance of the rest of the army. Our left wing was commanded by General Reynolds; the centre was more immediately under the command of General Meade; while the right, off towards York, was, I think, more under the command of General Sedgwick. On the 1st of July we were near Taneytown.

In view of these contingencies we had prepared lines of battle in different positions. One probable line was the line of Manchester and Ridgeville; the dividing ridge between the Monocacy and the waters running into the Chesapeake bay. Then we had another line under consideration on Big Pipe creek; [377] and orders were issued for that as the probable line of battle; and all the officers I could get were sent out to reconnoiter that line.

On the morning of the 1st of July we got information from General Buford that the enemy were moving down upon him at Gettysburg from the direction of Fairfield. I do not know how orders were issued; but I know that about that time General Reynolds moved forward to the support of General Buford, passing through the town of Gettysburg, and engaged the enemy there. This news came in very early in the morning. General Meade ordered me to go to Gettysburg to obtain information about it and examine the ground. In consequence of mistaking my road I went to Emmitsburg, a little out of the way. About at the same time that I left news came down that General Reynolds had been killed. General Meade then sent up General Hancock, with discretionary orders, I think, either to hold that place, if he thought it was a good one, or, if not, then to fall back to the line of Pipe creek, keeping General Meade informed. General Hancock got there a little before I did.

At that time General Reynolds's corps, the 1st corps, had fallen back pretty badly damaged; and what there was of the 11th corps, that had gone out to help him, was coming back in great confusion. General Howard was then on Cemetery ridge with one division. General Buford's cavalry was all in line of battle between our position there and the enemy. Our cavalry presented a very handsome front, and I think probably checked the advance of the enemy. General Hancock made a great deal of personal efforts to get our troops into position; and I think his personal appearance there did a great deal towards restoring order.

I went around over the ground with General Hancock, and we came to the conclusion that if that position could be held until night, it would be the best place for the army to fight on if the army was attacked.

Warren may have been engaging in a little self-promotion. No other sources confirm that he and Hancock examined the ground together or consulted each other on July 1.

General Hancock himself reported that to General Meade, who ordered all the army up to that position. It was a very difficult movement to make, for the 6th corps had to march over 30 miles to reach that position. I went back and reported to General Meade about midnight, and found him just ready to start out. All his orders had been given, and all the troops were moving.

The next morning as the troops arrived they kept going to position. By General Meade's direction I reconnoitered our position on the right; the most of our troops were coming up on the right; and General Meade had it in contemplation to order an assault from our right if his troops could be got into that position and be prepared for it before anything else took place. From the reconnaissance that I made I advised General Meade not to attack in that direction, because of the character of the ground.

Warren's reconnaissance on the right reflected Meade's determination to fight at Gettysburg on July 2, thus undermining previous testimony.

Soon afterwards I rode out with General Meade to examine the left of our line, where General Sickles was. His troops could hardly be said to be in position. There seemed to be some doubt about whether he should occupy a line in front, or the one on the ridge in the rear; and I am not sure but a report had come in from some of our officers that that position was not occupied. I know I had sent an officer there to ascertain and report. However, when we got on the ground the enemy were just about attacking, and General Sickles immediately began to arrange his troops on the advanced line. I suppose that was about the only thing that could be done at that time.

Warren had jumped into the brewing Meade-Sickles controversy with both feet. While not explicitly condemning Sickles's actions, Warren came down squarely on Meade's side.

I then went, by General Meade's direction, to what is called Bald Top, and from that point I could see the enemy's lines of battle.

This is Warren's version of the events on Little Round Top, or, as he called it, Bald Top. At the time of Gettysburg, the two hills which are known today as Big and Little Round Top were referred to variously by the opposing sides as Bald Top, Sugar Loaf, and "that rocky hill," among other designations. The names Big and Little Round Top did not become standard until the 1880s.

I sent word to General Meade that we would at once have to occupy that place very strongly. He sent, as quickly as possible, a division of General Sykes's corps; but before they arrived the enemy's line of battle—I should think a mile and a half long—began to advance, and the battle became very heavy at once. The troops under General Sykes arrived barely in time to save Round Top mill [hill], and they had a very desperate fight to hold it.

[378] I felt very well satisfied that General Sickles could not hold his position against the force brought against him; that his troops could not stand, and I so reported to General Meade; and other reports, either a call for reenforcements or something else, made me think it could not be done. A portion of the 2d corps went to help him, a division of General Slocum's corps, and, I believe, some of the 1st corps also, and all of the 6th that could come up were sent to fill up that line in rear of where General Sickles's corps was fighting. The enemy drove our lines back clear to the main ridge, and our troops

then drove the enemy back; that ended the fighting for that day. The repulse was mainly by the 12th, 1st, and 2d corps. I do not know which troops had the most prominent part in it. I only know they were all there.

Warren's account contradicted both Sickles's and Birney's testimony about the achievements of the Third Corps on July 2.

Whilst this attack was going on our left, the enemy also attacked on our right, and got possession of a part of the line General Slocum had established there, so that when his troops returned he found the enemy there. The enemy also attacked the line of the 11th corps just at dark; but, on the whole, they gained no essential advantage.

The next morning we began a fight on our right, to drive the enemy out, which was accomplished by General Slocum about 10 o'clock, I should suppose, and about 1 o'clock the enemy opened a very heavy artillery fire about on our left centre. After that had continued for about an hour and a half they assaulted us with a pretty large force, though I think not so large as the force they used the day before. That assault was repulsed and that ended essentially the battle of Gettysburg.

Question. That battle lasted for three days, I believe?

Answer. Yes, sir.

Question. Were any councils of war held during that engagement?

Answer. There was not held what I should call a council of war. The officers met together but merely for the purpose of explaining to each other how things stood.

Question. Were you present at those consultations?

Answer. I was part of the time. A great many of the officers slept in the same house. I knew what the opinion of all the officers was. I talked with nearly all of them, and everybody was for fighting it out; there was no necessity for any council. General Meade had so arranged his troops on our left during the third day that nearly one-half of the army was in reserve in that position. It was a good sheltered position, and a convenient one from which to re-enforce other parts of the line; and when the repulse of the enemy took place on that day, General Meade intended to move forward all the forces he could get in line and assault the enemy in turn. He ordered an advance of the 5th corps, but it was carried on so slowly that it did not amount to much, if anything.

Question. Who commanded that corps?

Answer. General Sykes. Instead of advancing the whole of the 5th corps, I believe only about one brigade was advanced.

With this account, Warren contradicted all previous testimony but Meade's. He also challenged two of the committee's key points about Meade's reluctance to fight. But Wade did not seek further information, instead switching to another subject.

Question. What was the condition of our army after the final repulse of the enemy; were our men much fatigued and discouraged, or were they in good spirits?

Answer. They were in splendid spirits; they were not fatigued then. Those three days had been days of rest for the most of them; but we had lost a great many of our most spirited officers. General Reynolds was dead, and General Hancock was wounded and carried to the rear.

Question. General Sickles was also wounded and carried off?

Answer. Yes, sir; and many officers of lower rank, but relatively of as much importance as they were, were killed or wounded. We were very much shattered in that respect; and there was a tone amongst most of the prominent [379] officers that we had quite saved the country for the time, and that we had done enough; that we might jeopard all that we had won by trying to do too much.

Warren pointed out a problem commonly overlooked by historians and students of Gettysburg. The records show that in addition to losses among corps commanders, of the nearly 5,500 officers present for duty, 29 percent, or nearly one in three, were killed, captured, wounded, or missing after the battle. The losses among officers who commanded brigades at some point in the battle were nearly as high, at 28 percent. In total, almost one-fourth of the Army of the Potomac was dead, wounded, or missing after those three days. The loss of these experienced men was keenly felt by the army and by Meade.[5]

Interestingly, Warren did not include Sickles among "our most spirited officers" until prodded by Wade. As a professional officer Warren may have looked down on Sickles, who was a political general. One incident in the battle of Chancellorsville may shed further light on the issue. On the night of May 3 a

5. *OR*, vol. 27, pt. 1, pp. 151, 187; *B&L*, 3:434–7.

council of the corps commanders was held. In writing his official report, Warren initially included an account of the council, which he deleted from the final draft. He wrote that at the council, Meade, Reynolds, and Howard favored advancing the next day, but Sickles thought that a withdrawal would not be fatal to the country, a victory was doubtful, and the "uncertainties were all against us." Hooker's mind was already made up, but the words of his friend Sickles during the council, and perhaps outside the council as well, surely reinforced his decision not to fight. On May 8 Warren wrote, "There was a want of nerve *somewhere . . . Our great weakness . . . is in the incompetency of many of our corps commanders." Though Sickles was not specifically mentioned, Warren may well have been alluding to him.*[6]

To this point, the last sentence of Warren's testimony is by far the most informative. Members of the committee believed that many of the corps commanders did not support the war effort, and Warren's statement corroborated their belief. It is obviously difficult to accept such an attitude among professional military officers. By the battle of Gettysburg, Lincoln had recognized that the destruction of Lee's army—and not the capture of Richmond—was the Union's primary military objective; yet the upper echelon of Federal officers had not reached the same conclusion. Indeed, Warren's testimony suggests that the conservatism in the officer corps went beyond normal caution, and that the corps commanders were satisfied with what was a tactical victory but a strategic draw. Lee's invasion had been repulsed, but his army was still in the field and still a threat to the Union. Why Wade did not pick up on Warren's comment is inexplicable.

Question. Do you know of any council of war held after the final repulse of the enemy?

Answer. Yes, sir; I think there was a talk that night about what to do.

Question. What was the opinion and decision of that council?

Answer. I am not certain whether there was a council of war before the night of the 4th of July. It is my impression that there was no council until the night of the 4th. On the morning of the 4th General Meade ordered demonstrations in front of our line, but they were very feebly made; and when the officers met together that evening to report the state of things in their front, there was so little definitely known as to the position and designs of the enemy that after some consultation they determined, I believe, to try and find out

6. Taylor, *Gouverneur Kemble Warren*, 110–1.

something before they did move. I know that was the result. I made the offer that night that if they would give me command of a division by 8 o'clock the next morning, I would tell them whether the enemy was retreating or not. It was not even known whether the enemy was retreating or not. On the morning of the 5th I went out with the 6th corps. General Meade gave orders for a division of the 6th corps to go with me, and for the whole corps to follow if I wanted.

Question. Are you certain there was no council of war held on the evening of the second day of the battle?

Answer. I do not know that there was; not what I would call a council of war. I think it probable that General Meade asked the opinion of all his officers about what they thought of their position.

Question. But you do not remember anything like a definite council, and a vote in that council?

Answer. No, sir; but a part of that evening I was asleep, being very tired, as we all were, of course. We were all in the same house together.

Warren did not mention that he had been shot in the neck on July 2. The shock of the wound, loss of blood, and exhaustion probably all contributed to his having slept through the July 2 council.

Question. Go on with your narrative of the way you got down to Williamsport.

Answer. We were considerably delayed in starting; but we found out that the enemy had gone, and we followed them up with the 6th corps to Fairfield. General Meade, during the day, issued orders for the whole army to move towards Frederick. On the evening of the 4th of July there was a discussion of the question whether we should move right after the enemy through the mountains, or move towards Frederick; that question was not decided, for the reason that we did not know enough about the enemy; and to have gone off the battle-field before the enemy did would have been giving up the victory to them. And then, if the enemy had gone, it was a question which way to go after him. To go right after him was a good way in one respect; but then we had to get all our provisions from Frederick.

Warren's point about the army's base of supply was an important consideration in the army's movements. He also emphasized the lack of sufficient information on which to base a pursuit, which was information that Pleasonton should have provided to Meade after the battle. Warren's comment about leaving the battlefield reflects the grip of tradition on the military mind; in earlier times, possession of the field was the indicator of victory. Though no longer valid, this idea still had resonance with many military men.

Warren's brief description of the council on July 4 hardly does justice to the importance of the meeting.

Question. You remained at Gettysburg two days after the battle was fought before your [*sic*] pursued much?

Answer. We commenced the pursuit with the 6th corps on the 5th of July, and on the 6th a large portion of the army moved towards Emmitsburg, and all that was left followed the next day. On July 7th the headquarters were at Frederick. On July 8th headquarters were at Middletown, and nearly all the army was concentrated in the neighborhood of that place and South mountain. On July 9th headquarters were at South Mountain House, and the advance of the army at Boonsboro and Rohrersville. On July 10th the headquarters were moved to Antietam creek; the left of the line crossed the creek, and the right of the line moved up near Funkstown. On the 11th of July the engineers put a new bridge over Antietam creek; the left of the line advanced to Fairplay and Jones's Crossroads, while the right remained nearly stationary. In my opinion we should have fought the enemy the next morning, July 12.

Question. Was there a council of war held about that time?

Answer. I think there was.

[380] Question. Of the corps commanders?

Answer. Yes, sir; almost every night they met. However, I think it probable that no council was held on the night of July 11th. The troops were not in position; we had got no very definite information of the enemy, and we had not heard of the columns on our right.

Warren's testimony makes it hard to see why he believed Meade should have attacked on July 12. His own words reveal that the army was obviously not ready for battle. Even a poor general, which Lee was not, would have been able to defeat the attack of an unorganized, undermanned army.

By Mr. Chandler:

Question. What was the impression in our army as to the amount of ammunition that the enemy had after such a severe engagement as that at Gettysburg?

Answer. I do not think that they considered it exhausted. I did not hear any one say that the enemy did not have ammunition enough. We always had enough. I do not know how it is with them; but we always carry along enough to fight two or three battles. I do not know whether they do or not. But from the best calculations I think it was considered that the enemy had enough ammunition yet to fight a battle, though I think it is very probable that he was somewhat short of ammunition. It would take me a long time to state the reasons that governed them for not fighting on a morning like that.

Warren was one of the few witnesses to appear before the committee who felt that the enemy had sufficient ammunition to fight.

Question. What troops had you in the way of re-enforcements that had not participated in the battle of Gettysburg? Had you any troops besides those that you had in the fight?

Answer. Yes, sir; we had probably some 5,000 or 6,000 under General French.

Question. And you also had some militia under General William F. Smith?

Answer. Yes, sir.

Question. What number?

Answer. I do not know what number he reported. I know that we did not consider them fit to put in battle.

Question. Then there was no use in having militia. Are they not good against a retreating enemy?

Answer. I could use them; I should have done what I could with them. But I know the report of the officer in command of them was that you could not rely upon them much, unless you mixed them up with other troops.

Question. You do not know the number of such militia?

Answer. No, sir; I probably knew at the time, but I have forgotten.

Question. You say it would take a great while to give the reasons for and against fighting the enemy at the river the night of the 11th or morning of the 12th of July?

Answer. Yes, sir; I should have fought on the morning of the 12th if I could have got my troops to fight.

Question. Was there any difficulty in that particular? You say the troops were in high spirits?

Answer. There was the same trouble that there had been before; worse than ever before. Having lost a great many of our good corps commanders, we could not get our troops well into line, for we could not get officers who understood that. The weather was also very stormy, and the roads were muddy. All of these things were great sources of trouble, so that none of them, I know, considered themselves ready to fight.

Warren again noted that the loss of experienced officers, combined with the stormy weather and bad roads, made an attack difficult.

Question. You knew that the enemy also had lost as many good officers as we had?

Answer. Yes, sir.

Question. Are they better disciplined, and can they handle their troops better than we can ours? Are they so superior to us that they can handle a defeated army better than we can handle a victorious army?

Answer. No, sir, I do not believe they can. The 12th of July was spent in trying to get the troops into position. General Meade then did have a council of war about what to do the next morning.

Question. Were you in that council?

Answer. Yes, sir.

[381] Question. What was the conclusion of the council?

Answer. They were opposed to an attack.

Question. All of them?

Answer. The most of them. General Wadsworth was not, and I think General Howard was not. But General Howard's opinion did not carry much weight with the rest, because his troops did not behave well. The conduct of his troops at Gettysburg was not such as to restore them to the confidence of the army.

Warren's comment about Howard provides an insight into the relationships of the corps commanders. The Eleventh Corps' performance at Gettysburg should have merited approval from their fellow soldiers. Basically flanked on both sides and pounded from the front, they had suffered heavy casualties in trying to stop Ewell's Second Corps. Yet their rout at Chancellorsville—along with a widespread prejudice against Germans, who made up a high percentage of the corps—had permanently branded them as unreliable. This attitude was reflected on Howard, as commander of the Eleventh Corps, and seems to have undermined the value of his opinions.

Question. Then the corps commanders were pretty generally of the opinion that they should not attack the enemy?

Answer. Yes, sir.

Question. What reason did they give for that? Were not our numbers equal to those of the enemy?

Answer. Yes, sir; I suppose they must have been. I do not know of any real reason they had for not attacking, except that they considered the enemy's positions and intrenchments were too strong to carry, and they quoted such instances as the first battle of Fredericksburg, and our own repulse of the rebel forces at Malvern Hill and Gettysburg. I do not think I ever saw the principal corps commanders so unanimous in favor of not fighting as on that occasion.

The July 12 meeting was an integral part of one of the committee's charges against Meade, since the vote by its participants allowed Lee to complete his escape. In addition to the seven infantry corps commanders (with Wadsworth attending in place of Newton, who was sick), Pleasonton, Warren, and the new chief of staff Humphreys were included. It was the majority opinion that an attack should be postponed.

Question. If you were not strong enough to fight their whole force, why not have fought some of them before they all got across the river?

Answer. They all got over in the night. At daylight on the 13th of June [*sic*] General Meade was out along the line, and ordered an attack to be made the next morning at daybreak. But when the troops, on the morning of the 14th, moved forward, the enemy was gone. One reason that operated on the mind of General Meade was this for not ordering an attack sooner; that if the enemy fell back across the river he could follow them into their own country and give them battle under, probably, as favorable circumstances as were there presented to him; that is, he thought if he lost that opportunity he could have another one. But he determined, finally, against the opinions of the others, to fight a battle there.

Question. Then all but General Meade and one or two others did not intend to fight them at all if the enemy had a mind to take up their quarters there? What, in your opinion, as a military man, would have been the effect of a general assault upon the enemy's position there by the river?

Answer. I think we should have cut them all to pieces; that was my opinion.

There followed a lengthy series of questions and answers about the Bristoe and Mine Run campaigns, which are not included verbatim here. In that testimony, however, Warren made various points that were related to the Gettysburg campaign.

During his questioning about the Mine Run campaign, Wade asked Warren if it was good generalship on Meade's part to have retreated and allowed Lee to destroy communications lines. Warren replied in the negative, but he went on to argue that Meade had been misinformed and "his information was so incorrect that he did not know what was going on. His cavalry deceived him very much; and I think some of his other officers failed him in spirit." As a concrete and personal example, Warren testified that when he had attacked at Centreville, Sykes had failed to help him without orders to do so.

Warren's criticism of the failure of the cavalry under Pleasonton was unusual. He was one of the few senior officers to speak openly of Pleasonton's failures, and his testimony should have set off alarm bells for the committee. If the cavalry—Meade's eyes and ears—had misled him, he was going after Lee in the dark, which could have had potentially disastrous consequences. Yet Pleasonton's failure went almost unnoticed. No one on the committee pursued Warren's criticism of the cavalry. Wade instead followed up on Warren's testimony about Sykes, wanting to know why frequently one corps did not help another. Warren stated that this lack of cooperation was due to the fact that the corps were not commanded by soldiers themselves. His testimony reinforced the committee's negative views of the professional officer corps.

There was a break in Warren's testimony and it was resumed the next day, March 10. Again, the Bristoe and Mine Run campaigns are omitted.

[384] By the chairman:

Question. Now, I want you, as an officer of experience, and one who has acted with this army of the Potomac for a long time, to tell me if you believe this army, just as it is now organized, is as efficient as it ought to be?

Answer. No, sir; I think that for offensive warfare it could be made immeasurably superior to what it is by properly organizing it.

Question. What do you mean by properly organizing it? What would you do?

Answer. For instance, I would consolidate this army into three corps.

This was essentially Burnside's three "grand divisions," which had been strongly espoused earlier by the committee.

Then I would get whoever should be the best man to command the army, and then I would allow him to have the choice of his own corps commanders.

Then I would allow these corps commanders to choose their subordinate commanders.

Question. And then hold them all to a strict accountability for what they did?

Answer. Yes, sir; and let them understand that their position depended upon their doing well; not merely excusing themselves, but accomplishing something.

Question. Now, for offensive warfare in an enemy's country, have you full confidence in the activity and spirit of our commanders?

Answer. No, sir, I have not, and I have never had, and now less of any time. I have the very highest confidence in General Hancock, but he is not with the army now; we have been operating without him ever since the battle of Gettysburg. At Gettysburg we lost General Hancock by wounds, General Reynolds by death, and then, by the change of commanders, we lost General Meade as a corps commander.

Question. And General Sickles by wounds?

Answer. Yes, sir. These were considered as fighting men by the army. They were men who handled their corps well, and stood well with their commands. I do not think that General Sickles is as good a soldier as the others; but he did the best he could, and with the corps he had he managed very well. His corps was composed of a little different material from the others.

Question. You considered him a man of resolution and courage, and one that would bring his corps into a fight well?

Answer. Yes, sir, he did very well. I do not think that General Sickles would be a good man to fight an independent battle, which a corps commander would often have to do. I think if he had been educated a soldier he might have stood very high. But when you come down to all the details of a battle, General Sickles has not had the same experience which others have had. The knowledge of those details do not make a soldier, but he should be possessed of them as much as he is of his own language.

Wade was trying to bolster the reputation of his star witness. Only a man looking for trouble could have answered as Warren did.

Question. Then, according to your view, there is eminent necessity for a reorganization of this army?

[385] Answer. Yes, sir; and I have maintained that on every ground since the battle of Gettysburg.

This was a potentially important point for the committee. If the army needed reorganizing, it would be easier to remove Meade from command.

[There followed more questions about the Mine Run campaign.]

[387] Question. Is it not your opinion that we have lost a great many opportunities by hesitating and waiting at the decisive points?

Wade's phrasing of this question is curious and seems to indicate that he already knew Warren's opinion.

Answer. Yes, sir. I will enumerate the points where, during the last year, I think we have lost opportunities. I think we should have advanced on the evening of the 3d of July, after the enemy were repulsed at Gettysburg, with all the force we had on our left. I think we should have attacked the enemy at Williamsport on the morning of the 12th of July. I think we were as ready then as we ever were, and the enemy was not ready at all. Then we lost another opportunity at Manassas gap, on the 23d of July, while the enemy was retreating. Then, again, we lost another opportunity when the enemy attacked me on the 14th of October at Bristow [*sic*]. Perhaps not at that point exactly, but during that movement, we missed an opportunity that we should be very glad to have again. Then, again, we lost a good opportunity after we recrossed the Rappahannock on the 8th of November. And another opportunity was lost in not making the junction we should have had at Robertson's tavern on the 27th of November. Nearly all these delays and failures, I think, are due not so much to General Meade as to his plans and expectations not being carried out.

[388] Question. And you think that, on the occasions you have enumerated, with promptness and energy of action, a serious injury might have been inflicted upon the enemy?

Answer. Yes, sir, almost amounting to his destruction.

Question. You have enumerated five or six of these opportunities lost. Is not that evidence of a defect either in the organization of the army, or in the character of its officers, or both?

Answer. Yes, sir. One great objection, one might say, is that we have too many corps; and as corps are independent bodies, to a great extent they require able and independent commanders; and of course it is more difficult to obtain five able and competent independent commanders than it is to obtain only three, and it is more difficult to manage five than three after you have got them. That is one trouble, that we have too many corps. And then, I think that our corps commanders have not all of them been equal to their positions; and I think there is enough in that to impair almost every plan and jeopard every chance, though I do not say it is owing altogether to that.

Question. And there seems to be a want of determination and resolution in our aggressive movements?

Answer. One defect in the corps commanders is that, I think, they do not go enough to the front to see for themselves; they rely too much upon the directions and information sent to them; they do not depend enough upon their own knowledge.

Question. Do they approach the enemy near enough to feel of him, and find out in that way?

Answer. I do not think they do. I think there is too much reporting "the enemy in force," or "the enemy in position," when there is nothing there. False reports have been the real cause of our failures.

Question. And this over-caution in approaching the enemy seems to be the reason that you do not know more of them?

Answer. Yes, sir; that is it.

Warren had certainly finished with a bang. He was well known for his blunt manner of speaking and his explosive temper; if he had any concern for army politics, he did not demonstrate it during his testimony. In short order he had managed to insult every corps commander in the Army of the Potomac. In later years Warren's volatile behavior would even call his sanity into question. On March 29, 1865, Colonel Charles Wainwright wrote in his diary of an outburst of temper by Warren, noting, "I have for some time past been convinced . . . that these awful fits of passion are a disease with Warren, and a species of insanity, over which he has no control."[7]

On balance, Warren's testimony had helped Meade's case, but it was not without criticism. Warren felt the army should have fought at Williamsport on July 12, though he admitted it was in no condition to do so. He testified further that Meade believed if he did not attack at Williamsport he would have an equally good opportunity to attack on the opposite side of the river.

Warren believed that Meade had missed other opportunities to attack—most notably on July 3, following Pickett's repulse, and on four other occasions during the Bristoe and Mine Run campaigns. This was valuable testimony for the committee.

7. Wainwright, *A Diary of Battle,* ed. Nevins, 509.

Warren supported Meade's testimony that he had wanted to fight at Williamsport but had been overruled by his corps commanders. In fact, Warren asserted that the corps commanders were mostly at fault for the army's failures. He said that the corps commanders were not the quality of officers that they should have been and that they did not go to the front often enough, which caused them to give false or misleading reports on the enemy. He also specifically cited Pleasonton as a source of some of Meade's problems.

10 Brigadier General Andrew Atkinson Humphreys

DESPITE THEIR SETBACK at the White House, both Wade and Chandler remained determined to remove Meade from command. Five of the first seven witnesses to testify before the committee were opposed to Meade. This meant, however, that the committee had a shrinking number of officers readily available to testify against Meade. To keep the hearings alive and maintain a semblance of impartiality, members of the committee had little choice but to call witnesses who generally supported Meade. Meanwhile, they continued to search for officers more amenable to the committee's point of view. In the interim the next witness to appear was Brigadier General Andrew Atkinson Humphreys.

Humphreys was an extremely competent soldier, considered by some as the "great soldier of the Army of the Potomac." As an engineer of considerable talent, he spent most of his prewar career in the Corps of Topographical Engineers surveying the Mississippi Delta. Humphreys was a professional soldier who had graduated from West Point, and during the Peninsula campaign he was McClellan's chief engineer (none of which, obviously, helped his standing with the committee). Not until September 1862 did Humphreys get a field command, a division in the Fifth Corps, which he "led with distinction in the Maryland campaign."[1]

Humphreys probably met Meade when they were both at West Point; however, Humphreys graduated the year Meade entered the academy and it is not likely they knew each other very well. Meade's appointment to command of the Fifth Corps in December 1862 began an association that would last until Meade's early death, when Humphreys was one of his pallbearers. Following

1. Quoted in Pfanz, *Gettysburg: The Second Day,* 135; Warner, *Generals in Blue,* 240–2; *MG,* 95.

Fredericksburg (where Meade noted that Humphreys "behaved with distinguished gallantry") and Chancellorsville, Humphreys was transferred to Sickles's Third Corps. Meade was sorry to lose Humphreys, as he considered him a "topnotch soldier and 'a splendid man.' "[2]

As a division commander at Gettysburg, Humphreys had only a limited knowledge of the events of interest to the committee. But he had the added value of being Meade's chief of staff after Butterfield left the army on July 5. Meade had asked Humphreys on June 28 to accept the position of chief of staff, but Humphreys had, in his words, "declined or deferred it." He felt that, with a battle looming, his place was with his division and Meade had reluctantly agreed. Other factors also influenced Humphreys's initial decision, however. He was ambitious and wanted a large command. Writing on July 12, after his appointment as chief of staff on July 8, he made his feelings perfectly clear. "I regard it as temporary, that is until I can get command of a Corps; less than that I cannot stand."[3]

Humphreys accepted the position as chief of staff principally out of loyalty to Meade and the enticement of a major general's commission, but he felt more than a little frustration over his situation. At Gettysburg he served under Sickles and then Birney, which he found both depressing and discouraging. He commented on July 16 that "my mortification at seeing men over me and commanding me who should have been far below me has destroyed all my enthusiasm."[4]

[388] Testimony of Major General Andrew A. Humphreys.

Washington, March 21, 1864.
Major General Andrew A. Humphreys sworn and examined.

By the chairman:

Question. When did General Meade succeed to the command of the army of the Potomac?

Answer. I received a note from General Meade on the 28th of June, asking me to come and see him, which I did. I learned from that he had that day been put in command of the army. I remained at headquarters for some hours, and

2. *MG*, 350; *LLM*, January 26, 1863, 1:352; *GC*, 39.

3. Henry H. Humphreys, *Andrew Atkinson Humphreys: A Biography* (Philadelphia: John C. Winston, 1924), 186–7, 201.

4. Ibid., 202.

then rejoined my division as it marched through Frederick. It was on that occasion that General Meade invited me to become his chief of staff, which I desired not to do until after the coming battle, and circumstances admitted of my postponing a decision until then. On the 29th of June we reached Taneytown. About midday of the 30th, as my division was encamped near Taneytown, we had orders to march, our march being directed towards Emmitsburg. I was sent for at the same time to go to general headquarters. General Meade being very much engaged at the time, I was informed by General Butterfield, who was still acting as chief of staff, of the object of my being sent for. He informed me of the positions of the different portions of the army, and told me that General Meade wished me, when I reached Emmitsburg, to examine the ground in that vicinity and see whether it would do to fight a [389] battle there, in the event of its being desirable to do so; and what ground we could occupy.

Though ignored by the committee and apparently forgotten by Butterfield, this is additional evidence that Meade was seeking a battle with Lee and that the Pipe Creek circular was a contingency order.

I think that the orders for our march were given under some information that Lee was moving towards us with his army. I understood there had been no very definite information received concerning his movements recently. But my division only moved about half way to Emmitsburg, some four or five miles, when I was told that the information under which we had marched had turned out to be erroneous, and my division remained where it was for the night.

This is another indication of the failure of the cavalry. Lee was certainly doing all he could to mask his movements; still, the incidence of wrong or misleading intelligence from the cavalry was high.

On the first of July we marched to Emmitsburg, and I posted my division about a mile out of town, on the Waynesboro pike. After conversing with General Sickles as to whether we should remain there or not, and finding that we should probably remain there some hours, I examined the ground very thoroughly in every direction. I was not satisfied with the ground at all; it was broken, complicated ground; the features of it were not of that bold, decided character that indicated any very good position in which to fight a battle; and

I was obliged to make my examination a very minute one. Upon returning to my division about four o'clock, I perceived that some of the troops had left the ground. In my absence orders had been sent to march up to Gettysburg at once. I immediately followed on as rapidly as I could, and when I got to the head of the column I found that orders had been received between three and four o'clock to march at once, leaving one brigade and one battery on the Waynesboro road, to watch it. We were directed to move up with all possible expedition to Gettysburg, and informed that the enemy had made their appearance there in force; that the 1st and 11th corps had been very hotly engaged, and that General Reynolds had been killed. Two brigades of the other division of the 3d corps were moving up the main road; I was to follow a road about two miles to the west of that one.

What follows is the well-known and fascinating tale of Humphreys's march to Gettysburg.

I learned that Lieutenant Colonel Hayden, assistant inspector general of the corps, was there with a gentleman from Gettysburg, who acted as a guide for the route that General Sickles wished me to take. I had a map of that country which I had purchased that morning that showed all the roads. My division did not reach the position which it occupied at Gettysburg until one o'clock in the morning. When about half way to Gettysburg, I received a note from General Sickles, which had been written to him by General Howard, telling him to look out for his left as he moved up (on the main road I suppose was meant) from Emmitsburg. I was to the left of this road, some two miles. Just after this I met a person who had conducted a portion of the first corps up in the morning, and he told me that there were none of our troops on the west side of the Emmitsburg road. Therefore when I came to where this road turned off to the right and united with the main road, I wished to move over to the right, but Colonel Hayden, who was there, insisted upon it that General Sickles had directed him to guide the division by the way of the Black Horse tavern, which was on the road from Fairfield to Gettysburg, the road by which some of the enemy came. I was convinced the enemy were on that part of the ground. Just previous to this conversation with Colonel Hayden, about dusk, a staff officer from General Sickles gave me directions from him to take position on the left of Gettysburg when I got up. I presumed the left, as we were then moving, was meant—that is, on the west side of the road. Therefore, upon Colonel Hayden's being so positive that General Sickles wished me to approach by the Black Horse tavern road, I moved over there. It occupied considerable time to move there, owing to the crossings of Marsh run. I took the precaution of directing my column to move quietly as it approached this road, and to close up, as I expected to fall in with the enemy. We found that the enemy were posted there in force. They were not aware of my presence, and I might have attacked them at daylight with the certainty of at least temporary success; but I was three miles distant from the remainder of the army, and I believed such a course would have been inconsistent with the general plan of operations of the commanding general. As soon [390] as I found what was the exact condition of things, I retraced my steps and moved my command by the route I have already indicated, bivouacking near Gettysburg about 1 A.M. on the 2d of July. This delayed me several hours, and fatigued my men a great deal. I mention it to explain why it was that I was so late in getting upon the field. It was a moonlight night, but hazy. I had to move back some distance after I found the enemy there. However, the fighting was over that day before any of the corps got to Gettysburg.

Years later, on a return visit to the battlefield, Humphreys spoke with the tavern keeper and his sons. They recalled that less than ten minutes after Humphreys had left, a group of twenty or thirty rebels arrived and spent the night. It was only by sheer luck that Humphreys had avoided them.[5]

Question. By the way, what is the reason that you generals never fight a battle by moonlight?

Answer. It is very dangerous to attempt anything of that kind by night, for if your troops are broken and dispersed it is almost impossible to rally them, and you are very liable to fire into your own men. A night operation is a very difficult one, and very rarely succeeds. Where you undertake to surprise a small force of the enemy, it may succeed, but it is very difficult and dangerous to attempt any offensive movement of magnitude at night.

I ought to mention that when I informed General Sickles of the circuitous route by which I had come, he informed me that it was altogether a misapprehension upon the part of Colonel Hayden to guide the division by way of the Black Horse tavern. But it shows what can be done by accident. If any one had been directed to take a division to the rear of the enemy's army and get up as close as I did unperceived, it would have been thought exceedingly difficult, if not impossible, to do it unnoticed.

5. Ibid., 189–90.

Early in the morning of the 2d of July my division was massed on the left of the 2d corps, on ground which, in my official report, I have called the Round Top ridge. It is in reality a ridge of elevated ground which runs between Cemetery hill and Round Top hill, and therefore might, perhaps, be as well termed Cemetery ridge. About 12 o'clock, or a little after, by direction of General Sickles, my division was formed some 400 or 500 yards in front of the position in which it had remained during the night. The first brigade was in line of battle, forming the front of the line. The second brigade was formed in line of battalions in mass in rear of the first, and the third brigade was massed in column of regiments in rear of the centre. This brigade had come up in the morning at 9 o'clock, having been ordered up by General Meade, as understood from the brigade commander. My left touched the right of the first division, commanded by General Birney. My right was opposite to the left of the 2d corps, General Caldwell's division, and I suppose some 500 yards in front of it. Afterwards, by direction of General Sickles, who commanded the corps, my third brigade moved down beyond my left, in a wood in rear of the first division, I being directed to give support from that brigade to General Birney if he needed it. At the same time I was authorized to call on General Caldwell, who commanded a division of the 2d corps in rear of my right, for such support as I might want. We remained in that position for some time.

Question. Your position was in advance of the general line somewhat?

Answer. Yes; my division was.

Question. So as to expose its flanks?

Answer. Not at that time. My orders first were to form with my right resting on the left of the 2d corps, and my left touching General Birney's right, and in line with him; but I could not do both; and when I learned from General Caldwell that he had no orders to move forward, I reported it to General Sickles, and was ordered to form as I did. It was at that time, I think, that I was authorized to call on General Caldwell for support. We were both of opinion that the distance I was then in front of him would make no very great difference. We were in a hollow, and this was simply a preliminary formation of the troops. I went to the front, as soon as we were formed, to examine the ground, and at once directed a regiment to occupy a little log-house [Daniel Klingle's house] on the Emmitsburg road, [391] and an orchard in front of and near the centre of my line. I also examined the enemy's position in front of me. They were in a wood something less than half a mile in front of us. I ought to have mentioned that during the morning, before 12 o'clock, by direction of the corps commander, I had sent out working parties and had all the fences taken down in my front, so that we could move readily in all directions.

There is no reason to doubt Humphrey's testimony that Sickles had issued an order to take down the fences in his front. Sickles was not the best corps commander in the Army of the Potomac, but he knew that fences delayed the movement of troops across fields. Yet it is curious that Sickles felt it necessary to issue such a direction to Humphreys, a professional military man. There is no record that Sickles issued a similar order to Birney, a political general. Birney did not remove the fences to his front, and his negligence created problems for the artillery in the battle, resulting in costly delays.

I did not see General Sickles in the morning, because I could not leave my division unless sent for. I therefore, at that time, had no knowledge of the general position of the other troops except what I could see on my right; the ground on my left was hidden by trees. I did not know how the ground was beyond where I could see the troops. I learned about mid-day, from an aide-de-camp of General Birney, Captain Briscoe, that there was an important position on our left, a high hill, which he thought we ought to occupy—an opinion in which I concurred from his description of it, and so told him.

Briscoe was obviously referring to Big Round Top. Humphreys thus contradicted Sickles and Birney, who both claimed in their testimony that the position had been occupied.

The ground where I formed was a hollow, from which the ground sloped up in my rear to the ridge which I have called Round Top ridge, and also up towards the Emmitsburg road in my front, which road ran along the crest of another ridge. As far as I could see, the ground fell off again towards the west just beyond the Emmitsburg road. Perhaps a little after 4 o'clock I received orders from General Sickles to move up near the Emmitsburg road, and at the same time I was authorized to call on General Hunt, the chief of artillery, if I wanted any more artillery than Lieutenant Seely's battery,[6] which had been assigned to me that morning. I immediately moved my command forward, placing my first brigade close up to the Emmitsburg road, just under the crest, perhaps fifty feet or so in some places from the road. I put Lieutenant Seely with his battery on the right of the log-house I have referred to. I increased my front line by a regiment from my second brigade, which remained in rear of my first brigade; my third brigade, from that time forward, was, by direction

6. Lieutenant Francis W. Seeley's Battery K, 4th U.S. Artillery.

of the corps commander, left to the control of General Birney. As we moved up the enemy opened with artillery upon our left, but it did not amount to much for some time, doing very little damage. I sent an aide-de-camp to General Sickles and asked whether I should attack the enemy, and received for answer No; to remain where I was. I had previously said to him that the enemy were in a pretty strong place in front, but, nevertheless, if he was to be attacked we were ready to go forward. The artillery fire went on increasing on my left, but on my front, or to my left front, it did not amount to a great deal. The enemy in my front made several demonstrations to attack, but they were nothing more than demonstrations.

When I found that my third brigade was to be used entirely for the support of General Birney, I think I sent to General Hancock, of the 2d corps, to inquire whether the division on his left, General Caldwell's, was ready to support me, and I am under the impression that I sent a request to him to throw forward some troops between my right and his left. The front line of my division was between a half and three-quarters of a mile in front of the main line, and in front of the troops from which I was to draw support, and there was this open space on my right. The orchards in my front and towards my right were very thick orchards, and a very heavy force of skirmishers could get pretty well into them without being seen by my command, and I felt a little uncomfortable about my right; probably it was in consequence of that message that General Hancock did send forward some artillery and a couple of regiments.

Humphreys's testimony before the committee about how various units were drawn off from his command is very professional and subdued, but his feelings at the time were quite different. On July 4, Humphreys raged against both Sickles and Birney in a letter to his wife, writing, "Had my Division been left intact I should have driven the enemy back, but this ruinous habit *(it don't deserve the name of system) of putting troops in position & then drawing off its reserves & second line to help others, who if similarly disposed would need no such help, is disgusting."*[7]

The fire of the artillery began to get pretty hot on my left. My own artillery had very little to do. I changed the position of Lieutenant Seely's battery from the right of the house a little further down to the left, so that he might fire bet-

7. Quoted in *GC*, 399.

ter into a battery that had annoyed us a little; and I sent for another battery, (Turnbull's[8] was sent me,) which I posted where Lieutenant Seely's had been. My left was near to General Graham's brigade of General Birney's division. I think it must have been as late as half past five before the musketry and artillery got to be serious. By that time it had reached to [392] something like the dimensions of a battle, and increased in hotness. During this time one of my regiments, Colonel Seawall's,[9] [*sic*] of the third brigade, reported to me and relieved the skirmishers of Graham's brigade, of Birney's division, who were in his front, and extended partly over my front.

It was a little after 6 o'clock when I received an earnest message from General Sickles, through a staff officer, to send a regiment to support Graham's brigade, as they were very hard pressed; at the same time he left it to my own judgment whether I could send it. I surmised, from the way the enemy were attacking, that I should be attacked in a very short time. I told those officers, from General Sickles and General Graham, that I was disposed to give them every assistance I could, but I could very ill afford it then, for I knew I might be attacked at any moment. While these officers were there, Colonel Sewall sent in word to me that the enemy were evidently deploying from the wood and were going to advance upon me. So urgent was the appeal, however, that I sent one of my regiments to General Graham, and at the same time sent a staff officer back to the 2d corps to send me up a brigade.

The enemy began to advance on me, and my artillery opened upon them. The space to my left, between a battery under General Graham and Lieutenant Seely's battery, was such that I could not throw any troops upon the front line. I found it was necessary to get my artillery out of the way as quickly as possible, intending to advance my whole line and pour in a fire as the enemy advanced. Just at that time I received an order from General Birney informing me that General Sickles was wounded, and that he had succeeded to the command of the corps, and that his division was going to fall back and form a line extending towards my right from the Round Top ridge, in rear of and oblique to my present line, and that I must change front and form on that line. In complying with this order I had to change front to the rear, under a heavy fire of infantry and artillery, just as I wanted to throw forward somewhat my troops to the attack. While I was making the movement the troops on my left,

8. Lieutenant John G. Turnbull's Battery F/K, 3rd U.S. Artillery.

9. 5th New Jersey.

that were to continue the line to the Round Top ridge, did not stop there, but passed to or beyond the Round Top ridge. I formed my line and extended it out to the left as far as possible to close up this aperture, and by that time was attacked on my flank as well as on my front. I never have been under a hotter artillery and musketry fire combined. I may have been under a hotter musketry fire. For a moment I thought the day was lost. I did not order my troops to fall back rapidly, because, so far as I could see, the crest in my rear was vacant, and I knew that when troops got to moving back rapidly it was exceedingly difficult to stop them just where you wanted to stop them.

At that moment I received an order to fall back to the Round Top ridge, which I did, falling back slowly, suffering a very heavy loss. I did not fall back rapidly, because I disliked to fall back at double quick before the enemy, and besides I did not suppose I could rally my troops, or that any troops could be rallied at the place where the line was to be formed, if the movement backward was made rapidly. I reached this ridge, leaving some three guns behind, the horses of which had been killed, and rallied my division, or the remnants of it, on the ridge. As the enemy came up they received the fire of the 2d corps on my right, and my troops joined in, and we drove those fellows back. My men brought back two, if not all three, of the guns we had left. I am under the impression we brought off all three of them ourselves, though I understand that the 2d corps claims that they brought off one of them. These men of mine did not wait for any orders, but went forward, and as there were so few of them I went with them to bring them back before they got too far from the main line. By that time it was dusk, and the fighting ceased for the day.

When I sent the regiment to General Graham, I immediately sent to General Hancock and asked him to send me as many troops as he could to support me, [393] and at the time I was changing front to the rear, two regiments of the 2d corps were brought out and posted very advantageously, and formed a protection to my flank. I lost about 2,000 men killed and wounded, out of something like 5,000 men. That is the part my division took in the battle of the 2d of July at Gettysburg.

Question. Did you consider your line of the 2d of July as really too far advanced from the main line?

Answer. Yes. I do not know what the enemy's plans would have been if we had occupied the main line and not the advanced line. I think, very probably, he would have done what he did the next day—that is, have attacked us on that Round Top ridge, advancing over somewhat the same ground from which

I had fallen back; but it will be seen that we were driven from this advanced position which we took up, and were not driven the next day from Round Top ridge, although we had a reduced force then.

Question. Suppose you had taken your position at first in the position to which you finally retired; would it not have been better?

Answer. Undoubtedly, as the result showed.

This was not the type of testimony the committee wanted. Humphreys's account was an indictment of their star witness and undermined Sickles's claim that he had saved the Union army by his unauthorized advance.

By Mr. Odell:

Question. Did not your advanced line, from a half to three-quarters of a mile, expose your division to the concentrated force of the enemy?

Answer. Undoubtedly; they waited until they broke the left before they attacked me. I saw all the troops on my left moving out of the way, and before I was heavily engaged I saw their artillery on the left approaching very much closer.

By the chairman:

Question. How did your troops behave?

Answer. I think they behaved very well. It is the most trying position in which troops can be placed. I wanted to move forward and attack, because there is always a great deal in the spirit of advancing, even though it be but a few paces. If I had not received the order to change my position to the rear, I should have attacked, and I do not think I should have suffered a great deal more than I did, and I should have punished the enemy very severely.

Question. Suppose you had advanced still further; would you not have been exposed to a still heavier fire?

Answer. I should have caught it very severely, but still I should have punished them more, and probably we should have been broken so much in a very short time that we would have been forced to move back very rapidly. The first corps was, I think, brought up in the mean time, and helped to fill the gap, but so far as I could see when we were falling back the gap was open, and I was afraid they would drive us through it.

By Mr. Odell:

Question. Did not your advanced position also expose our army to the danger of being cut in two?

Answer. No, I do not think it did. In one sense it was not a gap, and they would not attempt to go through there except when they pressed forward on me. They would simply attempt to drive me back and try to break me to pieces.

Question. That is what I mean. If you had been broken in pieces, was not all this space you were to occupy an open space?

Answer. Yes, sir, that would have been vacant, but another corps was brought up and put in there. The 1st corps and portions of the 6th corps came up and occupied ground on the left, and the 5th corps, or part of it, was brought up and occupied the Round Top, and the ground on its right.

For the more radical members of the committee, this was a dangerous line of questioning. If Humphreys had answered affirmatively to Odell's first question, he would have implied that Sickles's advance had in fact threatened the army with defeat. Such testimony would have seriously undermined Sickles's credibility and damaged one of Wade's favorite themes, that a lack of cooperation among the corps commanders caused much of the army's miseries.

Here, Odell seems to be trying to correct some of Sickles's most damaging testimony against Meade.

[394] By the chairman:

Question. This was on the 2d of July?

Answer. Yes, sir.

Question. And that finished that day's work?

Answer. Yes, sir; during that night I remained on the left of the position of the 2d corps. I received directions in the course of the evening to move to the rear and fill up my ammunition and get rations issued—some of my men had had no rations during the 2d, but that was their own fault. I requested to be permitted to remain until daylight, which was granted. At daylight I got up and began to move to the rear, when the enemy commenced shelling me very fiercely. I waited half an hour, perhaps an hour, to see what they were going to do, before I moved to the rear.

Humphreys was mistaken. The only report of an artillery bombardment of his division early in the morning of July 3 is that of Brigadier General Joseph B. Carr, commanding the First Brigade. Neither of the other two brigade commanders reported receiving artillery fire during the morning, nor was it mentioned in Humphreys's official report.[10]

10. *OR*, vol. 27, pt. 1, pp. 544, 559, 571.

I then moved there and got together with my first brigade, which was with the first division, and got together as many of my men as I could, and put my division into some shape. By direction of General Birney I then moved up and formed my division in masses in rear of the right of the 5th corps and the portions of the 6th corps which were towards the left of the line. I remained there until about 1 o'clock in the afternoon, when I was ordered to move quickly up towards the right and form my division into columns of attack, and be prepared to advance upon the enemy. I did so at once, and remained massed in rear of some batteries which were near the ground I had first of all occupied on the night of the 1st July. I sustained a loss there from the artillery fire of some very valuable officers and somewhat less than a hundred men. We did not advance to attack, and the enemy did not renew their attack. Towards night I returned to my position further to the left, where I remained until we marched from Gettysburg.

It is surprising that Wade did not pursue Humphreys's testimony about this aborted attack. He may have realized that an opportunity for an effective attack did not really exist. Humphreys commanded a single division and a severely mauled one at that. Moreover, the Union troops to Humphreys's front were hopelessly intermingled and would have been of little use in an attack, while Lee's artillery and the rest of the Army of Northern Virginia waited across the valley.

Prior to Pickett's charge, the idea of a counterattack was considered and abandoned by Meade. The assault would have been composed of the First, Second, and Third Corps. Yet in their official reports, both Newton of the First Corps and Birney of the Third Corps only reported providing support. Hancock of the Second Corps thought that an attack was planned, but he was wounded and taken from the field.[11]

Question. The battle of the 3d of July was the last of the fighting there?

Answer. Yes, it was the last battle there. I think I had between 2,500 and 3,000 men for duty on that day.

Question. What was your loss in that battle?

Answer. I lost, principally on the 2d of July, over 1,900 men in killed and wounded in my division of something less than 5,000 men for duty.

Question. Your division, then, lost as severely as any division in the army?

11. Ibid., 199, 262, 488; Jordan, *Winfield Scott Hancock*, 99–100; George Meade, *The Battle of Gettysburg: From the "Life and Letters of George Gordon Meade,"* ed. George Gordon Meade (1924; reprint, York, Pa.: First Capitol Antiquarian Book & Paper Market, 1988), 89.

Answer. I think it did. It was a fine division; the men were good soldiers.

Question. What was the condition of our army after that battle was over?

Answer. I remained very close with my division. I can only say that the spirit of my men was just as fine after the battle as at any time. I know that on the afternoon of the 3d of July, when I moved up, the greatest difficulty I had was to keep my men (a part of them) from jumping over the little breastwork in front of the artillery, and advancing against the enemy without any orders. They were full of fight, and felt angry at the way they had been cut up the day before. So far as my division was concerned, they were in fine spirits after the battle; they were not in the least disheartened.

Question. What was the reason you did not pursue after the enemy retired? They retired on the night of the 3d of July, did they not?

Answer. I think not; but I cannot tell you about that. We, our army, suffered very severely there; we never suffered as much in killed and wounded in any battle or series of battles. We lost some 17,000 or 18,000 men in killed and wounded. I do not know why we did not advance and attack them; they had also been damaged very severely.

As a division commander Humphreys's concern was with his own men; strategy was the purview of corps commanders and the army commander. From his vantage point Humphreys had no idea if the rebels were in general retreat or not.

Humphreys's estimation of losses was short of the mark. Actual losses were nearly 23,000 men.[12]

Question. They had had as hard a time of it as we had had?

Answer. It is estimated that they lost more than we did in killed and wounded.

Losses to the Army of Northern Virginia were almost exactly equal to losses in the Union army, though even today it is difficult to determine exact number of losses in Lee's army.[13]

Question. Was not the position of our army there rather a defensive than an offensive one?

12. John W. Busey and David G. Martin, *Regimental Strengths and Losses at Gettysburg* (Hightstown, N.J.: Longstreet House, 1994), 314. Losses placed at 22,813.

13. Ibid. Losses placed at 22,874.

Answer. Yes; the battle was a defensive battle, and to that I think is to be ascribed our success; we had the advantage in that.

This was not the answer Wade wanted. In his estimation, battles were won by aggressive generals. That a defensively fought battle was the greatest victory of the war to date was not welcome news.

[395] Question. What I wanted to know was whether they, who took the offensive, would not be more fatigued by such a fight then we, who acted upon the defensive alone?

Answer. As to that, I do not think there would be much difference, as moving up to this position or that position would fatigue us also. The loss would make a difference, and I have understood that their loss was considerably greater than ours.

Question. Which army do you think had the greatest numbers?

Answer. I think, from all I could learn, that if there was any superiority in the number of infantry it was with the enemy. It was estimated that they were superior to us in numbers. The 6th corps did not get up until the evening of the 2d of July; they made a march of 32 miles to get up to where we were. But that corps was not materially engaged in the battle; I understand they lost only 100 or 200 men out of the whole of that corps; and I am under the impression that this corps numbered something like 15,000 men. The absence of that corps from any active participation in the battle would reduce the number of those actually engaged very materially.

Officers in the Federal army had consistently overestimated Lee's strength, and would continue to do so. Humphreys testified that the army had actually fought at a numerical disadvantage, which made its victory even more impressive. Yet this was not the case. In the most exhaustive modern study of strengths and losses at Gettysburg, historians John Busey and David Martin place the strength of infantry at 71,816 for the Army of the Potomac and 57,544 for the Army of Northern Virginia.[14]

Question. The 6th corps was pretty fresh at the close of the battle?

Answer. Well, sir, that march of 32 miles would use them up; would fatigue them a great deal more than fighting the battle. And we had had a pretty severe

14. Ibid., 230.

time marching before that. I was very much fatigued myself the night I got there at 1 o'clock, as I had been actively engaged all day, which was a sultry one, making examination of the ground about Emmitsburg.

It is impossible to tell whether Humphreys saw where Wade's question was leading or whether he was just giving his opinion, but he was not helping Wade's case.

Question. Do you recollect at what time our army did advance in pursuit of the enemy?

Answer. The corps I belonged to did not march from there until the 6th of July; but we did not follow in direct pursuit, as that would have taken us to mountain passes in possession of the enemy. The 6th corps was moved forward in direct pursuit as far as the mountains, I understand; on what day I do not know. I did not leave my division, as I might receive orders at any moment, and did not, therefore, learn what was gong on outside of the corps. I did not go off the ground, not to my hospital even, which was a mile or two in the rear, though I sent my aides-de-camp down to see the wounded.

Question. General Sickles's corps was the first that was attacked on the 2d of July?

Answer. Yes, sir; they began the fight—that is, were the first engaged, though demonstrations of attack were made on other corps during the day, as I learn, but I do not know at all what attacks at other places amounted to. A division commander rarely knows more than what transpires on his immediate ground.

Ewell's Second Corps had made a none-too-determined attack on Culp's Hill and Cemetery Ridge shortly after Longstreet's attack on the Confederate right.

Question. You were down at Williamsport, where the enemy recrossed?

Answer. Yes; I accepted the position of chief of staff on the night of the 8th of July, while my division was on the march from Gettysburg towards Middletown.

Question. Some military men have thought that we ought to have attacked the enemy before he crossed the river there?

Answer. O, yes, undoubtedly.

Question. What is your opinion as a military man?

Answer. It certainly was that we should have attacked them as soon as possible. The army reached the Antietam on the evening of the 10th of July. On the 11th the right of the army was thrown forward, and strong reconnaissances were pushed out to feel the enemy, and see what his position was; and the different corps were directed to take such ground as would put them in connexion with each other.

The following series of questions reflects a lack of preparation not found with earlier witnesses. Wade jumped from one point to another, which suggests he was not getting the answers that he wanted from Humphreys and was searching for something to assist him. It also may indicate that earlier witnesses (with the exception of Meade) had discussed or even partially scripted their testimony with Wade prior to their appearance before the committee.

Question. The army received some re-enforcements after the battle of Gettysburg, [396] and before the enemy recrossed at Williamsport, did it not—some from Harpers Ferry?

Answer. I think General French had some 6,000 or 7,000 men, which he had taken from the force which had been at Harpers Ferry; I think he was near Frederick at the time of the battle of Gettysburg.

Question. He joined our army before the enemy recrossed the Potomac?

Answer. Yes; I think he joined the army on the 8th, and his division was attached to the 3d corps and formed a portion of it. I do not think the army received any material increase after that. I forget whether it was on the 11th or 12th of July that General William F. Smith reported that he was within available distance with a division. The numbers of that division I do not recollect, but it was composed entirely of raw troops. So far as I heard it mentioned, it was said General Smith did not have much opinion of the effectiveness of the troops that he commanded.

Question. After so fierce an engagement as that at Gettysburg, with such a heavy artillery fire, did it ever occur to you that the enemy, being so far from the base of his operations, must have been pretty short of ammunition?

Answer. I think he ought not to have been; I think that a general who starts out on an operation like that which General Lee was engaged in should above all things, see that he had ammunition enough for his purposes. He need not have troubled himself much about provisions, but I think he should be pretty careful about his ammunition train. The question of ammunition did not, at any time, enter very seriously into my mind. I recollect that it was said, when we were at Williamsport, that General Lee had an ammunition train advancing from Winchester. The expenditure of artillery ammunition by our army at Gettysburg was a little more than 100 rounds per gun. I do not think that we expended more than half our infantry ammunition, if that much. Lee's army did not probably expend more ammunition than we did. I have some indistinct recollection of its being reported that Lee had received some ammunition while at Williamsport, but I was very much occupied at that time, particularly on the 12th of July, when I received and sent off a very great number of despatches, which I wrote with my own hand.

This statement reveals Humphreys's opinion about the enemy's ammunition at Williamsport. Unlike most of the other witnesses before the committee, both Meade and Humphreys believed that Lee had received supplies of ammunition while at Williamsport.

Question. You were then acting as chief of staff?

Answer. I was chief of staff at that time; I began as such on the morning of the 9th of July.

Question. Were you consulted with as to whether an attack should be made there?

Answer. Yes, sir; in this way: On the morning of the 12th of July General Meade expressed to me his views, which were to move the army forward and feel the enemy, and to attack them at such points as he should find it best to attack. We knew something of the general character of their position, but it was a very general knowledge. General Meade asked my opinion. I replied that I coincided with him; that I was in favor of the operation he proposed, the advance of the army and a reconnaissance in force, as it is called, to be converted into an attack. We could not see the position of the enemy well; their skirmishers acted as a sort of curtain, to keep us from looking too closely at them. A circular note was therefore sent to corps commanders to meet at 8 o'clock in the evening at general headquarters; they were to be brought there for the purpose of receiving instructions, and to give all the information they had collected during the day concerning the position of the enemy, &c. They met, and were generally of the opinion that it was not proper to make the attack then.

By Mr. Odell:

Question. How many were there in the council?

Answer. I think there were seven corps commanders there. I do not include [397] the commander of the cavalry corps, though he was present during part of the time. I do not know that he took any part in the discussion, and I have never considered myself as forming a part of the council of war. I have been present at times, but I considered myself as being there rather for the purpose of giving any information that might be wanted. I do not think that the chief of staff forms part of the council properly, therefore I should take very little part in any discussion. In fact, it was hardly a discussion, but, as I understood, a presentation of such acknowledge [*sic*] as the corps commanders had of the enemy and the ground they occupied, and the expression of their opinion as to whether we ought or ought not to attack. I was in the tent part of the time, and part of it outside, the tent being small and crowded. I think there were two commanders, that is, General Howard and General Wadsworth, the latter temporarily commanding the 1st corps—General Newton being too unwell to be present—those two, I think, were the only corps commanders who advised an attack. I do not know that they advised it; they assented to advancing upon general principles, rather than upon special knowledge. General Warren, chief engineer, was present part of the time, and expressed himself in favor of General Meade's views. Finding this very positive opinion on the part of the corps commanders against attacking, General Meade deferred to them so far as to delay until he could examine our own ground and that of the enemy, so far as it was possible to do so. I rode with him the next morning, and we saw something of the general character of the ground, and some part of the ground in detail occupied by the enemy and by our troops, and upon returning, by direction of General Meade, I prepared instructions to the different corps commanders to move the next morning and make reconnaissances in force, supported by the whole army—a movement similar in most respects to the one which General Meade wanted to make that morning. They did advance on the morning of the 14th of July to make this reconnaissance in force, intending to feel the enemy and to attack him where he was weakest, if it promised to be successful. He had, however, retired in the night.

By Mr. Gooch:

Question. Did you counsel with General Meade that it was best to attack the enemy in that position?

Answer. Yes, sir, in the manner in which the advance on the morning of the 14th was made.

Question. Did you ever obtain any subsequent knowledge or opinion which led you to suppose that it would not have been advisable to make that attack?

Answer. Subsequent information showed that the enemy had a very strong position, and indicated that had we made an attack we should have suffered very severely. But it was proper that we should have made an attack at that time—that is, a reconnaissance in force, converting it into a battle upon circumstances warranting it.

Humphreys's reply could do nothing to challenge the incontrovertible fact that Meade had not attacked the enemy at Williamsport. It did reinforce his testimony that Meade had planned to do so, thus rebutting the charge that Meade had not wanted to fight. Humphreys also said that Meade was willing to take chances at the appropriate time. Attacking a position with limited knowledge of the enemy may not have been the bold, slashing move that the committee seemed to feel had been needed, but Meade's plan showed more aggressiveness than the committee gave him credit for.

Question. You still think that it would have been the better course to have made a reconnaissance in force?

Answer. I still think it would have been better to have made a reconnaissance in force, and have made an attack if we had found some parts of the enemy's line were not as strong as others. We might, perhaps, have found towards the right that we could have attacked them. It was very strong ground, and if we had made an attack there is no doubt that we should have lost very severely. But I cannot pretend to say now whether, if I had seen all that ground, I should or should not have counseled an attack. It would have been right for us to have made that reconnaissance in force, and to have been guided afterwards by the developments made by that reconnaissance.

I think that the public, and probably a great many officers, confound attacking field-works or intrenchments, where there is a small body of men posted, with attacking a whole army that has thrown up intrenchments. Now that is [398] a different thing altogether. You may take field-works, in which there are small garrisons, by assault; but when you have to attack a whole army, well intrenched, you will suffer terribly in getting up to them.

Question. If we had made a reconnaissance in force, as was suggested, and had been repulsed, would any serious disaster have followed to us?

Answer. I think we could have maintained our position there. We might have been broken, but we had pretty good ground to which to have withdrawn and withstood a return attack on their part; and I do not think, if they had attacked us in turn, that we could not have driven them back.

Question. Suppose, on the other hand, we had broken their lines, what would have been the consequence to them?

Answer. They would have suffered very severely; I suppose they would have endeavored to retreat rapidly up the Potomac.

Humphreys may well have been thinking of the mixed force of infantry and cavalry that General Benjamin F. Kelley had at Fairview, Maryland. On July 14, Kelley wired Halleck that he was moving on Williamsport as ordered. Later that morning Kelley received word that Longstreet's corps was within supporting distance of Williamsport and changed his mind about his advance. Evidently Humphreys, with some reason, thought little of the value of Kelley's troops.[15]

An army of 60,000 or 80,000 men is not to be knocked in pieces by any such battle as we have fought as yet. It is a rare thing to read of an army being completely broken in pieces, so that it cannot be collected together again and take up a position so as to make it difficult to dislodge them from it, especially in the country where we were. It is a broken country, full of good positions, where a good stand may be made. I do not think it would have been utter ruin to that army if we had defeated it there, though we should have done them a great deal of injury—damaged them very badly, no doubt.

Question. They would have been in about as bad a position or condition as an army of that size well could be?

Answer. Yes, sir.

By the chairman:

Question. While we could have made a reconnaissance in force, and felt them pretty smartly without any great hazard to ourselves, if we had been successful it would have been almost destruction to them. Was it not, then, unmilitary not to make the attempt?

Answer. We did make the attempt the morning of the 14th.

Question. But after the enemy had all gone.

Answer. The order was issued before they had gone; they moved away after the order was issued. There were no indications of their moving until the morning of the 14th.

Testimony on the Bristoe and Mine Run campaigns is omitted. One of Wade's questions about those campaigns is of interest, however, not for the information

15. *OR*, vol. 27, pt. 1, p. 85; pt. 3, pp. 698–9.

it sought but for what it revealed about the chairman's attitude toward the war. Wade prefaced a question with the phrase, "When you invade an enemy's country." Such rhetoric infuriated Lincoln, who had rebuked army officers (including Meade) for using similar language. Wade was one of the most powerful men in the Senate, and his equation of the Confederacy with "enemy's country" surely would have been deeply troubling to Lincoln. Wade's language suggests that he sought to subjugate and occupy the Confederacy, not welcome the South back into the Union.

[402] Question. It is the enemy's policy, undoubtedly, to spin out and protract this war as much as possible, and your policy to finish it as quickly as you can?

Answer. Yes. Yet there is this to be said: the commander of that army can never forget that he is to protect Washington, as well as to carry on an offensive war. And the difference of numbers in our favor is not great enough to admit of our making such movements as will oblige the enemy to fight us with equal advantages of ground. For instance, suppose we had had force enough when we made that movement on Mine run to have left a heavy column near Culpeper, and had moved on his flank and brought his army away from the Rapidan. Then having this column in position, concealed, which might have [403] been done, we could have thrown it on those portions of the enemy's lines which were not occupied, and have moved it to attack his left flank, in connection with an attack on his front. If we had had force enough for that, there would have been no question as to the result. But such movements as these, being double movements, require a very great force, a very large superiority of numbers in order to be carried on successfully. That is the experience of military men.

Humphreys had offered the best defense of Meade yet presented before the committee. By testifying that he had been ordered to look for a possible battlefield in the Emmitsburg area, he demonstrated both that the Pipe Creek circular was only a contingency plan and that Meade was seeking a battle. Humphreys also asserted that Gettysburg had been won precisely because it was a defensive battle.

Humphreys agreed with the committee that an attack should have been made at Williamsport and pointed out that Meade had tried to do so. Though delayed a day by the decision of his corps commanders, Meade had issued an order for an attack.

11 Major General Winfield Scott Hancock

THOSE TESTIFYING ON Meade's behalf represented some of the best of the officer corps. Among them was Major General Winfield Scott Hancock, who commanded the Second Corps at Gettysburg. Nicknamed "Hancock the Superb" by McClellan for his actions on the Peninsula in 1862, he was widely considered one of the best officers in the Army of the Potomac.[1]

Born in Pennsylvania in 1824, Hancock graduated from West Point in the bottom third of his class of 1844. Following frontier service Hancock was stationed in Los Angeles during the early months of the Civil War. When he finally arrived in the East, McClellan secured for him a commission as brigadier general in the volunteers. With exemplary service in the Peninsula and Maryland campaigns, Hancock rose to major general as of November 29, 1862. He distinguished himself at Fredericksburg and Chancellorsville, where he commanded the First Division, Second Corps. Following Chancellorsville Hancock was given command of the Second Corps.[2]

Hancock's reputation among his fellow officers led to repeated rumors that he would be offered command of the Army of the Potomac to replace Meade, his close friend. In December 1863, following the Bristoe and Mine Run campaigns, Halleck intimated as much to Hancock (who promptly relayed the story to Meade). Such talk appeared again in July 1864 after a visit to the army by Senators Chandler and Morton S. Wilkinson of Minnesota. As late as October 11, 1864, Grant wrote Stanton of the possibility of Hancock replacing Meade in command of the army.[3]

Except for Grant's letter to Stanton, these offers were all related to various

1. Jordan, *Winfield Scott Hancock,* 44.

2. Warner, *Generals in Blue,* 202–3; Boatner, *Civil War Dictionary,* 372.

3. *MG,* 272–3; *LLM,* 2:163–4; Jordan, *Winfield Scott Hancock,* 169.

people by Hancock himself and do not appear to have any official foundation. Unfortunately for Hancock, there was no real probability of his promotion. Two things worked against him. First, he was and remained a close friend of McClellan. In the eyes of the committee and many members of Congress, this fact alone disqualified him from high command. Secondly, and even more damning, Hancock was a Democrat, which made him totally unacceptable to radical Republicans. He believed that the Federal government had no right to interfere with a domestic institution such as slavery. Yet he believed fervently in the Union. With the outbreak of war, his choice had been simple: "he was a northern man and would adhere to his people, even though he knew they were wrong." Hancock's stand for the Union might have been popular with members of the committee, but his disapproval of the Emancipation Proclamation was not. Hancock believed that the proclamation was unconstitutional, and that it had expanded the goals of the war beyond reuniting the states. He was not happy about the change.[4]

In looking at Hancock one is often reminded of the twentieth-century general Douglas MacArthur, whose father had served in the Civil War. Like the more famous MacArthur, Hancock had political ambitions, eventually losing the 1880 presidential election to James Garfield by only 7,018 popular votes. Like MacArthur, Hancock was also very aware of the power of the press; in 1864 he went so far as to place a reporter, Finley Anderson of the *New York Herald,* on his staff as an adjutant. Long after the Civil War, George Alfred Townsend, another reporter for the *Herald,* said that Hancock had told him that "he did not wish any personal laudation." Yet he had become irritated when he thought that Townsend was following his instructions too literally. Hancock "certainly considered that the proper care of his public image was essential."[5]

[403] Testimony of Major General W. S. Hancock.

Washington, March 22, 1864.
Major General W. S. Hancock sworn and examined.

By the chairman:

Question. Go on with your narrative of the operations of the army of the Potomac after General Meade took command of it.

4. Quoted in Jordan, *Winfield Scott Hancock,* 33, 59.
5. The electoral vote was more decisive, 214 to 155. Ibid., 58–9, 306, 327–8 n. 5.

Answer. I arrived in Frederick on the 28th of June. General Meade had probably been placed in command on the night of the 27th. On the 29th the whole army moved, making very long and rapid marches. I marched with my whole corps, (the 2d corps,) of which I then had the command, from 32 to 34 miles that day—from Frederick city to Uniontown, arriving there about 10 o'clock that night. It was very sultry weather, and my troops were much exhausted when I got there. I found that the rebel General Stuart, with his cavalry, was at Westminster, six miles ahead of me. I knew that General Gregg, of our cavalry, was to have been in Westminster that night; but I knew that he would not be there, because I had met him on the way, and the roads being narrow, the artillery of his column had been interfered with by our infantry. General Sedgwick had also been ordered to march to Westminster with his corps; but knowing the very long march I had made, and that General Sedgwick had the outside of me, I felt certain that he could not get there that night. We took up a line, as it were, along the general direction of the Baltimore turnpike. I was to have gone to Frizelburg, but General Meade authorized me to stop at Uniontown.

As soon as I found that Stuart, with his cavalry, was at Westminster, I sent a note to General Meade, giving him the information. General Meade sent for General Pleasonton, who denied that Stuart was there, saying that he had received information from his staff officers that General Gregg was there. The mistake arose in this way, I have no doubt; General Gregg had got to New Windsor, and the name of Windsor was confounded with that of Westminster. My report of the matter was not credited, and no effort was made to catch Stuart. If there had been, I have no doubt we should have inflicted serious damage upon him; indeed, I do not believe he could have gotten away. At all events, that rapid march of our whole army had one grand effect—it placed us so near Stuart that instead of marching up to Gettysburg, as he probably would otherwise have done, he was forced over towards the Susquehanna, which I have no doubt prevented him from joining Lee earlier in the action, which was an advantage to us. I remained at Uniontown during the next day, the 30th, because my troops were very much exhausted; but other movements were probably in operation.

Hancock was largely correct. The fast movement of the Army of the Potomac had forced Stuart east, but he was already a day and a half late in meeting with Ewell's Second Corps. This delay was caused in no small part by Stuart's refusal to abandon some 125 captured supply wagons. His appearance at Gettysburg late on July 2 was then, and is now, criticized as one of the reasons for Lee's defeat.

Hancock's biographer David Jordan blames Pleasonton's "ignorant posturing" for the lost opportunity in regard to Stuart, but Jordan's explanation lacks a comprehensive analysis. Brigadier General David Gregg's Second Cavalry Division was near New Windsor, about ten miles from Westminster. Gregg's troops were the closest Union forces to Stuart; they were, however, totally exhausted. Captain William E. Miller of the Third Pennsylvania wrote, "The men fell asleep in their saddles . . . and whenever the column halted . . . horses would also fall asleep." Gregg and his senior brigade commander, Colonel John B. McIntosh, were both sick with an intestinal ailment, leaving Colonel Pennock Huey in command. But Huey was so distrusted by both Gregg and McIntosh that for many hours no one told him of the situation.[6]

Meanwhile, Hancock's corps had completed a fourteen-hour march of over thirty miles with packs of fifty pounds "under the broiling sun in the hottest month of our year." Hancock notified Meade of Stuart's location around 10:00 P.M.; it was 12:15 A.M. when Hancock received the mistaken report of Gregg's men. If Hancock had marched to Westminster at that time, he could have reached Stuart before he left. Yet it is debatable whether tired, slow-moving infantry could have done more than chase off the rebel cavalry.[7]

On the morning of the 1st of July I received an order to march to Taneytown. I arrived there about 11 o'clock, and massed my troops. I then went to the headquarters of General Meade and reported to him. While I was there General Meade told me all his plans. He said he had made up his mind to fight a battle on what was known as Pipe creek; that he had not seen the ground [404] but judging from the map it presented more favorable features than any other position that he could see; that he had sent his engineers there to examine the position and note all its strong features, and that he was then preparing an order for that movement. Shortly after that conversation General Meade received a message from General Reynolds, who at Gettysburg was really a mask, in order to allow this movement (occupying the line of Pipe creek) to go on in his rear. But it turned out that the enemy started to march down the same road a little earlier than was anticipated. Therefore, when General Reynolds attempted to move up from a point between Emmitsburg and Gettys-

6. Quoted in Longacre, *Cavalry,* 170–1.

7. Jordan, *Winfield Scott Hancock,* 79; *OR,* vol. 27, pt. 1, p. 1084; *GC,* 669 n. 91.

burg to Gettysburg, where he had been directed to move that morning, it became a race between him and the enemy which should first get to Gettysburg. But General Buford, by a persistent deployment of his cavalry, and continually attacking the enemy, held them in check until General Reynolds beat them to Gettysburg. General Reynolds at once advanced to the relief of Buford, and engaged the enemy, knowing that it was no time to inquire about future operations, and that the only thing was to attack the enemy and delay him until the commander of the army should come to some decision. Whether General Reynolds had received this order designating Pipe creek as the line of battle which General Meade told me was in preparation, I do not know. General Reynolds engaged the enemy and the 11th corps, under General Howard, came to his assistance.

To this point, Hancock's testimony on the Pipe Creek line must have been encouraging to the committee. Hancock asserted that Meade had definitely decided on the Pipe Creek line as the place to do battle, in contradiction to Meade's own testimony.

General Meade heard, about the time I have stated, that this affair was going on at Gettysburg. He felt that the matter was being precipitated very heavily upon him, and he felt the responsibility. Shortly afterwards he heard that General Reynolds was either killed or mortally wounded. I had returned at that time to my troops.

I soon received an order, dated 1.10 P.M., directing me to proceed to the front, and in the event of the death of General Reynolds, or his inability to command, to assume the command of all the troops there, consisting of the 1st, 3d, and 11th corps. (Order appended, marked A.)

There were actually two orders issued to Hancock. The first, timed 12:30 P.M., noted that Meade did not know if Reynolds had received the Pipe Creek circular, which would leave the center of the army's position open. Hancock was ordered to move to Gettysburg, with instructions for his actions under various circumstances.[8]

After Meade received word of Reynolds's death, he issued his second order. This order, timed 1:10 P.M., instructed Hancock to transfer command of his Second Corps to Brigadier General John Gibbon and go immediately to Gettys-

8. *OR*, vol. 27, pt. 3, p. 461.

burg where, if Reynolds was dead, he was to take command of the First, Third, and Eleventh Corps. Hancock was also to determine if Gettysburg was better ground than the proposed Pipe Creek line; if so, Meade would scrap his plans and concentrate the army at Gettysburg.[9]

There is a difference between the copy of Meade's order attached to Hancock's testimony and the one submitted by Meade as Exhibit H. Meade's copy reads, "If you think the ground and position there a (better) suitable one to fight a battle," while Hancock's copy reads, "If you think the ground and position there a better one to fight a battle." In later years, Hancock admirers cited Hancock's copy of this order as evidence that Meade put the choice of battlefield on Hancock's shoulders.

I started a little before half past 1, turning over the command of my corps to General Gibbon, under General Meade's directions. General Gibbon was not the next in rank in that corps, but he was the one General Meade directed should assume the command, as he considered him the most suitable person for it.

Brigadier General John C. Caldwell, commander of the Second Corps, First Division, was senior to Gibbon.

Several such instances occurred during that battle. General Meade, prior to the battle, showed me or told me of a letter he had received from the Secretary of War on this subject. The government recognizing the difficulty of the situation, believing that a battle was imminent, and might occur in one, two, or three days, and not knowing the views of General Meade in relation to his commanders, the Secretary of War wrote him a note, authorizing him to make any changes in his army that he pleased, and that he would be sustained by the President and himself. That did not make it legal, because it was contrary to law to place a junior officer over a senior. At the same time it was one of those emergencies in which General Meade was authorized, as before stated, to exercise that power. I was not the senior of either General Howard, of the 11th corps, or General Sickles, of the 3d corps. My commission bore date on the same day with theirs; by my prior commission they both ranked me. Of course it was not a very agreeable office for me to fill, to go and take command of my seniors. However, I did not feel much embarrassment about it, because

9. Ibid.

I was an older soldier than either of them. But I knew that legally it was not proper, and that if they chose to resist it, it might become a very troublesome matter to me for the time being. Whether or not General Meade, when he gave me the order, knew about this relative rank, I do not know. I say this because I have since understood that he did not. When I spoke to him about it before departing, however, he remarked, in substance, that he was obliged to use such persons he felt disposed to use; that in this case he sent me because he had explained his views to me, and had not explained them to the others; that I [405] knew his plans and ideas, and could better accord with him in my operations than anybody else.

Hancock's concern with the legality of his command was well placed. Howard initially refused to recognize Hancock's authority over him, though a cooperative arrangement was worked out. Yet Hancock's testimony probably carried little weight with committee members. An earlier witness, Doubleday, had charged that Meade was in the habit of violating the "organic law" of the army to place his personal friends in power, and that this favoritism benefitted "McClellan men." Hancock—a friend of McClellan's—had clearly benefitted from Meade's favor.

I went to Gettysburg, arriving on the ground not later than half past 3 o'clock. I found that, practically, the fight was then over.

There is considerable uncertainty about Hancock's actual time of arrival at Gettysburg. His official report gave his arrival time as 3:00 P.M. In a dispatch to Meade timed 5:25 P.M., Hancock said he had "arrived here an hour since." Howard wrote Meade at 5:00 P.M. that Hancock had arrived at 4:00, and Doubleday placed Hancock's arrival at "about 3:30." Years after the battle, C. H. Morgan, Hancock's Second Corps chief of staff, noted Hancock's arrival time as 3:30.[10]

The rear of our column, with the enemy in pursuit, was then coming through the town of Gettysburg. General Howard was on Cemetery hill, and there had evidently been an attempt on his part to stop and form some of his troops there; what troops he had formed there I do not know. I understood af-

10. *OR*, vol. 27, pt. 1, pp. 366, 368, 696; Doubleday, *Chancellorsville and Gettysburg*, 150; Hancock, *Reminiscences*, 189.

terwards, and accepted it as the fact, that he had formed one division there prior to this time. I told General Howard I had orders to take command in the front. I did not show him the orders, because he did not demand it. He acquiesced.

"Acquiesced" seems to be a face-saving word for Howard's benefit. Howard was "mortified" by Hancock's assignment and wrote Meade that Hancock had "assisted me in carrying out orders which I had already issued." Some twelve years after Gettysburg, Howard wrote that Hancock had greeted him, "General Meade has sent me to represent him on the field." Howard replied, "All right, Hancock. This is no time for talking. You take the left of the pike and I will arrange these troops to the right. . . . It did not strike me then that Hancock, without troops, was doing more than directing matters as a temporary chief of staff for Meade."

Major E. P. Halstead, who later claimed to have been present at the meeting, reported that Hancock had announced that Meade had sent him to take command of the three corps. Howard responded that he was the senior officer, whereupon Hancock replied that he had a written order if Howard wished to see it. Howard did not doubt Hancock's word, according to Halstead, but had told him, "you can give no orders here while I am here." At that point Hancock had said, "Very well, General Howard, I will second any order that you have to give."

Halstead's version of events does not accord with Hancock's character. Hancock may not have wanted to be put in the position of claiming command over a senior officer, but his orders were to do so; it is unlikely that he would have agreed to split that command with anyone. His actions on July 1 (corroborated by the reports of others) show he took the lead in command until Slocum arrived.[11]

I exercised the command until evening, when General Slocum arrived, about 6 or 7 o'clock. His troops were in the neighborhood, for they apparently had been summoned up before I arrived, by General Howard possibly, as well as the 3d corps. When General Slocum arrived, he being my senior, and not included in this order to me, I turned the command over to him. In fact, I was instructed verbally by General Butterfield, chief of staff, before I left for the front, that I was to do so.

11. *OR*, vol. 27, pt. 1, pp. 696–7; quoted in Jordan, *Winfield Scott Hancock*, 83; *B&L*, 3:285.

Slocum's slowness in coming up to Gettysburg is another of the many controversies concerning Gettysburg. At noon his Twelfth Corps was at Two Taverns, only five miles southeast of Gettysburg. In spite of urgent requests from Howard for Slocum's aid and counsel, as well as two requests from members of Howard's staff for Slocum to come forward and take command as the ranking major general in the army, Slocum moved slowly and refused to come forward to take command. He eventually arrived sometime after 5:00 P.M.[12]

When I arrived and took the command I extended the lines. I sent General Wadsworth to the right to take possession of Culp's hill with his division. I directed General Geary, whose division belonged to the 12th corps, (its commander, General Slocum, not then having arrived,) to take possession of the high ground towards Round Top. I made such disposition as I thought wise and proper. The enemy evidently believing that we were reenforced, or that our whole army was there, discontinued their great efforts, and the battle for that day was virtually over. There was firing of artillery and skirmishing all along the front, but that was the end of that day's battle. By verbal instructions, and in the order which I had received from General Meade, I was directed to report, after having arrived on the ground, whether it would be necessary or wise to continue to fight the battle at Gettysburg, or whether it was possible for the fight to be had on the ground General Meade had selected. About 4 o'clock P.M. I sent word by Major [William G.] Mitchell, aide-de-camp, to General Meade, that I would hold the ground until dark, meaning to allow him time to decide the matter for himself. As soon as I had gotten matters arranged to my satisfaction, and saw that the troops were being formed again, and I felt secure, I wrote a note to General Meade, and informed him of my views of the ground at Gettysburg. I told him that the only disadvantage which I thought it had was that it could be readily turned by way of Emmitsburg, and that the roads were clear for any movement he might make. I had ordered all the trains back, as I came up, to clear the roads.

It is apparent that Meade had decided to fight at Gettysburg before Mitchell arrived. Around 4:30 P.M. Meade had ordered the Third, Fifth, and Twelfth Corps to Gettysburg, along with six batteries of the Reserve Artillery. The large Sixth Corps had been ordered to Taneytown. At 6:00 P.M., before Mitchell's arrival,

12. *GC*, 312–5.

Meade sent a message to Hancock saying that a "battle at Gettysburg is now forced upon us."[13]

General Meade had directed my corps, the 2d corps, to march up towards Gettysburg, under the command of General Gibbon. When I found that the enemy had ceased their operations, I directed General Gibbon to halt his corps two or three miles behind Gettysburg, in order to protect our rear from any flank movement of the enemy. Then my operations in the front being closed, I turned the command over to General Slocum, and immediately started to report to General Meade in detail what I had done, in order to express my views clearly to him, and to see what he was disposed to do. I rode back and found General Meade about 9 o'clock. He told me he had received my messages and note, and had decided, upon the representations I had made, and the existence of known facts of the case, to fight at Gettysburg, and had ordered all the corps to the front. That was the end of operations for that day.

Lieutenant Frank Haskell, an aide to Brigadier General John Gibbon, who was temporarily in command of the Second Corps, wrote that Gibbon met Hancock about 9:00 P.M. *just south of Round Top. Modern scholars have generally indicated that Hancock arrived around 10:00. 10:00 or later is probably correct.*[14]

In light of Warren's earlier claim to have surveyed the field with Hancock, it is odd that Hancock does not mention Warren in his testimony.

The next morning, some time after daylight, I again reported to General Meade, at Gettysburg, and assumed the command of my own corps after it arrived. I was placed on the line connecting Cemetery hill with Little Round Top mountain, my line, however, not extending to Round Top, probably only half way. General Sickles was directed to connect with my left and the Round Top mountain, thus [406] forming a continuous line from Cemetery hill (which was held by General Howard) to Round Top mountain.

Everything remained comparatively quiet during that morning, except that the enemy attacked General Slocum; but that was on the other part of the line, the extreme right, directly behind the position I have just referred to. There was fighting going on there all the morning with portions of Ewell's

13. *LLM,* 2:40–1; *GC,* 325; *OR,* vol. 27, pt. 3, p. 466.

14. Byrne and Weaver, eds., *Haskell of Gettysburg,* 101; Jordan, *Winfield Scott Hancock,* 86; *MG,* 138.

corps, but we did not know at that time whether that was going to be the main attack or not. In fact, when I arrived on the ground in the morning, General Meade thought there would be a formidable attack by the enemy on the right of our line, and when my corps arrived on the ground it was formed facing in that direction, but shortly afterwards was marched over to the position which we held during the subsequent battle.

Everything remained quiet, except artillery and engagements with pickets on our front, until about 4 o'clock that afternoon, when General Sickles moved out to the front. I happened to be present with my corps at the time. I knew that the fight was expected to commence, but the object of General Sickles moving to the front I could not conceive. I recollect looking on and admiring the spectacle, but I did not know the object of it. I soon saw, however, that it was going to involve a fight in front of our line, because the enemy were only a certain distance from us and parallel to us, and I thought it would be disadvantageous to us.

Very shortly the fight commenced with General Sickles's corps, and in the course of the afternoon involved everybody along the line. One of my divisions, General Caldwell's, was sent over to the left of General Sickles; but it was sent to report to General Sykes, and it was posted, I believe, by one of his staff officers. I imagine that the reason it was ordered to report to General Sykes was, that after General Sickles advanced General Sykes was ordered to hold Round Top, and probably his own troops had not gotten up, although he was there in person, and I judge it was intended that that division of mine should hold the position until General Sykes's command should arrive.

Sickles had testified that his men had occupied Little Round Top, which was not correct. Hancock's testimony directly contradicted Sickles.

In fact, I was told at the time that the division would be returned to me as soon as General Sykes's troops had arrived; but it became involved in the fight, and fought there all the afternoon. The enemy succeeded late in the afternoon in turning the left of the 3d corps by passing between it and Round Top mountain, and, making the attack upon the flank of the 3d corps, forced it back. General Gibbon, of my command, had sent out two regiments and a battery to connect the right of General Sickles with our line. There was a little brick house in front of our line which seemed to be a good point to rest the right upon, and, in order to strengthen General Sickles, he sent out these regiments and a battery. The remaining troops of my corps remained as they were, except as I have stated. As the 3d corps formed part of the original line of battle, and this division of mine (Caldwell's) which I had sent to the assistance of that corps also formed a part of that line, it followed, of course, that the moment those commands were forced back there was a vacancy in the original line of battle from Round Top up to the point where the right of this first division had rested.

Hancock recognized Sickles's position as part of the original battle line even though apparently Sickles had not done so at the time.

The 3d corps and Caldwell's division of the 2d corps did not return to the original line that day, but were forced behind that line. The enemy breaking through at different places, it required us to patch up that line all the latter part of the afternoon and evening. Detachments of the 12th corps came over from the right, and also greater detachments of the 1st corps came up. The enemy made an attack along the whole front there, and on the 2d corps. But although the enemy had actually gotten in our line at more than one place, yet when night came we had managed to repulse them, and had driven them back, so that we held exactly the position we had started out with, which was the direct line from Cemetery hill to Round Top. But we did not hold any of the advanced ground which was attempted to be taken. [407] Things then remained in that condition. After we had successfully disposed of that force of the enemy, I heard a heavy firing on the front of General Howard and General Slocum. As it appeared to be coming nearer, I directed General Gibbon, then commanding the 2d corps, to send a brigade and two regiments, under Colonel Carroll, to that point, and they very materially assisted to repulse the enemy, who had made a very vigorous attack upon General Howard.

There was a council held that evening at General Meade's headquarters. All the corps commanders were sent for. I was present. Some of this fighting was going on at twilight, and after we had assembled in council. The 12th corps, on their return from the left centre, or the portion of it which had been sent over there, found that the enemy had taken a part of their intrenchments, and they went to work to drive them out. They did not succeed that night, but they did early the next morning. I should have stated that after General Meade received notice that General Sickles was wounded so as to be unable to continue in command, he sent word to me to go and take command of the 3d corps. I then turned the command of the 2d corps over to General Gibbon. When I went out to the front I took with me a brigade of my own corps, which

I had been directed a few minutes before to send to General Birney, who was then in command of General Sickles's corps. I got down on the original line of battle, from which General Sickles had marched out just in time to be enabled to stop the enemy there. There we met the enemy, for that was the first point which they attempted to break through. I soon found that the 3d corps was all gone as a force for that occasion. I met General Birney, and he so informed me, when I told him I had been sent to take command. A small part of General Humphreys's division stopped on the line. I then exercised a general command on the left centre, in virtue of rank and verbal orders I had received from General Meade, and used the troops sent to me and with me to drive the enemy back. General Birney went to collect his division. I never really exercised any command over any part of the 3d corps in action, save the fragments of General Humphreys's command, (many 3d corps men, individuals, stopped on our line when directed to halt there,) because the command was in the condition represented. They were scattered, and could not be collected then. That was the end of it as a corps for that day.

It is interesting to compare Hancock's testimony to Birney's on this point. Birney did not mention that Hancock assumed command, nor did Birney reveal the shattered nature of the Third Corps.

That night this council was held. After each corps commander had reported the actual condition of things along his front, the question was submitted to the council. General Meade being present, and General Butterfield questioning the members whether we should remain there or the army fall back to a better position—I understood with a view of protecting our supplies—one corps commander, I think it was General Newton, said he did not think the position of Gettysburg a very good one. General Gibbon, who was the junior officer, I believe, and voted first, said that he had not seen the entire ground, but he had great confidence in General Newton's military eye for these matters, and he voted in accordance with that view of the case, except that he objected to anything that looked like a retreat. I understood afterwards that General Newton really had the same view, and did not propose to make a retreat. But all the other commanders, I understood, said they wished to fight the battle there, and General Meade announced that to be the decision. The council then adjourned, and that was the last operation of the second day of the fight.

On the third day, in the morning, the enemy and General Slocum were a good deal engaged. About 1 or 2 o'clock in the afternoon the enemy commenced a terrific cannonade, from probably 120 pieces of artillery, on the front of the line connecting Cemetery hill with Round Top, the left centre, commanded by me. That line consisted of the 1st, 2d, and 3d corps, of which I had the general command. I commanded that whole front. General Gibbon commanded the 2d corps in my absence, General Newton the 1st corps, and General Birney [408] the 3d.

In fact, Hancock had resumed command of his own corps around 1:00 P.M. on July 3 and made no claim of a general command in his battle report. Meade's battle report made one reference to Hancock as commanding the "left center" but did not define what was meant by it. At the same time, however, Meade reported that Gibbon was in command of the Second Corps when Gibbon had actually returned to command his division. Whether Hancock commanded a "left center" or not, he acted as though he did.[15]

That cannonade continued for probably an hour and a half. The enemy then made an assault at the end of that time; it was a very formidable assault, and made, I should judge, with about 18,000 infantry. When the columns of the enemy appeared it looked as if they were going to attack the centre of our line, but after marching straight out a little distance they seemed to incline a little to their left, as if their object was to march through my command and seize Cemetery hill, which I have no doubt was their intention. They attacked with wonderful spirit; nothing could have been more spirited. The shock of the assault fell upon the 2d and 3d divisions of the 2d corps, and those were the troops, assisted by a small brigade of Vermont troops,[16] together with the artillery of our line, which fired from Round Top to Cemetery hill at the enemy all the way as they advanced whenever they had the opportunity. Those were the troops that really met the assault. No doubt there were other troops that fired a little, but those were the troops that really withstood the shock of the assault and repulsed it. The attack of the enemy was met by about six small brigades of our troops, and was finally repulsed after a terrific contest at very close quarters, in which our troops took about thirty or forty colors and some 4,000 or 5,000 prisoners, with great loss to the enemy in killed and wounded. The repulse was a most signal one, and that decided the battle, and was prac-

15. *OR*, vol. 27, pt. 1, pp. 117, 372–4.
16. Brig. Gen. George J. Stannard's Third Brigade, Third Division, First Corps.

tically the end of the fight. I was wounded at the close of the assault, and that ended my operations with the army for that campaign. I did not follow it in its future movements.

Question. And that also ended the fighting at Gettysburg?

Answer. That practically ended the fighting of the battle of Gettysburg. There was no serious fighting there after that, save on the left, in an advance by a small command of the Pennsylvania reserves, made very soon afterwards, and based upon our success. I may say one thing here: I think it was probably an unfortunate thing that I was wounded at the time I was, and equally unfortunate that General Gibbon was also wounded, because the absence of a prominent commander, who knew the circumstances thoroughly, at such a moment as that, was a great disadvantage. I think that our lines should have advanced immediately, and I believe we should have won a great victory. I was very confident that the advance would be made. General Meade told me before the fight that if the enemy attacked me he intended to put the 5th and 6th corps on the enemy's flank; I therefore, when I was wounded, and lying down in my ambulance and about leaving the field, dictated a note to General Meade, and told him if he would put in the 5th and 6th corps I believed he would win a great victory. I asked him afterwards, when I returned to the army, what he had done in the premises. He said he had ordered the movement, but the troops were slow in collecting, and moved so slowly that nothing was done before night, except that some of the Pennsylvania reserves went out and met Hood's division,[17] it was understood, of the enemy, and actually overthrew it, assisted, no doubt, in some measure, by their knowledge of their failure in the assault.

What had actually happened was that Meade had ordered Major General George Sykes's Fifth Corps to make a reconnaissance in force. Sykes had Brigadier General Samuel H. Crawford, commander of his Third Division, send forward Colonel William McCandless's First Brigade and one regiment of Colonel Joseph W. Fisher's Second Brigade, the Eleventh Pennsylvania Reserves. For some reason Crawford did not think this force sufficient for a reconnaissance, also asking for the First Brigade, Third Division.[18]

In a masterpiece of fiction, Crawford later claimed to have driven back Hood's division and to have captured two hundred prisoners of Confederate

17. Maj. Gen. John Bell Hood's division of Longstreet's First Corps. After Hood's wounding on July 2, the division was under the command of Brig. Gen. Evander M. Law.

18. *GC*, 534; *OR*, vol. 27, pt. 1, pp. 654, 685.

Brigadier General George T. Anderson's brigade. In fact, Crawford had hit the Fifteenth Georgia of Brigadier General Henry L. Benning's brigade, which reported only ninety-nine men missing for the entire battle. Hood's and McLaws's divisions were well on their way back to a new line along the Emmitsburg road at the time.[19]

There were only two divisions of the enemy on our extreme left, opposite Round Top, and there was a gap in their line of one mile that their assault had left, and I believe if our whole line had advanced with spirit, it is not unlikely that we would have taken all their artillery at that point. I think that was a fault; that we should have pushed the enemy there, for we do not often catch them in that position; and the rule is, and it is natural, that when you repulse or defeat an enemy you should pursue him; and I believe it is a rare thing that one party beats another and does not pursue him, and I think that on that occasion it only required an order and prompt execution.

Hancock's only criticism of Meade was his failure to counterattack, though Hancock tempered this criticism by adding that Meade had ordered an attack but it had not been carried out due to the slow movement of the troops involved.

When this assault first commenced I was on the extreme left of our line. As soon as I saw the skirmishers coming over the hill I knew the assault was coming, and I followed it up to see where it was going to strike, and as I passed General Caldwell, who commanded the left division of the 2d corps, I told [409] him this: "If the enemy's attack strikes further to your right I want you to attack on their flank; why I say so is this—you will find the 5th and 6th corps on your left, and they will help you." He did not attack on their flank; why, I do not know. Perhaps it would not have been wise for him to do so, because the 5th and 6th corps did not make the movement.

There is no confirmation for Hancock's story, but there is no reason to doubt it either. Caldwell reported one killed and only a few wounded in the cannonade of July 3. Perry's and Wilcox's brigades, which had attacked on Caldwell's front, retired well short of his position. Caldwell must have seen the Fourteenth and Sixteenth Vermont's flank attack, but he did not move.

19. *OR*, vol. 27, pt. 1, 654; *GC*, 534; Busey and Martin, *Regimental Strengths and Losses at Gettysburg*, 281.

By Mr. Chandler:

Question. Do I understand you to say that there was a gap of a mile in the enemy's line?

Answer. There must have been practically a gap to that extent, because it took a mile of troops in position to have made that attack in column as it was made.

Such a gap, which did not actually exist, would have made the lack of a counterattack all the more inexplicable.

By the chairman:

Question. Was all of their artillery thus left without infantry support?

Answer. This shattered mass of the enemy's forces rushed to the rear over the ground on which their artillery was posted and through it, and I judged there was nothing of any importance left with their batteries, but the artillerymen, as I understood the only two divisions the enemy had on their extreme right were Hood's and McLaws's, and they were evidently in a pretty shattered condition, because they had been heavily engaged the day before. I judge of their condition from the fact that this small command of the Pennsylvania reserves overthrew Hood's division by their advance. General Meade gave the order for the 5th and 6th corps to advance, but he said the troops were so slow in moving that they allowed the remaining hours of daylight to pass by before much was accomplished. I think we would have won a greater victory had the advance been promptly made and with spirit; and I have stated the reasons why it ought to have been done, for the intention was announced even beforehand that the 5th and 6th corps were to make a movement.

Caldwell ran into only one regiment, not Hood's division. Both Hood's and McLaws's divisions were available to meet any counterattack.

Question. We seem always to have failed to follow up a victory?

Answer. And we shall never reap the just fruits of a victory until we do follow it up promptly.

Question. I have observed that neither the enemy nor ourselves, when we come in collision with our great armies, seem to gain a decisive victory.

Answer. That is generally so, and one reason for that is this—unless the very moment is seized it passes away, because the troops on both sides have become so inured to war, that if you give them time to collect again they are ready for another fight. They know the advantage of collecting together as soon as possible, and if you allow them time to do it you lose all the benefits of your victory, or at least of that condition of things which immediately follows a victory. The men will fight again—not with the same spirit, perhaps, but still they will fight, as I have seen on many occasions.

Question. After the furious cannonade in that battle, and the expenditure of so much ammunition, what was the opinion of our officers as to the enemy having a supply of ammunition left?

Answer. I do not know, because, after the cannonade, I was intensely occupied and interested until the close of the fight; after I was shot, I had only time to dictate that note, which I have already referred, to General Meade, when I was taken from the field.

By Mr. Chandler:

Question. What would then have been your opinion?

Answer. If the matter had presented itself to my mind at all, I should have considered that the enemy must at least have exhausted their ammunition upon the field, because their artillery fire was most terrific, and they must have exhausted an immense deal of ammunition. It was the most terrific cannonade I ever witnessed, and the most prolonged.

[410] By the chairman:

Question. Which side had the most artillery on the field at that time?

Answer. The enemy had the most in operation at the time; we used as little as possible, for the reason that we were separated from our supplies by a distance of twenty-five miles; we had brought up but a limited quantity of ammunition; we were short of ammunition, and were continually husbanding it, and, frequently, during that cannonade, orders were sent to expend as little ammunition as possible, or it would be exhausted. On the night of the 2d of July, when we went to fill up our boxes for the next day's fight, we were not able to refill them completely, even from the artillery reserve.

Hancock was mostly at fault for his lack of ammunition, having brought only half of his ammunition train to Gettysburg contrary to Meade's orders. Hunt, well aware of the tendencies of infantry commanders to shorten their trains to speed their march, had begun to carry extra ammunition at Chancellorsville. He assured Meade on the morning of July 2 that there was "enough ammunition for the battle, but none for idle cannonades, the besetting sin of some of our commanders." According to Lieutenant Cornelius Gillett, ordnance officer for the Artillery Reserve, Hancock's corps drew 2,825 rounds from the Artillery Reserve, only 175 less than the Third Corps (who drew the most artillery ammunition). Hunt was a meticulous officer, and it does not seem probable that he was at fault if Hancock got fewer rounds than he needed.[20]

There was no shortage of ammunition for the Army of the Potomac. Nearly 20 percent of the original supply—4,694 rounds—was still on hand.[21]

Question. And if we were short of ammunition the enemy must have been still more so?

Answer. I have no doubt the enemy regarded the success of their assault as certain, so much so that they were willing to expend all their ammunition. They did not suppose that any troops could live under that cannonade, but they met troops that had been so accustomed to artillery fire that it did not have the effect on them that they expected. It was a most terrific and appalling cannonade—one possibly hardly even paralleled.

Question. Was there ever, in any battle of which you have read, more artillery brought into action than in that battle?

Answer. I doubt whether there has ever been more concentrated upon an equal space, and opening at one time. I think there has been more artillery engaged in many battles, but do not believe there has been more upon both sides concentrated on an equal space.

Question. You did not follow the army from there?

Answer. No, sir; I left the field the moment the fight was over.

Question. When did you join the army again?

Answer. I did not join it again until some time in December, when active operations had ceased. I was then ordered by the Secretary of War into the States from whence the regiments of my corps came, to fill them up by recruitment, and I am now on my return to the army.

Question. You were not with the army when it retired from Culpeper to Centreville?

Answer. No, sir; I have not been with it during any of its movements since the battle of Gettysburg.

20. *OR*, vol. 27, pt. 1, pp. 372, 879; Henry J. Hunt, "The Second Day at Gettysburg," *B&L*, 3:297–300.

21. *OR*, vol. 27, pt. 1, p. 879.

Question. You have been with the army of the Potomac during all its important operations, and have been in a great many battles. What do you say of the spirit of our troops and that of the enemy?

Answer. I think the spirit of our troops is always good—as good as that of the enemy; but as a general thing I think the attacks of the enemy are made with more vivacity than our attacks are made. I think our men have fought better in defensive positions than the enemy have. I think the enemy, from peculiarity of characteristic and climate, and possibly other reasons, attack with more vivacity, but I do not think they continue the fight with the same energy as our troops do when serious resistance is made.

By Mr. Chandler:

Question. But with equal numbers you would not hesitate to attack the enemy anywhere under equal circumstances?

Answer. No, sir, I would not. In fact there is no finer army, if as fine, in existence in the world than the army of the Potomac. The troops will do anything if they are only ordered. If they have not made this or that attack, it is because their commanders did not order them to make it.

By the chairman:

Question. And if they do not attack with as much vivacity as the enemy, [411] may that not be owing to the fact that this army has not been accustomed to take the offensive?

Answer. It may be so; they have not been in the habit of it. That has not been our system of fighting; our practice has habitually been to seek a defensive position and receive an attack.

Question. Does it not require more coolness to receive an attack than to take one?

Answer. I think, with equal education, it does. I think it is more difficult to stand and receive an attack—see it coming on before you are called upon to take part in it—than in any other operation of war.

By Mr. Gooch:

Question. Why has it been generally true that this army has waited to be attacked, instead of itself taking the offensive?

Answer. I think it has depended entirely upon the temperament or policy of the commander; I can see no other reason for it, because our troops are always anxious to attack. I have always had troops that were eager to attack, and I judge it has been owing to the policy or temperament of the commander that that has not been our system.

By the chairman:

Question. Is not this overcaution derived from the fact that all the fights of the army of the Potomac have been rather in defense of our capital?

Coming from Wade, this is an odd question. While it indirectly laid partial blame for the army's failures at the foot of the administration, it also partially exonerated the army's commanders.

Answer. I have no doubt that has had its effect. I think the very fact that we have been defending something has placed us to a certain extent in the position to lead us all to feel that we are fighting a defensive fight; without being able to point to any distinctive fact that seems to prove it, other than that the capital is under our protection.

Question. Suppose that our fortifications about this capital were manned and supported, say by 30,000 troops, would not that baffle an army of the enemy until our army could come up and engage the enemy?

Answer. They ought to do so. But I have been stationed in Alexandria at times when the enemy were approaching the capital, and I have always thought that unless we had a very large force of infantry there, under judicious commanders, who knew these fortifications well, the enemy had it in his power to penetrate between our forts with great impunity, particularly at night. We have always allowed free ingress and egress of people; there has been no time apparently when peace ceased and war commenced. While the enemy are approaching the gates of the capital, the country seems to be open. There is no consolidation of troops, and no system, and I have not much confidence in that kind of defenses.

Question. That is a defect in the organization of the forces?

Answer. I think so. I think, with the disciplined army the enemy have in front of us, it would take a very large army in those works to defend them, because the works occupy a great deal of ground; and you must have a large body of troops at each of the different prominent points—the great centres.

Question. I do not mean to indicate that our troops should make a permanent defense here; but would not they detain the enemy until our army should come up?

Answer. There is no doubt that they ought to do so; that the fortifications have not performed their functions unless they can do so.

Question. That, I suppose, was the object of the fortifications?

Answer. No doubt; and it ought to be known what command of infantry, in conjunction with these forts, could defend them.

Question. Do you know the number of troops in and about Washington at the time of the battle of Antietam?

[412] Answer. I have no doubt that there were quite a number here, because I know some divisions of the army of the Potomac that were not in the battle of Antietam; and some of these I understood were in Washington.

Question. In your opinion as a military man, I will ask whether or not our army should have attacked the enemy before he recrossed the Potomac at Williamsport?

Answer. I was not there, but my impression is that I should have voted for an attack. My military opinion may not be good for much, because I have not seen the ground, but my impression is that the enemy should have been attacked there.

By Mr. Odell:

Question. During the battle of Gettysburg did you know anything about an order of General Meade's to retire from that position?

Answer. No, sir.

Question. Would you have known of such an order if it had been published?

Answer. I suppose so; the movement could not have been made without my knowledge.

Hancock's statement further undermined the committee's charge that Meade had intended to retreat at Gettysburg.

A.

Headquarters Army of the Potomac,

July 1, 1863—1.10 P.M.

Commanding Officer 2d Corps:

The major general commanding has just been informed that General Reynolds has been killed or badly wounded. He directs that you turn over the command of your corps to General Gibbon; that you proceed to the front, and by virtue of this order, in case of the truth of General Reynolds's death, you assume command of the corps there assembled, viz.: the 11th, 1st, and 3d, at Emmitsburg. If you think the ground and position there a better one to fight a battle under existing circumstances, you will so advise the general, and he will order all the troops up; you know the general's views, and General Warren, who is fully aware of them, has gone out to see General Reynolds.

Later—1.15 P.M.

Reynolds has possession of Gettysburg, and the enemy are reported as falling back from the front of Gettysburg. Hold your column ready to move.

Very respectfully, your obedient servant,
D. BUTTERFIELD
Major General and Chief of Staff
January 13, 1864.
Official copy:
S. WILLIAMS, *A. A. G.*

Hancock made a very impressive witness. As one of the best soldiers in the Army of the Potomac, he carried himself in such a way as to command respect. For the most part, his testimony helped Meade. Noting that Meade had intended to fight on the Pipe Creek line, Hancock affirmed that Meade was a flexible commander who had concentrated the army rapidly once the battle was joined on good ground. Although Hancock criticized Meade for failing to push a counterattack following Pickett's repulse, he blamed the slowness of the Fifth and Sixth Corps—not Meade—for the absence of an effective attack. Had Meade's orders been promptly executed, Hancock believed there had been a good chance to have captured all of Lee's artillery.

While Hancock avoided testifying to events about which he had no firsthand knowledge, Wade was able to get him to say that the Union would never enjoy the fruits of victory until its armies followed up their successes on the battlefield. This was the type of statement that could be used against Meade. Out of context, it could be taken to mean that Hancock blamed the escape of Lee's army on Meade's failure to order a prompt pursuit.

12 Brigadier General James Samuel Wadsworth

THE COMMITTEE MOVED from the consummate professional to the amateur with its next witness, Brigadier General James Samuel Wadsworth, who commanded the First Division, First Corps at Gettysburg. A political general, Wadsworth was born in Geneseo, New York, where his father was one of the largest farmers in the state. Wadsworth's youth was devoted to learning the responsibilities inherent in his position as an eventual leader of local society.[1]

Wadsworth was a lawyer by training; he entered politics out of a sense of duty rather than from any burning political motive. Initially he was a Democrat, and he spent considerable time in the South, where he became acquainted with leading and influential Southerners. Eventually, however, he became disenchanted with southern influence on the Democratic Party and the Democrats' support of slavery. In 1848 he became one of the organizers of the Free-Soil Party, which would later became a part of the Republican Party.[2]

Wadsworth was opposed to slavery, and he sought a peaceful resolution to the brewing conflict. In 1861 he was a member of the Washington Peace Conference, an unofficial gathering of moderates hoping to prevent civil war. Although the conference was attended by delegates from various states, radicals of both North and South ignored its proceedings. With the failure of the conference and the outbreak of war, Wadsworth offered himself and his fortune to the Union cause.[3]

Aware of his complete lack of military knowledge, he served as a volunteer aide on the staff of General Irvin McDowell at First Bull Run. At Bull Run, ac-

1. Warner, *Generals in Blue,* 532–3.

2. Ibid.; *New York Times,* May 11, 1864.

3. Warner, *Generals in Blue,* 532–3.

cording to his obituary in the *New York Times,* he "had a horse shot under him, and behaved with conspicuous and serviceable gallantry." As a result, McDowell had Wadsworth appointed a brigadier general as of August 9, 1861. Admittedly a political move, it was hoped that Wadsworth's promotion to general would strengthen the loyalty of onetime Democrats now in the fledgling Republican Party by showing that they had been fully accepted. Interestingly, Wadsworth had been offered the twin stars of a major general in the state militia at the outbreak of the war by the governor of New York, which he had turned down. Later he was again offered a commission as a brigadier general of volunteers. He was at first hesitant, suggesting a regular army officer instead, but when none were available he accepted, saying, "I am better than a worse man." Events would prove him right.[4]

With McClellan's assumption of command of the Army of the Potomac, well-meaning neophytes were expendable. Too well connected to be totally shunted aside, Wadsworth became military governor of the District of Columbia in March 1862. He ran for governor of New York on the Republican ticket but was defeated by Horatio Seymour, a Democrat and anti-administration candidate. The off-year elections turned out to be a disaster for the Republicans generally, and Wadsworth's defeat was hard felt, both by the party and Wadsworth himself.[5]

With McClellan's ouster from command, Wadsworth once again returned to field duty and was assigned to command the First Division in Reynolds's First Corps. In December 1862, Charles Wainwright wrote, "Wadsworth having been defeated in his efforts to be governor of New York gets the First Division as a balm. He commanded a brigade in it while McDowell had the division last winter, but has been in charge of Washington ever since and has not seen any active service." Wadsworth's division was not significantly engaged at Chancellorsville, but more than made up for its inactivity at Gettysburg, where it stalled the Confederate attack of July 1.[6]

[412] Testimony of Brigadier General James S. Wadsworth.

Washington, March 23, 1864.
General James S. Wadsworth sworn and examined.

4. *New York Times,* May 11, 1864; *DAB,* 10:308–9.
5. *New York Times,* May 11, 1864; Warner, *Generals in Blue,* 533; *MG,* 84.
6. Wainwright, *A Diary of Battle,* ed. Nevins, 149.

By the chairman:

Question. You were at the battle of Gettysburg?

Answer. Yes, sir.

Question. What was your position there?

Answer. I commanded the 1st division of the 1st corps during that battle. This was the first division that engaged the enemy on the morning of the 1st of [413] July. I commanded the division during the engagement, and until the army crossed the Potomac.

Question. How many men did you lose from your division?

Answer. A little more than half of them.

Question. Will you give us a brief but clear account of the first day's fight?

Answer. I do not know under what orders General Reynolds moved that day. He was, generally, very particular in communicating his orders to his division commanders, but on that occasion he communicated none, if he had any. He rode up to my headquarters, on the morning of the 1st of July, and asked what order I had received from General Doubleday, who then commanded the corps, General Reynolds being then in command of two corps, the 1st and 11th. I told him that I was waiting for the other divisions to pass, as I was ordered to move in rear of the other two divisions. He said that that was a mistake, and that I should move on directly. This was about four miles from Gettysburg.

I moved on the road with him until we got within a mile of Gettysburg, when we heard the report of guns. General Reynolds then received a report from General Buford that the infantry of the enemy were advancing in some force and driving his cavalry back. It was a matter of momentary consultation between General Reynolds and myself whether we would go into the town or take a position in front of the town. He decided that if we went into the town the enemy would shell it and destroy it, and that we had better take a position in front of the town. We moved across the fields to Seminary ridge, about half a mile west of Gettysburg. [The First Corps initially formed along McPherson's Ridge.] Before we had time to form our line we were engaged with the enemy. The only battery[7] in my division was placed in position by the side of the road leading to Cashtown. At that time only one brigade[8] was up.

General Reynolds told me to take three regiments to support the battery

7. 2nd Battery, Maine Light Artillery, under Capt. James A. Hall.

8. Brig. Gen. Lysander Cutler's Second Brigade, First Division, First Corps, was the first brigade up.

on the right, and he would go to the left and place the balance of the division there. I went on the right of the battery with three regiments, and he went on the left, but was almost immediately killed. I, however, did not hear for some time that he was killed. I contended with the enemy for two hours alone. General Doubleday came up in person in about half an hour, and the other divisions of the 1st corps in about two hours. The 11th corps came up about the same time and took position on our right, on the north of Gettysburg. I was driven back with my three regiments on the right.

Wadsworth's regiments had been flanked by Davis's brigade. The hasty withdrawal had left Captain Hall's battery unsupported and Hall had lost one gun in his retreat, which he later recovered. Hall and Wadsworth had words of "rather an animated nature," and Hall angrily described the abandonment of his battery as a "cowardly operation." Wadsworth later explained to Hall that he had been looking out for Reynolds, not knowing that Reynolds had been killed.[9]

We retired in order, keeping up the contest, and the left of my division swung around and captured about 800 of the enemy, including Brigadier General Archer.

Brigadier General James J. Archer, commanding the Third Brigade, Heth's Division, of Lieutenant General A. P. Hill's Third Corps, thus obtained the dubious distinction of being the first general officer captured since Lee had assumed command. The exact number of Confederates captured is unknown, with figures ranging from 60 to Doubleday's 1,000. The return of casualties for the Army of Northern Virginia set the number of captured or missing for this brigade for the entire battle at 517.

I then formed my division on the same ridge, a little in front of Seminary ridge, under orders from General Doubleday, and held that position until four o'clock in the afternoon. And so far as anything in front of us was concerned I could have continued to hold it. We had a very good position for the artillery, and had some six or eight Napoleon 12-pounders throwing grape and canister, and the enemy could not have driven us from that position. But the 11th corps

9. John D. Bachelder, David L. Ladd, and Audrey J. Ladd, eds., *The Bachelder Papers,* 3 vols. (Dayton, Ohio: Morningside House, 1994), 1:305–7.

having broken on the right, and the other portions of the 1st corps on our left having been driven back, the enemy got on to our flanks and nearly surrounded us.

General Howard had ridden over to see me about 2 o'clock, and told me to hold the position as long as I could, and then to retire. This was the only order I received after General Reynolds's death, except one before referred to from General Doubleday. When we found that we were very nearly surrounded, and my division was reduced to a very small force, I retired to Cemetery hill. This was 4 o'clock P.M. Very few of my division were taken prisoners, but a great many prisoners were taken on the right from the 11th corps, and from one division of the 1st corps that went into position on the right. The next morning I had but 1,600 men answer to their names, out of about 4,000 men that went into the action.

Wadsworth's testimony about his losses was misleading. The official reports of one of his regimental commanders, with two not reporting losses, show 308 officers and men missing after the battle. Most had been killed or captured on July 1. Historian Edwin Coddington has estimated that about 2,000 of First Corps were captured. Comparatively, he estimated that about 1,500 of the Eleventh Corps were captured.[10]

[414] We think that we punished the enemy so severely in that contest, and that they lost so heavily, that they were in no condition to continue the attack after we had retired to Cemetery hill from Seminary ridge. The report which we have from the enemy, especially from some English officers who were among them, were that they suffered very much in the first day's fight, and were not disposed to continue the contest until they had completed the concentration of their army. We who were engaged in that day's fight claim the credit of having held the enemy in check until General Meade concentrated his forces at Gettysburg.

I was on the evening of the first day assigned, with my division, to a position on the mountain ridge [Culp's Hill] on the right of Gettysburg. The enemy attacked us there the next morning, by which time, however, we had got up a pretty good line of breastworks. They continued the attack until about 9 o'clock at night, driving a portion of the 12th corps, which was on our right, out of their rifle-pits; but we recovered the next morning. I sent two reg-

10. *OR,* vol. 27, pt. 1, pp. 269, 274, 277, 286, 288; *GC,* 305, 307.

iments, the 14th Brooklyn and ______ [blank in original],[11] to assist in this work.

On the morning of the third day of the fight the enemy renewed the attack on the right, taking advantage of a valley which broke the mountain at the point where my division joined to the 12th corps. It was a very furious assault, but it was repelled by the 12th corps, and my division of the 1st corps. The balance of the 1st corps was over on the left, separated from us. My division did not lose much on the second and third days of the fight, as they were protected by breastworks.

Question. What portion of our army was engaged on the field of battle at Gettysburg?

Answer. Every man in the army was available. The whole army was concentrated on about three miles square; the reserve was within thirty minutes' march of any part of the line. The position was such that the enemy could not attack on our right and left simultaneously; and that left our right at liberty to re-enforce the left, if necessary, or vice versa.

Question. You say all our men were available for that battle?

Answer. Yes, sir; our left rested on Round Top mountain, which protected us perfectly from being outflanked in that direction. Our right rested upon a ridge of mountains running easterly, which protected us on the right, except in a valley in which the enemy did attack us. But the distance from this point to the left of the line was estimated at several miles, the enemy having to make a large detour round Gettysburg, that place being commanded by our guns on Cemetery hill, so that they could not attack at that point and on the left at the same time, without dividing their army. So far as I know, this is the only battle the army of the Potomac has ever fought in which our whole army was available, or in which even much more than one-third of it was engaged at one time.

Wadsworth gave an excellent description of the advantages of interior lines, an advantage which is often overlooked by students of the battle.

On the morning of the third day Ewell's corps attacked us on the right, and made repeated and furious assaults to break the line in the valley which I have mentioned, and across which our line was formed. Having failed in that,

11. The 14th Brooklyn (84th New York) under Col. Edward B. Fowler was accompanied by the 147th New York, under Lt. Col. Francis C. Miller.

his troops, except a few skirmishers, were moved around Gettysburg, a march of six or seven miles, to our left, and precipitated in the attack on our left, which was very fierce, particularly the artillery fire.

Some of the artillery of Ewell's corps participated in the bombardment prior to Pickett's charge, but none of Ewell's infantry was involved in the assault.

I do not think the army at any moment was in jeopardy from this attack, as the whole army could have been concentrated to meet it in twenty or thirty minutes.

Question. What was the condition of our army after the battle was over on the third—I mean in morale and spirits?

Answer. The slaughter had been terrible; but the spirit of the troops was unimpaired, and, in my opinion, our troops were in good condition to have taken the offensive, and they would have taken it with alacrity.

Question. Do you know why they did not then take the offensive?

[415] Answer. I do not; they were not ordered to take it. I think that General Meade did not, perhaps, appreciate fully the completeness of his victory. The terrible slaughter of our men produced, of course, a great impression upon the officers of our army. General Meade's headquarters were almost in the line of battle, and were surrounded by great havoc. A large number of horses were killed in the yard of the little house which he occupied.

Question. Do you suppose the slaughter on our side was greater than it was on the side of the enemy?

Answer. I think not; I think the slaughter was greater on the side of the enemy than on our side on every day of the battle. I am sure it was on the first day; I know we almost annihilated one or two brigades that came against us on the first day. They came up within canister range of our guns, and our men claim to have utterly annihilated them.

Question. You then followed the enemy down to Williamsport?

Answer. Yes, sir.

Question. What was the condition of things down there?

Answer. General Meade, on the 12th of July, formed a line on the southwest side of the Antietam creek, which was then swollen by heavy rains, and a very formidable stream to cross except at the bridges. The moment the line was formed we commenced a line of breastworks, which by dark was nearly completed, and was quite formidable. About dark the corps commanders were summoned to meet at General Meade's headquarters, five or six miles in the rear. General Newton being ill at that time, I was in command of the corps temporarily, and I attended the council. We assembled about 8 or 9 o'clock in the evening. General Meade stated briefly the condition of our forces, giving his estimate of our army, and the best information he had as to the number of the enemy; stating, as I think, that he believed we were superior to them in numbers, and he asked the corps commanders, commencing with the ranking officer, General Sedgwick, what they thought of the expediency of attacking the enemy the next morning. General Sedgwick, General Slocum, General Sykes, General French, and General Hays, who was temporarily commanding the 2d corps, pronounced decidedly against the attack. General Howard, General Pleasonton, and myself, advised an attack. General Meade stated that he favored an attack; that he came there to fight the enemy, and did not see any good reason why he should not fight them. But he said he could not take the responsibility of bringing on a general engagement against the advice of his commanders.

It will be observed that four of the officers who opposed the attack were the ranking officers of the army, next to General Meade, and held, in every respect, the highest positions in the army. The reasons for and against an attack were not discussed for some time, and I believe not until I asked that those generals who opposed the attack should state their reasons for it. General Sedgwick did not give at any length his reason against an attack, but stated generally that General Meade had won a great victory, and he thought he ought not to jeopard all he had gained by another battle at that time. General Sykes and General French gave as reason for not making an attack, as nearly as I can remember, that there was nothing between the enemy and Washington except our army, and that if it was overwhelmed, Washington and Baltimore would be open to the enemy.

By Mr. Odell:

Question. Was not that true?

Answer. There was no force of any moment but that army, not enough to have resisted General Lee. General Warren, the engineer officer of General Meade's staff, made a strong and able argument in favor of an attack; and General Pleasonton likewise urged an attack. General Howard, who had voted for [416] an attack, did not enter much into the discussion. I did not myself, except to meet the objection that there was nothing between the enemy and Washington but our army, which I did by urging that our line of breastworks, the Antietam creek, and South mountain gave us defensive lines, where we certainly could hold the enemy if repulsed in our assault; and that we had every reason to believe that the enemy were demoralized by their retreat, and were short of ammunition. Some of the officers—I do not recollect whom—took the ground that the enemy would attack us if we did not attack them. I said that I did not believe that the enemy had ever come there to fight a battle; that so good an officer as General Lee never would take a position with his back on the river to fight a battle.

Wadsworth favored an attack at Williamsport for the same reasons given by others testifying before the committee: the demoralized state of the enemy, their shortage of ammunition, and the fact that they were pinned with their backs against the river. Wadsworth also believed that Lee had no intention of fighting. All these opinions were incorrect.

By the chairman:

Question. What is your opinion now, as a military man, with all the light upon the subject you have since obtained, as to the result had you attacked the enemy then?

Answer. I believe there is very little difference of opinion in the army now as to the expediency of making an attack then. Most of the officers I have met think it should have been made. We know now that the enemy then was very short of ammunition; that he had already got a great deal of his material across the river; that he was prepared to cross and commenced to cross at two o'clock in the afternoon of the very day we should have attacked him.

Meade had testified that after viewing the Confederate position he felt an attack would have been disastrous, but Wadsworth was ultimately right.

Question. And a vigorous attack on our side, with our army in good spirits, as you say they were, must have been destructive to Lee's army under the circumstances?

Answer. I believe almost everybody in the army admits that now. I have not talked with many officers upon the subject, but I do not think there is much difference of opinion in the army about it.

Question. Did you follow the army on to Culpeper?

Answer. No, sir; I left the army of the Potomac about that time.

Question. Did you participate in any of the councils held on the second or third day of the fight at Gettysburg?

Answer. No, sir; that was the only time I was at headquarters during the whole affair. I know nothing of any other council.

By Mr. Gooch:

Question. Who selected the position occupied by our army at Gettysburg?

Answer. I cannot answer that question. I think the necessity of the case forced us to fight near that point.

Question. What reason had you for supposing the army of the enemy to be short of ammunition at Williamsport?

Answer. The very profuse use they had made of ammunition at Gettysburg, and the difficulty of transporting it to where they were. I have never seen ammunition thrown away as they threw it away at Gettysburg. I thought, from their using it so profusely there, that they had staked everything upon that battle. The whole army of the enemy was so handled as to show that they staked everything on that struggle. Their assaults were very furious, and even reckless.

By Mr. Chandler:

Question. They expected to destroy us, or to be destroyed themselves?

Answer. Yes, sir.

Question. And if they failed they expected nothing but annihilation?

Answer. Yes, sir. Colonel [Henry A.] Morrow, of the 24th Michigan volunteers, who was taken prisoner there, heard a conversation between General Ewell and one of [417] his subordinate officers, in which the subordinate officer reported to him that they had failed and could not force the line on our right. General Ewell replied, with an oath, that he knew it could be done, and that it should be done, and that the assault should be renewed; and the fact is that they did assault our line there three times on the evening of the second day, and made three or four assaults on the morning of the third day. They were repulsed with terrible slaughter; the ground was covered with their dead.

By Mr. Gooch:

Question. How long was it after the final repulse of the enemy on our left before you became satisfied that the enemy would not renew the attack, and were retreating, or meditating a retreat?

Answer. I was satisfied of it when they did not renew the attack on the morning of July 4. Had they intended to renew the attack, they would certainly have done it by daylight that morning. They were short of provisions, had no chance of getting up re-enforcements, and had nothing to gain by delay, and we had everything.

By Mr. Odell:

Question. It has been said that General Meade never intended to fight that battle at Gettysburg, but had ordered a retreat to Pipe creek?

Answer. I know nothing about that.

Question. Did you ever see anything that indicated any but an advance movement from the time the battle began?

Answer. No, sir. General Meade or his chief of staff could tell you all about it; I know nothing about it.

Question. Would not your position in the army have given you such information?

Answer. From my position in the army I would not have heard of any movement until its execution commenced.

Wadsworth gave perhaps the most honest testimony of all the witnesses called before the committee. He did not testify to things he knew nothing about, and he gave sound, if not always correct, reasons for his opinions.

In Meade's favor, Wadsworth noted that the entire army had been available during Pickett's charge, which was the first time he could remember that happening. As a result, he did not believe that the charge posed a real danger to the army. On the other hand, Wadsworth did not think Meade fully appreciated the magnitude of his victory at Gettysburg.

Wadsworth testified that Meade had favored an attack at Williamsport; yet he admitted that Meade believed he should not go against the advice of his commanders and bring on a general engagement. Wadsworth tried to soften this potentially damaging testimony by pointing out that the generals opposed to the attack were, after Meade, the four ranking generals of the Army of the Potomac. Yet he felt that most of the officers believed they should have attacked at Williamsport.

13 Major General Daniel Butterfield

NOTWITHSTANDING THE BOMBASTIC rhetorical attacks of Daniel Sickles, the most damaging witness against Meade before the committee was Major General Daniel Butterfield. As chief of staff for both Hooker and Meade, Butterfield offered the committee a unique insight into the actions of the two commanders.

The son of John Butterfield, president of the Overland Mail and one of the founders of the American Express company, Daniel Butterfield had a "genius for organization, an indomitable will, and a natural ability for promoting large enterprises." After graduation from Union College in 1849 he traveled throughout the South, where he became convinced of the inevitability of civil war. On his return to New York, Butterfield went to work for American Express and became superintendent of the eastern region. He also had a lively interest in military affairs, which led him to the New York militia. By the outbreak of the Civil War he was colonel of the Twelfth New York militia regiment. When the regiment was taken into Federal service Butterfield—unusually—was commissioned lieutenant colonel in the regular army. This commission, and another as brigadier general of volunteers on September 7, 1861, were primarily due to political influence. Moving rapidly through various commands, he led the Fifth Corps at Fredericksburg as a major general.[1]

There was certainly no love lost between Butterfield and Meade. Butterfield's grievances with Meade began in December 1862, when Meade, who was senior to him by eight days, replaced him as commander of the Fifth Corps. Butterfield was bitterly disappointed at being replaced, since he had been assured by then army commander Burnside that his command of the Fifth

1. *DAB*, 3:373, 8:372; Pfanz, *Gettysburg: The Second Day*, 14.

Corps was a permanent assignment. When Hooker gained command of the army he appointed Butterfield as his chief of staff. Butterfield had a reputation as a good organizer, but political connections may also have played a role in his selection. The influential Salmon P. Chase backed both Butterfield and Hooker.[2]

While it might be too harsh to characterize Butterfield as one of the "most universally unpopular general[s] in the Union Army," he was certainly not among its most well-liked officers. Colonel Charles Wainwright, commander of the First Corps Artillery Brigade, wrote that to his surprise Butterfield often seemed to lack common sense and was not a very good chief of staff. Wainwright dubbed Butterfield the "little Napoleon," and wrote that he was "most thoroughly hated by all officers at headquarters as a meddling, over-conceited fellow." Brigadier General Marsena R. Patrick, provost marshal of the Army of the Potomac, complained that "Butterfield delights in papers and orders" and "thinks himself very smart, but is in reality nearly a fool about some things—I am utterly disgusted with him." Meade's opinion of Butterfield was not much higher. Two weeks after Hooker's elevation to army command, he wrote his wife, "I do not like his [Hooker's] *entourage*. Such gentlemen as Dan Sickles and Dan Butterfield are not the persons I should select as my intimates."[3]

When Meade took command of the Army of the Potomac, he retained Butterfield as chief of staff only because A. A. Humphreys, Seth Williams, and Gouverneur K. Warren in turn all declined the position. Apparently Meade's search for a new chief of staff was hardly a secret. Wainwright noted, "Butterfield remains with him [Meade] at present, but Warren I understand will be the new chief of staff." Unfortunately for Meade, Butterfield knew the job and there was no time for an extended search for a replacement.[4]

It did not take Meade long to become dissatisfied with Butterfield's performance. When Butterfield was hit by a piece of shrapnel during the preliminary bombardment for Pickett's charge on July 3, Meade had the perfect opportunity to remove him. Butterfield left the army on July 5, "fortunately for him & to the joy of all," as General Patrick caustically observed.[5]

2. Julia Lorrilard Butterfield, ed., *A Biographical Memorial of General Daniel Butterfield* (New York: Grafton, 1904), 112. It should be noted that the editor was Butterfield's wife. Gerard Patterson, "Daniel Butterfield," *Civil War Times Illustrated* 12, no. 11 (Nov. 1973): 16.

3. Patterson, "Daniel Butterfield," 13, 15; Wainwright, *A Diary of Battle,* ed. Nevins, 215; quoted in Swanberg, *Sickles the Incredible,* 169; *LLM,* February 13, 1863, 1:354.

4. *CCW,* 388; *B&L,* 3:413; Wainwright, *A Diary of Battle,* ed. Nevins, 227.

5. Quoted in *GC,* 558.

Despite face-saving statements by both Meade and Butterfield, he was in essence fired. He had returned to work with Meade on July 4, an indication that his wound was not disabling. Upon leaving the army he was given a thirty-day furlough, which was extended once. On August 22, less than two months after being wounded, Butterfield was assigned to assist Hooker in writing his reports as commander of the Army of the Potomac. In early September Butterfield joined Hooker in several "brilliant" dinners in Washington before joining him in the West in October. Whitelaw Reid, the famous newspaper correspondent for the *Cincinnati Gazette,* wrote soon after Gettysburg, "It has been telegraphed and re-telegraphed and telegraphed again from headquarters, that General Butterfield was badly wounded. He received a slight blow on the back Friday afternoon from a spent fragment of shell, I believe; but it did not even break the skin."[6]

The details surrounding Butterfield's appearance before the committee are worthy of note as well. At the time of the hearings Butterfield was with Hooker and the Army of Tennessee in the West. Distance was not, however, a deterrent to the committee. The exact circumstances of Butterfield's arrival in Washington are somewhat cloudy, but it is clear that Butterfield was absent without leave from the army when he appeared in Washington at the end of February 1864. On his arrival he contacted Sickles, who then wrote to Chandler:

> Butterfield is at Willards—He has not received permission from Genl. Halleck to come here & apprehends it will be refused—Allow me to suggest that, as in Birneys [*sic*] Case, he be subpoenaed regularly—He comes only by *request* from Senator Wade.
>
> It is very important that you have Brig. Genl. S. Williams Ast. Adjt. Genl. Army of the Potomac here *with all orders & Communications* bearing on the Gettysburg Campaign—*original* drafts & *Copies* as received at Head Quarters—this is *all important* for you to have before you *when Butterfield is Examined*—Then you will get the *real history* of the Campaign.[7]

6. Gary W. Gallagher, ed., *Two Eyewitnesses At Gettysburg: The Personal Accounts of Whitelaw Reid and A. J. L. Fremantle* (St. James, N.Y.: Brandywine Press, 1994), 77; Butterfield, ed., *Biographical Memorial of General Daniel Butterfield,* 116; Hebert, *Fighting Joe Hooker,* 249–50; *LLM,* 2:125.

7. According to Freeman Cleaves, Butterfield requested permission from the War Department to come to Washington to testify before the committee and it was denied. Yet Cleaves's account is suspect on this point due to Sickles's note to Chandler. Swanberg gives the date of the note as February 30. *MG,* 231; Swanberg, *Sickles the Incredible,* 253.

The tone of the note indicates that Butterfield's appearance would come as no great surprise to Chandler. Sickles's suggestion that Butterfield be subpoenaed "as in Birneys [*sic*] Case" shows the depth of his involvement in the hearings (or at least his desire to appear important). Though it doubtless would have occurred to Wade and Chandler on their own, Sickles's suggestion that Butterfield should be called gave him a flimsy, if belated, excuse for being in Washington.

For a man illegally absent from the army, Butterfield did not keep a very low profile. On March 9, 1864, a *New York Tribune* article speculated about the reasons why Butterfield had been summoned to testify before the committee. By March 24 Stanton was "very indignant at his coming [to Washington] . . . and has ordered him back to his post." Meade also knew by then of Butterfield's presence in Washington, as well as the main point of his testimony, the so-called retreat order of July 2. Butterfield had been talking, and not just to committee members. In February 1864, he had told General "Baldy" Smith in Chattanooga that he had a rough draft of the retreat order. Prior to March 5 the committee knew the essence of Butterfield's testimony, though why they waited another three weeks to call him is not clear.[8]

[417] Testimony of Major General Daniel Butterfield.

Washington, March 25, 1864.
Major General Daniel Butterfield sworn and examined.

By the chairman:

Question. What was your rank and position in the army of the Potomac at the time General Meade took command of it?

Answer. I was major general of volunteers and chief of staff of that army.

Question. Give us a narrative, in your own way, of what occurred in the army of the Potomac after General Meade assumed the command. If any questions occur to me I will put them as you go along.

Answer. On the 27th of June General Hooker telegraphed a request to the

8. *LLM,* March 24, 1864, 2:183; Letter from Meade to Gibbon, March 15, 1864, Gibbon, *Recollections,* 185–8. The manuscript of this book was completed in 1885, though it remained unpublished for forty-three years. Meade wrote that the committee had announced that "Gen. Meade having denied the charges of issuing such orders, the committee has sent for *Gen. Butterfield* who wrote them!" Letter from Meade to Gibbon, March 9, 1864, Gibbon, *Recollections,* 189–90.

War Department to be relieved from the command of the army of the Potomac. On the morning of the 28th, about four o'clock, a staff officer, Colonel Hardee [Hardie], arrived from the War Department with orders relieving General Hooker from the command of the army, and assigning General Meade to the command in his place.

Question. Why did General Hooker ask to be relieved from the command of that army at that time?

Answer. General Hooker had had in mind, as part of his operations, to use the garrison at Harpers Ferry, which consisted of 10,000 or 11,000 men, under [418] General French. On the morning of the 27th of June he left me at Poolesville, with instructions to take the portion of the army near there to Frederick. He asked me if I knew of any reason why the garrison at Harpers Ferry should be retained there. I said that I did not, in view of the then condition of General Lee's army. He said: "I wish you would telegraph to General Halleck, in my name, asking him if there is any reason why that garrison should remain at Harpers Ferry, and I will go personally to Harpers Ferry and look over the place; and when you telegraph ask that a duplicate of the answer be sent to Harpers Ferry and to Frederick. I will go to Harpers Ferry, and take General Warren (of the engineers) with me, and look over the ground and see if I can find any reason why that garrison should be kept there, and I will be at Frederick to-night."

General Hooker's intention had been to take that garrison with General Slocum's corps, near Knoxville, the two making about 25,000 men, throw them rapidly in rear of General Lee's army, cut his communications, destroy the bridges and capture his trains, and then reunite with the main army for the battle. He had assembled three corps at Middletown, under Reynolds, with a view to this movement, so that if the enemy turned back to attack this force in their rear, the corps at Middletown holding the mountain passes could fall on their flank. General Lee's report, since made, shows his anxiety as to his communications and his rear, and what effect that would have had.

On the surface this plan appeared to hold some promise, but in reality it had major problems. The troops Butterfield spoke of using actually numbered around 16,000 men instead of 25,000. The garrison from Harpers Ferry, which made up half the total, consisted of 5,000 untried men and 3,000 men from the rout at Winchester, who French described as "ready to take the rear at the first alarm."[9]

9. *OR*, vol. 27, pt. 1, 70, 151; pt. 3, p. 440.

Another problem with this plan was the presumption that Lee had a conventional supply line and would have reacted to a threat to his line. In fact Lee intended to, and did, live off the land. Hooker's movement would have inconvenienced Lee, but not enough to have made him change his plans.

General Halleck telegraphed back that the post of Harpers Ferry was a very important one, and that the garrison should not be taken away, or something to that effect; I cannot give the exact language of the dispatches. General Hooker then telegraphed, asking to be relieved from the command of the army.

That evening General Hooker came down to Frederick and informed me that he had asked to be relieved from the command of the army. I was surprised, and asked him why he had done so. He replied that he had too much respect for the position to remain in command of the army when he was not allowed to command it; that he would rather go into the ranks as a soldier than to stand there and be thwarted at such a time, when it was for every man to be used for the safety of the country and the destruction of Lee's army; that they would appoint a successor to him who would be allowed everything, while he would trust to history for a right judgment in regard to his motives. Many other remarks were made by him that I do not at present recall. The next morning he was relieved.

General Meade came up very early in the morning to headquarters. It had been General Hooker's intention that the army should move on the 29th of June, the following day; allowing the 28th, Sunday, for the army to rest at Frederick. I went into General Hooker's tent, and asked him if I should prepare orders for the movement the next day. The general told me that I had a new commander; that General Meade was in command of the army, and I better apply to him.

I saw General Meade shortly afterwards; he came to me and asked me what I desired to do. I replied that if I had been put in command of that army at half past four in the morning, without any previous advice of it, there was no major general who should tell me what he wished to do—that they should do as I wanted them to do; that I had nothing to say; that I would serve him in any capacity and in any way, most cheerfully, and to the best of my ability; that I recognized without question his right to select his chief of staff, and that if he did not desire me to act in that capacity, I should not have the slightest feeling about it, for I had been in the field constantly since the breaking out of the war, and would not object to a rest. He said I would relieve him from embarrassment if I would express my preference. I told him that if he placed it on that ground, I would say most decidedly that my preference had never been for that position; that I preferred to command troops; that I had accepted [419] that position, as I had done everything else, because I was ordered to do so. It was thought then that I could render valuable assistance. He said he was very much obliged to me for my course; that it certainly was very patriotic and very kind; he would take the matter into consideration, and let me know during the day what he intended to do with me.

Towards afternoon General Meade came to me and said, "General Butterfield, I have made up my mind that I cannot get along without you; I desire you to remain as my chief of staff." I said I would serve him to the best of my ability; and if I did not act according to his ideas, it was only necessary for him to suggest what he wished. I then said, "General, since you have selected me for this position, it is necessary this army should be moved to-morrow." He desired to know the reasons why. I explained to him that one corps of General Lee's army (Ewell's) was in the vicinity of York and Carlisle, and the others had passed through Hagerstown; that if it was General Lee's intention to cross the Susquehanna and move towards Harrisburg and Philadelphia, we must prevent it and try to catch him while crossing.

Question. Were you in possession of General Hooker's plan of operations?

This question had implications beyond the hearings. Beginning in December 1863, Congress had taken up the matter of allotting the honors of war. Grant was voted a gold medal, and a joint House-Senate resolution of thanks was unanimously passed on his behalf. Generals Nathaniel P. Banks and Ambrose Burnside also received the thanks of Congress for their actions in the West.

Politics played an even more decisive role for honors in the East. Hooker, championed by Secretary of the Treasury Salmon Chase and many of the radicals, and General O. O. Howard, supported by Vice President Hannibal Hamlin, were both nominated. Meade merely got a nod for his "skill and heroic valor." It was maintained that Hooker had planned the Gettysburg campaign, Butterfield had taken care of the daily logistics, and the actual fighting had been done by the corps commanders. Meade, it would seem, had only been along for the ride.[10]

During the congressional debates, Sickles—always the self-promoter—tried to have Meade's name removed and his own name inserted in the resolution.

10. *MG*, 216; *LLM*, 2:164.

He asserted that Howard had selected the position at Gettysburg, but that he and his corps had done all the fighting. Hearing of Sickles's claim, Meade sarcastically wrote his wife that "before long it will be clearly proved that my presence on the field was rather an injury than otherwise." Sickles's efforts failed, however. Although the inclusion of Howard as the only corps commander brought protests and grumbling in the army, the resolution passed February 1, 1864, listing Hooker, Howard, and Meade in that order.[11]

Answer. That will appear when I state all this conversation. I said that if it was General Lee's intention to go around our right into Baltimore, we had to prevent that; that we must not let him get too far away from us; that we had to move up and cover the approaches around the mountains—there was a pass near Emmitsburg and Gettysburg—and prevent him getting on in that direction. General Meade said he had not had time to give the subject as much reflection as he ought to give it, having been so pressed with the duties incident upon taking command. I asked him if he had a full and free conversation and understanding with General Hooker in regard to his plans and purposes. He said yes, but it was very early in the morning, and he had been taken so completely by surprise in being placed in command of the army that he did not know that he could recall it all, though he had a general ideal of General Hooker's views and plans. I asked General Meade if he desired me, as his representative, to have an official conversation with General Hooker concerning his plans and purposes, and he replied that he desired I should do so. I then went to General Hooker's tent and said to him, "General, General Meade has selected me as his chief of staff, and I have come officially from him to have an official conversation with you in regard to your plans and purposes. I do not consider it necessary, in order to enlighten me any further in regard to what you intended to do; but it is better that it be in that shape, in order that there may be no misunderstanding about it." General Hooker then went over his plans and purposes with me, as he had done before; repeated his intentions, and I returned and repeated the substance of the conversation to General Meade.

Question. Can you tell us what those intentions and purposes were?

Answer. I can hardly do so understandingly without a map. General Hooker's plans were, of course, interfered with by the, to him, unexpected refusal of the troops within the line of his operations. After repeating the conversation

11. *MG*, 216; *CG*, 38th Cong., 1st sess., February 1, 1864, p. 421.

General Meade said that was what General Hooker had told him, and directed that the movement should be made as proposed—that is, to move the army, in three columns, up towards Gettysburg, and the line of the Northern Central railroad, across from Gettysburg. The only change made in General Hooker's plan was the leaning a little to the right, so as to use the Northern Central road as a line of supply in case of necessity, possibly separating the army a very little more, which was in accordance with the opinions and views of General Hooker, and the orders were issued accordingly.

Butterfield's testimony implied a more essential role for himself than in fact was the case. He also described Meade as befuddled and in shock upon assuming command. Yet Meade was a decisive man, and once he had been briefed on the position of the Army of the Potomac he quickly formulated his own strategy. As early as 7:00 A.M. Meade telegraphed Halleck a broad outline of what he was going to do. That Meade's strategy had many of the same elements as Hooker's was not surprising. Hooker's plan, as far as it went, was good. Moreover, based upon available information about Lee's movements, Meade had very few options.

Shortly after the order had been prepared, and General Meade had looked it over and assented to it, a telegram came from the Secretary of War announcing that there was a force of the enemy at Winchester, north of the Potomac. General Meade said he could not move the army as proposed, for here was a dispatch from the Secretary of War that there was a force of the enemy at [420] Winchester. I stated that, in my opinion, there was no force of the enemy at Winchester; that our information was very accurate, very correct in regard to Lee's army, and that it was that it had all crossed over the Potomac; that if there was any force of the enemy there, it was probably only a regiment or two, or at most a small brigade, to keep Lee's line of communication with the river open, and to guard his trains and despatches. General Meade said he could not disregard a despatch from the Secretary of War, who was the highest official authority, and that he did not think he was justified in moving the army as had been proposed, after having received this notice from the Secretary of War of a force of the enemy at Winchester. I told him I thought he ought to telegraph to the Secretary of War that if this force was there it might stop his contemplated movement. After some discussion, General Meade decided that the movement should go on.

This is another example of Butterfield's habitual self-presentation: here again, his calm reasoning convinced Meade to do the right thing. Yet there is no record of such a dispatch from the secretary of war. One of Halleck's dispatches mentioned an enemy force south of the Potomac, but Meade did not believe it to be true.[12]

I then asked him if he intended to use the garrison at Harper's Ferry. He said, no; that it had been refused to General Hooker, and it would create a great disturbance if he should take it. I told him that the question was not one of any disturbance; that it was a question of what had best be done; that our information showed us that Lee had 91,000 infantry, 12,000 cavalry, and 275 pieces of artillery. Lee's army, as it passed through, had been counted by several citizens of Hagerstown from the commencement to the end; they had counted it at different points, comparing notes every night; our own spies and scouts had brought us information; and coming from several sources, the information was reliable.

This is an excellent example of the consistent overestimation of Lee's army. Based upon supposedly reliable information, Lee's army was estimated at 103,000 men and 275 guns. This, of course, was not Butterfield's fault. Like Meade, he could only operate with the information given to him. But such inflated numbers reveal the overall poor intelligence-gathering capabilities of the Army of the Potomac and the failure of Pleasonton's cavalry to penetrate Stuart's cavalry screen.

I said to General Meade that, with the marches we were making, when we came to fight the battle, which we should certainly within a week, we might fall short that number of infantry, while we would have a superiority of artillery; that the garrison at Harper's Ferry would be of no possible use there while Lee's army was in or beyond Hagerstown; that if we failed, that garrison would have to leave Harper's Ferry; and if we took it away and succeeded, it could be replaced; that his orders and authority from General Halleck and the Secretary of War gave him the command of all the troops in the vicinity, and of General Couch's command; and in case of his failure, he would be responsible for not using them; while in case of his success, no one would ever ques-

12. *OR,* vol. 27, pt. 1, pp. 61–3.

tion his use of them. I said that if we went on, the present line of supply—the railroad from Baltimore to Frederick—would have to be guarded; and if we did not bring those troops from Harpers Ferry up to Frederick to do that duty, we would have to detach forces from our own army for that purpose; and I considered it altogether advisable to use this garrison. After General Meade had reflected upon the subject for some time, he directed an order to be issued, directing General French to move up with that garrison to Frederick, which was done.

The army made the march decided upon on the 29th of June, and on the 30th it continued its march. I happen to have a copy of the order of march which were issued on the 30th of June. They are as follows:

"Order of March for July 1.
"Headquarters Army of the Potomac,
"June 30, 1863.
"Orders.
"Headquarters at Taneytown.
"3d corps to Emmitsburg.
"2d corps to Taneytown.
"5th corps to Hanover.
"12th corps to Two Taverns.
"1st corps to Gettysburg.
"11th corps to Gettysburg, (in supporting distance.)
[421] "6th corps to Manchester.

"Cavalry to the front and flanks, well out in all directions, giving timely notice of positions and movements of the enemy.

"All empty wagons, surplus baggage, useless animals, and impediments of every sort, to Union Bridge, three miles from Middleburg—a proper officer from each corps with them. Supplies will be brought up there as soon as practicable."

We came across a railroad there which nobody seemed to know was in existence. It was not indicated upon any of the railroad maps. Although I supposed I knew every railroad in the country, I found a railroad there of the existence of which nothing was known to us before, and it was determined to make use of it at once.

"The general relies upon every commander to put his column in the lightest possible order. The telegraph corps to work east from Hanover, repairing the line, and all commanders to work repairing the line in their vicinity between Gettysburg and Hanover."

The army was then moving up in fan-shape, and would cover the line of railroad from Gettysburg over to the railroad to Baltimore, and cover the line of retreat if it was found that General Lee was moving from the Susquehanna.

"Staff officers to report daily from each corps, and with orderlies to leave for orders; prompt information to be sent in to headquarters at all times; all ready to move to the attack at any moment.

"The commanding general desires you to be informed that, from present information, Longstreet and Hill are at Chambersburg, partly towards Gettysburg; Ewell at Carlisle and York; movements indicate a disposition to advance from Chambersburg to Gettysburg. General Couch telegraphs, 29th, his opinion that the enemy's operations of the Susquehanna are more to prevent cooperation with this army than offensive. The general believes he has relieved Harrisburg and Philadelphia, and now desires to look to his own army and assume position for offensive or defensive as occasion requires or rest to the troops. It is not his desire to wear his troops out by excessive fatigue and marches, and thus unfit them for the work they will be called upon to perform. Vigilance, energy, and prompt response to the orders from headquarters are necessary, and the personal attention of corps commanders must be given to reduction of impediments. The orders and movements from these headquarters must be carefully and confidentially preserved, that they do not fall into the enemy's hands.

"By command of Major General Meade."

I may say that this is a copy which I always required the Adjutant General to furnish me, that I might have one with me. And it was one of the few documents I did not send back to the army, it being unnecessary to do so, as the original was there. The following is an addendum to the foregoing order:

"Headquarters Army of the Potomac,

"June 30, 1863.

"The movements indicated in the enclosed orders are to be made as early tomorrow as their receipt and the condition of the troops will permit. The trains sent off must be subordinate to these movements. Maps, whenever possible, must be obtained from citizens.

"By command of Major General Meade."

The army moved under these orders. The headquarters of the army were moved to Taneytown. At Taneytown, I think, on the morning of the 30th of June, General Meade came to me with an order which he proposed to issue. That order, as issued, I have a copy of; it is as follows:

[422] (See papers accompanying testimony of General Meade, the one commencing with this paragraph:)

"From information received, the commanding general is satisfied that the object of the movement of the army in this direction has been accomplished, viz.: the relief of Harrisburg, and the prevention of the enemy's intended invasion of Philadelphia, &c., beyond the Susquehanna."[13]

The order, as General Meade brought it to me, was in his own handwriting, and somewhat different from the one issued, of which this is a copy. Some additions were made to the order by me, with his approval, in regard to the details. I think General Williams may have the original, as prepared by General Meade, with the additions which I made with his consent. If he has, the committee can obtain it from him if they desire it.

When General Meade presented this order to me, I stated to him that I thought the effect of an order to fall back would be very bad upon the morale of the army, and that it ought to be avoided if possible. General Meade seemed to think that we were going ahead without any well-understood plan, and that by reason of that we might be liable to disaster. I spoke to General Hancock, who was at headquarters at the time, with regard to the order; I also spoke to General Ingalls, and I think, to some others. I stated to them that I thought an order indicating a practical falling back would have a bad effect upon the morale of the army, and that it ought to be avoided if possible. And I requested of them that, if those were also their views, they would express them to General Meade should he have any conversation with them in regard to the order—that which I have read in the corrected order as issued. I am not sure whether the original of the order directed the falling back immediately or not. That is why I speak of it. This is the order that was sent out.

Wade and Chandler must have been mentally dancing with joy upon hearing this testimony. Here was evidence that Meade had not intended to fight at Gettysburg but rather to retreat in the face of the enemy. Such an intention, could it be convincingly demonstrated, might have convicted Meade not merely of timidity and incompetence, but of cowardice or even treason.

13. The entire order can be found in *OR*, vol. 27, pt. 3, p. 458.

Butterfield's testimony was not entirely accurate, however. He failed to read the entire order into the record at this time, leaving out two key lines. The first omission is the very next sentence after where he left off, which said that Meade would suspend forward movement until Lee's movements or position rendered "such an operation certain of success." In other words, Meade had not given up the offensive; he simply was still uncertain about Lee's intentions and wanted to wait until they became more clear before committing his army to offensive operations. The second omission, buried farther down in the order, said, "Developments may cause the commanding general to assume the offensive from his present positions." This clearly suggested that Meade would assume the offensive if Lee did not attack him in his present location.

Unfortunately for Meade, the order's emphasis on withdrawal exposed him to attacks from his critics. Without a careful reading, the order can appear to be what Butterfield claimed it was—proof of Meade's confusion and paralysis.

During the day intelligence was brought in that General Reynolds had got in collision with the enemy at Gettysburg. Shortly after news of the death of General Reynolds came in. I stated to General Meade that, in the event of the death of General Reynolds, I thought it his duty to go upon the field in person, or send me as his representative. There would be inevitable confusion on the field if the chief commander was killed, and that it was necessary to decide at once whether he would fight the battle there at Gettysburg, or, in case of that being considered an unfavorable position, to maneuver for position elsewhere; that the question must be decided then whether we should fight at Gettysburg or elsewhere. General Meade replied that he could not go himself; that the enemy was, as stated in this last order, at Emmitsburg, Two Taverns, Taneytown, &c., and that he could not spare me. I replied that if he thought he could not go himself or send his chief of staff, he ought to send some one on the field fully possessed of his views and intentions to represent him, and decide whether to fight there or to fall back, and where the army should be concentrated for battle. He asked who there was to send. I replied, if I was in command of the army, and felt that I could not go myself or send my chief of staff, I should in trust that duty to General Hancock, whom I considered entirely competent, and in whose ability I had great confidence. He was close at hand, too, for the duty. General Meade then requested me to get my horse and go to General Hancock, and to write an order for the purpose. General Hancock was then at Taneytown, a short ride from headquarters. Before I could get my horse General Meade rode off to General Hancock's headquarters.

Meade's failure to rush to the battlefield when informed of Reynolds's death was not without its critics. But had he done so, he would have been out of touch with, and out of control of, events at Gettysburg.

Butterfield's testimony that he suggested Hancock to a bewildered Meade is patently false. Hancock was the logical choice for Meade. Earlier that very morning the two men had had a long discussion about Meade's thoughts and plans for battle. After Reynolds, Hancock was the man Meade may have trusted most in the army.[14]

Butterfield's testimony that he wrote out Hancock's orders at headquarters is also false. The orders were written after Meade and Butterfield had arrived at Hancock's headquarters and after further discussions between Meade and Hancock. Butterfield probably was trying yet again to bolster his own role in events and to undermine Meade.[15]

I prepared the order, of which the following is a copy:

"Headquarters Army of the Potomac,

"July 1—1.10 P.M., 1863.

"Commanding Officer, 2d Corps:

"The major general commanding has just been informed that General Reynolds has been killed or badly wounded. He directs that you turn over the command [423] of your corps to General Gibbon;[16] that you proceed to the front, and by virtue of this order, in case of the truth of General Reynolds's death, you assume command of the corps there assembled, viz.: the 11th, 1st, and 3d, at Emmitsburg. If you consider the ground and position there a better one to fight a battle, under existing circumstances, you will so advise the general, and he will order all the troops up. You know the general's views; and General Warren, who is fully aware of them, has gone out to see General Reynolds.

"Later—1.15 P.M.

"Reynolds has possession of Gettysburg, and the enemy are reported as falling back from the front of Gettysburg. Hold your column ready to move."

I followed General Meade to General Hancock's headquarters. General Meade had some conversation with General Hancock, explaining his views,

14. *LLM,* 2:33.

15. See among others, *GC,* 284–5; *MG,* 136; Jordan, *Winfield Scott Hancock,* 81.

16. Brig. Gen. John Gibbon, commander of the Second Division, Second Corps. Brig. Gen. John C. Caldwell of the First Division, not Gibbon, was the senior officer.

which I did not hear. He read the order I had prepared and gave it to General Hancock, who jumped into an ambulance, in order that he might have an opportunity to consult his maps, leaving directions for General Gibbon to assume command of his corps and move it up on the road at once, and started for Gettysburg. Meanwhile, during the time of General Hancock's absence, and before his return, orders had been issued to other corps to move towards Gettysburg. General Hancock came back in the evening and made his report to General Meade.

Before General Hancock left for Gettysburg I stated to him my views of the matter. I told him that I hoped, as he was vested with this authority, he would not, if circumstances were such that it could be avoided, have the army fall back; that I thought the effect upon the morale of the army would be bad. General Hancock said that he would not fall back if there was any other way of doing anything, or something to that effect. I ought to say here that in all the conversations I report, I do not express the precise language, but my recollection of the substance of the conversations.

In the evening General Hancock came back and made his report to General Meade, who determined to go on the field of Gettysburg. He went up that night, leaving me at Taneytown, with instructions to remain there until I could get a reply from General Sedgwick, whose corps had been ordered up from Manchester. We had sent two or three staff officers and two or three orderlies, but we had got no reply from General Sedgwick. General Meade himself had waited for some time for the purpose of having an interview with General Sedgwick, and himself giving him his views. In order that I might correctly and without any mistake convey General Meade's views to General Sedgwick, I took a memorandum, the original of which I have with me. I was to state as follows to General Sedgwick:

"General Meade presumes that the condition of General Sedgwick's troops, upon their arrival at Taneytown, will be such that he can hardly get on the field at Gettysburg before the matter is pretty well settled. General Meade proposes making a vigorous attack upon the enemy to-morrow. He thinks that General Sedgwick, after resting at Taneytown, better move forward as far as possible and take up a position in line of battle at some strong point, so that in the event of General Meade's being compelled to withdraw, General Sedgwick can cover his withdrawal, and if General Meade is successful General Sedgwick can push forward and aid him. The inhabitants represent that there is a very strong position on this side of Willaloway creek, a high commanding ground. The engineer battalion is placed under General Sedgwick's orders, who can use them to prepare any works that may be necessary."

Butterfield failed to mention that shortly after sending this dispatch Sedgwick's orders were changed, and the Sixth Corps was ordered to march to Gettysburg immediately by the shortest route. Without the Sixth Corps, Meade felt that the Union army would be considerably outnumbered.[17]

My instructions were to remain at Taneytown and communicate the view and wishes of General Meade to General Sedgwick in person. I got no word from General Sedgwick, though I waited all night. I sent out several times, [424] but hearing nothing from him, at daylight in the morning I concluded that, under the circumstances, it was my duty to go on to the field and disregard the order requiring me to remain, as it was possible that General Sedgwick might have gone by some other route. I did so. On my arrival at headquarters General Meade informed me that he had received word during the night from General Sedgwick that he was on his way up by another route, instead of through Taneytown—a little shorter route; that he would be up during the day, and that everything was up but the 6th corps, and that he was glad I had arrived.

General Meade then directed me to prepare an order to withdraw the army from that position. I stated to him that it would be necessary that I should know the exact position of the troops.

This was one of the major reasons Butterfield had been called before the committee. Whereas Sickles's and others' testimony on this point had been hearsay, Butterfield claimed to have been personally involved in preparing an order to retreat. His testimony to that effect, however, is disproved by his own work at Gettysburg. Meade had initially decided to make a "strong and decisive attack" from his right, using the fast-approaching Sixth Corps. Butterfield did not include this planned attack in his testimony, but he was aware of it. In a message sent after 9:30 A.M., Butterfield had notified Slocum, "The commanding general desires you to make your arrangements for an attack from your front on the enemy."[18]

Meade devoted his second appearance before the committee to refuting this charge by Butterfield.

Question. What day of the fight was this?

Answer. This was on the morning of the 2d of July, before the battle of that

17. *OR,* vol. 27, pt.1, pp. 467–8.
18. Ibid., pt. 3, pp. 480, 486.

day had commenced. I stated to General Meade that I could not prepare that order properly without first going over the field and ascertaining the position of each division and corps of the army with relation to the roads. General Meade replied that he could not wait for that—that he could show me where the troops were. He then took a pencil and a piece of paper and made a rough sketch showing the position of the different corps. I stated to him that the order was one requiring a great deal of care in its preparation; that it involved something more than logistics, as we were in the presence of the enemy, and that while I was preparing it I must not be interrupted by anybody coming to me with despatches or orders. He said, "Very well, you shall not be interrupted." I told him I thought I could not prepare the order without a more accurate sketch, and I would have to send out to the corps commanders to give me a report of the position of their troops in regard to the various roads; that in the mean while I could be studying the maps. He said, "Very well, do so." I then went up stairs, and, after carefully studying the maps, I prepared the order for the withdrawal of the army from the field of Gettysburg. After finishing it, I presented it to General Meade, and it met with his approval. I then stated to him that it would be a great deal better, if that order was to be executed, as it might involve grave consequences if not properly executed, to submit it for careful examination to such general officers as were then present, with a view of giving them an opportunity of finding any fault with it then, so that no misunderstanding should arise from the manner in which it was worded or expressed. He said there was no objection to having that done. I called General Gibbon, who was present, and, I think, General Williams and General Ingalls, and stated to them that I had been directed to prepare this order, and that I would be very much obliged to any of them if they would look it over and point out any faults in it then, rather than after it was put into execution; that I desired it scrutinized carefully with a view of discovering anything in it which might be misunderstood. Some of these officers—I do not now remember which; I am very sure General Gibbon was one—I think General Hancock was there, but whether he read it over or not I am not sure—some of the officers read it over and said that they thought it was correctly prepared.

The corps commanders were then sent for by General Meade to report to headquarters. The order which I had prepared was given to General Williams, and was copied by the clerks, or was in the process of being copied by them. As General Sickles rode up to headquarters, in pursuance of the request of General Meade, the battle broke out in front of General Sickles's corps, and there was no council held. General Sickles returned immediately, and every corps commander there rode immediately to his command. Without my memoranda I cannot fix the hour of this, but it was during the 2d day of July.

[425] General Sickles's corps was very severely attacked. General Hancock went to his relief with two brigades; other re-enforcements were sent from the left. General Sickles was wounded and taken from the field, and the enemy were finally repulsed.

After night-fall, General Meade summoned a council of the corps commanders.

Question. Did this collision of General Sickles's corps with the enemy prevent the order being executed which you had prepared?

Sickles used this line of argument to justify the advance of his line on July 2.

Answer. It is impossible for me to state that, because General Meade had not communicated to me his intention to execute that order regardless of the opinions of the corps commanders, or whether he intended to have the order submitted to them. He merely directed me to prepare such an order, which I did. It is for him to say whether he intended to execute it or not. He may have desired it prepared for an emergency, without any view of executing it then, or he may have had it prepared with a full view of its execution.

Whether a show of restraint (as historian Edwin Coddington has called it) or an admirable job of acting, Butterfield's answer also served to cover himself. He had cast his lot with the anti-Meade camp, but he did not burn all his bridges behind him. Butterfield surely realized that his version of events would receive little support from the corps commanders; he sought a fallback position in the unlikely event that the committee failed to have Meade removed from command.[19]

Question. The collision of Sickles's troops with the enemy broke up the council?

Answer. It prevented any consultation of the corps commanders at that time. That evening, after the enemy were repulsed, a council of corps commanders was held. I kept minutes of that council, which I sent to General Williams, who informs me that they have been lost.

19. *GC*, 340.

Butterfield may have been trying to suggest a sinister motive behind the disappearance of the minutes, but the committee did not give him an opportunity for further dramatics.

The general question put to the corps commanders present at that council was, whether our army should remain on that field and continue the battle, or whether we should change to some other position. A vote of the corps commanders was taken in regard to that, and a majority were in favor of remaining on the field and fighting it out. General Slocum gave the first opinion; his answer was, "Stay and fight it out." I will not be positive as to what corps commanders differed with him; but the majority were for remaining on the line which the army then held, and fighting it out.

Question. Can you give the opinion of each corps commander? Because, perhaps, in justice to them, that ought to be known.

Answer. My impression is, that those generals can tell how they voted. I am clear in my memory that General Slocum voted to stay and fight it out, and that General Sykes so voted; that General Newton entered into a long discussion to show that that position was a disadvantageous one; that he was not prepared to vote to leave it, but he wanted the council to understand that he had objections to it. General Birney, I think, voted to stay and fight it out, as did General Hancock also. I do not remember what General Sedgwick's vote was, nor do I remember how General Howard voted; I think he had a great deal to say upon the subject. The reason I do not remember the votes exactly is, because I intrusted the matter to the memorandum which I sent General Williams. After the council had finished, General Meade arose from the table, and remarked that in his opinion, Gettysburg was no place to fight a battle; but it was settled to remain there, and the council dispersed.

This was confirmation that Meade had not wanted to fight at Gettysburg but had been forced to do so by his corps commanders.

The minutes of the July 2 council resurfaced in 1881 among Meade's papers. There were actually nine, not seven, general officers voting at the meeting. They were: Newton, who commanded the First Corps after Reynolds's death; Hancock and Gibbon, Second Corps; Birney, Third Corps; Sykes, Fifth Corps; Sedgwick, Sixth Corps; Howard, Eleventh Corps; Slocum and Brigadier General Alpheus S. Williams, Twelfth Corps.

There were three questions put to the council: whether to stay at Gettysburg or retire; whether the army should attack or defend, if it stayed; how long the army should wait to be attacked, if it took a defensive stance. Except for suggestions for minor adjustments in the line, the opinion was unanimous to stay and fight, but to wait for Lee to attack.[20]

The remark Butterfield attributed to Meade was another attempt to discredit him. Gibbon, whose version of this meeting is the accepted one, attributed such a statement not to Meade but to Newton, though in a different context than Butterfield suggested.[21]

In anticipation of Butterfield's testimony, Meade on March 10 had sent a circular memorandum to those officers he felt to be friendly—Gibbon, Newton, Sedgwick, Slocum, Sykes, and A. S. Williams—asking for their recollections of the meeting. Slocum did not reply, but none of the others had the impression Meade had wanted to retreat. Why Meade did not send the circular to Howard and Hancock, both of whom supported him, is not known.[22]

On the next day, the 3d of July, matters were very quiet along the lines until about noon, when the enemy opened a terrific artillery fire on our left front and centre.

Question. About what number of guns had they in operation in your judgment?

Answer. I should judge from 125 to 150. It was a very terrific cannonade, but our troops behaved with the greatest composure. During this artillery fire, and before the enemy made their assault with infantry, I was wounded and sent over to General Meade's headquarters, on the Westminster turnpike. While I was lying on a bed there, word was brought to me by some person that General Hancock was severely wounded and desired to see me. I made an effort to get out; was lifted on my horse, and rode as far as General Slocum's position, when I found I was unable to go any further, and dismounted there and [426] laid down for a time. Appearances on the field indicated to me that we were successful. I sent for General Slocum and asked him his opinion in regard to it, and he agreed with me. I then said to General Slocum that there was a great chance for him; that his command, though it had had hard fighting, had been well protected and had not met with heavy loss; that I hoped if there was any intention to pursue, he would not be one to say that he could not pur-

20. Also present, but not voting, were Meade, Butterfield, and Warren (who slept through the meeting). *B&L*, 3:314.

21. Gibbon, *Recollections*, 140.

22. *OR*, vol. 27, pt. 1, pp. 123–7.

sue, but that he would have his command ready to move out, and tear the enemy in pieces; that he would get up ammunition and rations, and if there was any intention to pursue, that he would not hesitate to offer to go out, for he would thus have a great opportunity to make a reputation and a name, and to do a very brilliant thing. General Slocum assented to what I said, and said that within half an hour he would be ready to pursue. After resting for some time, I was again lifted on my horse, and rode over on the field. The enemy had retired and withdrawn, and there was very little firing going on. It was some time before I found General Meade. When I did see him he seemed to think that General Lee had only withdrawn into the mountains with the view of inducing him to follow and to attack him in a stronger position. He did not seem much inclined to make a vigorous pursuit. No council was held on the night of the 3d of July.

On the night of the 4th of July a council was called. I have with me the minutes of that council as I kept them at the time.

On the morning of the 4th of July a very heavy rain came up. We were almost drowned out of headquarters, down in the woods, and had to leave there and go into the house where General Neal [Neill] had his headquarters. Heavy details were made to go out and collect our dead and bury them; and I believe a portion of the troops were ordered out to make a pursuit, but, as I was wounded, I did not make out any of these orders. I cannot speak positively as to what orders were then issued, but the records of headquarters will show.

I have here the minutes I kept of the council of the 4th of July. That council was held at the headquarters of General Neal. He gave up his headquarters to General Meade. The council was opened by General Meade explaining his instructions and asking the corps commanders for their advice as to what course he should pursue.

Question. Can you state what General Meade said his instructions were?

Answer. I think he said his instructions were to cover Washington and Baltimore. He said he had no knowledge of General Foster's movements. There was a rumor that General Foster was coming up from Washington with re-enforcements. General Meade said he desired the earnest assistance and advice of every corps commander. The corps commanders commenced giving their opinions, beginning with General Slocum, and followed by General Sedgwick and General Howard. Their advice, according to my memorandum here, was as follows:

General Slocum would move on an interior line as far as Emmitsburg, and then, if the enemy had not gone from Gettysburg, hold on there, and push out a force at once with a view of preventing the enemy from crossing the Potomac.

General Sedgwick would wait at Gettysburg until certain that the enemy were moving away.

General Howard would like to remain at Gettysburg and ascertain what the enemy were doing, but thought it would do no harm to send a corps to Emmitsburg.

General Meade then determined to change the manner of procedure in the council, and the following questions were written by his instructions. A portion of these questions are in his handwriting, and a portion in mine.

The first question was, "Shall this army remain here?" that is, at Gettysburg.

Second. "If we remain here, shall we assume the offensive?"

[427] Third. "Do you deem it expedient to move towards Williamsport, through Emmitsburg?"

Fourth. "Shall we pursue the enemy if he is retreating on his direct line of retreat?"

To the first question General Newton answered no; to the second question, No; and to the third question, Yes.

General Slocum answered to the first question, No; the second question was involved in that answer; to the third question, Yes; to the fourth question, To pursue on the direct line of retreat, with cavalry moving with the infantry, to cut him off.

General Sedgwick, to the first question, answered, Would remain here (at Gettysburg) until positive information concerning their movement; to the second question, No; to the third question, Yes; to the fourth question, Only cavalry.

General Howard, to the first question, did not exactly say yes, and did not exactly say no, but would commence a movement to-morrow; to the second question, No; to the third question, Yes; to the fourth question, By a show of force.

General Sykes, to the first question, as to remaining at Gettysburg, answered, Until we know where the enemy is gone; to the second question, No; to the third question he made no answer, his answer to the first question involving that; to the fourth question he answered, He would pursue with cavalry only.

General Birney, to the first question, answered, Yes, until we see; to the second question, No; to the fourth question, He thinks not.

General Pleasonton, to the first question, answered, No; to the second question, No; to the third question, Move by that route; to the fourth question, Would pursue with infantry and cavalry.

General Hays answered to the first question, Yes, until we find out where the enemy are, and what they are doing; to the second question, No; to the third question, Yes, if we move; to the fourth question, No, only with cavalry.

General Warren, as to the first question, whether we should remain there, answered, Yes, until we see what they are doing; to the second question, about assuming the offensive, Not if the enemy remains.

Those are the questions to the corps commanders, and their answers. The summary which I made for General Meade in the council of the answers to the first question, whether we should remain at Gettysburg, was—

Those in favor: Birney, Sedgwick, Sykes, Hays, and Warren.

Opposed: Newton, Pleasonton, and Slocum.

Doubtful: Howard.

By this memorandum I see that the corps commanders reported about 55,000 infantry on the field. That was not from actual returns, but that was their estimate. I have noted here what each one reported on the 4th of July, and also what was the force we had on the 11th of June.

Question. Was there any discrepancy between their estimates and the real facts about our force?

Answer. Yes, sir; that is always the case after a battle. A great many commanders come in and say that half their force is gone; the colonel reports that half his regiment is gone; that is reported to the brigade commander, who reports that half the brigade is gone, and so on.

Question. How many troops had we, in fact, there at that time?

Answer. I have never seen the actual returns, because I left that army soon after that.

By Mr. Gooch:

Question. How many did the corps commanders estimate at that time?

Answer. The estimate then made was as follows: 1st corps, 5,000; 2d corps, [428] 5,000; 3d corps, 5,676; 5th corps, 10,000; 6th corps, 12,500; 11th corps, 5,500; 12th corps, 7,838; making altogether 51,514 infantry. This was merely their judgment; it was not given as the exact numbers.

This is nearly 10 percent lower than the figure Butterfield had given the committee a moment earlier.

By Mr. Chandler:

Question. How many had they when the battle began?

Answer. I can state what they had on the 10th of June. The 1st corps had 11,250; 2d corps, 11,361; 3d corps, 11,898; 5th corps, 10,136; 6th corps, 15,408; 11th corps, 10,177; 12th corps, 7,925; making in all 78,245.

By the chairman:

Question. What do you understand were our losses at Gettysburg?

Answer. I left the army of the Potomac soon after that, and have never been back since, and have never seen the returns of our losses. I believe General Meade gives them in his official report. I have never seen a copy of that but once, and then only for a moment, and have forgotten what is stated there to have been our losses.

By Mr. Gooch:

Question. Had there been any considerable change in the army between the 10th of June and the time the battle of Gettysburg was fought?

Answer. Yes, sir.

Question. What change?

Answer. A portion of the Pennsylvania reserves, some 4,000 or 5,000, had been added to the 5th corps; General Stannard's Vermont brigade had been added to the 1st corps, but were to go out of service very shortly; General Lockwood, with the Maryland brigade, of about 2,500 men, had joined the 12th corps. I have a memorandum among my papers at Lookout valley which will show all the additions made to the army of the Potomac. I do not remember the exact figures now. I was suffering so much from my wound during the occurrences of the 4th and 5th of July that I was unfitted for much duty; still I was anxious to work all I could, but I finally had to succumb; and, by the advice of the medical director of the army, I left on the 6th of July and went home. I had prepared an order for the movement of the army through Frederick and Middletown, to intercept General Lee. It was not executed, at least until after I left. What occurred after the 6th of July, when I left, I have no knowledge of, except from hearsay.

By the chairman:

Question. You say that at the time the enemy made their last assault at Gettysburg, they opened upon our lines with from 125 to 150 pieces of artillery?

Answer. I will explain. On the afternoon of the 3d of July they made their last assault. In making that assault they had placed in position about 125 pieces of artillery, with which they opened upon that portion of our line held principally by General Hancock's 2d corps, and to his right and left. They kept up their artillery fire I should think for an hour or more, and while their artillery fire was going on they were forming their infantry columns for the assault. When they ceased their artillery fire they made their assault with their infantry. But during that artillery fire I was wounded and left the field.

Question. What was the condition of the enemy's artillery after their infantry attack had been repulsed? Where was it, and why could we not have taken it?

Answer. The range of artillery is much greater than that of small-arms; their artillery was further from our lines than their infantry. I have no doubt that if a prompt pursuit had been made by us after they were repulsed, all that artillery, or the most of it, would have fallen into our hands.

Question. Where was General Sedgwick, with his corps, when that attack had been repulsed?

[429] Answer. He had been in reserve principally on the left of the centre. What his position then was I do not know, as, while I was lying down at General Neal's after being hit, his position might have been changed.

Question. Suppose he had made a vigorous advance at the time the enemy were repulsed; what would have become of the enemy's artillery?

Answer. A better opinion than mine would come from those who were there at the exact time. I think we should have captured a large number of guns.

Question. Did you ever state, in Baltimore, say about the 7th of July, that General Lee would escape across the Potomac?

Answer. I did say so.

This is obviously a rehearsed question, for it refers to a private conversation.

Question. What reasons had you for expressing that opinion?

Answer. That was a private conversation with General Schenck. General Schenck came to me at the Eutaw House, in Baltimore, to see if he could do anything for me, and assist me in getting through. He asked me whether Lee's army would be destroyed: I said, no. He asked me why I thought so. I told him that I had not seen that inclination to pursue that would have pleased me; that Lee was an able engineer, and would get away, if he was not followed up right sharply. General Schenck asked me how Lee would get across the Potomac. I told him that Lee would find a way to get across the Potomac by making bridges; and I did not think he would be hurt before getting across; that that was my judgment from the complexion of affairs at headquarters before I left. That is my recollection of the conversation.

Question. Have you had any correspondence with General Meade since the battle of Gettysburg, which would be proper to be laid before the committee?

This is a transparent attempt to give Butterfield a chance to put his version of being replaced as chief of staff into the record.

Answer. I have had some correspondence with him. Shortly after the battle of Gettysburg General Meade sent me, unsolicited, the following letter:

"Headquarters, Army of the Potomac,

"July 14, 1863.

"Dear General: I owe you an apology for not having sooner written to you; but I need hardly make it to you, who know so well how difficult it is for me to find time to write.

"After you left, in view of the suffering you seemed to experience from your wound, and the probability of the length of time you might be kept from the army, together with my knowledge of the fact that the position you occupied was not altogether one of choice, I deemed it proper to appoint a successor, which I did by having General Humphreys made a major general.

"I hasten to explain to you the reasons for my so doing, and at the same time to express my grateful sense of the value of the services you rendered me during the time intervening between my assuming command and your being wounded. I shall never cease to remember and to bear testimony to the efficient assistance you so heartily rendered me, and without which I hardly know how I should have gotten through with the new and arduous duties imposed on me.

"Trusting, my dear general, you will understand the necessity which compelled me to appoint a successor, and that you will believe my assurance that it did not arise from any want of confidence in you, and hoping you may soon be restored to perfect health,

"I remain most sincerely and truly yours,

"GEO. G. MEADE,
"Major General."

I replied to that letter, but I have not a copy of my reply. There were several letters of a friendly character passed between us.

One such letter, which Butterfield did not produce for the committee, contains a clue to the cause of his grievances against Meade. Written by Meade around the end of July 1863, it appears to be in response to a letter from Butterfield asking if he had been relieved and therefore no longer had a job with the Army of the Potomac. Meade replied that no order had been issued relieving him, and that since he was on leave it was only necessary to announce the appointment of Humphreys as his replacement. Meade did not know whether Butterfield should report to the army or to Washington at the expiration of his leave, but said that he could not promise him anything if he came to the army. If there had been any question in Butterfield's mind about whether he had been relieved or not, this letter should have settled it.[23]

[430] I had no more correspondence with General Meade until the publication of General Halleck's report, in which there appeared this paragraph:

"Our force at Harpers Ferry at this time was supposed to be about 11,000. It was incorrectly represented to General Meade to be destitute of provisions, and that he must immediately supply it or order the abandonment of the place. Accordingly, a few hours after he assumed the command, he assented to an order drawn up by an officer of General Hooker's staff, directing General French to send 7,000 men of the garrison to Frederick, and with the remainder—estimated at 4,000—to remove and escort the public property to Washington. This order, based on erroneous representations, was not known in Washington till too late to be countermanded. It, however, was not entirely executed when General Meade very judiciously directed the re-occupation of that important point."

As soon as I saw that report I considered that the paragraph I have read unjustly reflected upon me. I addressed this letter to General Meade:

"January 23, 1864.
"Major General Meade:

23. Butterfield, ed., *Biographical Memorial of General Daniel Butterfield*, 126–7.

"General: I find the following most extraordinary statement in the annual report of the general-in-chief: (Extract from report.)

"Although it does not mention me by name, it will be considered by the public that I was the officer alluded to, as I was, before your assuming command, serving as chief of staff to the army under General Hooker, and am now temporarily serving in that capacity with him, although at the time alluded to I was no more an officer of General Hooker's staff than Generals Williams, Hunt, Ingalls, or any of the officers serving on the general staff of that army.

"Under the presumption that he may allude to me, it is proper, before taking the steps I propose to in the matter, that I should ascertain whether the entirely erroneous statement made by the general-in-chief in the premises is based upon anything he may have received from you officially or otherwise.

"You will certainly well remember that the garrison had an abundance of supplies, and it was so stated to me by you. You will also remember that no order was drawn up until after we had conversed upon the subject, and you had directed the order to be drawn; also, that the grounds upon which I advised it were generally, first, that Lee's army, to our then certain knowledge, numbered 91,000 infantry, 12,000 cavalry, and about 275 pieces of artillery; that, without this garrison, and taking into consideration our rapid marches, we should be likely to fall short of that number of infantry; that your having an order which gave you control of that garrison would make you responsible in the event of failure for not making use of them; that in such an event they would in all probability be required to leave that post; that in the event of success they could be returned at once.

"You will also doubtless remember that the bringing on of the general battle at Gettysburg sooner than you expected by Reynolds's collision with Hill and the events that followed prevented French reaching us in time, and it being determined that he could not reach us, orders were given him for his movements, contingent upon our success or failure, as the battle would be decided before he could reach us. The telegraphic and other correspondence will show this.

"I recall these facts to your recollection, knowing the duties suddenly imposed upon you at the time may have caused you, while giving attention to other and more pressing duties, to fail to fix decidedly in your mind these points. I shall be glad to know, if such is the case, that some other person than myself is alluded to.

[431] "In conclusion, I would repeat the purpose of this communication,

and respectfully and earnestly request a reply at your earliest convenience, as to whether the statement given above of the general-in-chief is based upon anything he may have received from you officially or otherwise."

This letter General Meade replied to as follows:

"Philadelphia, February 4, 1864.

"General: I am in receipt of your letter of the 23d ultimo. I have never made any official communication to the general-in-chief upon the subject of the withdrawal of the troops from Harpers Ferry, except such as were made at the time.

"Some time after the battle of Gettysburg, the first time I saw the general-in-chief, I did in private conversation say to him 'that my own judgment was in favor of leaving the garrison at Harpers Ferry intact, although I agreed with General Hooker that it was of no importance as a crossing place of the Potomac river, but I did think it of importance to hold it as a debouche into the Cumberland valley; that after much discussion I yielded to your arguments, and directed 4,000 men to be left to garrison Maryland heights, and the balance, 7,000, to be brought to Frederick to guard the Baltimore and Ohio railroad; that late on the night of the 28th, understanding from you that the supply of subsistence stores with the garrison was limited, and that owing to the difficulty of protecting the canal and railroad the communication with the place would be precarious, I ordered the abandonment of the place, and directed the 4,000 men to escort the public property to Washington.

"This communication was private, and was made in explanation of my course, but with no expectation that it would be officially used by the general-in-chief.

"You will see from it that I did not repudiate the responsibility of the act, but that I did state that it was based on arguments used by you and information derived from you.

"I shall greatly regret if my recollection of the facts differ from yours; but it is proper I should state that my recollection is clear and distinct as given above.

"Respectfully yours,

"GEORGE G. MEADE,

"Major General.

"Major General D. Butterfield,

"U.S. Vols., Headquarters 11th and 12th Corps, Lookout Valley, Tennessee."

I have answered this letter, but have not a copy of my answer with me. I will append the copy to my testimony when I come to examine it.

It is not clear why Butterfield introduced these two letters into the record. They certainly did not increase his standing before the committee or supplement his earlier testimony. Butterfield may have been making yet another attempt to protect his reputation. His reply to Meade is not in the record.

Question. What number of troops had General Meade after the close of the battle of Gettysburg with which he might have pursued the enemy?

Answer. According to the statements of the corps commanders of the 4th of July, which I have already given, he had 51,514 men; that was their actual strength, according to the best of their judgment.

Question. But, in fact, they must have had much more than that, when you consider the real amount of our loss at Gettysburg and the re-enforcements that had been received after the 10th of June. That is, was not their estimate manifestly an under estimate?

Answer. I think it was rather under than over.

Question. What was the condition of our troops after that battle, and what was their ability to pursue?

Answer. They were in splendid spirits, very exultant, and I think would have undergone any privations with a view to pursuit.

Question. How was it with the 6th corps under General Sedgwick? Had they been engaged in the battle enough to have become much fatigued?

[432] Answer. They had not been so much engaged as some of the other corps.

Question. In your judgment, as a military man, what should have been done after the final repulse of the enemy?

Answer. They should have been pursued immediately.

Question. How did you consider their ammunition to have been after that terrific cannonade: considering that they were so far from their base of operations, could they have had much ammunition on hand, or did you, as a military man, suppose that their artillery ammunition was nearly exhausted?

Answer. My opinion was that their supply of ammunition must have been very limited. We had no knowledge at that time that General French had broken their bridges and stopped their communications. But it was generally estimated that their supply of ammunition was short.

Question. It has occurred to me a great many times to ask why it was, when Lee had crossed over into Maryland, and it was known there would be a general engagement, the troops from Baltimore, Washington, Suffolk—all our disposable forces—were not brought into action. Was that ever a subject of deliberation?

Answer. Some time in May, I think on the 28th of May, General Hooker telegraphed to Washington that General Lee was about to renew his campaign of the year previous. That was before Lee had commenced his movement at all, and General Hooker asked permission, in the event of Lee's moving, to execute certain movements. I will refer to that more in detail in another part of my testimony.

Butterfield did not come back to these "certain movements" in his testimony, if in fact they existed.

And at that time General Hooker telegraphed to Washington, requesting that all the troops in the departments of Washington, Baltimore, Fortress Monroe, Western Virginia, all the troops that could possibly operate upon General Lee's army, should be placed under one commander, in order to secure unity and concert of action; and that his motives might not be misunderstood and unappreciated, General Hooker expressly requested that some general other than himself should be that commander.

Question. Was there any more difficulty for General Foster to bring his troops up before the battle than after?

Answer. It only took a certain length of time for him to bring them up. It depended upon when he should get the order. I presume he could just as well have brought them up a week sooner if he had been ordered to do so.

Question. Do you know why it was that General Halleck refused to General Hooker the garrison at Harpers Ferry, and immediately afterwards allowed General Meade to take it?

Answer. It is true General Halleck refused the troops at Harpers Ferry to General Hooker; but his order to General Meade I do not think expressly contemplated that General Meade would use them. It merely gave him control over them. The letter which General Meade had when he assumed command will show that. I must say, however, that General Hooker was always under the impression that General Halleck did not support him cordially.

Question. What is your opinion about that?

Answer. As General Halleck, as chief of staff of the armies, is my superior, I prefer not to express an opinion upon that subject.

Question. Can you tell why the enemy were not followed up more promptly after the battle of Gettysburg?

Answer. General Meade was under the impression that General Lee had drawn past into the mountain passes and taken a strong position there, where it would be unwise to attack. The telegraphic correspondence and reports from headquarters at that time with Washington and General Couch will probably express the views entertained.

Butterfield's language gave the erroneous impression that Meade had made no effort to find out Lee's position. Meade was not merely "under the impression" that Lee's forces had taken up a strong position in the mountain passes; he knew it for a fact.

By Mr. Odell:

Question. Was not that the fact, that those mountain passes were very strong positions?

[433] Answer. Mountain passes are generally strong positions.

Question. Was it not the fact that those positions were very strong?

Answer. I did not go through them; they were reported as strong positions.

Odell scored some strong points for Meade with these questions.

By Mr. Gooch:

Question. Have you the order for the retreat of the army from Gettysburg which you prepared under the direction of General Meade on the morning of the 2d of July?

Answer. I have not. It was given to General Williams to be copied by his clerks, but was never issued.

Question. Did you, when you were preparing that order, understand that it was to be issued immediately, or that it was to be issued only in certain contingencies?

Answer. I understood, when I prepared the order, that it was General Meade's intention to consult with his corps commanders, and that it was a matter of precaution to have the order in readiness in case it should be decided upon to retreat. That is my recollection of it. General Williams can produce that order, and the wording of it will tell a great deal in regard to that.

As the leading interrogator, Wade should have asked these questions not only of Butterfield but of all the witnesses. Butterfield's testimony here that the order to retreat was simply a precaution contrasts sharply with his earlier testimony that Meade was preparing to retreat and had directed him to prepare an order to withdraw the army.

Question. Did you understand the circular of the 1st of July was intended by General Meade as an order to retreat to the point indicated, or was it dependent upon contingencies?

Answer. I would suggest that that question can be more properly answered by General Meade.

Question. If it was his original intention to move the army back to that position, do you know what he supposed the enemy would do?

Answer. The natural inference is that he supposed the enemy would attack him there.

This "natural inference" had not been mentioned by Sickles and was dragged from Butterfield.

Question. Was the battle-ground of Gettysburg selected by design and intent, or was its selection merely the result of accident?

Answer. My testimony shows that I was at Taneytown when the collision occurred between General Reynolds and the enemy before Gettysburg. General Hancock was sent up there when General Reynolds fell, and, as I understood it, General Hancock selected the ground where the battle was fought. It rests between General Hancock and General Howard as to who selected the lines on which the battle was fought. My impression is that it was done by General Hancock and approved by General Meade when he went on the ground.

Question. How soon was it understood by the officers of our army, after the last assault of the enemy, that they did not intend to renew the attack?

Answer. Owing to my being wounded and unfit for constant duty, I cannot answer that question properly.

By Mr. Odell:

Question. At the time of the issuing of the circular of the 1st of July was there at headquarters any well-defined opinion, or satisfactory information, as to the intention and purposes of the enemy?

Answer. Some thought that Lee intended to move up into Pennsylvania, crossing the Susquehanna; others thought he intended to move around our right towards Baltimore. On the morning of the 30th General Meade asked General Couch if he could keep Lee from crossing the river.

Question. In that uncertainty, was not that circular a prudent one, as indicating a place for the concentration of our forces?

Answer. I would rather you would not ask me that question.

This was a strange response and in effect a stall. The committee then adjourned for the weekend, to resume the following Tuesday. On Monday the committee asked the secretary of war for copies of all orders, dispatches, and communications of Generals Halleck, Hooker, and Meade while they commanded the Army of the Potomac. One has to wonder why the committee had waited so long to ask for this material. At any rate, someone had at last asked the questions of Butterfield that were fairly screaming to be asked. His answers, if not entirely satisfactory, at least brought out some of the weakness of his testimony.

It should be noted that the journal of the committee contains several errors in regard to dates. The dates noted by committee stenographers are more often correct. In this case, the journal shows that Butterfield resumed his testimony on Monday, March 28, rather than Tuesday, March 29. The journal is also occasionally inaccurate about which committee members were in attendance. On March 29, Julian and Loan are recorded as absent. In fact, Loan completed the questioning of Butterfield due to Wade's absence.

[434] Tuesday, March 29, 1864.
Major General Daniel Butterfield recalled and examined.

By Mr. Loan:

Question. The chairman of the committee, who is now absent, has handed me some questions which he desires me to ask you. What were the tendencies of General Hooker's remarks to yourself and other officers of the staff of the army of the Potomac at the time General Hooker was relieved from the command, as to their course towards his successor?

Answer. Most of the officers called upon General Hooker in a body to pay their respects to him before his departure. The general made a few remarks to them, stating that it was all for the best that General Meade had the command of the army; that he thought his own influence was impaired; that General Meade was a brave and gallant man, who would undoubtedly lead them to success; and he hoped that all who regarded him, or his wishes, or his feelings, would devote every energy and ability to the support of General Meade, or words to that effect. I do not undertake to repeat the exact language he used.

Question. That was the tendency of the language he used?

Answer. Yes.

Question. From what you know, do you think General Meade was honestly and cordially supported at Gettysburg by the entire army?

Answer. In my experience with that army I have never seen an officer supported more cordially and earnestly by everybody in it, from highest to lowest, than General Meade was there.

Question. Were there any flags of truce after the battle of Gettysburg?

Answer. Yes; on the morning of the 4th of July, a little after daybreak, or very early in the morning, a letter was sent in to General Meade from General Lee, under flag of truce, containing a proposal, for the convenience of both armies, to exchange the prisoners that each army held. General Meade asked me what I thought of it. I told him that I thought it was a device of the enemy to gain time. General Meade did not seem to so regard it at first; but, after a little reflection, he declined the proposition, and an answer was returned to that effect. That is the only flag of truce that I know of.

Question. Were there any other communications from rebel officers than by flag of truce after the battle? If so, what were they?

Answer. There were a great many rumors of communications. I know nothing positively about any, except one from a rebel general who had lived in Baltimore—General Trimble, I think—who sent a note to General Meade, saying that he was wounded and had been left on the field without care or accommodation, and asking, as a favor from an old acquaintance, that General Meade would send an ambulance and bring him in and have him cared for, and General Meade ordered it to be done. Before the battle was over (on the night of the 2d) it was reported that General Barksdale was on the field wounded, and desired to be brought in; but he died before we reached him. I sent for him, but he was dead when found. General Armistead was also wounded, but that was within our lines. No communication from him came in from the outside. There were several reports brought in of rebel officers of various ranks who had been left wounded in barns and buildings, and wanting assistance. But the only formal communication was this one received from General Trimble, which I have stated.

Question. What was the general character of the report received from the front after the battle of Gettysburg?

Answer. Everybody that came in reported that all the barns and houses were full of the enemy's wounded, most of them without anything to eat, and all of [435] them acknowledged that they had been very badly whipped; that the enemy's wounded were suffering very much, and that medical supplies, and stores should be sent out to them at once; that every barn and house, so far as anybody had gone, were filled with the enemy's wounded, who had been left behind and abandoned.

Question. Was there any attempt made to secure the co-operation and aid of General Couch's troops with the army at Gettysburg?

Answer. Despatches were sent to General Couch, informing him of the relative positions of both armies, and asking his co-operation and assistance. General Couch was under General Meade's orders. The exact nature of those despatches I do not remember, whether they were in the character of peremptory orders, or whether they were of the nature of information merely to General Couch of our position, leaving it to him whether to come down or not. My impression is, that they partook of the latter character, or both. General Couch was under General Meade's command, and he had authority to order him down; but I do not think he did so peremptorily. General Smith's command, which was a portion of General Couch's, first opened communication with us on the afternoon on the 4th of July; a staff officer from General Smith arriving to announce that his column was near.

Question. Any orders or information sent to General Couch were sent by direction of General Meade?

Answer. Yes, certainly. No order or instructions were made out or sent to any command except by his order.

Question. When you were before the committee last Friday you stated, in reply to a question, that at the time the order was issued to form our army in line on Pipe creek, it was thought by some that Lee intended to cross the Susquehanna and move into Pennsylvania; by others that he intended to move around over night towards Baltimore. And then, when asked whether, in that uncertainty, that circular of the 1st of July was not a prudent one, as deciding upon a place for the concentration of our forces, you declined to answer. Will you answer that question now, and what were your reasons for declining to answer it then?

Butterfield now had a chance to atone for his disingenuous reply on Friday and finish his testimony on a high note. Over the weekend he possibly had conferred with Sickles, Wade, or Chandler, who may well have helped him formulate an answer for when the committee reconvened.

Answer. My reasons for declining to answer the question then was, that I did not like to pass unfavorable criticisms upon a superior officer, as the answer to that question would have been. But I will answer the question now, for fear my refusal may be misunderstood or misrepresented.

I do not think that circular was a judicious one. I do not think the position designated in that circular was a good one. And I think if we had gone back there it would have resulted in the destruction of our army; and the movement would not have prevented either of the movements that Lee was supposed or expected to make. It was the business of our army then to find Lee and fight him.

Question. You think the movement down to Pipe creek would have been injudicious?

Answer. Extremely so; and I so expressed myself at the time to officers of the staff.

Butterfield's testimony, despite some false starts, was invaluable to the committee. He had supported testimony that the Pipe Creek circular was an order to retreat and that Meade had planned to retreat on July 2. His testimony was all the more valuable because he had actually drawn up the retreat orders.

He also offered testimony that helped rehabilitate Hooker's tarnished reputation. Butterfield argued that one of the reasons Hooker had resigned from command was his lack of adequate support by Halleck. Halleck was not in favor with the committee, and Butterfield's charge could be used against him.

Butterfield also testified that at Gettysburg, Meade had merely followed Hooker's plans. This was meant to imply that Hooker, not Meade, had directed the army toward contact with Lee; it reaffirmed Hooker's superiority over Meade as a general and discredited Meade for any positive actions leading up to the battle.

14 Brigadier General John Gibbon

The next witness to appear before the committee was Brigadier General John Gibbon, who commanded the Second Division, Second Corps at Gettysburg. With almost two dozen division commanders for the committee to choose from, Gibbon seems an odd choice to call as a witness. He represented nearly everything the committee members opposed: a West Pointer, a Democrat, an admirer of McClellan, and a friend of Meade's.

Gibbon had one other dubious attribute: he had been appointed to West Point from North Carolina. Although he had been born in Philadelphia, his family had moved to Mecklenburg County, North Carolina, when he was around ten years old. His Southern background and connections—he had three brothers and two brothers-in-law in the Confederate service—put him in a peculiar position. Nonetheless, he was successfully able to overcome suspicions of his background to rise in rank.

Prior to the Civil War, Gibbon saw service in Mexico, Florida, and on the frontier. He also spent five years at West Point as assistant instructor of artillery and quartermaster. It was during his tenure at the academy that he published *The Artillerist's Manual,* which became the standard work on artillery for both sides in the Civil War.[1]

With the outbreak of hostilities, Gibbon's climb up the promotion ladder ran into an unusual problem. Nominated brigadier general in early 1862, Gibbon later wrote that "there was no North Carolina senator present to second my nomination . . . there was no one present with any information in regard to me and my name was passed over in accordance with a rule of the Senate." His nomination may have died there except for his new army friend James S. Wadsworth, who Gibbon told of his problem. Wadsworth "at once sat

1. Warner, *Generals in Blue,* 171–2.

down and wrote a note to, I think, Senator Wilson of Massachusetts and in a few days the nomination was confirmed." Senator Henry Wilson was the very influential chairman of the Senate Committee on Military Affairs.[2]

Assigned a brigade of western troops, Gibbon quickly shaped them into the famous Iron Brigade. His ability to fashion the tough westerners into one of the best brigades in the army marked him as an officer with a future. Gibbon was given command of the Second Division, First Corps, at Fredericksburg, where he was slightly wounded in the wrist. After his return to active duty he commanded the Second Division, Second Corps at Gettysburg, where he was again wounded.[3]

Gibbon's writings do not indicate any active involvement in the political morass of the time. He had friends of both political parties, as his close relationship with Republican Wadsworth indicates. Gibbon's heart, however, was with McClellan and the Democrats. He considered McClellan the ideal general and enjoyed his patronage. Though not overtly active in politics, Gibbon did take a limited role in the 1864 presidential election. As a staunch McClellan supporter, he was listed by McClellan as someone to whom Democratic literature could be sent for distribution.[4]

Gibbon's noninvolvement in politics was probably due to his low opinion of politicians who meddled in military affairs, a feeling that stemmed from their treatment of McClellan. Just prior to Gibbon's promotion to brigadier general, he wrote that the "politicians had better let McClellan alone and attend to their own business." The next day he added that the battle of Yorktown "would not have been as hard a one if the politicians had let Gen. McClellan pursue, undisturbed, his own plans instead of interfering in a matter they did not understand." Nor was his opinion tempered with the passage of time. In 1885, he wrote of politicians and political considerations, "That they worked a very great harm, there can be no question."[5]

[439] Testimony of General John Gibbon.

Washington, April 1, 1864.
Brigadier General John Gibbon sworn and examined.

2. Gibbon, *Recollections,* 26–7.

3. Ibid., 104.

4. Byrne and Weaver, eds., *Haskell of Gettysburg,* 22; *MG,* 85–6; Stephen W. Sears, ed., *The Civil War Papers of George B. McClellan: Selected Correspondence, 1860–1865* (New York: Da Capo Press, 1992), 600–1.

5. Gibbon, *Recollections,* 22, 24–5.

By the chairman:

Question. What is your rank and position in the army?

Answer. I am a captain in the 4th regular artillery and a brigadier general of volunteers, commanding a division in the 2d corps of the army of the Potomac.

Question. We are inquiring now more particularly about the battle of Gettysburg. You were in that battle?

Answer. Yes, sir, I commanded a division there.

Question. Will you state to us in your own way such facts and circumstances connected with that battle as you may deem material or interesting?

[440] Answer. I can only tell my own part of it; I do not know much about any of the rest. I was put in command of the 2d corps on the afternoon of the 1st of July, at Taneytown, General Hancock having been ordered to the front, at Gettysburg, when news arrived of General Reynolds having been killed or very seriously wounded. I was ordered to march to Gettysburg, and began the march; but about sundown I received orders from General Hancock to put the corps in position on the Taneytown road, about three miles from Gettysburg. That night, about 12 o'clock, General Meade passed my headquarters on his way to Gettysburg, and shortly afterwards I received orders to push the corps forward to Gettysburg. I got in motion shortly after daylight, and got upon the field early that morning. The corps—General Hancock resuming command of it—was put in position on the ridge to the left of Cemetery hill. During the most of that forenoon I understood that the troops were coming into position, taking their places in the line. There was not much fighting going on until General Sickles's movement took place, about 4 o'clock in the afternoon. I understood his position to be on the left of our line, extending our line along the ridge in the direction of Round Top hill, quite a prominent hill on our left flank.

This puts another hole in Sickles's story. If Gibbon understood where Sickles's line was supposed to be, why didn't Sickles?

About 4 o'clock in the afternoon I was standing on the hill within the limits of my division, and noticed troops moving out to our left and front. It turned out to be the 3d corps, under General Sickles; they were taking up their position obliquely to our line and to the front, somewhere along the Emmitsburg road, which ran just to the front of the right of my division, and obliquely to the line. I was standing there with General Hancock, and noticed the position of Sickles's line. There was quite a thick wood away off to the left of Sickles's line, and I asked General Hancock if he supposed there was anything in those woods; and very shortly afterwards the enemy brought out his guns and commenced firing, and there was more or less fighting whilst General Sickles's corps was being put in position. They then commenced their attack on Sickles's left. After fighting for some time the corps was evidently giving away; had to change its position. I had several messages from General Humphreys, I think, asking me to send troops out to their assistance. General Hancock was there, and I consulted with him, and, by his direction, sent two regiments, I think. I also sent two regiments to connect Sickles's right with our line, and prevent the enemy from coming in and cutting him off entirely from our line. Those regiments became very heavily engaged, when the troops began to fall back, and lost both of their commanding officers.

Soon afterwards I saw the enemy's lines advancing after our troops directly in my front. I went up to the batteries which were on the most prominent part of the line and directed them to fire solid shot over the heads of our own men at the advancing enemy. I was afraid to fire shell for fear they might explode too soon and injure our own men.

Gibbon's justified fear of using exploding shells was broadly shared on both sides. The shells' unreliable fuses often caused premature explosions, resulting in friendly casualties.

The smoke soon became so thick on this hill that nothing could be seen at all, and I had to discontinue the firing. I understood that our men came back in a great deal of confusion, but I could see very little myself on account of the smoke being so thick.

I was riding down to the left of my line, where General Meade sent for me. He was coming up with a portion of the 12th corps. Those men went in and the enemy was beaten back. I think, however, that the enemy were forced back from our line before any re-enforcements came up. I understood they ran over several batteries that were in position on the outside of our line; but the guns were immediately recovered when our troops advanced. That was about all the fighting that took place on the 2d of July that I know anything about.

After we had repulsed one attack there was heavy firing over on the right of Cemetery hill. I received a message from General Howard, commanding the 11th corps, asking for re-enforcements. Just about the same time General Hancock became alarmed at the continued firing, and desired me to send a brigade, [441] designating Colonel Carroll's, and afterwards three other regiments from my division, to the assistance of our right centre. Colonel Carroll moved off promptly, and, as reported to me, arrived on the right of Cemetery hill to find the enemy actually in our batteries and fighting with the cannoniers for their position. He gallantly moved forward with his command, drove the enemy back, retook the position, and held it till the next day.

By Mr. Gooch:

Question. When you say that the enemy were forced back from our line before the re-enforcements came up, which line do you mean—the advanced line taken by General Sickles, or the line subsequently taken?

Answer. I mean the line upon which the battle of Gettysburg was fought; the line which we subsequently took, extending along the ridge from Cemetery hill to Round Top.

Question. Do you know why General Sickles took the advanced line which he did?

Answer. I do not; I have no knowledge of his reasons for taking that line.

Question. Was it or not, in your opinion, a judicious position in which to place his men?

Answer. I should think it was not.

Question. Will you state the disadvantages of that advanced line?

Answer. In the first place we had our line established, and General Sickles was in a position where he would very naturally have support on both flanks. To put himself out in that position he would isolate his corps from the rest of the army, and necessarily weaken the position, without having the same support to his wings which he would have had if he had remained in the continuous line. Then, again, I think the position he put his corps in, as it turned out, invited an attack upon his left flank, and such an attack is almost always disastrous, particularly to volunteer troops who are not thoroughly disciplined. You will see necessarily how his troops had to change their position when the attack was made on them from the direction of the Emmitsburg road. Those troops had to change their position, and in doing so were fired upon by the enemy.

By the chairman:

Question. What do you know about any councils of war being held on the 2d of July?

Answer. There was a council of war held on the night of the 2d of July.

Question. Were you there?

Answer. Yes, sir; although properly I ought not to have been there. I had commanded the corps on the afternoon of the 1st of July, in the absence of General Hancock. When I came up to Gettysburg with the corps General Hancock, of course, resumed the command of it. During the retreat of Sickles's corps, General Hancock turned the command of the corps over to me, as he had done the day before, in order, as he informed me, to take command of the 3d corps after General Sickles was wounded. At night, after the fighting was over, the staff officer, in summoning corps commanders to the council, summoned me, and I went there. General Hancock also went there, so that the 2d corps really had two representatives there. I spoke to General Meade about it after the council was over. I was present at the council in that way. During a portion of the sitting of the council there was fighting off to the right of our line somewhere; I did not know exactly where.

The fighting was along Culp's and Cemetery Hills.

As the corps commanders came in, the result of the day's fighting was ascertained, each one reporting what had taken place near his position. The subject was very thoroughly discussed. We were sitting in a room not half as large as this one, very close together, of course, and we were all discussing the result of the day's fighting. During the conversation General Newton made some objections [442] to the position we occupied. He is an officer of engineers, and I supposed had examined the whole position; which I knew nothing at all about it, except my own part of the field. The matter was discussed in regard to the military position. After we had been sitting there for several hours, there were a number of points written out by direction of General Meade, upon which the council was to decide. Among the rest was the question—

Should the army remain upon its present ground, or should it retire and take up some other position?

Being the youngest member of the council, I had the first vote on it, and I therefore had probably more full discussion with General Newton in regard to his objections to the position. Finally, when the question was put, my vote was that we should rectify the position as far as possible, but not to leave it so far that anybody could construe it into a retreat from our position. General Newton, I think, voted substantially the same as myself, because I recollect there was a little sparring between us as to whether he was agreeing with me or I with him. Every other member of the council, according to my recollection, voted simply to stay there and fight. I recollect very distinctly General Meade's announcement, when the vote was taken: "That, then, is the decision." There was great good feeling among all present as far I could understand, and we were all unanimous upon the subject.

In his Recollections, *Gibbon recounted an interesting exchange with Meade. Noting that the council had decided to await Lee's attack the next day, Meade said, "If Lee attacks tomorrow, it will be* in your front." *Gibbon asked why he thought so, and Meade replied, "Because he has made attacks on both our flanks and failed and if he concludes to try it again, it will be on our centre." Gibbon's story is also confirmed by the* Official Records. *At 8:00* A.M. *on July 3 Butterfield notified Slocum, commander of the Sixth Corps, that "it is their [the Confederates'] intention to make the attempt to pierce our center." Meade had correctly anticipated Lee's next move.*[6]

There is a matter connected with a report in regard to the retreat of the army from Gettysburg, which I think it proper to mention in my testimony. It is this: some time during the day of the 2d of July, but before this fight with General Sickles's corps had taken place, I was at General Meade's headquarters, as I frequently was during the day; I consequently knew a great deal of the dispositions made, and orders given, for the troops to come up. I had been urged frequently in the morning of that day, by General Meade, to hurry up to the field, and I heard of the other corps that were coming up; I therefore had but one idea in regard to General Meade's intention, which was to concentrate the whole army there for the purpose of fighting a battle; when, therefore, on coming out of the little room in which he had his office, I met General Butterfield, his chief of staff, and he asked me to read over with him, and compare with a map he had there, a draught of an order which he had, and I asked him what it was, and he told me that it was an order for the army to retreat, I was struck with a great deal of astonishment, and I recollect very well my exclamation, "Great God! General Meade does not intend to leave this position?" General Butterfield did not say that General Meade did intend to leave; he merely said something to the effect that it was necessary to be prepared, in case it should be necessary to leave, or some remark of that kind. He then showed me the order, and either he read it over and I pointed out the places on the map, or I read it over and he pointed out the places to which

6. Ibid., 145; *B&L*, 3:313–4; *OR*, vol. 57, pt. 1, p. 1068.

each corps was to go. When he got through, I remarked that it was all correctly drawn up.

Until very recently I supposed that the order which General Butterfield showed me was an order in regard to the army falling back to a position which I heard General Meade had selected on Pipe Clay creek. But I am satisfied now that order must have been some different order from the one I had been thinking it was. Being firmly convinced, as I was at the time, that General Meade had no idea of falling back from the position there, it struck me as very remarkable that his chief of staff should be making out an order to retreat; and I still think so.

Gibbon's testimony is at odds with Sickles's and Butterfield's testimony. Butterfield had hinted that, as one of the officers who had read the order, Gibbon could confirm it as an order to retreat.

By Mr. Gooch:

Question. Do you know what was the opinion of General Meade, at the time the council was held on the night of the 2d of July, in regard to remaining on the ground where you were?

[443] Answer. I can only judge of that from his manner after the decision of the council was made, because I do not recollect that General Meade said much upon the subject during the council. He appeared to me to be waiting to listen to the reports and opinions of his corps commanders. I do not recollect having heard him express a decided opinion one way or the other. I certainly did not hear him express any preference for retreating.

Question. At the time of your interview with General Butterfield, do you remember whether or not that you understood that the order which had been prepared for the army to retreat was one that was to be executed?

Answer. No, sir. I understood from him that it was merely preparatory, in case we might be called upon to retreat.

With this testimony, Gooch scored two excellent points in Meade's defense.

By the chairman:

Question. Will you go on with your narrative?

Answer. On the morning of the 3d of July skirmishing commenced pretty early, but I do not recollect any serious fighting—there was none on our part of the line—until about 1 o'clock, when the enemy opened their artillery fire upon us. I do not believe there was ever a hotter fire of artillery in the world; it was the most terrific scene I ever witnessed. That fire continued almost an hour and a half.

Question. Which side had the most guns in position there?

Answer. I am not able to answer that question. I know they had a great many more than I wanted to see there. But we kept up a pretty heavy pummeling all the time, too. I suppose that fire must have continued an hour and a half or two hours, when the enemy's lines of infantry appeared coming out of the woods in our front, line after line, a heavy line of skirmishers, then a line of infantry, then another line behind that, and, I believe, a third behind that; and, from my position near the left centre of my division, as far as I could see, these lines were coming up against us in most beautiful style.

Question. How many men do you judge there were in that assault?

Answer. I had no time to calculate. I had no idea how many there were; the lines to our right and their left extended as far as I could see. Over to our left they did not extend so far. And their line was broken in one part as they came upon my division. I rode to the left of my division, and was trying to get some regiments to wheel outside of the little breastworks they had thrown up, and attack this assaulting line in flank. And I am satisfied that if I had been able to get these men to do what I wanted, we would have captured a great many more than we did.

Question. What was the difficulty?

Answer. It was the want of proper discipline. Men get very much excited in battle; they are all yelling, hallooing, shooting, and, unless they are very well drilled and disciplined, they do not wait for the orders of their colonels.

Question. In the heat of battle can a commanding officer have much control over his men?

Answer. Not after the men become thoroughly engaged. But if men are well disciplined and accustomed to listen implicitly to the voice of their officers they can have an immense influence over them, if they (the officers) stand by them and direct them. I was wounded about the time, I suppose, the enemy's second line got into our batteries, probably a little before that. As described to me afterwards, the result, I think, will carry out my idea in regard to it; because the enemy broke through, forced back my weakest brigade, under General Webb, got into our batteries, and the men were so close that the officers on each side were using their pistols on each other, and the men frequently clubbed their muskets, and the clothes of the men on both sides were burned by the powder of the exploding cartridges. An officer of my staff,

Lieutenant Haskell, had been sent by me, just previously to the attack, to General Meade, with a message [444] that the enemy were coming. He got back on top of the hill hunting for me, and was there when this brigade was forced back; and, without waiting orders from me, he rode off to the left and ordered all the troops there to the right. As they came up helter-skelter, everybody for himself, with their officers among them, they commenced firing upon those rebels as they were coming into our batteries, and took them in flank, and the rebels laid down their arms by hundreds. And if I had got these regiments in a little sooner they would have taken the rebels in flank before they got into the batteries.

Question. At what time of the day were you wounded?

Answer. I must have been wounded somewhere about 3 o'clock.

Question. Where was the 6th corps during this assault?

Answer. I cannot tell; it was on our left and rear somewhere, but I do not know its position.

Question. After the enemy had been repulsed that day, was there any council of war held that you know of?

Answer. Not that I know about; I was in the hospital.

Question. You did not accompany the army as it followed the enemy to Williamsport?

Answer. No, sir; I have not been with the army since.

Question. Do you desire to place on record any other observations in regard to that battle?

Answer. I do not know that I have, particularly. I think it was one of the hardest fought battles of this war, and one of the best fought.

Question. You have studied the history of battles a great deal. Now, in the battles of Napoleon had they at any time half as many artillery engaged as there were at Gettysburg?

Answer. I am not sufficiently conversant with military history to tell you that. I think it very doubtful whether more guns were ever used in any one battle before. I do not believe Napoleon ever had a worse artillery fire.

Question. Which army had the most men in that battle, as near as you can ascertain?

Answer. I do not know. I have had no opportunity of judging. I could not tell you what our own force was. I should imagine we had about the same force as they had; however, that is a mere rough guess.

Question. Are our troops as well disciplined as those of the enemy, as a general thing?

Answer. I do not think they are.

Question. What reason do you give for that?

Answer. I think they are fully aware of the fact that they cannot get along unless they do have strict discipline, and I am sorry to say that we seem to have a notion that we can. There are some volunteer regiments that are as well disciplined as any men I ever want to see. I had several such regiments in that battle. A great deal of it depends upon the kind of officers they have. I think we ought to have some kind of rule for promoting officers for efficiency and gallantry in the field.

Question. Have they any articles of war, or rules of proceeding that will enable them to discipline their men better than ours?

Answer. I do not know that they have. But I believe that all their forces are under the control of the central government. I do not know how that is, but that is my idea. I think the central government makes all the appointments, but I will not be certain of that. But I am satisfied of one thing: that men in their service get their promotion from military recommendations. In our service, the governor of each State has the appointment of officers from his State, though he appoints none higher than colonels; and very frequently they will insist upon appointing men who are not competent in a military point of view. The general government, however, has the power of dismissing officers; [445] that will enable us to get rid of the worst officers in time, but we have no system which will enable us to get the good officers in position, and sometimes the bad ones are put back upon us.

Question. The rebels, of course, must have selected many of their officers from civil life, as we have done?

Answer. Yes, sir. Do not misunderstand me. I do not want men of military education, but I want men who have shown themselves in the field to be competent. There are two kinds of military ability—one theoretical, and the other practical. We have plenty of volunteer officers who have shown themselves to be really competent soldiers, but they do not get promotion. There was one young man [Franklin A. Haskell] on my staff, who has been in every battle with me, and who did more than any other one man to repulse that last assault at Gettysburg, and he did the part of a general there, yet he has been only a first lieutenant until within a few weeks. I have now succeeded in getting the governor of Wisconsin to appoint him to a colonelcy, and I have no doubt he will, before long, come before you of the Senate for a star. He is an excellent soldier, and has distinguished himself in every battle; and I have also got the general government to recognize his services, and he is appointed a major in the Adjutant General's department.

Question. Does not that arise from the necessity of having rules by which it is rendered very difficult to supersede an officer? If a vacancy happens anywhere in the regular army, the next in rank moves up, so that it is very difficult, is it not, to break through these rules, and reward merit?

Answer. We have broken through that rule during this war. Suppose we had promoted in the regular army altogether according to the rule of seniority; you would not have had one officer who has distinguished himself in this war, unless you had promoted all the older officers and then retired them.

This is the rule which I say will give us a good army, the best in the world: We have the best material upon the face of God's earth of which to make an army; I am convinced of that. In the first place, let us commence with the regiment. After a regiment goes into service, if the colonel is not fit for his place, put him out, either by a court-martial, which is slow, or by a board, which a great many people say is unjust; and then put a competent man in command of the regiment; and then never make a promotion to a captaincy or field officer in that regiment unless upon the recommendation of that colonel. And as long as that colonel tells you that this or that captain of his regiment is a competent military man, never make a promotion in his company except in accordance with his indorsement. If the colonel tells you that the captain is not a competent man, and insists upon having somebody that he knows to be competent promoted, take the colonel's word and promote accordingly.

Question. Your colonel may have his favorites, and dispense his recommendations accordingly?

Answer. That is true. But how are you going to avoid these partialities? Who is going to decide upon them? Suppose the colonel is an indifferent military man—is not fit for his place; he will have his prejudices as much as anybody else. The only question is, whether the competent military man will not be the surest source from which to make those appointments, who will make them with an eye solely to the good of the service, and will be a more competent man to judge than a man who is not declared by military authority to be the right man for the position. In both cases you will probably have partiality; but in the one case you have partiality governed by military principles; in the other you have partiality governed by politics, relations, anything else, you do not know what.

Question. Suppose this very excellent, competent young staff officer of yours had been placed in command of a regiment at once; would not the morale of [446] that regiment have been destroyed or seriously impaired by placing the junior officer over the others, notwithstanding his great merits?

Answer. He has gone out to Wisconsin, and in a few weeks his regiment has been raised for him.

Question. That is all very true; he has raised a new regiment. But suppose you had placed him over all the officers in an old regiment?

Answer. I can only answer that in this way; I will instance two Wisconsin regiments. I commenced with what is known as "the iron brigade," and those two regiments were in it. One of the regiments was commanded by a graduate of the Military Academy, who, however, was not in the service when the war commenced. The other was commanded by a man who had no military education whatever, but who was naturally a disciplinarian and a soldier. Those two regiments, the 2d and 6th Wisconsin, were, and are yet, what is left of them, two of the finest regiments that ever fought on any field. The principle in those regiments was to promote only competent men; and I attribute their discipline and the reputation which they have gained to that fact alone. I believe there was some objection to it at first; but the governor of Wisconsin finally almost always promoted those who were recommended by the colonels.

I tried once to get this very same young staff officer of mine, Lieutenant Haskell, before I knew so much about him as I know now, made a lieutenant colonel; but the pressure was too strongly in favor of the major of the regiment, who was a very good soldier too, and whom I have also recommended for promotion.

Now, in other States they do not pay that regard to these recommendations which I think they ought to do. I think, also, these recommendations should always go up through the regular military channel. For instance, if a colonel, no matter from what State he comes, recommends such a captain for promotion to the position of major, I think that recommendation should receive the indorsement of the brigade commander, and then go up for the indorsement of the division commander. I do not know that it should go further than that, for those officers are the ones who have the best opportunity to observe the ability and conduct of the one recommended.

Now, to show you how the other rule works, I will give an instance that occurred in this very division of mine at the battle of Fredericksburg last May. When we went down at one o'clock at night, to take possession of Fredericksburg, the colonel in command of one of my brigades was found by me to be so intoxicated that he was utterly unfit for command, and I had to relieve him from his command and give it to some one else. I preferred charges against him, and a court of volunteer officers was ordered. He was tried and dismissed [from] the service for drunkenness when going into action. The lieutenant colonel, who commanded the regiment at Gettysburg, had not been mustered in as colonel when he was killed at the head of his regiment. Now, the government here, for some reason or other, rescinded the order dismissing this colonel from the service, and he has been reinstated, by the governor of New York, as the colonel of that regiment. They hold in New York that the rescinding of the order of dismissal was a kind of recommendation to the governor of New York to reappoint him. I told the adjutant general of the State of New York that the rescinding of the order dismissing that colonel from the service did not make him either a sober man or a competent officer, and that if the State of New York had bad troops in the field she need blame nobody for it but herself, for we were inclined to do everything we could to improve them, for it was a matter of life and death with us to have good soldiers under us. I speak for myself: we will not recommend any other than competent men for promotion. I do not think you can leave the matter to better judges than military men, though we may make mistakes sometimes in the matter.

[447] By Mr. Julian:

Question. Can you not illustrate your idea by the case of an Indiana brigadier general now absent on sick leave?

Answer. Yes, sir, very well. I had in my brigade—"the iron brigade"—three Wisconsin regiments and one Indiana regiment. The colonel of the Indiana regiment I soon found was a marked contrast to at least two of the other colonels. I found him always opposing every plan of mine to render that brigade more efficient. He had not the first principle of a soldier in him; he was altogether disqualified for his position. I asked that he should be brought before a board of examination, but it was never done. In the first place he was very much opposed to my coming into the brigade. Like a great many other volunteers he had prejudices against regular officers, which only needed contact with them to remove. He made complaints to the War Department against me for my military administration of the brigade. After the first fight we got into, which was on the 28th August, 1862, in General Pope's campaign, when I lost 600 men in about an hour and twenty minutes, this man seemed to have changed in his sentiments towards me, and I always supposed he was a great friend of mine. We went up into Maryland and fought the battle of South mountain. My brigade was charged with the duty of going up into a gorge along the turnpike and carrying that position. This colonel had command of his regiment along the left of the turnpike; opposite to him was another regiment, and behind him were the other two regiments of the brigade. The enemy were posted behind a stone-wall and a great deal protected there. While this man was marching up with his regiment I sent him word to throw out two companies on his left into a little skirt of woods, to keep along through the woods to see that there was nothing there to fire on his flank. Instead of doing that, he changed front forward on his left company and faced the woods, thus exposing his flank to the fire of a rebel battery. Now, my main object was to push forward rapidly and get engaged before the darkness came on, but this delayed us. And this very Lieutenant Haskell, of whom I have spoken, had to go down there and give him commands to put his regiment back into its old position, and then I had to send orders to Colonel Fairchild to push the other regiment into action. This Indiana regiment had the finest material in it in the whole brigade, and yet it was the worst regiment I had.

This was the Nineteenth Indiana under Colonel Solomon Meredith. Meredith was a Republican politician with no previous military experience and a favorite of Indiana governor Oliver P. Morton. After Gibbon left the brigade, and over his objections, Meredith became commander of the Iron Brigade.

At the battle of Antietam my brigade led off in the attack on the right, and lost very heavily. The colonel of this Indiana regiment was not in that battle at all; he came here to Washington on sick leave. When he came back to the army he had a brigadier general's strap on.

Question. How did he get it?

Answer. Through the recommendation of General Hooker; which was obtained because the pressure from very high authority was so strong that General Hooker could not refuse. I protested against his appointment, and wrote a letter to the Adjutant General of the army, telling him the man was totally disqualified for any such position.

Gibbon's characterization of Meredith was unfair. Meredith was wounded twice during the war (including at Gettysburg) and had a distinguished war record.

Gibbon made some good points for Meade. His testimony was of the greatest value on a subject that he himself brought up, the contingency retreat order. Gibbon testified that he had read the order, but was told by Butterfield that it was a "merely preparatory" order. This directly contradicted Butterfield's testimony and was another blow to Sickles's testimony.

15 Major General George Gordon Meade (Second Appearance)

When news of Butterfield's testimony reached Meade, he determined to make a second appearance before the committee to refute the accusation that he had been preparing to order a retreat on July 2. Yet even as Meade prepared for his second appearance before the committee, outside events affected both Meade himself and the committee hearings.

After the failure of Wade and Chandler's attempt to have Meade removed from command, the clamor in the press for Meade's removal had gained momentum. The most damaging article against Meade appeared on March 12, 1864, the day after Meade had made his first appearance before the committee. Writing under the pseudonym "Historicus," someone who identified himself as an eyewitness of Gettysburg published a letter in the *New York Herald* entitled "The Battle of Gettysburg. Important Communication from an Eye Witness. How the Victory was Won and Its Advantages were Lost. Generals Halleck's and Meade's Official Reports Refuted." The author claimed his only motive was "to vindicate history, do honor to the fallen, and justice to the survivors when unfairly impeached." In fact, the letter was a slanderous attack on Meade and an attempt to promote the role Dan Sickles played in the battle. It was quickly assumed by nearly everyone that the author was Sickles himself. More recently, Meade's biographer Freeman Cleaves has argued that the letter was written by John B. Bachelder, who had been at Sickles's headquarters at Gettysburg; but Cleaves's argument is not convincing. The riddle of Historicus is still unsolved.[1]

1. Historicus, "The Battle of Gettysburg. Important Communication from an Eye Witness. How the Victory was Won and How Its Advantages were Lost. Generals Halleck's and Meade's Official Reports Refuted." *New York Herald,* March 12, 1864; *OR,* vol. 27, pt. 1, pp. 127–36; *MG,* 229–30; Sauers, *A Caspian Sea of Ink,* 50 n. 30.

Meade himself was certain of Historicus's identity, however. Writing to the War Department on March 15, he enclosed a copy of the offending article, complaining that whoever wrote it had access to official documents and papers not yet made public. He continued, "I cannot resist the belief that this letter was either written or dictated by Major General D. E. Sickles." Meade then asked the War Department to ascertain whether Sickles and Historicus were the same person. If so, he wrote, he would request a court of inquiry to investigate the subject fully and make the truth known.[2]

Meade's request for a court of inquiry caused a flurry of concern in the Lincoln administration. A public feud between two high-profile figures such as Meade and Sickles was bad enough; to drag the matter before a court would inevitably weaken the administration's war effort by splitting both the army and the general public into different camps. A court of inquiry would also play into the hands of the radical Republicans by producing testimony that Lee's escape was the result of Meade's conservative generalship, which could then be used to confirm the joint committee's contention that conservative generals such as Meade should be replaced.

Damage control, in an effort to soothe Meade's feelings, soon followed. Halleck wrote a confidential letter to Meade on March 20, in which he agreed with Meade on the authorship of the Historicus letter but pointed out that Meade would never be able to prove that Sickles was its author. Nothing would suit Sickles better, said Halleck, than to embroil Meade in a personal or newspaper controversy. Halleck counseled Meade to ignore the situation, writing that Sickles could not, with one newspaper article, even slightly injure Meade's military reputation.[3]

Meade, though not mollified, perhaps recognized the truth of Halleck's words. On March 22, he replied, "I am not as philosophical as you are, nor do I consider it good policy to permit such slanders as have been circulated to pass entirely unnoticed. They have an influence with many people to whom I am a stranger; indeed, even my friends, believing me innocent, have still been puzzled to account for and understand these charges." Nonetheless, Meade offered to withdraw his letter to the War Department if Halleck and Stanton thought it better to keep quiet.[4]

This was exactly what Halleck, Stanton, and Lincoln wanted. Soon after

2. *OR*, vol. 27, pt. 1, pp. 127–36.

3. Ibid., 137.

4. Ibid., 137–8.

Meade's letter to Halleck, George Harding, an old law associate of Stanton's from Philadelphia, visited the aggrieved commander. Harding informed Meade that Stanton would not grant a court of inquiry and, like Halleck, advised him to pay no attention to "such a person as Sickles." Stanton later explained to Meade that a court of inquiry was just what Sickles wanted. While it might exonerate Meade, it would not necessarily incriminate Sickles; and Stanton believed that "on the whole, it was deemed best not to take any action." Lincoln was in full agreement with his secretary of war. On March 29 he denied Meade's request for a court of inquiry. "The country knows that, at all events, you have done good services; and I believe it agrees with me that it is much better for you to be engaged in trying to do more, than to be diverted, as you unnecessarily would be, by a Court of Inquiry," the president wrote.[5]

Nor was the controversy surrounding the Historicus letter the only tribulation Meade had to bear. The night before his initial appearance before the committee, he was attacked in the Senate by Morton S. Wilkinson, Republican of Minnesota. Comparing Meade unfavorably with Grant, Wilkinson ridiculed Meade for allowing Lee to escape. Reverdy Johnson, a Maryland Democrat, came to Meade's defense on the Senate floor. On Meade's return to the army from Washington he found a note from Johnson saying he had assumed the responsibility of denying Wilkinson's statement and asking if his defense of Meade was correct. Meade promptly wrote to Johnson indicating where he thought Wilkinson "had been misled."[6]

Johnson, for whatever reason, began showing Meade's letter to friends, and a copy of it wound up in John Froney's *Washington Chronicle,* where it quickly came to Stanton's attention. Incensed, Stanton wrote to Meade demanding to know "by what authority" he had written to a senator about military operations. Meade testily replied that his note was private and not intended for publication or circulation, and that he was not aware he required any permission to write private letters defending himself. In addition, he had written of military operations that had taken place some nine months before, and of which official reports were already published.[7]

The matter rested there until Meade returned to Washington for his second appearance before the joint committee. Stanton then told him that his letter to Johnson had been a "great mistake." Stanton explained that Johnson

5. *LLM,* March 26, 1864, 2:183–4 and April 2, 1864, 2:186, 2:336.

6. *CG,* 38th Cong., 1st sess., March 2, 1864, pp. 898–9; *LLM,* March 6, 1864, 2:169 and March 10, 1864, 2:177.

7. *LLM,* March 10, 1864, 2:177.

was showing the letter to everyone, making it appear he was Meade's chosen defender, "and that Johnson's political status was such that any identification with him could not fail to damage [Meade]."[8]

Stanton had again protected Meade from his political naïveté. The Democrat Johnson was naturally suspect as far as the radicals on the committee were concerned; the fact that he had defended McClellan in the Senate in opposition to the committee sealed his reputation. Fortunately for Meade, he ran into Johnson on a street in Washington and asked him to keep the letter private while "borrowing" it to copy for War Department files. There is no mention of its ever being returned.[9]

[435] Testimony of Major General George G. Meade.

Washington, April 4, 1864.

Major General George G. Meade appeared before the committee and said: I desire to add a little to my testimony, with the permission of the committee.

The chairman: Certainly, you are at liberty to make such additional statements as you please.

[436] The witness: I wanted to say a few words to the committee, in extension of the remarks which I made the last time I was here, in reference to a charge which I expected then would be made against me, and which I understand has since been made against me, to the effect that I intended that an order should be issued, on the morning of July 2, withdrawing the army from the position it then occupied at Gettysburg and retreating, before the enemy had done anything to require me to withdraw.

It is proper that I should say that the fact of such a charge having been made here, or such a report given here, has reached me through outside sources, but in such a way that I can hardly disbelieve that such a statement has been made; and that it was made by an officer who occupied a very high and confidential position on my staff—the chief of staff, Major General Butterfield. Now, indulging in the utmost charity towards General Butterfield, and believing that he is sincere in what he says, I want to explain how it is possible that such an extraordinary idea could have got into his head.

I utterly deny, under the full solemnity and sanctity of my oath, and in the

8. Ibid., March 14, 1864, 2:178.

9. Sears, ed., *Civil War Papers of George B. McClellan*, 568–9, 626; *LLM*, March 14, 1864, 2:178.

firm conviction that the day will come when the secrets of all men shall be made known—I utterly deny ever having intended or thought, for one instant, to withdraw that army, unless the military contingencies which the future should develop during the course of the day might render it a matter of necessity that the army should be withdrawn. I base this denial not only upon my own assertion and my own veracity, but I shall also show to the committee, from documentary evidence, the despatches and orders issued by me at different periods during that day, that if I did intend any such operation, I was at the same time doing things totally inconsistent with any such intention.

I shall also ask the committee to call before them certain other officers of my staff, whose positions were as near and confidential to me as that of General Butterfield, who, if I had had any such intention, or had given any such orders as he said I gave, would have been parties to it, would have known it, and have made arrangements in consequence thereof; all of whom I am perfectly confident, will say they never heard of any such thing. I refer to General Hunt, chief of artillery, and who had artillery, occupying a space of from four to five miles, drawn out on the road, and who, if I had intended to have withdrawn that army, should have been told to get his trains out of the way the very first thing, because all the troops could not move until the artillery moved. I would also ask you to call upon [Brigadier] General [Rufus] Ingalls, my chief quartermaster, who had charge of the trains; also General Warren, my chief engineer, who will tell you that he was with me the whole of the day, in constant intercourse and communication with me; and that instead of intending to withdraw my army, I was talking about other matters. All these officers will corroborate what I say, that I never mentioned any such purpose to any of them.

Hunt appeared before the committee later that same day; Warren had testified earlier. Ingalls was not called.

General Butterfield remained at Taneytown on the night of the 1st of July, and did not join me on the field until about 9 or 10 o'clock in the morning of the 2d, I having arrived there at 1 o'clock. Soon after he arrived I did direct him to familiarize himself with the topography of the ground, and I directed him to send out staff officers to learn all the roads. As I have already mentioned in my previous testimony here, I had never before been at Gettysburg, and did not know how many roads ran from our position, or what directions they ran. My orders to General Butterfield were similar to this:

"General Butterfield, neither I nor any man can tell what the results of this day's operations may be. It is our duty to be prepared for every contingency, and I wish you to send out staff officers to learn all the roads that lead from this place, ascertain the positions of the corps—where their trains are; prepare to familiarize yourself with these details, so that in the event of any contingency, you can, without any order be ready to meet it."

[437] It was in anticipation of possible contingencies, and not at all that I had made up my mind to do anything of that kind.

I would furthermore call the attention of the committee to the absurdity of such an idea. If I had directed the order to be issued, why was it not issued? With General Butterfield's capacity it would not have taken him more than ten or fifteen minutes to prepare such an order. We were furnished with what you call manifold letter-writers, so that after the frame work of an order is prepared, ten or a dozen copies may be made at once. Why was the order not issued, or if issued, why was it not executed? There was no obstacle to my withdrawing that army, if I had desired; the enemy presented none. There was not a moment from the time the first gun was fired at Gettysburg until we knew the enemy had retired that I could not have withdrawn my army. Therefore, if I had entertained such an idea, it seems to me extraordinary that I did not execute it.

I will now read the documentary evidence that I proposed to lay before this committee. The first is a despatch to Major General Slocum, commanding the 12th corps, as follows:

"July 2, 1863—9.30 A.M.

"General: The commanding general desires that you will at once examine the ground in your front, and give him your opinion as to the practicability of attacking the enemy in that quarter.

"Very respectfully, your obedient servant,

"S. WILLIAMS,

"Assistant Adjutant General.

"Major General H. W. SLOCUM, Commanding."

Then there is a despatch at 10 A.M., addressed to General Slocum, written by General Butterfield himself, directing him to make an attack:

"HEADQUARTERS, ARMY OF POTOMAC,

"July 2, 1863 (supposed about 10 A.M.)

"Major General Slocum:

"The commanding general desires you to make your arrangements for an attack from your front on the enemy, to be made by the 12th corps, supported by the 5th.

"He wishes this a strong and decisive attack, which he will order so soon as he gets definite information of the approach of the 6th corps, which will also be directed to co-operate in this attack; for this purpose he has sent an officer to ascertain the whereabouts of General Sedgwick, and report.

"I am, very respectfully, your obedient servant,

"DANIEL BUTTERFIELD,

"Major General and Chief of Staff."

At 10 o'clock I was ordering General Slocum to make the attack; at the same time I sent General Warren, my chief engineer, to consult with General Slocum as to the advisability of making the attack. General Warren went, and then returned and reported to me. I also received the following note from General Slocum:

"Headquarters, July 2, 1863—10.30 A.M.

"Major General Meade,

"Commanding Army of Potomac.

"General: Your note of 9.30 A.M. is received. I have already made a better examination of the position in my front than I was able to do, now that [438] we have taken up a new line. If it is true that the enemy are massing troops on our right, I do not think we could detach enough troops for an attack to insure success. I do not think the ground in my front, held by the enemy, possesses any peculiar advantages for him.

"Very respectfully, your obedient servant,

"H. W. SLOCUM,

"Major General, Commanding."

General Warren, furthermore, reported to me that he did not think an attack advisable from our right flank; I therefore abandoned that attack, and waited for the 6th corps to arrive, intending to move the 5th corps over to the left, as I did, and then, if the enemy did not attack me, to make an attack myself from the left.

I find on the records of the Adjutant General's office of the army of the Potomac a document, supposed to have been issued at 10 o'clock A.M. of the 2d of July, which is in confirmation of what I consider my orders to General Butterfield. It is as follows:

"Headquarters Army of Potomac,

"July 2, (supposed about 10 A.M.) 1863.

"The staff officers on duty at headquarters will inform themselves of the positions of the various corps—their artillery, infantry, and trains—sketch them with a view to roads, and report them immediately as follows:

"3d corps, Colonel Schriver.

"2d corps, Lieutenant Colonel Davis.

"1st corps, Lieutenant Perkins.

"12th corps, Lieutenant Oliver.

"5th corps, Captain Cadwalader.

"It is desired to know the roads on or near which the troops are, and where their trains lie, in view of movements in any direction, and to be familiar with the headquarters of the commanders,

"By order of General Meade.

"S. WILLIAMS,

"Assistant Adjutant General."

That was the sum and substance of the instructions I gave to General Butterfield, to familiarize himself with the position, and be ready, in case I should desire to retreat or do anything else, to issue the necessary orders.

In further confirmation of that, I find among my papers my despatch to General Halleck, informing him of what I proposed to do during the rest of the day, if in my power to do so. The despatch to General Slocum to make the attack was at 10 A.M. This despatch to General Halleck was at 3 P.M., and is as follows:

"Headquarters Army of Potomac,

"July 2, (3 P.M., near Gettysburg,) 1863.

"Major General Halleck, Washington:

"I have concentrated my army at this place to-day. The 6th corps is just coming in very much worn out, having been marching since 9 P.M. last night. The army is fatigued.

"I have to-day, up to this hour, awaited the attack of the enemy, I having a strong position for defense. I am not determined as yet to attacking him till his position is more developed. He has been moving on both my flanks apparently, but it is difficult to tell exactly his movements. I have delayed attacking to allow the 6th corps and parts of other corps to reach this place, and to [439] rest the men. Expecting a battle, I ordered all my trains to the rear. If not attacked, and I can get any positive information of the position of the enemy which will justify me in so doing, I shall attack. If I find it hazardous to do so, or am satisfied the enemy is endeavoring to move to my rear, and interpose between me and Washington, I shall fall back to my supplies at Westminster. I will endeavor to advise you as often as possible.

"In the engagement yesterday the enemy concentrated more rapidly than we could, and towards evening, owing to the superiority of numbers, compelled the 11th and 1st corps to fall back from the town to the heights on this side, on which I am now posted.

"I feel fully the responsibility resting on me, and will endeavor to act with caution.

"GEORGE G. MEADE,
"Major General."

The committee will perceive that I tell General Halleck that I was waiting the arrival of the 6th corps before I should commence any active operations myself; that I had been expecting an attack up to that moment; that, after the 6th corps arrived, if the enemy did not attack me I should attack him if I thought it advisable to do so.

There is no doubt, as I mentioned here before, and as I have no hesitation to say again now, whatever influence it may have upon my reputation as a general, that it was my desire at Gettysburg to receive the attack of the enemy, and fight a defensive rather than an offensive battle, for the reason that I was satisfied my chances of success were greater in a defensive battle than an offensive one, and I knew the momentous consequences dependent upon the result of that.

That General Butterfield may have misapprehended what I said to him; that he may himself have deemed a retreat necessary, and thought we would be compelled to retreat in the course of the day, and in the excess of zeal and desire to do more than he was called upon to do, may have drawn up an order of that kind, I do not deny; but I say he never showed me any such order, and it had not my sanction or authority.

After Meade's first appearance before the committee, he wrote to his wife concerning the missing order to withdraw. Meade had ordered his adjutant gen-

eral, Seth Williams, to search the records for a copy of this order, knowing that the existence of such an order would be of great utility to his enemies. Williams reported that no "vestige" of it existed and assumed that it had been destroyed within a day or so of its preparation. The clerks at headquarters remembered that such an order had been prepared, but that not being needed it was "destroyed as worthless." Although Sickles claimed to have a copy of this order, he never produced it for the committee or anyone else.[10]

I have only further to say that I have brought with me a map of the field of Gettysburg. I consider the map accurate. It contains on it, in blue lines, the position which General Sickles thought proper to take, and, in red lines, the position I designed him to occupy. [This map is not included in the committee's papers.]

Meade gave a solid defense against the July 2 order. In an emotional statement Meade solemnly denied ever having intended to withdraw from Gettysburg. He pointed out that his actions that day were totally inconsistent with any intention to withdraw. He also produced documentary evidence to support his case, which was something notably lacking from his critics. Meade introduced several dispatches to Slocum concerning his proposed attack on the morning of July 2, as well as one message to Halleck sent that afternoon.

Meade took a somewhat aggressive stance when he acerbically noted that Butterfield himself may have wanted to retreat or had thought a retreat might be necessary and had prepared the order out of zeal.

The one weak point in Meade's testimony was his admission that he had wanted to fight a defensive battle. The committee wanted aggressive generals to lead the war, not generals who would wait for the enemy to attack them. To the committee, Meade's statement could be seen as an admission to the charge of timidity.

10. *CCW,* 466; quoted in *GC,* 340.

16 Brigadier General Henry Jackson Hunt

BRIGADIER GENERAL HENRY J. HUNT, chief of artillery for the Army of the Potomac at Gettysburg, followed Meade's second appearance before the committee. Like Gibbon, Hunt was the antithesis of what committee members thought made a good officer. From a military family—he was both the son and grandson of professional military officers—Hunt was a Democrat who had graduated from West Point. He was also the best artillery commander in the Union army.

After West Point Hunt fought in Mexico before settling into the quiet life of the antebellum regular army in the East. His most notable service during this time was on a board to revise the system of light artillery tactics. The board's report was adopted by the War Department in 1860 and used by both sides throughout the war.[1]

With the coming of war Hunt distinguished himself at First Bull Run and Malvern Hill, where his guns were credited with smashing the Confederate attack. In September 1862, he was made a brigadier general of volunteers. Still, promotions in the artillery were slow and Hunt complained long and loud all during the war about what he thought were too few field and staff officer positions in the artillery.

The reorganization of the army into "grand divisions" by Burnside destroyed the artillery arm's command structure. In 1862 the War Department had announced that field officers of artillery were an unnecessary expense and forbade the enlistment of new ones. Many promising artillery officers found the only route to promotion was a transfer to the infantry. Hunt stayed in the artillery, but despite commanding all the artillery for the Army of the Potomac

1. Warner, *Generals in Blue*, 242–3.

and all the siege operations at Petersburg, he was not made a major general until the end of the war.[2]

Unlike most professional officers in the army, Hunt took an active part in politics. A close personal friend of McClellan's, Hunt corresponded with him and quietly distributed Democratic campaign literature during the election of 1864. The depth of Hunt's involvement in politics can be seen in a letter he wrote to McClellan in September 1864, suggesting that McClellan use the Mexican War as an example to show that an armistice could lead to peace. McClellan thought Hunt's idea "worth attending to."[3]

[447] Testimony of General Henry J. Hunt.

Washington, April 4, 1864.
Brigadier General Henry J. Hunt sworn and examined.

By Mr. Gooch:
Question. When were you restored to the full command of the artillery?
Answer. General Meade took command on the 28th of June, I think, and moved the next morning. I had no opportunity then of saying anything whatever [448] to him about my position. I proceeded to do everything I could, as I always had done, to forward whatever was necessary to be done.

Hunt had had full command of the artillery under McClellan and Burnside, but with Hooker's reorganization of the army the batteries had been distributed to various commands and placed to a large extent under their control. Hunt was relegated to merely administrative duties.[4]

Hunt's resumption of active command of the artillery appears to be predicated on the idea that the job of the chief of artillery entailed active command. This contrasts with Meade's view that chief of cavalry was an administrative job, indicating that perhaps Meade had less faith in Pleasonton than in Hunt.

At Taneytown I received orders from General Meade with regard to selecting positions for the artillery at Pipe creek and examining the country there, and I accompanied him to Gettysburg, which place we reached about one

2. Ibid.; Hunt, "First Day at Gettysburg," *B&L,* 3:259.

3. Wainwright, *A Diary of Battle,* ed. Nevins, 473; Sears, ed., *Civil War Papers of George B. McClellan,* 611.

4. Wise, *Long Arm of Lee,* 2:546; Hunt, "First Day at Gettysburg," *B&L,* 3:259.

o'clock at night. As soon as the position was explained to General Meade by some officers there, he directed me to immediately select the positions for the artillery, which I proceeded to do, so far as the darkness would permit. I could see our own ground, but not that of the enemy. General Meade accompanied. About dawn of day General Slocum reported to General Meade that there was a gap in his lines, which should be filled by a division which was not there, and that he apprehended an immediate attack. I was lying down near the root of a tree there. General Meade immediately asked for me; and when I reported to him, he gave me directions to take immediate measures for stopping that gap, and if an attack was made to repulse it. I looked upon that as no opportunity to come to an explanation with him; but I regarded it, and his previous order to look to the positions of the batteries, as, in fact, recognizing the position I had held both under General McClellan and General Burnside. At all events, I proceeded at once to act upon that assumption; ordered artillery from wherever I could find it, where I thought it could be spared, without any regard to the commands of others, except to inform them that it was necessary; took possession of all the ground that covered the position, put the batteries on it, and covered that gap until the troops took their position there, when I distributed the artillery back to its former positions.

At the request of General Meade I sent for the artillery reserves, which had been kept behind us, and from that time I exercised all the duties of commander of the artillery, as recognized in modern armies, in the same way as at Antietam, where General McClellan told me on the field that he held me responsible for everything in connexion with the artillery, and that I might make every use of his name if I came across anybody that ranked me; that is, I took full control of the artillery where, by the regulations and necessities of the service, it was not under the exclusive command of others.

It was in discharge of my duties as commander of the artillery of the army that I went to every point of attack, where it was frequently necessary to use the artillery of adjoining corps, together with portions of the reserve artillery brought up for the purpose, and which, of course, no one corps commander could take charge of. I gave all the orders I found necessary under these circumstances at all the points of attack.

The day after we recrossed the Potomac General Meade called me, and stated that there was some mismanagement in the marching of the heavy ammunition trains of the reserve artillery and the general park. I explained to him that they had crossed a long pontoon bridge, where the wagons could not keep close together, but were compelled to have a certain distance between them; that after crossing they were compelled to move rapidly, in order to catch up with those in front, or leave wide openings, and of course some confusion had occurred in regard to regularity of march; that it could not be wondered at that the lines should be cut by infantry troops crossing the adjoining bridge. I asked the general why he spoke to me about it, and said that under existing orders—those of General Hooker—I had no authority to interfere; that the orders given to the artillery reserve were not given through me; that I had not had an opportunity to bring the subject to his attention, as he was engaged in matters of more importance; that I had been able to get things along as they were without any particular authority, but now I wished him to define my duties.

A few weeks afterwards, when we had got into camp, the subject was taken up. The command of all the artillery not attached to troops was given to me; and all the management and responsibility, as to movements, equipments, &c., of [449] the troops of the artillery that were attached to other troops, were also put under my direction. In fact, it amounted to giving me the command of the whole of the artillery, as in other armies. One by one, since that time, as occasion has arisen, when it has been necessary to decide, I believe all, or nearly all, the powers of a corps commander have been conferred upon me under special orders, so that now I occupy a position very much like that of the commander of the cavalry, and it is, to all intents and purposes, the same that was given me at first.

Question. Will you give to us a concise description of the battle of Gettysburg?

Answer. The first day of the fight, July 1, I was not on the ground; I was at headquarters. I accompanied General Meade to Gettysburg. On my arrival there I examined the ground and posted the batteries, or approved of the positions where the batteries had been placed, and placed such additional batteries as were required the next morning.

As my attention was drawn more particularly to my own arm of the service, I can give a description of the battle only in general terms. On the morning of the 2d of July I examined all the positions along the whole line. I think the 3d corps was just coming up to its ground on our extreme left; next to them was the 2d corps; then the 11th, and I think the 1st corps, on Cemetery ridge; then on their right was the 12th corps. I do not remember distinctly the relative positions of the 1st and 11th corps. In fact, I was so busy with the artillery that I did not fix in my mind the relative positions of the infantry corps.

The majority of the Third Corps was already in camp at Gettysburg. Hunt was probably referring to the two brigades and two batteries left behind at Emmitsburg, which rejoined the Third Corps around 9:00 A.M.

On the morning of the 2d the reserve artillery, with its heavy trains of ammunition, which had been left behind some three or four miles, was brought forward by direction of General Meade, and parked about the centre of the field, between the Baltimore pike and the Taneytown road, near which I think the 5th corps was in support of the 12th and 11th corps, the 6th corps not having yet arrived.

About 11 o'clock, I had just come into headquarters from an inspection of the ground, when General Meade sent for me and told me that General Sickles, who was there at the time, wished me to examine his line, or the line that he wanted to occupy; and General Meade wished me to go with General Sickles and examine the line. I think he added that General Sickles had no good position for his artillery. At that time I did not know anything of the intentions of General Meade—whether it was to occupy a line with a view to attack, or a defensive line, or a defensive and offensive line. As we left the room I asked General Sickles what his idea was. He said he wished to throw forward his line from the position in which it was then placed, and where it was covered in its front by woods and rocks, with a view to cover the Emmitsburg road. Whether I asked him the question if that was his view or not, or whether he stated it, I do not remember; I may have asked him that. The orders were to bring up the ammunition of the corps and the reserve; and I had learned that General Sickles had left his ammunition behind on that road, and I thought, among other things, he was naturally anxious to control that road until it should get in.

I examined the position with him and told him that the right of his proposed line was out where it would not be connected with the 2d corps; that it would have to be connected, perhaps, by throwing out the left wing of the 2d corps, and that that could not well be done unless a wood in our front, in which I saw no enemy, was under our control, so that the enemy could not take possession of it. We met a couple of countrymen just then, who told us that the wood in front of us was a narrow strip with open ground beyond it, and I was told that we had some cavalry in the open ground.

The troops were from Buford's First Cavalry Division, which had already been removed earlier that morning by mistake.

General Sickles said he would send in a couple of companies of Berdan's sharpshooters[5] to examine the wood and see whether the enemy was there.

[450] About this time a very heavy cannonade was opened at the cemetery, which continued, and made me anxious about that point, for I was even worse off in regard to field officers at Gettysburg than I was at Chancellorsville, and that made it necessary to go myself to every point of attack and look after it. I told General Sickles that I would follow the line from the position he mentioned down to the Round Top on our left, and report its condition to General Meade. He asked me, as far as I remember, something about whether it would be proper to move forward his line, and I said, "No; that he should wait orders from General Meade"; for, as far as I was concerned, I had no authority in the matter.

In their testimony before the committee, Hunt and Sickles disagreed about this meeting. In fact, Hunt gave at least two slightly different versions of it himself. In his article "The Second Day at Gettysburg," Hunt wrote that he and Sickles went directly to the Peach Orchard, which he had examined that morning. He also claimed credit for insisting that Sickles order a reconnaissance of the woods to the front. Credit for this reconnaissance was also claimed by Sickles, Colonel Hiram Berdan, and General Birney.[6]

In contrast, Sickles asserted that he and Hunt examined the entire position of the left "in reference to . . . the best line for us to occupy, and . . . the movements of the enemy." Sickles also testified that Hunt had told him that while he could not speak for Meade, the proposed line seemed good, and that he would "undoubtedly" receive orders to occupy the line once Hunt had reported to Meade. Sickles did not mention that Hunt had any reservations about the line.

I moved down that road; it was a very good line to occupy, provided it was necessary to watch our left flank and prevent a movement by the enemy, or from which to make an offensive demonstration; but one which exposed both its own flank and the flank of the 2d corps, which would have to move forward to join it, to a cross-fire, if the enemy should take position in the strip of woods of which I have spoken.

I returned to headquarters, on my way to Cemetery ridge, and went in and made a report, very briefly, to General Meade. I stated to him that I had exam-

5. Col. Hiram Berdan's 1st and 2nd U.S. Sharpshooters.

6. Hunt, "Second Day at Gettysburg," *B&L,* 3:301–2; *GC,* 724 n. 121.

ined the line; that, so far as it was a line for troops to occupy, taken by itself, it was a very good line; but before putting any troops on it, or occupying it, I would advise him to examine it for himself; that I would not give any advice in the matter. I did this because I did not know General Meade's intentions, and I supposed he would soon be out there and examine it for himself if he thought it necessary. I went up to the Cemetery hill, on which an attack was being made, at that time principally by artillery, and some troops thrown out as sharpshooters. Some demonstrations were made by moving down by our right. I remained there until I saw the attack would not be a very serious one, and, feeling anxious about the position of General Sickles, I returned directly towards the position he wanted his right to occupy. On approaching it, Captain Randolph, who commanded the artillery of the 3d corps, came riding towards me, stating that he was glad I had come; that he was ordered to post a couple of batteries in a peach orchard there, and wished me to select the position. I asked if General Sickles had ordered it, and he said yes. The skirmishers were already engaged. I dismounted and went in with him, bringing us under a warm musketry fire. I told him if the batteries were to be placed there, the place he had selected was as good a position as he could find; pointed out another position for another battery, and sent immediately to the artillery reserve for some rifled batteries, as I saw the enemy's artillery moving in heavy force around our left, and beyond the reach of our smooth-bores. As soon as I had given these instructions I started back immediately to find General Sickles. On approaching him I saw he was in conversation with General Meade. I supposed, of course, that General Meade had come out there, and had approved of his occupying that line. I therefore returned to Captain Randolph and assisted him in putting his batteries in position, when we were opened upon by a very heavy artillery fire, at close range, from this strip of wood in front of General Sickles's new line. Having given instructions to one of the field officers of the reserve artillery whom I found on the ground for the posting of the batteries that I had sent for to the reserve, I proceeded at once to the extreme left of the line, where I knew there was a battery to be placed in a position very difficult of access, but which, if once attained, would give a very effective fire upon the batteries of the enemy that were then playing upon our right as it went into position. On reaching the position I found that three of the guns of [Captain James E.] Smith's battery—4th New York—had been got up quite a precipice, and were in the desired position. I had a fire opened immediately, which very much interfered with the enemy's batteries, and relieved our right a great deal from their fire. At the same time some of the enemy's batteries that I had seen passing round to our left had got into position, and opened, partly on Sickles's right, partly on [451] Smith's battery, which he answered with effect. I then left him to proceed along the line of Sickles's front, looking to the position of the batteries, giving such directions as I found necessary, and sending for such additional batteries as I wanted. I continued there until nearly sunset. I found that the time had passed very rapidly, and that I had been absent from General Meade a long time, and fearing that he might want me, I returned to headquarters. Soon after I arrived there, all at headquarters got up suddenly and left—the bulk of them going down the Tenallytown [Taneytown] road, under the lead of General Butterfield. I remained, with two of my staff officers and an aid[e] of General Meade, with him, and accompanied the re-enforcements which were then going up to the position originally occupied by Sickles's corps, and from which the enemy were driven back.

In the mean time an attack had taken place on the 12th corps, on our right. But by the time we had got through with the battle of the 3d corps, it had got so dark that I saw there would be no further use for the artillery over there; and being pretty well worn out, I did not go over to that affair, but proceeded to the park of the artillery reserve, to supervise the reorganization of the batteries and the necessary repairs.

The next morning an attack by our own troops took place where the 12th corps was, and I went over and took charge of the artillery there.

This was the reoccupation of earthworks abandoned the previous day, as the men were sent to bolster the left against Longstreet's attack.

I then went to the position of the 11th corps on Cemetery ridge, where another cannonade had commenced between the enemy's batteries and our own.

I moved from there along the ridge to Round Top, as I saw the enemy were placing batteries in position in the woods opposite our line—whether with a view to opening upon us preparatory to an attack, or fearing an attack from us, I could not judge. I gave orders to the artillery along the line what should be done. I had just reached the extreme left battery on the hill of Round Top, when the bombardment of the enemy commenced, I think about 1 o'clock. The enemy opened upon us with some 115 or 120 guns, to which we could bring but about 70 to reply effectively.

Hunt's estimate of the number of Confederate guns at Gettysburg grew with time. In his article "The Third Day at Gettysburg," he claimed to have opposed nearly 150 rebel guns, while having only 77 guns himself. The number of guns on the Confederate line is generally accepted as having been approximately 115. In his book The Long Arm of Lee, *historian Jennings Wise puts the number of rebel guns at roughly 150, but this figure is too high.*[7]

The number of guns used on the Federal side is even more difficult to determine because they were constantly being withdrawn and replaced throughout the bombardment. In his battle report Hunt gave the number of Union guns as 80, but he did not seem to include the guns on Cemetery Hill. The total of Union guns involved at any one time appears to have been about 118.[8]

This bombardment continued for an hour and a half, I should judge. It was very destructive to our material, but was replied to very effectively by our artillery, until I ordered them, commencing at the cemetery, to slacken their fire and cease it, in order to see what the enemy were going to do, and also to be sure that we retained a sufficient supply of ammunition to meet, what I then expected, an attack.

In this instance Hunt and Meade were thinking along identical lines. Meade had issued orders at about the same time for the guns to cease fire in order to save ammunition and draw out the Confederate attack. In "The Third Day at Gettysburg," Hunt recalled that after giving his order to cease fire, he went to get fresh batteries from the Artillery Reserve. On the way he met Major Bingham of Hancock's staff, who informed him that Meade's aides were looking for him with cease-fire orders.[9]

At the same time batteries were ordered up to replace those guns which had been damaged, or which had expended too much ammunition.

By the time these batteries had reached the ground, I saw directly in front of the 2d corps the enemy forming their column of attack, or rather their lines of attack. It turned out to be Pickett's division of the rebel army.

7. Henry J. Hunt, "The Third Day at Gettysburg," *B&L*, 3:371; *OR*, vol. 27, pt. 1, p. 239; Wise, *Long Arm of Lee*, 2:670.

8. Wise, *Long Arm of Lee*, 2:670.

9. Meade, *Gettysburg*, 91; Hunt, "Third Day at Gettysburg," *B&L*, 3:374; Ladd and Ladd, eds., *The Bachelder Papers*, 1:229.

The well-known Pickett's charge was not commanded by Pickett, nor were his troops the majority of its participants. The attack was under the command of Lieutenant General James Longstreet, commander of the First Corps, and Pickett's men were outnumbered by Heth's division of Lieutenant General A. P. Hill's Third Corps.[10]

In his fascinating and highly detailed book on Pickett's charge, George Stewart demonstrates that the total number of Confederate troops was closer to 10,500, rather than the commonly cited 15,000.[11]

They advanced directly towards the 2d corps, and our artillery in reach was turned upon them very effectively. But they continued to advance very handsomely, and made a direct attack upon our position. As soon as their troops had got so nearly joined to ours that it was unsafe any longer to fire canister upon them, I found that our men were giving way. As the supports had not come up, I left the batteries and went up to assist in keeping the men up. My horse was soon killed, which brought me down; and before I could get remounted and back there again the struggle was over, and we captured all of the enemy who did not run away or were not killed.

As soon as that attack was over, and the enemy saw that their men had given up, they opened their batteries at once, and upon their own men and ours at the same time, and after that cannonade they formed another column of attack, which advanced, but more upon our left, opposite the 3d corps. That attack was more easily disposed of than the other, as the enemy, I suppose, were somewhat disheartened by the repulse of their first attack. We were enabled to bring our guns all to bear upon them, so that they did not get within a hundred [452] yards of our line, but went back under cover of a little stream which was covered by a growth of small bushes. I can only say that my knowledge of the battle of Gettysburg is very much circumscribed, as I was kept busily occupied by my own special duties.

Question. Had you any knowledge of any order being prepared during the battle of Gettysburg for the withdrawal of the army from the position it then occupied?

Answer. No, sir. I know of no such order, and no such intention. I presume if any such intention had been entertained I should have known of it as soon

10. George R. Stewart, *Pickett's Charge: A Microhistory of the Final Attack at Gettysburg, July 3, 1863* (Boston: Houghton Mifflin, 1959), 172–3.

11. Ibid.

as anybody, as the first thing to have been done was to get rid of the large reserve artillery and ammunition train under my charge, and which had been brought up on the morning of the 2d of July, under, or by the direction of, General Meade.

Question. You say you had no knowledge or intimation of any such thing during the battle?

Answer. None at all. The only time I ever had a thought such an idea might be entertained was on the night of the 2d of July. On that night I was down at the artillery reserve, refitting and reorganizing the batteries that had been cut up that day. I received a message from General Mead's headquarters—I do not now recollect whether it was from General Meade himself or from General Butterfield—stating that both General Tyler, who commanded the reserve artillery, and myself, were wanted at headquarters. I told General Tyler that it was impossible for me to go up just then, but that if the question came up about falling back, to cast my vote against it. He remained for some time, and I went up with him, perhaps a half an hour afterwards. On arriving at headquarters, I understood that the question had been spoken of as to what they should do, and there was no person at all in favor of leaving the ground we had then; that was just as the consultation closed.

Just about daylight on the 2d of July General Meade ordered the reserve artillery brought up. I sent my aide for it, and it came up about 8 o'clock in the morning, I think; so that at that time there could have been no question of leaving.

Question. The meeting of our troops with those of the enemy at Gettysburg was not premeditated, was it? It was an accidental conflict between the two armies as they were moving, was it not?

Answer. As I have always looked upon it, the army was moving up there to see as to the position of the enemy. From the orders that were issued at Taneytown it was evident that the enemy had seen the necessity of concentrating; and it was certain that if he concentrated he would have to attack us, and arrangements were made looking to the collecting of our troops behind Pipe creek. I cannot say, however, that the battle of Gettysburg was accidental. It necessarily followed from the concentration of the enemy there, unless General Reynolds had seen fit to fall back.

Question. Do you mean that the battle of Gettysburg followed necessarily from the concentration there of the troops of the enemy, or the concentration of our troops there?

Answer. The enemy would necessarily have to concentrate when he found us in his neighborhood. And so soon as our movements up there had shown him that we were getting together he did commence concentrating his troops at Gettysburg, and of course he would attack any portion of our troops he might find there. It is a natural place, I should think, for an attack of that kind to be made, so many roads meeting there. If he wanted to concentrate, it would be the most natural place for him to do so.

Question. Why did General Meade select Pipe creek as the point at which he proposed to concentrate?

[453] Answer. He had several corps of his troops out in a fan shape looking for the enemy and feeling for him. He supposed, of course, they would concentrate as soon as possible and attack him. He had to select some position at which to concentrate his own troops, and I suppose he selected that from the appearance of the map as a good line, and also from what he considered the absolute necessity of the enemy's attacking him; for it could hardly be supposed that, having gone up into Pennsylvania, they would fall back without attacking us. I know of no particular reasons for selecting that line, except that, from the appearance of the map, it appeared to be an eligible place, and it was considerably nearer than Gettysburg to Manchester, the place where we had our supplies; and it was a question, too, of battle-fields. General Meade had not had time to examine the ground at different points. As soon as General Hancock came down and reported the nature of the ground at Gettysburg, General Meade immediately gave the order to concentrate there.

Question. What do you say of the position which we held at Gettysburg? Was it a very advantageous one for us?

Answer. I think it was a very advantageous position. If the enemy attempted to turn us, of course, being upon the outer circle, he would have to scatter his forces a great deal. At the time he attacked General Sickles it appeared to me, from what I saw of his movements, in the hurried examination I made, that he was making a movement in that direction, that is, towards turning our extreme left. The position was a very strong one; that is, the ground was very favorable for the use of our arms, of the infantry in particular. There was a ridge extending from the cemetery for half or three-quarters of a mile, which was open in front, and over which the enemy could not advance without exposing themselves to the sweep of our artillery. The results was that they were enabled to concentrate more guns upon us in the heavy cannonade of July 3 than we could bring to reply to them.

Question. Was the advanced line selected by General Sickles, on Emmitsburg road, under all the circumstances, a judicious selection; and did advantage or disadvantage result to us from the adoption of that line by him?

Answer. That would depend upon circumstances. If the battle was to have been a purely defensive one, based upon the almost certainty that the enemy must attack us, I suppose our policy would have been to have taken up a strictly defensive line. In that case the line should have extended, as it was ordered, from Cemetery ridge direct to Round Top, along the crest. If there was fear of our left being turned, our line might have been thrown forward to prevent the attempt, but that should have been done by placing it in *echelon* instead of changing the direction of the line by throwing forward the right flank, as was done of Sickles's corps. I suppose the occupation of that advanced position compelled the enemy to attack us there, even if they had started to turn our left flank. I do not know enough about the numbers of the troops we had there on our left at the time to judge what would have been the result of the enemy turning our position, because I was so taken up with my own duties that it was impossible for me to learn all of those particulars. I know it led to a very severe and a very bloody battle. And it gave great advantages to the enemy on General Sickles's right flank, for they occupied the wood in front, which I said to him must be in our possession, or at least not occupied by the enemy.

On the whole, I cannot say whether it would have been better or not for him to have remained behind. Excepting on that right flank, it was probably as well to fight there as anywhere else. It would have been well, however, if the general commanding had known of it sooner, so as to dispose of troops behind; yet I was informed that they came up in good time. The only disposable [454] supports at that time, as I understood, was the 5th corps, which was left in support of the 12th corps on the Baltimore pike, and which was only to leave there when the 6th corps showed itself on that road. I have understood, but I do not know it of my own knowledge, that the 6th corps came up in very good time, or at least in sufficient time to enable General Sykes to move his corps over to the left early. My attention was taken up so entirely with the artillery that I did not take time to find out the position and strength of the infantry troops.

Question. Immediately after the final repulse of the enemy, on the 3d of July, were we not in a condition to have attacked the enemy, and why was not that done?

Answer. I think we might have attacked the enemy there if the troops in hand had been formed so that they could push forward at once. But our troops were very roughly handled where they were attacked. I thought that the troops that were on the right of the point of attack, near the 2d corps, and which moved out beyond their lines, and continued to move down the front of our line after the first assault was repulsed, might have joined in an attack upon the right of the enemy, of course taking the chances of his position.

On the evening of the 2d of July, when the re-enforcements came up, just at dusk, I thought it would be well to move forward. But on the evening of the 3d I did not feel so positive about it by any means, because I did not see a disposable force sufficiently large, immediately on the ground, to attack the enemy in position in those woods, where I knew, from my experience of that day, that they had more than one hundred guns in position, a much larger force of artillery than we could bring to bear against them. And they had been planted behind that wood long enough to have made such defenses as were found so effective where the 12th corps was. It was one of those cases where it was a question of risk and opportunity, and the general commanding must decide for himself whether he will run the risk or not.

In later years, Hunt concluded that Meade had been right in not counterattacking on July 3. As he wrote, "This *was not a 'Waterloo defeat' with a fresh army to follow it up, and to have made such a change to the offensive, on the assumption that Lee had made no provision against a reverse, would have been rash in the extreme. An advance of 20,000 men from Cemetery Ridge in the face of the 140 guns then in position would have been stark madness; an immediate advance from any point, in force, was simply impracticable." Elsewhere he wrote that Meade "was right . . . in not attempting a counter-attack at any stage of the battle."*[12]

Question. At what hour on the 3d were the enemy finally repulsed?

Answer. What I looked upon as the final repulse—for his attacks afterwards did not amount to much—was about 4 o'clock. I suppose after that they formed quite a heavy column of attack, which moved over and came within about two hundred yards of us. But the first troops, which came out on the right of the 2d corps, had moved down towards their lines, and when the enemy saw them they turned and ran back in confusion to their lines.

Question. Were you present at any council of war at Gettysburg after the final repulse of the enemy?

12. Hunt, "Third Day at Gettysburg," *B&L*, 3:376; *MG*, 185 n. 7.

Answer. I was not present at any council at that time. I had no field officers, and had so much duty to attend to that I was scarcely ever at headquarters at the time those things occurred.

Question. What is your opinion as to an immediate attack upon the enemy, or a pursuit if the enemy was retreating?

Answer. My idea was that our cavalry should have been so used as to have made that movement of his getting off almost impossible, although I perhaps do not know enough of the country to decide who is to blame for that not having been done. On the 4th it stormed terribly, so that afternoon it would have been almost impossible to move. We might have organized an attack on the morning of the 4th if the general had seen reason to do so; and, of course, had we seen the enemy move we should have followed up at once. The moment there was good reason to believe the enemy were withdrawing we should have followed at once without losing any time.

By the chairman:

Question. Do you know whether the enemy used oxen to get their artillery on or off the field?

[455] Answer. Not that I know of. I never heard of it. I heard a great deal about the enemy being out of ammunition, but I do not believe that.

Question. What supports had their artillery after the repulse of their final charge?

Answer. I do not know; they had the cover of a wood. I do not know what they had behind there. From the maps, and their works, and what I afterwards saw on the ground, I learned that they had rifle-pits, and troops in them. Their artillery was very much cut up by our fire; their losses, both in material and horses, were as great as ours. I saw graves, showing that our fire had passed over the artillery and struck infantry supports. I found evidence of great losses on their part; but what troops they had behind there I do not know.

Question. Was the 6th corps in the fight of the last day?

Answer. I do not think the 6th corps was engaged heavily; I do not know very much about that corps. It came up and was in reserve. I know its artillery was not much engaged, if at all.

Question. Where was that corps stationed at the time of that final repulse?

Answer. On our left, as I heard. When I reached the extreme left, just before the cannonade commenced, I heard that General Sedgwick was near there, and I meant to see him. I was prevented by the opening of the enemy's fire, and the fact, until now, had escaped my memory.

Question. Those troops were fresh; had not been much engaged?

Answer. They were fresh so far as fighting, but not so far as marching was concerned, for they had done very hard marching.

Question. Suppose an immediate and vigorous attack had been made after that repulse, what is your opinion as to their getting off their immense line of artillery there?

Answer. If the attack had been successful, we should most likely have captured all of it. I do not know what would have been the result of the attack; but our troops were very good.

Question. Were the troops in good spirits?

Answer. Our troops were in very good spirits.

Question. In your judgment, as a military man, what would have been the effect of a sudden advance along our line after their repulse and retreat? What would have become of their artillery?

Answer. If we had been successful, we probably would have got all their artillery, and I would have liked to see the attack made. It is very difficult to give a decided opinion upon these matters. If I had been asked, I should have advised an attack as soon as troops to make it could have been collected, though I did not know all the conditions of our army. We must risk to win.

Question. You had got over the heavy fighting, and then was the time to reap the harvest?

Answer. Yes, sir, if circumstances would permit.

By Mr. Gooch:

Question. Were you consulted in relation to attacking the enemy while he was at Williamsport?

Answer. I was not.

Question. In your opinion, should or not an attack have been made upon the enemy at Williamsport?

Answer. I did not have an opportunity to examine the ground there, as I was kept at headquarters of the army. From what I could hear at the time, I was in favor of moving up to our right and attacking the enemy. I was told afterwards that the position the enemy occupied was a very strong one from the character of the ground. It was described to me as rolling ground, with ridges presented towards us, each of which could have been made a line [456] of defense by the enemy; but from all I could learn, we could have got rid of that difficulty by moving up to our right, and moving down upon the enemy from that direction.

Question. Knowing as you did that the enemy had been repulsed, and were falling back with the intent to recross the Potomac river, which at that time was in a swollen condition, in your judgment should not such steps have been taken as would have enabled you to attack that army, either before it made the crossing, or while it was in the act of crossing?

Answer. I thought then, and I have seen no reason since to change my opinion, that a comparatively small force, which might have consisted mostly of cavalry, with some infantry, could, if thrown across the river, whether from that army, or pushed up from Frederick or from Washington, have prevented their crossing, and have shut them up on the north side of the river, where they would have been compelled to stand an attack from us—in which case we could have taken our time about it, and we had a large force of artillery—or, from all I heard of the character of the roads behind them, they would have been compelled to abandon the most of their material, in order to escape up the river, by the Hancock road, and cross above. I was then under the impression that we should have made an attack.

Question. If we had attacked them at that point, and our attack had been successful, it would have resulted in the destruction of that army, would it not?

Answer. Yes, sir; or rather in the loss of much material and many men. The destruction of an army is no easy matter.

Question. And could we not have made an attack in such manner as to have withdrawn, in the event we had found ourselves unable to cope with the enemy with any serious disaster to us?

Answer. I do not see why we could not have organized an attack, nor can I see why such an attack could not have been made consistently with proper precautions against a disaster in case of an adverse result. I will add that these opinions are based on the facts of the case as then presented to my mind. As I have already stated, I was not called into council, and I may not have been in possession of all the facts bearing on the subject and necessary to the forming of a sound judgment.

By Mr. Loan:

Question. What opportunities did you have for knowing what order General Meade issued from day to day, during the continuance of the battle of Gettysburg?

Answer. I received from day to day the circulars and orders that were issued regarding the movements of troops involving those of the artillery; and I had the same opportunities that others on his staff had. My headquarters are with the general, and though I have not been so much with him as others have been, still he could hardly have given any orders affecting extensively the movements of the army without my knowing them.

Question. I am speaking now particularly of the battle of Gettysburg; were you the chief of artillery there?

Answer. Yes, sir.

Question. Were you on General Meade's staff as chief of artillery?

Answer. Yes, sir.

Question. At what time were you assigned to duty as chief of artillery on General Meade's staff?

Answer. On assuming command he found me chief of artillery of the army. I continued chief of artillery of the army; no order was necessary to confirm it, and none was issued.

Question. At what time were you appointed chief of artillery on the staff of General Hooker?

[457] Answer. He found me chief of artillery upon his assuming the command. As such, I do not form part of the personal staff of the commander, but of the general staff of the army.

Question. At what time did General Hooker appoint you as chief of artillery on his staff?

Answer. I will not say now that he appointed me at all; he found me there, and I continued so.

Question. I understood you to say that you were upon his staff as chief of artillery?

Answer. Yes, sir; that is, I have been chief of artillery of the army of the Potomac from September 5, 1862 to this time.

Question. At what time did he issue an order assigning you to that duty?

Answer. I cannot remember positively that I was ever announced in orders; I would continue on duty as chief of artillery until relieved.

Question. Did General Meade, on assuming command, assign to duty the staff officers of General Hooker, in the positions they occupied on General Hooker's staff at the time General Meade took the command?

Answer. I have seen no orders from General Meade about the staff. He brought his personal staff with him. He recognized or continued the chiefs of "the staff" of artillery and of engineers as they stood when he took the command. At least he did not relieve me from my duties.

Question. Not have been assigned to any duty upon his staff, what particular facilities or opportunities did you have for knowing what orders he issued during the three days' battle at Gettysburg?

Answer. As chief of artillery of the army of the Potomac I was furnished with all orders that it was necessary I should know for the movements of the artillery, the positions they occupied, with the positions and movements of the troops, so that I should know where they were. I suppose I had the same facilities that any other person at headquarters had.

Question. Did you have any other facilities that you can name?

Answer. I was furnished with copies of all the orders that were issued.

Question. How do you know you received all the orders?

Answer. I mean circular orders. I simply assume that I received all the orders, because I received copies of all the orders that I saw or heard of. I know of no general movements that took place of which I did not receive notice.

Question. Had you any means of knowing what private orders General Meade issued to corps commanders?

Answer. No, sir; I know nothing about his private orders. When his special orders affect me I am furnished with them.

Question. Had you any means of knowing any orders or intentions of General Meade, excepting such as were promulgated to officers occupying your grade?

Answer. No, sir, except so far as my *position,* which is independent of grade, gives them to me, and what I can infer from the circumstances of the case. My position, in this respect, would put me on a footing with a corps commander, or the chief of engineers; and in other armies the officer occupying it would have the rank due to the position. The question is not one that can be determined by the grade of the officer. I do not think that any order involving the movements of troops could have been given without my knowing it, for the simple reason that the first thing to be provided for in falling back was the movements of heavy trains of ammunition and the reserve artillery under my charge, and which would be the first thing to see to. There were some very heavy guns left behind at Westminster. All wagons and supply trains of every kind, including large portions of the medical wagons, were left behind, so that there should be as little to cumber the roads as possible. But it was necessary to bring up the artillery, and with that very large trains of ammunition. [458] My facilities for knowing of any orders relating to the general movements of troops not only were as good, but I suppose better than those of most others in one respect, because the movements of those trains were involved in any such orders. I had all the facilities that anybody about headquarters had.

Question. The same as the adjutant general?

Answer. No, sir; not perhaps the same as those who write the orders; I refer to others than those who write the orders; an order might be lost on its way to me.

Question. Was it usual at that time, when special orders were sent to individual officers, to send copies to others whether they related to their actions or not?

Answer. No, sir; only those that related to their action.

Question. Then your means of knowledge related only to such general orders as were issued to officers of your grade, and such special orders as related particularly to your arm of the service?

Answer. That is all; I mean to include officers of my position as well as grade.

Congressman Benjamin Loan did not speak often in the hearings, but he made strong points in his cross-examination of Hunt. Implicit in his question about adjutant generals was the point that Butterfield, as chief of staff, was responsible for writing the orders and thus would have been more informed than Hunt of the situation at Gettysburg.

Question. Do I understand you rightly, that you were not present at the council of war held on the night of 2d of July?

Answer. I was not present at the time, though I was sent for.

Question. Nor were you present at the next council?

Answer. I was present at no council held there.

[The questions about the Bristoe and Mine Run campaigns are omitted.]

On balance, Hunt's testimony was about a draw. He had denied that there was any order to withdraw on July 2, aptly pointing out that he would have been among the first to have been notified. On the other hand, Hunt thought the army should have attacked at Williamsport, based on what he heard at the time.

Unusually, Gooch opened the session; he and Loan asked most of the questions. Wade asked only nine questions of Hunt.

17 Major General John Sedgwick

After a long weekend, the hearings resumed with Major General John Sedgwick, commander of the Sixth Corps at Gettysburg. Like McClellan, Sedgwick held a special place in the heart of the Army of the Potomac; he was affectionately known among the men as "Uncle John." Sedgwick was among the several West Pointers and Democrats who appeared before the committee. He made no secret of his warm personal feelings for McClellan, which were returned in kind by Little Mac. Upon receiving the corps badge worn by Sedgwick at the time of his death in the Battle of the Wilderness, McClellan wrote, "I am sure that no one was more warmly attached to John Sedgwick than I was."[1]

Following graduation from West Point, Sedgwick's career followed the typical path, with distinguished service in the Mexican War and against the Seminoles. In 1855 Sedgwick was appointed a major in the newly formed First U.S. Cavalry commanded by Colonel Robert E. Lee. With Lee's resignation to join the Confederacy, Sedgwick became colonel of the First Cavalry. Commissioned brigadier general of volunteers in August 1861, Sedgwick was promoted to major general in less than a year. He was given command of the Sixth Corps before the battle of Chancellorsville, where his failure to carry out impossible orders from Hooker sparked a heated controversy. Despite Hooker's oft-repeated criticism, Sedgwick retained command of his corps. At Gettysburg the Sixth Corps was used primarily as a reserve unit, and as a consequence it sustained relatively few casualties.[2]

Through his friendship with McClellan, Sedgwick became ensnared in an

1. Sears, ed., *Civil War Papers of George B. McClellan,* 604–5.

2. Warner, *Generals in Blue,* 430–1.

affair that almost cost him his position and career. Before the 1864 Democratic Convention in Chicago, Sedgwick backed a testimonial for McClellan. Such testimonials were hardly unusual—both Sedgwick and Meade had received them—but a testimonial for McClellan, as a serving military officer and a candidate for president, was a different matter. Moreover, in an instance of spectacularly bad timing, at about this time Sedgwick took on his staff McClellan's younger brother, Captain Arthur McClellan. (Prior to and since McClellan's removal from command of the Army of the Potomac, young Arthur had been serving on his brother's staff.)

Although its origins are murky, the McClellan testimonial came to involve a circular letter and a cash subscription from officers and enlisted men in the Army of the Potomac. On behalf of himself and the men of the Sixth Corps, Sedgwick pledged twenty thousand dollars. As news of the testimonial spread, the press branded it as an obvious political move to boost McClellan. Journalists were not the only ones to reach this conclusion, and members of the Lincoln administration persuaded Meade to put a stop to it. Nonetheless, Secretary of War Edwin Stanton was so incensed by the political implications of the testimonial that he had papers drawn up dismissing several of the participating officers (including Sedgwick, Sykes, and Hunt). Although Stanton was talked out of issuing the order, Sedgwick must have known he was on very thin ice.[3]

Though the Republicans were denied the opportunity openly to show their ire, it may have been vented unofficially. On several occasions rumors circulated that Sedgwick was being considered for command of the Army of the Potomac. Nothing ever came of these rumors. Sedgwick claimed to have no interest in the post, writing his sister in late 1863, "I know my name has been mentioned and I think I could have had it if I had said the word, but nothing could induce me to take it." Whether he could have had the post in light of his political leanings is doubtful; as a professional soldier, his claim not to be interested in it seems contrived. As one historian has written, Sedgwick heard the news of Meade's appointment while on the march, whereupon he " 'struck his spurs into his gigantic and phlegmatic steed' and led his men at a quick gallop for some time. The general vented his emotions in this

3. See Richard Elliot Winslow III, *General John Sedgwick: The Story of a Union Corps Commander* (Novato, Calif.: Presidio Press, 1981), 134; Wainwright, *A Diary of Battle*, ed. Nevins, 284.

way and did not say anything. . . . Sedgwick was disturbed that a general, junior to his grade, had obtained this nod from the administration."[4]

Though the committee journal indicates that Wade was present for Sedgwick's testimony, no questions were recorded from him, and Representative Daniel Gooch took the lead. Given Wade's dominance of the committee, it is likely that he was absent and the journal is in error.

[459] Testimony of Major General John Sedgwick.

Washington, April 8, 1864.
Major General John Sedgwick sworn and examined.

By Mr. Gooch:

Question. Were you connected with the army of the Potomac at the time General Meade assumed the command?

Answer. I was.

Question. Will you give us an account of the operations of the army from that time forward until General Lee recrossed the Potomac?

Answer. I do not know that I can give a detailed account of it, except so far as my own corps was concerned. Frequently the corps were separated for long distances, and I did not know the positions of the other corps.

[460] Question. Give us an account of that which came under your own observation.

Answer. On the night of the 1st of July my corps was at Manchester, about thirty miles from the field of Gettysburg. About 7 o'clock that night I received orders from General Meade to march to Taneytown, which at that time was his headquarters. After proceeding about seven or eight miles, I received another order to make a forward march to Gettysburg, and I immediately commenced the movement. I arrived at Gettysburg about 2 o'clock on the afternoon of the 2d of July, having marched thirty-five miles from 7 o'clock the evening previous. I received on the way frequent messages from General Meade to push forward my corps as rapidly as possible, as a battle was imminent, and it was important I should be there. I received no less than three messages by his aide, urging me on. I arrived on the field, as I have said, about 2 o'clock.

4. Wainwright, *A Diary of Battle,* ed. Nevins, 308; Winslow, *General John Sedgwick,* 88, 95–6.

The message that put Sedgwick and the Sixth Corps into motion was actually the second one Meade sent. In his first message, Meade notified Sedgwick of his general plans and told him to be ready to move in any direction. Meade's second message informed Sedgwick of Reynolds's death and directed the Sixth Corps to Taneytown. It was sent at 4:30 P.M. At the same time Sedgwick was told that one of his division commanders, Major General John Newton, was to take over Reynolds's First Corps. This lends credence to the contention that Doubleday was replaced because of Hancock's note incorrectly saying the First Corps broke.[5]

A third message was sent at 7:30 P.M., directing the Sixth Corps to march to Gettysburg by the shortest route possible. Sedgwick did not mention to the committee that this message also instructed him to report "in person, without delay" to Meade at Taneytown, and that Meade was waiting for Sedgwick before going to the front. For whatever reason, Sedgwick did not go to headquarters and Meade left around midnight for Gettysburg.[6]

Another message was sent at 5:30 A.M. on July 2, repeating the gist of the previous messages and enclosing a memorandum outlining what Meade wanted Sedgwick to do. This message said that the "general proposes to make a vigorous attack upon the enemy to-morrow." Since Butterfield wrote the message, he knew at this time Meade had no intentions of withdrawing.[7]

Sedgwick's times are faulty. He testified that he received his marching orders at 7 P.M. and also that he began his march at 7 P.M. The start time most commonly mentioned by historians is around 9 P.M. His arrival time of 2 P.M. also seems inaccurate. In his battle report Sedgwick only wrote that he arrived in the afternoon, but two of his division commanders reported an arrival time of between 4 and 5 P.M.[8]

I immediately reported to General Meade's headquarters, but found that he had gone out to the position of the 3d corps, and I waited until his return, a few minutes, to see him; for I knew nothing about the dispositions of the troops at that time. General Meade said that he had been out to the front; that General Sickles had not taken the position he had directed, but had moved out from a quarter to three-quarters of a mile in advance. I asked General Meade

5. *OR,* vol. 27, pt. 3, p. 465.
6. Ibid., 467–8.
7. Ibid., 484–5.
8. *GC,* 715 n. 17; *OR,* vol. 27, pt. 1, pp. 665, 675.

why he had not ordered him back. He replied that it was then too late; that the enemy had opened the battle.

I received my orders from him, and returned to my corps to carry them into execution. The orders were to take a position near the left of the line, between the 5th and 3d corps. But General Sickles, in the mean time, had been forced back, leaving an opening that was filled up by, I think, a portion of the 5th corps. A portion of my corps went in and occupied the position the 5th corps had left. We arrived there just in time to throw two brigades into line of battle and assist in checking and repulsing the enemy.

My corps did not take any important part in the battle of Gettysburg. It was frequently sent to different parts of the field to re-enforce and support other troops that were more vigorously engaged.

On the morning of the 5th, as soon as it was ascertained that the enemy were retreating, I was ordered with my corps in pursuit, and pursued them as far as Fairfield, perhaps eight miles, when I was recalled, and joined the rest of the army in its movement.

Question. Were you present at any councils of war at Gettysburg?

Answer. Yes, sir; at two.

Question. Please state at what councils you were present, and what was done in those councils.

Answer. I think the first council was on the 2d of July, at night. The question submitted, I believe, was, whether we should attack the enemy, or wait in position and receive the attack.

Question. Were you present at any other council there?

Answer. I think there was one on the evening of the 4th of July, in which the question was whether we should pursue the enemy directly, or move in a parallel line and endeavor to cut him off, or attack him. I believe the council were unanimous to move on a parallel line.

Question. When the enemy had been finally repulsed, on the 3d of July, why was he not immediately pursued and attacked by our army?

Answer. He held a very strong position. I presume he was with equal force to our own. I do not think it would have been expedient to have attacked him. I think that was pretty much the opinion of most of the general officers present there.

Actually Sedgwick and Meade were a minority of two in thinking that a counterattack would not have been "expedient."

Question. Can you tell how many men we had who could have participated in an attack at that time?

[461] Answer. I think our army numbered 55,000 infantry, and perhaps 12,000 or 15,000 cavalry and artillery; that included our whole force. Of course, they were most of them available.

Question. Do you think the enemy had that number of effective men after that final repulse?

Answer. I believe they had; and that was the general opinion.

Question. Have you any knowledge of the preparation of any order for the withdrawal of the army at any time during the battle of Gettysburg, or the retreat of the army from the position it then held?

Answer. I never heard of any such order until within the last four weeks; and when I first heard it I denied most positively that any such order could have been given. I was the second in command there, and reported to General Meade at a critical time; and if he contemplated so important a move, he would have informed me. Besides, his urging my corps forward shows that he intended to fight the battle there. General Meade undoubtedly was apprehensive that the enemy might turn his flank; and in that event he would have had to take up a new position; but I do not think he ever contemplated any retreat.

By Mr. Odell:

Question. Had it been the intention of the commanding general to retreat the army, was not the order to you to come up in direct conflict with any such intended movement?

Answer. It certainly was. In the course of the night of the 1st and the morning of the 2d of July I received no less than three verbal messages from him to hurry up with all possible despatch.

By Mr. Loan:

Question. Where was your corps stationed during the battle of the third day, relative to the point of attack, for instance?

Answer. I had two brigades stationed between two divisions of the 5th corps, on the left of the point of attack as we faced the enemy. I had three brigades on the left of the Round Top, beyond the divisions of the 5th corps of which I have spoken. My other brigades were detached to different parts of the field in support of troops actively engaged.

Question. You had five brigades of yours convenient to the point of attack?

Answer. Yes, sir, in close vicinity.

Question. The 5th corps was there?

Answer. The 5th corps occupied the Round Top, and to the right.

Question. What troops occupied the valley to the right of Round Top, where the enemy made their assault?

Answer. A portion of the 5th corps, two brigades of my corps, the 3d and 2d corps, commanded by General Hancock.

Question. The enemy made their assault there about 2 or 3 o'clock on the evening of the 3d, and that assault was repulsed?

Answer. Yes, sir.

Question. In what condition did that repulse leave the artillery of the enemy at that time?

Answer. I have no means of knowing; I was not on that part of the field.

Question. You do not know the condition it was left in?

Answer. I do not.

Question. Did you receive any orders that evening to pursue the enemy after they were repulsed?

Answer. I did not receive any.

Question. Do you know whether General Sykes received any such orders?

Answer. My impression is that General Sykes was ordered to send out a strong reconnoitering party to ascertain if the enemy were retreating, or if he could force them to retreat.

[462] Question. Was that order obeyed?

Answer. It was. I was present with General Sykes when he gave the order, and was present when the troops returned. They met the enemy in considerable force, which checked them, and the force then returned.

Question. At what time in the evening did that force return?

Answer. I cannot state with any certainty.

Question. Do you know at what point they met the enemy in force to check them?

Answer. It was directly in front of the position which General Sykes occupied on the right of Round Top.

Here Sedgwick supported Meade's earlier testimony before the committee.

Question. After the assault had been repulsed, do you know any reason why General Sykes's corps could not have continued to drive the retreating enemy?

Answer. I do. It is not likely that the whole of their forces were engaged in that assault, and that the troops General Sykes's forces met were no part of the assailing party, and were in such position as to check his troops.

Question. If I remember rightly, you said you were present when General Sykes gave the order to a part of his command to advance?

Answer. Yes, sir.

Question. At what time was that?

Answer. I think it was soon after the attack, but I cannot remember the hour; it might have been 4 o'clock—perhaps a little later.

By Mr. Gooch:

Question. Did those troops return before dark?

Answer. I think they returned about dark. They had a very sharp skirmish; I was in a position where I could see it.

Question. Will you state why the enemy was not attacked at Williamsport by our army?

Answer. They occupied a very strong position there. I think they were at that time quite as strong as we were, for we had received no re-enforcements. In the council held there I voted against any attack, and my subsequent information confirmed me in the opinion that I was right in so voting: that the enemy occupied too strong a position for General Meade to attack.

Question. What subsequent information did you get?

Answer. In passing over the ground they had occupied and seeing their works.

Question. You knew at that time that it was the intention of General Lee to cross his army over the Potomac, if possible?

Answer. I presumed he had retreated to that point for that purpose.

Question. Did not the fact that he was intending to cross that river afford you a very favorable opportunity to attack him while he was in the act of crossing, and why was it that he was permitted to escape without being attacked?

Answer. He occupied a very strong position in front of Williamsport, and he withdrew in the night. It certainly would have been very advantageous to have attacked him while he was withdrawing, but not while he was in position there. I believe if we had attacked him we would have received a severe repulse.

Question. Was it impossible to ascertain when he commenced the movement of his army across the Potomac?

Answer. I do not know that it was impossible, but I think it was impracticable.

Question. Why so?

Answer. We could not force his lines to ascertain what was behind him. I think we had information afterwards that he was two or three days in crossing over his sick and wounded, and bringing over supplies both of ammunition and rations.

Question. Bringing supplies over to the Maryland side?

[463] Answer. Yes, sir; I think our information was that he at least received supplies of ammunition from the other side.

Question. Was it before or after it was possible for us to have made the attack that he received those supplies?

Answer. During the time he was occupying that position. All the time he was lying there I think he was transporting his sick, and probably his baggage, to the Virginia side; and the small number of boats he had to take them over brought back ammunition and probably other supplies.

Question. Could not an attack have been made upon him sufficient to ascertain his strength without endangering our force?

Answer. I scarcely know how to answer that question.

Question. I will say—without seriously endangering our forces?

Answer. It is very difficult to withdraw troops after they have once become seriously engaged, without having them severely handled. I recollect the vote of the different officers composing the council of war regarding the attack.

This is the best and most complete explanation given by an officer opposed to the attack at Williamsport.

Question. What was that vote?

Answer. General Wadsworth represented General Newton, who was commanding the 1st corps. General Wadsworth voted for an attack; General Howard also voted for an attack. Those were the only two corps commanders who did vote for it. The others all strongly opposed it. I think General Pleasonton, in command of the cavalry corps, voted for it; and I believe General Meade expressed himself in favor of an attack, but of course he did not vote. He acquiesced in the decision of the council. Whether General Meade expressed himself so at the council or not I am not positive, but I am sure he did in conversation with me.

Question. What prevented our placing troops on the south side of the Potomac sufficient in number to so far impede the crossing of the enemy as to enable the main body of our army to attack him while making the crossing?

Answer. I do not think that we had the troops; but I think that as soon as possible bridges were laid at Harpers Ferry, and General Meade ordered all the cavalry, or at least such portion of it as he could spare, to cross over, and probably if he had other troops they would have been ordered over.

By Mr. Odell:

Question. In this council of war at Williamsport, where the question was discussed of attacking the enemy there, did or not this consideration enter into your deliberations—the exposed condition of Baltimore and the capital, should you attack and be repulsed?

Answer. It did in mine, and I presume it did with the others.

Question. If you had been repulsed and defeated, was there any force between you and the capital that would have resisted the progress of the enemy?

Answer. I know of none.

Question. Had you any evidence, at any time during or after the battle of Gettysburg, that the enemy were destitute of ammunition?

Answer. No, sir, I do not know of any. I did understand at Williamsport, while lying there, that the batteaux that crossed over their sick and wounded returned with ammunition; I understood that from citizens of Williamsport, who resided there; I heard it myself at the time.

By Mr. Gooch:

Question. Will you give us a concise account of the operations of the army subsequent to the crossing of Lee's army over the Potomac? I do not desire a detailed statement of everything, but a concise account of such movements and operations as you deem of importance.

Answer. I have not thought of that matter much of late, and I have none of my papers with me.

Mr. Gooch. —You can then prepare such a statement and append it to your testimony, when the manuscript of what you have already given shall be submitted to you for revision.

[Since it is beyond the scope of this work, Sedgwick's subsequent statement is omitted.]

Sedgwick had provided some excellent information for the committee, even if most of it was not what they wanted to hear. He had correctly pointed out that as second in command he would have been told if Meade had thought about retreating on July 2. In response to a question from Moses Odell, who supported

Meade, Sedgwick had agreed that his orders to hurry to the front were in conflict with any theoretical order to retreat.

Sedgwick's responses to questions about Williamsport were well considered and possibly suggest advance preparation for his appearance before the committee.

18 Brigadier General Seth Williams

Brigadier General Seth Williams served as assistant adjutant general of the Army of the Potomac for two and a half years before becoming inspector general under Ulysses Grant. His lengthy record of service as adjutant general is all the more remarkable considering the dissimilar natures of his commanding officers—McClellan, Burnside, Hooker, and Meade.

Only an outline of Williams's military service is available. He graduated from West Point and, following some routine garrison duty, served as an aide-de-camp of General Robert Patterson during the Mexican War. After a tour as adjutant at West Point, Williams transferred to the adjutant general's department. He served as an assistant adjutant general until his death in 1866. (It should be noted that there was only one adjutant general in the army, and he was in Washington. All others were assistant adjutant generals.)[1]

With the outbreak of the Civil War, Williams was not General McClellan's first choice as adjutant general; McClellan had initially asked for FitzJohn Porter, but the appointment was not made. The job primarily entailed managing the vast sea of paperwork that all generals curse but armies need to survive. Messages to and from headquarters, orders for troop movements, and documents about promotions, leaves and courts-martial all passed through the hands of Williams or his staff. The adjutant general was also responsible for keeping copies of all paperwork.[2]

Williams's job required daily contact with his superior whenever the commander was at headquarters. It appears that McClellan developed a genuine

1. Warner, *Generals in Blue*, 562–3.

2. Sears, ed., *Civil War Papers of George B. McClellan*, 17–8.

affection for him; in letters to his wife, McClellan habitually referred to Williams as "Seth." Such familiarity was not developed between Williams and the shy Meade.[3]

[464] Testimony of Brigadier General Seth Williams.

Washington, April 18, 1864.
Brigadier General Seth Williams sworn and examined.

By the chairman:

Question. What is your present rank and position in the army?

Answer. I am a lieutenant colonel in the adjutant general's department of the regular army, a brigadier general in the volunteer service, and at present on duty as assistant adjutant general of the army of the Potomac.

Question. How long have you been connected with the army of the Potomac?

Answer. Since its organization.

Question. You are now on the staff of General Meade?

Answer. Yes, sir. During the time General Burnside was in command I was inspector general of the adjutant general's department.

Question. We have been inquiring into the administration of that army from the time General Meade took command until the present time, and we desire your account of what took place under your observation. In the first place, I will ask what do you know in regard to the plan of the battle of Gettysburg?

Answer. I think when General Meade took command of the army his first idea was to move in the direction of the Susquehanna, supposing that he would there find the army of General Lee. But subsequent information induced him to move towards Gettysburg, and he put the army in motion in that direction.

[465] Question. There has been a great deal said as to what General Meade's intentions and purposes were, and what dispositions of troops he intended to make, and whether he intended to fight the battle where it was fought or somewhere else. I do not know whether it is very material, but such questions have been made. What do you know in regard to those points?

3. Ibid., 16–8, 124, 230, 530.

Wade was being less than honest. The Pipe Creek circular, showing Meade's preferred line of battle, was an integral part of the committee's charge that he had not wanted to fight at Gettysburg. In this light, the question of where Meade had intended to fight was very material.

Answer. I think that as soon as General Meade heard that the enemy was moving in the direction of Gettysburg, and as soon as he learned the general result of the engagement on the 1st of July in front of Gettysburg, and the character of the ground at Gettysburg, he made up his mind to fight the battle at that place, and he concentrated the army there with all possible rapidity. I think his orders were all in accordance with that idea.

Question. Have you now, with you, any of the orders that were issued on that battle-field?

Answer. No, sir; I did not bring them. I did not know that the committee desired to have them.

Question. We told General Meade that we desired you to bring with you, all the papers relating to that battle. How happened it that the battle took place where it did?

Answer. I do not think that either General Lee or General Meade had at first any idea as to where the battle would be fought. I think General Meade was desirous to bring on the battle at the earliest possible moment, and with as much advantage to himself, of course, as might be attainable. He learned that the position at Gettysburg was a good position for a battle, and he assembled his troops and put them in position there, designing to fight the battle out at that place.

Question. Do you not consider that the ground on which the battle was fought was well chosen?

Answer. Remarkably well chosen.

Question. What do you know about the disposition of General Sickles's corps there?

Answer. Of my personal knowledge I know nothing. I only know what I heard at the time and what I have heard since, that General Sickles did not assume the exact position which General Meade designed he should take up, but extended his left considerably in advance of the ground it was intended he should occupy. I was not on that part of the field, and do not personally know anything about the disposition made of the third corps.

Williams's neutrality about Sickles's advanced line is a little surprising. Except for Sickles himself, all other witnesses had criticized the advance.

Question. You were with General Meade during the battle?

Answer. I was with him at the field headquarters, but did not always accompany him to the front, and was generally left at headquarters to prepare and send out orders and instructions, as well as to receive and dispose of communications addressed to me by the different commanders. On the third day I was with General Meade on the field a considerable portion of the time.

Question. Is there anything pertaining to that battle in any part of the field that you would be likely to know that he did not see or know?

Answer. I think not. I was not over the field except when with him; my duties required me to be at the field headquarters for the most part.

Question. Were you there when the final charge was made by the enemy on the third day?

Answer. I was at the field headquarters a part of the time, and a part of the time with General Meade as he rode along the line.

Question. Do you know anything about an order on the 2d of July to withdraw the army?

Answer. The orders for the movements of the army, under the present arrangement, are generally prepared by the chief of staff, and the manuscripts of the orders are turned over to me to have copies prepared for those to whom they are to be distributed, and I am held responsible that the orders are correctly [466] copied, and that they are delivered to the persons for whom they are intended. In regard to the order of the 2d of July, to the best of my recollection and belief, the chief of staff either handed to me or to my clerk an order looking to a contingency which possibly might happen of the army being compelled to assume a new position. To the best of my belief such an order was prepared, and I presume it may have been signed by me, and possibly the copies may have been prepared for the corps and other commanders. Orders of such a character are usually made out in manifold in order to save time. The particular order in question, however, was never distributed; no vestige of it is to be found among any of the records of my office, and it must have been destroyed within a day or two after it was prepared. I have no reason to suppose, other than the fact that the order was given to me or my clerk by the chief of staff, that General Meade had any knowledge of it. It was not for me to look beyond the orders of the chief of staff. Whether or not a copy of that order was given to Major General Butterfield, who was then acting as chief of staff, I am unable to say, and I cannot certainly state whether the rough draught was ever handed back to him. I only know that there is nothing in relation to that order to be found among the records in my charge. The order was never recorded, or issued in any sense. I do not now remember the exact tenor of the order, but to the best of my belief it was an order which, if carried out, would have involved a retrograde movement of the army.

Williams's testimony seems to be well thought out. He obviously knew that he would be asked about an order to retreat.

Question. What was the condition of our troops after the battle ended on the third day there?

Answer. So far as I could see, the troops were in efficient condition, although our losses had been very heavy.

Question. I mean in what spirits were our troops?

Answer. The troops were in fine spirits as far as I had an opportunity of observing.

Question. At what time on the third day did it become known that the enemy were retreating?

This question was based on the presumption that the enemy retreated on the third day, which they did not.

Answer. I do not think it was exactly known at all during that day that the enemy was actually on the retreat. The enemy had fallen back to the woods from which he emerged when he made the attack. I do not think it was until the next morning and along in the forenoon that we were certain he had abandoned his position.

Question. What is your opinion as a military man? Ought our army to have advanced or not as soon as it was ascertained the enemy were retreating?

Answer. I think that as soon as we found out certainly what direction the enemy had taken, orders to march were given for the purpose of coming up with him again by way of the South Mountain passes.

Question. After the army had reached Williamsport, what was the reason that a general attack was not ordered before the enemy recrossed the Potomac?

Answer. I was not present at any of the consultations that General Meade had with his chief of staff or with his corps commanders, and I am unable to say what influenced his action on that occasion.

Question. You have been a long time in the service. As a military man, what is your opinion as to whether the enemy should have been attacked before they recrossed the river?

Answer. Inasmuch as I did not see the ground at the time, I do not think my opinion would be entitled to the same weight as the opinion of those who did see it. From what I have heard I think the enemy had a very strong position indeed, and that it is doubtful whether we could possibly have carried it. I was not at the extreme front, but I have always understood that the position held by the enemy was naturally a very strong one, and that an attack upon it, would be by no means certain of success.

[467] Question. Have you the custody of the despatches and orders written and issued during that period?

Answer. Yes, sir.

Question. Where are they now?

Answer. The most of the papers are in an office we have in this city.

Question. Would they throw any light upon any of these subjects?

Answer. I think General Meade has already handed to the committee the most of the papers they would desire to have. He certainly has had me make copies of the most essential papers.

Question. If you think of anything else in regard to that battle and campaign which will throw any light upon the subject, will you please state it?

Answer. I have not much personal knowledge respecting the plan of the campaign and its principal operations, except what I have derived from the orders and instructions issued as they have passed through my hands. I think General Meade's intention, after assuming command of the army, was to fight a battle as soon as possible, and he moved the army with great rapidity, and, as I supposed, with that object in view. His design was to bring on a battle, but at the same time to gain for himself, of course, what advantage he could in the way of position, presuming the enemy to be equal or a little superior to himself in effective force.

Question. The understanding was that the troops of the enemy were equal in numbers to ours?

Answer. Yes, sir, I think so. I think it was supposed that, numerically, he was a little stronger than we were.

Question. What was the reason that before that battle our army was not strengthened by the troops around Washington, Baltimore, &c.?

Answer. I am unable to say; I have no idea as to the reasons that controlled the authorities in the matter.

Question. Do you know whether that subject was ever mooted among the officers?

Answer. I think the impression was that it was one of those occasions when all troops that could possibly be spared from other points should be sent to the army. When the army crossed the Potomac there was some little anxiety as to where the battle would be fought and how re-enforcements could be forwarded. I think General Meade himself expected to fight the battle somewhere on the Susquehanna or in that direction.

[There followed a series of questions concerning the Bristoe and Mine Run campaigns, which are omitted.]

[468] By Mr. Gooch:

Question. Did you have any conference whatever with General Meade, at any time during the operations at Gettysburg, in relation to an order for a withdrawal of the army from that place?

Answer. No, sir, none at all. I have very good reason to suppose that General Meade knew nothing of the existence of such an order.

Question. Why did you suppose that?

Answer. I think all his actions that day lead irresistibly to the conclusion that he intended to fight at Gettysburg, because the 6th corps, some distance in the rear, was hurried up, orders were repeatedly sent to the commander of the corps to move up as rapidly as possible, and all of General Meade's arrangements looked to fighting the battle in the position in which it was finally fought.

Question. When you received the order and had the copies prepared, were you instructed at that time not to issue them; or what would have been the regular course?

Answer. To the best of my belief the chief of staff handed me or my clerk the manuscript of the order, with the understanding that no copies were to be sent out until I received further instructions from him, and I infer this from the fact that no copies of the order were sent out. The order was prepared a short time before the engagement on that day commenced. I only know such an order was in fact never issued.

By Mr. Odell:

Question. If General Meade had intended to have retired his army, would you have known it?

Answer. I must have known it, because I should have seen the preparations going on around me—should have seen the ammunition and other trains sent to the rear; and I should doubtless have had something to do with, or some knowledge of, the instructions issued for such a movement.

Question. Would he have ordered his troops to come forward?

Answer. I should suppose not, because he would have been blocking up the road. I have no idea that he could for a moment have entertained the idea of withdrawing, except as a last extremity. I think if he gave any orders it was that the country might be explored for the purpose of ascertaining in what direction the army should fall back in case we were compelled to do so. All that I saw led me to believe that General Meade fully intended to fight the battle at Gettysburg.

Question. Was it not the part of a prudent commander to ascertain the avenues of retreat in case of disaster?

Answer. In my opinion it would have been his duty as a skillful commander to prepare to meet every contingency that might happen, and to gain all the information with respect to the country that he might be able to obtain, so that in the event of the occurrence of the alternative of a disaster the army might move in the direction determined upon without any confusion. I have no reason to suppose that General Meade expected a reverse.

Williams was an exceptionally strong witness for Meade, and Wade was unable to elicit any criticism of Meade from him. Williams seriously undermined Sickles's and Butterfield's testimony about an order to retreat on July 2. Under friendly questioning by Gooch and Odell, Williams reiterated that Meade had never known of an order to retreat, which was simply a contingency order and never issued. He also added that Meade had done his duty in preparing for every eventuality at Gettysburg.

19 Brigadier General Samuel Wylie Crawford

THE LAST WITNESS OF note to testify in the Meade hearings was Brigadier General Samuel Wylie Crawford, commander of the Third Division, Fifth Corps. Crawford had an unusual background for a division commander. Born in Franklin County, Pennsylvania, just across South Mountain from Gettysburg, he graduated from the University of Pennsylvania medical school. Entering the army as an assistant surgeon, Crawford served along the frontier until 1860. The outbreak of the Civil War found him in Fort Sumter. Though a surgeon, he commanded a battery during the siege.[1]

Within a year, the surgeon turned soldier was a brigadier general of volunteers commanding a regiment. Soon he led a brigade. At Antietam, where he was severely wounded, he had command of a division. When Crawford returned to duty he was given the Pennsylvania Reserves—a brigade Meade had once commanded—which was then stationed around Washington. With Lee's invasion of Pennsylvania, Crawford's command was ordered to the Army of the Potomac and formed the Third Division, Fifth Corps.[2]

Crawford seems not to have been a man of strong convictions; he was more interested in being on the winning side. Charles Wainwright noted in his diary that Crawford was "quite a politician, strong on the side of those in power." Crawford's instincts failed him during the Meade hearings, however, where he seems to have tried to be on both sides at once.[3]

1. Boatner, *Civil War Dictionary,* 207–8; Warner, *Generals in Blue,* 99–100. The last witness actually called in the Meade hearings was Brig. Gen. Marsena Patrick, who appeared before the committee ten months after Crawford. Patrick's testimony is extremely brief and adds nothing of substance to the case, so it was not included in this edition.

2. Warner, *Generals in Blue,* 99–100.

3. Wainwright, *A Diary of Battle,* ed. Nevins, 472–3.

An interesting story about Crawford, which gives some insight into his character, was told by Lafayette McLaws, commander of McLaws's Division, Longstreet's First Corps, at Gettysburg. McLaws related that when he was living in Augusta, Georgia, several years after the war, a gentleman called on him and introduced himself as General S. Wiley Crawford, U.S. Army. According to McLaws, Crawford announced that he was the man who had found Lee's lost order during the Antietam campaign and had handed it to McClellan. (This claim was false. Lee's order had been found by Private B. W. Mitchell, Twenty-seventh Indiana Regiment. After traveling up the chain of command, it was handed to McClellan by General A. S. Williams. Crawford never touched Lee's order.) Crawford then spoke of Gettysburg, telling McLaws that if he would state in writing that Crawford's Pennsylvania Reserves had driven back McLaws's division at Gettysburg, "it would be worth a grade in the army to him." McLaws refused to do so, since it was not the truth. According to McLaws, Crawford had also called on Longstreet while Longstreet was visiting New York after the war. Crawford had asked which of Longstreet's troops he had attacked and driven back at Gettysburg. Longstreet told Crawford that "he was not aware that anyone had attacked him at Gettysburg."[4]

When Crawford appeared before the committee, Wade, Harding, and Gooch were out of town investigating the Fort Pillow Massacre. Chandler thus served as the acting chairman, but he asked no questions. Instead he left the questioning to Representative Benjamin Loan.

[468] Testimony of Brigadier General S. W. Crawford.

April 27, 1864.

Brigadier General S. W. Crawford sworn and examined.

By Mr. Loan:

Question. General, will you state what your present employment is; if you are in the army; what your rank is, and what command you are connected with?

[469] Answer. I am a brigadier general of volunteers, in command of the third division, 5th army corps. I have been in command of that division since last April.

Question. Go on now, in a narrative form, and state what you know of the battle of Gettysburg; how you got to the field, and what occurred there.

4. Glenn Tucker, *Lee and Longstreet at Gettysburg* (Indianapolis, Ind.: Bobbs-Merrill, 1968), 66–7.

Answer. I was ordered to join the army of the Potomac from the defences of Washington, and I carried along two brigades of the division, the first and third; the second, though placed under my orders, was detailed at the solicitation of the authorities in Alexandria, General Slough refusing to allow the colonel commanding that brigade to obey the order I had sent him to join me on the Leesburg turnpike. I marched forward and crossed the Potomac at Edward's ferry the following day. I received, in crossing the Potomac, orders to report to the 5th corps, General Meade commanding.

When Meade took command of the army on June 28, he was replaced at the Fifth Corps by Major General George Sykes.

I joined the army of the Potomac on June 28, 1863, at Frederick, Maryland, when General Meade had assumed command of the whole army. We lay for two days at Frederick, and the whole army was placed in motion. I was in the rear division of the corps, and on the evening of the 1st of July I marched through Hanover and along the road through McSherrystown, marching until between two and three o'clock in the morning, and bivouacked at a town called Brushtown; and before dawn on Thursday, the 2d of July, a staff officer of General Sykes, then commanding the corps, rode to my headquarters and directed me to march my men, without giving them any coffee, at once to the field. I placed the column in motion and arrived before noon in the rear of the other divisions of the corps. They were on a spot called Wolf's hill, near Rock creek, and to the left of the Baltimore and Gettysburg turnpike, in rear of the order of battle, behind the first and second divisions of the 5th corps. I there rested my men. About twelve o'clock I received an order from General Sykes, stating that I was to go to the field with my division at three o'clock, and that a staff officer would come to indicate to me the road to the field of battle—that part of it to which he wished me to go with my division. My division was to follow the second division of regulars.

This was the Second Division, Fifth Corps, under the command of Brigadier General Romeyn B. Ayres. Two of its three brigades were regular army troops.

At three o'clock, no staff officer having reported to me, I placed the column in motion; went to the left around Wolf's hill, and struck a road running along the woods [Granite Schoolhouse Lane]. The regular division were marching on my left, but were suddenly halted and marched to the right. As this did not lead towards the field of battle, in my judgment, I did not follow, expecting the officer to arrive who would show me the proper place to go. At this moment an officer arrived, very much excited; pointed over in the direction of some hills, which were directly in my front, and said that the enemy were attacking those hills; that it was most important to hold them, and that the troops there were in need of assistance. I asked him who he was. He said he was Captain [Alexander] Moore, of General Meade's staff. I said to him, "Very well, that is sufficient authority for me. If you give me General Meade's order I will go at once, if you will show me the direction. I am expecting an officer from General Sykes's staff, who commands the corps, to show me the way he wishes the division to go; but if you give me General Meade's order I will go at once." He said, "I cannot give you General Meade's order." I said, "There are some general officers to my right. General Slocum is there, commanding the 12th corps. Bring me his order, and I will go."

He galloped down the road, and in a few minutes returned with the order from General Slocum. I moved the column rapidly with him, and arrived in a few moments on the field. I crossed the Taneytown road, on a cross-road running from it to the Emmitsburg road, and to the right of Little Round Top. I rode at once and reported to General Sykes. He said to me he was gratified to see I was so promptly upon the field, and that the other division had just come up. He directed me to mass my command in a field of scrub oak, to the right, and hold them in readiness for any movement. Before I could complete the movement I received an order from him to move to the left, across this [470] cross-road that runs from Emmitsburg to the Taneytown road, and there to support our men, in case they were compelled to fall back. I crossed the road and formed my division on the slope of Little Round Top, to the right of the summit. The movement was scarcely completed before I received another order from General Sykes, directing me to send a brigade to my left and rear, to the support of a brigade of Barnes's division, which had demanded re-enforcements. I detached the 3d brigade, under Colonel J. W. Fisher, consisting of five regiments, and gave him the order to go at once to report to the officer commanding that brigade. At this moment the firing was exceedingly heavy in our front; some of my men had fallen. I heard the cheers of the enemy, and looking in front, across a low ground, I saw our men retreating in confusion; fugitives were flying across in every direction; some of them rushed through my lines. I then ordered one of the regiments that belonged to Fisher's brigade, which had not yet marched to the left, to remain with McCandless, of the 1st brigade. The plain in front was covered with the flying men. The regular division had marched out past my left flank. A wheat field lay between two masses of woods directly in my front. A stone wall skirted these roads from right to left. The enemy in masses were coming across this wheat field, having driven everything before them. Their line of skirmishers had crossed the stone wall, and their column was coming across the low ground towards the hills upon which we stood. I ordered an immediate charge upon the enemy by the whole division. The division moved forward at once; two volleys were fired, when the whole command started at a double quick. We met the enemy on the low ground, drove them back to the stone wall, for the possession of which there was a short struggle, and at which two regiments, which had been massed on the flanks of the line, were deployed, drove the enemy through the woods and over the wheat field, over to the ridge beyond. The line was there permanently established.

This description of a gallant charge by McCandless's brigade is colorful but a little overdrawn. McCandless's charge had met relatively little resistance.[5]

I sent back to General Sykes and begged him to send me supports; that I had advanced far ahead of our line and driven the enemy back, and that I needed support. He said he had none to send. I returned myself at a later period, and again asked him for supports. He said he would wait until morning, and if he then saw fit he would send them. At this moment I met an aid[e] from Colonel Rice, who succeeded to the command of Vincent's brigade, and to whom the regiments of Fisher's brigade had been sent. He said he came from Colonel Rice to say that a hill in his front [Big Round Top] was yet unoccupied by our troops, and he wanted to occupy it. I asked him who Colonel Rice was. He replied that he was with those troops on that hill, pointing to Little Round Top hill. I told him I was going there. On my way I met an aid[e] to Colonel Fisher, who stated that the hill was occupied by the enemy, not in great force, and representing the necessity of taking it. I rode at once to the summit of Little Round Top, where I met Colonel Fisher, and asked him in regard to this. He informed me that the enemy was at the hill in advance, which is the main top; that he could hear him moving about up there, and that he would like permission to move up his regiments there and take it. It was of vital importance to take this hill. I directed Colonel Fisher to take two of his regiments and deploy a line of skirmishers, and move up and occupy the hill.

5. Pfanz, *Gettysburg: The Second Day,* 398; *GC,* 409.

He replied that Colonel Rice desired to co-operate with him in the movement. I told him I had no objection, but to move up the hill at once, before it got any darker. I then rode back to my command.

Question. Where did you remain on Thursday night?

Answer. I was in advance of Little Round Top with the command that had carried the wheat field.

Question. Did Colonel Fisher take the main Round Top that night?

Answer. Fisher remained there that night.

Question. Your command lay on the ridge where they crossed the wheat field?

[471] Answer. They lay in advance of the stone wall. I had driven the enemy back, and the left of our line was secure.

Colonel Fisher reported to me that he deployed the 20th Maine in his front as skirmishers, and moved up with the 5th and 12th regiments to occupy the Round Top. I found them on its summit in the morning.

Question. If I understand you rightly, your men were in advance at the stone wall, and Fisher occupied the Round Top?

Answer. Yes, sir. That was the relative position of the forces that night.

The command held its position all night. Bartlett's division of the 6th corps were, early on Friday morning, moved up in support of my advanced line.

Crawford was in error. He was referring to Brigadier General Joseph J. Bartlett, who actually commanded the Second Brigade, First Division, Sixth Corps. The division commander was Brigadier General Horatio G. Wright.

No attempt was made by the enemy on the extreme left during Friday. The prisoners taken belonged to Anderson's and McLaws's divisions of Longstreet's corps.

Major General Richard H. Anderson's division belonged to Lieutenant General Ambrose P. Hill's Third Corps. Crawford has confused him with Brigadier General George T. Anderson's brigade of Major General John B. Hood's division.

On the afternoon of Friday General Meade came to the Little Round Top [following the repulse of Pickett's charge]. He was accompanied by several general officers. He asked what command it was that was occupying the line of the stone wall. He was answered that it was my division. He directed General

Sykes to order me to advance and clear the woods in my front; that if I found too strong a force I was not to engage them. I directed the command at once to advance. It consisted of McCandless's brigade, and one regiment of Fishers's brigade—the 11th [Pennsylvania Reserve] of Fisher's brigade. Hardly had the men unmasked from the hill, before a battery of the enemy, stationed on a ridge beyond the wheat field, opened with grape and canister. I directed Colonel McCandless to deploy a strong body of skirmishers towards the battery, and discover whether there was any strong infantry support; if not, to advance with his command and take the battery. As soon as the skirmishers opened fire on the cannoneers, the battery limbered up and fled. I then formed a line and directed it to cross the wheat field and clear the woods. In doing this they came upon a brigade of Hood's division under General Anderson or General Bonham, composed of Georgia troops; they attacked them, capturing over 260 prisoners, the battle flag of the 15th Georgia, retaking nearly all the ground that had been lost, and over 7,000 stand of arms, besides one 12-pound Napoleon gun and three caissons, and all the wounded, which had lain entirely uncared for. We permanently held that line. Hood's division was driven entirely off for a mile distance.

There was no General Bonham in command of Georgia troops at Gettysburg. Crawford must have been referring to Brigadier General Henry L. Benning of Hood's division, whose command included Colonel M. Dudley DuBose's Fifteenth Georgia. Except for this regiment there were no other units of Benning's brigade in the area.[6]

Crawford's testimony, except for the very basic facts, is a classic example of self-aggrandizement. Although Crawford repeatedly implied that he took direct command of the operation, he was not even present for it. In his own battle report he placed the advance under the "immediate direction of Colonel McCandless."[7]

Crawford also ignored the fact that at his own request Colonel David J. Nevin's Third Brigade, Third Division, Sixth Corps formed behind and in support of McCandless's advance, as did the Sixty-second New York on McCandless's left and the 139th Pennsylvania on his right.[8]

In both his battle report and his testimony, Crawford claimed to have taken

6. Evander M. Law to Bachelder, June 13, 1876, Ladd and Ladd, eds., *The Bachelder Papers,* 1:494.

7. *OR,* vol. 27, pt. 1, p. 654.

8. Ibid., 654, 685.

on and driven off Hood's division. This was a gross exaggeration. He encountered only the Fifteenth Georgia of Hood's division, which was already moving back to a new line at the time. Crawford's claim to have captured 7,000 enemy weapons was also false. In his battle report he wrote that the arms captured on both July 2 and 3 totaled 3,672. McCandless reported the number of weapons as between 2,000 and 3,000, the "majority of which had been piled on brush heaps, ready to be burned." This indicates that the arms were not seized as a result of McCandless's advance, but were taken from wounded or dead in previous actions.[9]

Question. What time during the day was this on Friday?

Answer. Towards evening.

Question. Will you state about the time that General Meade directed you to make this charge?

Answer. It was about half past four or five o'clock.

Question. You had remained, then, from the night before, up until about five o'clock, holding that position, without any orders to change?

Answer. Yes, sir.

Question. State what was your relative position to that of General Hancock, of the 2d corps, on Friday.

Answer. General Hancock was on my right; how far I do not know.

Question. Who was on your immediate right, between you and Hancock?

Answer. The 6th corps, I think. There were so many that came and changed again that I cannot say positively.

Question. During Friday while you were lying at the stone wall, can you tell who it was that was on your immediate right in the direction of our line of battle?

Answer. I think I was next to Hancock's corps, though I believe I saw Newton there, and I think a fragment of the 1st corps was there.

Question. Where was Sedgwick's corps?

Answer. In my rear, in the rear of the Round Tops, in rear of the line of battle entirely.

Question. Did you see that charge made upon the 2d corps? [This was Pickett's charge.]

[472] Answer. I witnessed it. It was made upon Hancock's corps.

Question. State if, while in your position, you were in advance of the line of battle, relatively, to Hancock's position?

9. Ibid., 656, 658.

Answer. I was in advance of Hancock's position. I was on the right flank of the charging line of Pickett when making the charge upon Hancock's corps; but I was some distance from it, so as to leave a space of considerable extent between us. The enemy left a gap between Hood's division and a division on his left.

Question. What time was it that Hancock repulsed that charge on Friday?

Answer. That was about noon, or a little after it. There had been a terrible bombardment all day, and the enemy moved immediately after it.

Pickett's advance began around 3:00 P.M. and for the most part was over around 3:30. The time is important in that a noon charge would have left some five to six hours to organize a counterattack. Meade had previously testified that he had only an hour or so to mount an advance, and darkness would have fallen by the time an attack was organized.

Question. After that repulse what prevented the 5th and 6th corps following up the enemy?

Answer. The repulse at night?

Question. After that on Friday. After the repulse of the charge on Hancock's command, I understand they were repulsed?

Answer. Yes, sir.

Question. Now, if I understand, Sedgwick was in your rear. What was to prevent the unemployed men of the 5th and 6th corps being thrown right on the retreating enemy?

Answer. Nothing at all, that I know of.

Crawford did not and should not have been expected to know the situation and condition of the Sixth Corps or even other divisions in his own corps. The Sixth Corps units had been doled out piecemeal as emergencies arose, and five of its eight brigades were not in the area of the Round Tops.

An attack by an unsupported Fifth Corps would have been suicidal.

Question. What was the condition of their artillery at the time of their repulse? If I understand it, they had massed their artillery there, and had opened a very heavy bombardment on our lines, and after firing for an hour or so they organized this assaulting column and made this charge. In what condition did it leave their artillery as regards supports, and what prevented its capture?

Answer. I do not know.

Question. Can you tell whether there were supports for that artillery?

Answer. I cannot. They opened 140 or 150 pieces, I think. It was as heavy a bombardment as I ever saw except that at Fort Sumter.

Question. You know of nothing to prevent the unemployed portion of the 5th and 6th corps from pursuing the broken columns of Pickett's division?

Answer. There was nothing, to my knowledge, to prevent it.

Question. What further occurred?

Answer. I remained on the field all that night, holding this advanced line. The enemy made no further demonstrations. The next morning their picket line was there quite close to us. On the morning of Saturday a reconnaissance was ordered, which consisted of the regular division and some supports. They advanced a short distance beyond my line, developed the enemy's line of battle, and returned.

Question. Where was that line of battle found on Saturday morning?

Answer. I cannot say. I did not go with them, but Colonel Day, who made the reconnaissance, told me that the enemy were there.

Question. What time did Lee's retreat commence?

Answer. On the morning of Sunday I was ordered to advance my picket line, and to find the position of the enemy. The picket lines on my right and left were also ordered to advance. I crossed the ground in front of the Round Tops and advanced beyond my position on the ground that we had held, and across the fields towards the ridge where the enemy had intrenched himself on Friday night. My men there took some prisoners, one or two, who had been left behind in the enemy's retreat. At two o'clock on Sunday morning they left that part of the line, according to the statement of the prisoners.

Question. At what time was pursuit made by your command?

Answer. Immediately after the reports were received that no enemy could be [473] found, Sedgwick's corps was thrown at once to the front, and marched to the Emmitsburg road.

Question. What time was that?

Answer. I advanced the picket line at half past 8 o'clock, in connexion with the line on my right and left. I advanced to the enemy's position and found that he had retreated.

Question. At what hour was it that you arrived at the enemy's position, and found he had retreated?

Answer. About 9 o'clock I arrived at the enemy intrenchments and found that he had entirely gone. I sent back word immediately, and reported it to General Sykes.

Question. About what hour in the day was it that Sedgwick's command moved in pursuit?

Answer. About 11 o'clock.

Question. Do you know anything about the pursuit?

Answer. I do not; I heard his guns soon after, and I reported to General Sykes. When I made the report to General Sykes that I had taken Round Top on Thursday evening, he did not understand where the locality was, and its position was subsequently explained to him by one of my staff officers by means of a diagram. The whole army then moved in pursuit of the enemy. We met the enemy in the neighborhood of Williamsport. The enemy immediately in my front had intrenched themselves strongly. The 5th corps were moved to the left, which brought us down to near the Hagerstown pike, and that force moved to the left, which brought us down in front of St. Mary's college. We were ordered to remain in line of battle and hold ourselves in readiness at any moment to move. The pickets were quite close, and the enemy distinctly visible.

Question. You say you found the enemy strongly intrenched at Williamsport?

Answer. Yes, sir, and he appeared to be so at every part of his lines, and could be very easily seen, at any place, digging.

In the night of July 13 I received an order from Major General Sykes, enclosing to me an order of General Meade, requiring a reconnaissance in force to be made of four divisions of the army. My division was selected from my corps. I was ordered to advance at 7 o'clock the following morning to drive in the enemy's pickets, to drive in the supports, and develop their line of battle. If strongly posted, or in great force, I was to await support before attacking. I moved precisely at the hour indicated. The division of the 6th corps, under Brigadier General Wright, was on my right. The division of the 2d corps was on my left, under Brigadier General Caldwell; and a division of the 12th corps, under Brigadier General Williams, was on its left. We advanced and found the enemy had retreated. I advanced towards his fortifications, which were very strong. The whole position had been selected with great care. I found some negroes, who told me that the enemy had retreated at 7 o'clock the night before. I reported at once to General Sykes that the enemy had retreated. I advanced my division over the Williamsport and Boonsborough road, when I received a message from the cavalry in my front, that a large body of infantry had not yet crossed the river. I pushed on my whole division at once, came up with Buford's cavalry, and in conference with that general found that the enemy had entirely crossed, and had taken up the bridge. The cavalry fight had taken place during my march. Finding that he was not in need of support, and the enemy had retreated, I returned.

Question. What prevented taking him as he was crossing the river?

Answer. Night, and the uncertainty as to when the movement was made.

Question. Which battle of Fredericksburg were you at?

Answer. I was wounded at Antietam. I was not at Chancellorsville. I have not been at any defeats of the army.

As a division commander, Crawford should not have been expected to provide much fuel for the committee's case, and he did not. Although he asserted that Pickett's charge had occurred around noon, thus leaving Meade time to mount a counterattack, his testimony was contradicted by all other witnesses before the committee. While Crawford agreed that nothing had prevented a counterattack by the Fifth and Sixth Corps, he had prefaced all his answers with a "that I know of."

Crawford's testimony about Williamsport gave a good front line view of the situation. He recalled that the Confederates were strongly entrenched along the entire line, and said that they could be very easily seen digging. In his earlier testimony, Warren had faulted the corps commanders for not going to the front often enough. Crawford's testimony also suggested as much.

20 The Committee's Report

THE FINAL REPORT ON the Meade hearings was published on May 22, 1865. Signed by Benjamin Wade, it made little impact on a public weary of hearing about lost battles, bad generals, and wartime corruption. The war was over, and the nation's euphoria over the surrender of Lee's Army of Northern Virginia had turned to grief over the assassination of Lincoln. In an effort to boost the country's sagging morale, a large victory parade was planned for May 23 in Washington.

With Lincoln dead by a Southerner's hand, conservative dreams of a smooth reunification were dashed. Tough-talking Andrew Johnson became president. Radical Republicans viewed Johnson, an original member of the Joint Committee on the Conduct of the War, as an improvement over the soft-hearted Lincoln. The work of Reconstruction would not be guided by Lincoln's dream of reuniting a nation; instead, it would proceed under the vindictive heel of a conqueror. As Congress took up the task of punishing their rebellious brethren, the committee's report was stillborn.

[lv] GENERAL MEADE.

The assigning General Meade to the command of the army of the Potomac, which he assumed on the 28th of June, 1863, seems to have been attended by no immediate changes other than the transferring to that army of the force at Harpers Ferry, under General French, which force had been refused to General Hooker by General Halleck; the assigning General Couch and his force to his command, and the conferring upon him full powers for the organizing and officering his army. The plans and view of General Hooker were fully made known to him by General Butterfield, who continued to act as chief of staff.

General Warren states that "the troops continued to move on just the same as if the command had not been changed."

One of the charges against Meade was that he had merely followed Hooker's plans and did not deserve credit for the Gettysburg campaign. The issue had surfaced when Congress was debating who should be accorded honors for the campaign, and Meade himself had raised the subject before the committee during his initial appearance. Butterfield was the only other person to testify that had been present at the meeting between Meade and Hooker, and Butterfield's testimony does not correspond to Meade's.[1]

Warren's quotation was taken out of context. The relevant sentence from his testimony reads, "He [Meade] assumed command on Sunday morning, and the troops continued to move on just the same as if the command had not been changed." Warren seemed to want to convey the idea that the transfer of command went smoothly. The committee's final report implies that Warren had said there were no changes and that Meade simply followed Hooker's plans.

The two armies were approaching each other so closely that it was apparent a collision could not long be avoided, and the most important question undoubtedly was the selection of the field for the coming battle. General Pleasonton says that he several times informed General Meade that, from the knowledge of the country he had acquired the previous year during the Antietam campaign, he was satisfied that there was but one place to fight the enemy, and that was Gettysburg. With that view General Pleasonton, on the 29th of June, sent his strongest division of cavalry, under General Buford, to occupy Gettysburg, with instructions to hold that position to the last extremity until the army could be brought up there.

General Meade, however, decided upon making a stand at another point for the purpose of receiving the attack of the enemy, and selected a position the general line of which was Pipe creek, the left resting in the neighborhood of Middleburg, and the right at Manchester, [lvi] and even down to somewhat late in the day of the 1st of July was engaged in making arrangements for occupying that position as soon as the movements of the enemy should indicate

1. *MG*, 215–6.

the time for doing so. To that end, on the morning of the 1st of July, a preliminary circular order was issued, directing his corps commanders to make the necessary preparations for carrying the order into effect as soon as circumstances should arise to render it necessary or advisable in the opinion of the commanding general; and it was not until information reached General Meade, in the afternoon of July 1, that the cavalry, under General Buford, had come in contact with a large force of the enemy near Gettysburg, and that General Reynolds, who had gone to his assistance with the 1st and 11th corps, had been killed, that the attention of General Meade seems to have been seriously directed to the position at Gettysburg for meeting the enemy. He sent General Hancock there to report the condition of our troops and the character of the ground. General Meade says that before he received the report of General Hancock he had decided, upon information received from officers from the scene of action, to concentrate his army at Gettysburg, and it was done that night and the next day, and the battle was there fought.

That circular order, with other orders and despatches of the same date, indicate the views of the commanding general and the circumstances which led him to turn his attention to the position of Gettysburg for the purpose of meeting the enemy. They are given here in full, as furnished by General Meade, and are as follows:

[Circular.]

"HEADQUARTERS ARMY OF THE POTOMAC,

"Taneytown, July 1, 1863.

"From information received the commanding general is satisfied that the object of the movement of the army in this direction has been accomplished, viz.: the relief of Harrisburg and the prevention of the enemy's intended invasion of Philadelphia beyond the Susquehanna.

"It is no longer his intention to assume the offensive until the enemy's movements or position should render such an operation certain of success. If the enemy assume the offensive and attack, it is his intention, after holding them in check sufficiently long to withdraw the trains and other impediments, to withdraw the army from its present position, and form line of battle with the left resting in the neighborhood of Middleburg, and the right at Manchester, the general direction being that of Pipe creek.

"For this purpose General Reynolds, in command of the left, will withdraw the force at present at Gettysburg, two corps, by the road to Taneytown and Westminster, and, after crossing Pipe creek, deploy towards Middleburg.

The corps at Emmitsburg will be withdrawn, by way of Mechanicsville, to Middleburg, or, if a more direct route can be found, leaving Taneytown to their left, to withdraw direct to Middleburg.

"General Slocum will assume command of the two corps at Hanover and Two Taverns and withdraw them *via* Union Mills, deploying one to the right and one to the left after crossing Pipe creek, connecting on the left with General Reynolds, and communicating his right to General Sedgwick at Manchester, who will connect with him and form the right.

"The time for falling back can only be developed by circumstances. Whenever such circumstances arise as would seem to indicate the necessity for falling [lvii] back and assuming this general line indicated, notice of such movement will at once be communicated to these headquarters and to all adjoining corps commanders.

"The 2d corps, now at Taneytown, will be held in reserve, in the vicinity of Uniontown and Frizelburg, to be thrown to the point of strongest attack, should the enemy make it. In the event of these movements being necessary, the trains and impedimenta will all be sent to the rear of Westminster.

"Corps commanders, with their officers commanding artillery, and the divisions, should make themselves thoroughly familiar with the country indicated, all the roads and positions, so that no possible confusion can ensue, and that the movement, if made, be done with good order, precision, and care, without loss, or any detriment to the morale of the troops.

"The commanders of corps are requested to communicate at once the nature of their present position, and their ability to hold them in case of any sudden attack at any point by the enemy.

"This order is communicated that a general plan, perfectly understood by all, may be had for receiving attack if made in strong force upon any portion of our present position. Developments may cause the commanding general to assume the offensive from his present positions.

"The artillery reserve will, in the event of the general movement indicated, move to the rear of Frizelburg, and be placed in position, or sent to corps, as circumstances may require, under the general supervision of the chief of artillery.

"The chief quartermaster will, in case of the general movement indicated, give directions for the orderly and proper position of the trains in rear of Westminster. All the trains will keep well to the right of the road in moving, and in case of any accident, requiring a halt, the team must be hauled out of the line, and not delay the movements.

"The trains ordered to Union Bridge, in these events will be sent to Westminster.

"General headquarters will be, in case of this movement, at Frizelburg.

"General Slocum as near Union Mills as the line will render best for him.

"General Reynolds at or near the road from Taneytown to Frizelburg.

"The chief of artillery will examine the line and select positions for artillery. The cavalry will be held on the right and left flanks after the movement is completed; previous to its completion, he will, as now directed, cover the front and exterior lines well out.

"The commands must be prepared for a movement, and, in the event of the enemy attacking us on the ground indicated herein, to follow up any repulse.

"The chief signal officer will examine the line thoroughly and at once, upon the commencement of this movement, extend telegraphic communications from each of the following points to general headquarters, near Frizelburg, viz.: Manchester, Union Mills, Middleburg, and the Taneytown road.

"All true Union people should be advised to harass and annoy the enemy in every way; to send in information, and taught how to do it—giving regiments by number of colors, number of guns, generals' names, &c.; all their supplies brought to us will be paid for, and not fall into the enemy's hands.

"Roads and ways to move to the right and left of general line should be studied, and thoroughly understood. All movements of troops should be concealed, and our dispositions kept from the enemy. Their knowledge of these dispositions would be fatal to our success, and the greatest care must be taken to prevent such an occurrence.

"By command of Major General Meade.

"S. WILLIAMS,

"Assistant Adjutant General."

[lviii] "HEADQUARTERS ARMY OF THE POTOMAC, July 1, 1863.

"Commanding Officer, 1st Corps:

"The telegraphic intelligence received from General Couch, with the various movements reported from Buford, seem to indicate the concentration of the enemy either at Chambersburg, or at a point situated somewhere on a line drawn between Chambersburg and York, through Heidlersburg, and to the north of Gettysburg.

"The commanding general cannot decide whether it is his best policy to move to attack, until he learns something more definite of the point at which the enemy is concentrating. This he hopes to do during the day. Meanwhile he would like to have your views upon the subject, at least so far as concerns your position.

"If the enemy is concentrated to the right of Gettysburg, that point would not, at first glance, seem to be a proper strategic point of concentration for this army. If the enemy is concentrating in front of Gettysburg, or to the left of it, the general is not sufficiently well informed of the nature of the country to judge of its character either for an offensive or defensive position. The number of the enemy are estimated at about 92,000 infantry, with 270 pieces of artillery, and his cavalry from six to eight thousand. Our numbers ought to equal it, and with the arrival of General French's command, which should get up to-morrow, exceed it, if not too much weakened by straggling and fatigue.

"The general having just assumed command in obedience to orders, with the position of affairs leaving no time to learn the condition of the army as to morale and proportionate strength compared with its last return, would gladly receive from you any suggestions as to the points laid down in this note. He feels that you know more of the condition of the troops in your vicinity and the country than he does.

"General Humphreys, who is at Emmitsburg with the 3d corps, the general considers an excellent adviser as to the nature of the country for defensive or offensive operations. If near enough to call him to consultation with you, please do so, without interference with the responsibilities that devolve upon you both. You have all the information which the general has received, and the general would like to have your views.

"The movement of your corps to Gettysburg was ordered before the positive knowledge of the enemy's withdrawal from Harrisburg and concentration was received.

"S. WILLIAMS,

"Assistant Adjutant General."

"Headquarters Army of the Potomac, July 1, 1863.

"Commanding Officer, 6th Corps:

"I am directed by the commanding general to state that it would appear from reports just received that the enemy is moving in heavy force on Gettysburg. (Ewell from Heidlersburg, and Hill from Cashtown Pass,) and it is not improbable he will reach that place before the command under Major General Reynolds, (the 1st and 11th corps,) now on the way, can arrive there. Should such be the case, and General Reynolds finds himself in the presence of a superior force, he is instructed to hold the enemy in check, and fall slowly back. If he is able to do this, the line indicated in the circular of to-day will be occupied to night. Should circumstances render it necessary of the commanding general to fight the enemy to-day, the troops are posted as follows for the support of Reynolds's command, viz.: On his right at 'Two Taverns,' the 12th [lix] corps; at Hanover, the 5th corps; the 2d corps is on the road between Taneytown and Gettysburg; the 3d corps is at Emmitsburg.

"This information is conveyed to you that you may have your corps in readiness to move in such direction as may be required at a moment's notice.

"S. WILLIAMS,

"Assistant Adjutant General."

"HEADQUARTERS ARMY OF THE POTOMAC,

"July 1, 1863—1.10 P.M.

"Commanding Officer, Second Corps:

"The major general commanding has just been informed that General Reynolds has been killed, or badly wounded. He directs that you turn over the command of your corps to General Gibbon; that you proceed to the front, and by virtue of this order, in case of the truth of General Reynolds's death, you assume command of the corps there assembled, viz.: the 11th, 1st, and 3d, at Emmitsburg. If you think the ground and position there a (better) suitable one to fight a battle under existing circumstances, you will so advise the general, and he will order all the troops up. You know the general's views, and General Warren, who is fully aware of them, has gone out to see General Reynolds.

"Later—1.15 P.M.

"Reynolds has possession of Gettysburg, and the enemy are reported as falling back from the front of Gettysburg. Hold your column ready to move.

"DANIEL BUTTERFIELD,

"Major General, Chief of Staff."

"HEADQUARTERS FIRST CAVALRY DIVISION,

"July 1, 1963—3.20 P.M.

"General Pleasonton:

"I am satisfied that Longstreet and Hill have made a junction. A tremendous battle has been raging since 9 1/2 A.M., with varying success. At the present moment the battle is raging on the road to Cashtown, and in short cannon range of this town; the enemy's line is a semicircle on the height from north to west. General Reynolds was killed early this morning. In my opinion there seems to be no directing person.

"JOHN BUFORD,

"Brigadier General of Volunteers.

"We need help now.

"BUFORD."

"5.25.

"General: When I arrived here an hour since, I found that our troops had given up the front of Gettysburg and the town. We have now taken up a position in the cemetery, and cannot well be taken; it is a position, however, easily turned. Slocum is now coming on the ground, and is taking position on the right, which will protect the right. But we have as yet no troops on the left, the third corps not having yet reported, but I suppose that it is marching up. If so, his flank march will in a degree protect our left flank. In the mean time Gibbon had better march on so as to take position on our right or left to our rear, as may be necessary, in some commanding position. General G. will see this despatch. The battle is quiet now. I think we will be all right until night. I have sent all the trains back. When night comes it can be told better what had best to [lx] be done. I think we can retire; if not we can fight here, as the ground appears not unfavorable with good troops.

"I will communicate in a few moments with General Slocum, and transfer command to him.

"Howard says that Doubleday's command gave way.

"Your obedient servant,

"WINFIELD S. HANCOCK,

"Major General Commanding Corps.

"General Warren is here,

"General Butterfield, Chief of Staff."

"HEADQUARTERS ARMY OF THE POTOMAC,

"July 1, 1863—7 P.M.

"Commanding Officer, 5th Corps:

"The major general commanding directs that you move up to Gettysburg at once upon the receipt of this order, if not already ordered to do so by

General Slocum. The present prospect is that our general engagement must be there. Communicate with General Slocum, under whose directions you are placed by the orders of this morning. The general had supposed that General Slocum would have ordered you up.

"DANIEL BUTTERFIELD,

"Major General, Chief of Staff."

"HEADQUARTERS ARMY OF THE POTOMAC,

"Taneytown, July 1, 1863—7:30 P.M.

"Commanding Officer, 6th Corps:

"The major general commanding directs me to say that a general battle seems to be impending to-morrow at Gettysburg. That it is of the utmost importance that your command should be up. He directs that you stop all trains, or turn them out of the road that impede your progress. Your march will have to be a forced one to reach the scene of action, where we shall probably be largely out numbered without your presence. If any shorter road presents itself without difficulty in getting up, you will use your discretion in taking it, and report the facts to these headquarters.

"General Sykes has been ordered up from Hanover to Gettysburg and General Slocum from Littletown, and General Hancock's corps from here. The whole army is there, (Gettysburg,) or under way for that point. The general desires you to report here in person without delay the moment you receive this. He is waiting to see you here before going to the front. The trains will all go to Westminster and Union Bridge, as ordered.

"DANIEL BUTTERFIELD,

"Major General, Chief of Staff."

The use of dispatches only from July 1 is misleading. In several dispatches from June 30, also submitted by Meade, Gettysburg is mentioned as a possible point of concentration for Lee. Of particular interest is Meade's exhibit H, "Orders," dated June 30, which ordered the First and Eleventh Corps to Gettysburg.

On the morning of the 1st of July, General Buford, with a division of cavalry, was fiercely attacked by the enemy in the immediate vicinity of Gettysburg. He held his ground with great gallantry, and General Reynolds, upon hearing of the attack, immediately moved up to his support with the 1st and 11th corps. The fighting on that day was on and near Seminary ridge, immediately west of the town of Gettysburg, and was conducted on our side entirely by the cavalry division of General Buford, and the 1st and 11th corps of infantry. Quite early in the fight General Reynolds was killed, and the command devolved upon General Howard, of the 11th corps. The fighting continued [lxi] until about four o'clock in the afternoon, when our troops retired through the town and took up a position on Cemetery ridge, and the fighting ceased for the day. General Sickles, with the 3d corps, which, with the 1st and 11th, had constituted the command of General Reynolds, was at Emmitsburg, about ten miles distance. Upon hearing of the action at Gettysburg, General Sickles immediately put his troops in motion, and they began to arrive at Gettysburg about five o'clock in the afternoon, and were at once placed in position by General Hancock, who had arrived and assumed command shortly after the position upon Cemetery ridge had been taken by General Howard. The 12th corps, under General Slocum, arrived at Gettysburg about the same time. General Meade determined to concentrate his army at Gettysburg, and during the night of the 1st and morning of the 2d of July, the 2d, 5th, 12th, and most of the 6th corps were moved there, and placed in position upon Cemetery ridge, and other high ground connected therewith, as far as what is known as Round Top mountain; the line extending from Round-top mountain on the left to Culp's hill on the right.

The morning of the 2d of July was passed in strengthening the position of our army, and placing the troops in line to receive the attack of the enemy. Skirmishing began before noon, but the enemy did not make their attack in force until about half past three in the afternoon. The attack was directed mainly upon the 3d corps, under General Sickles, which was posted near the left of the line. It was very fierce, and the fighting continued until about seven o'clock, when the enemy retired. The 3d corps suffered severely in this day's engagement, and General Sickles received a wound resulting in the loss of a leg. General Meade and others criticized General Sickles for the disposition he made of his troops before the fighting commenced; claiming that by throwing forward his corps from the regular line he exposed himself to and invited the attack of the enemy. General Sickles in his testimony gives his reason for the course he pursued, and holds that the movement he made prevented a disastrous flank attack on our left, which was threatened, besides being advantageous in other respects. Some troops of the 2d and 5th corps were also engaged in support of the 3d corps.

There is testimony to show that during the 2d of July General Meade contemplated abandoning his position at Gettysburg and retiring to some other position. As there is some controversy on that point, your committee will quote from the testimony of various witnesses upon the subject. General Butterfield, who was acting as chief of staff to General Meade, says:

"General Meade then directed me to prepare an order to withdraw the army from that position. I stated to him that it would be necessary for me to know the exact position of the troops.

"Question. What day of the fight was this?

"Answer. This was on the morning of the 2d of July, before the battle of that day had commenced. I stated to General Meade that I could not prepare that order properly without first going over the field and ascertaining the position of each division and corps of the army with relation to the roads. [lxii] General Meade replied that he could not wait for that; that he would show me where the troops were. He then took a pencil and a piece of paper and made a rough sketch, showing the positions of the different corps. I stated to him that the order was one requiring a great deal of care in its preparation; that it involved more than logistics, as we were in the presence of the enemy, and that while preparing it I must not be interrupted by anybody coming to me with despatches or orders. He said, 'Very well, you shall not be interrupted.' I told him I thought I could not prepare the order without a more accurate sketch, and I would have to send out to the corps commanders to give me a report of the positions of their troops in regard to the various roads; that in the meanwhile I could be studying the maps. He said, 'Very well, do so.' I then went up stairs, and after carefully studying the maps I prepared the order for the withdrawal of the army from the field of Gettysburg. After finishing it I presented it to General Meade, and it met his approval. I then stated to him that it would be a great deal better if that order was to be executed, as it might involve great consequences if not properly executed, to submit it for careful examination to such general officers as were there present, with a view of giving them an opportunity of finding any fault with it then, so that no misunderstanding should arise from the manner in which it was worded or expressed. He said there was no objection to having that done. I called General Gibbon, who was present, and, I think, General Williams and General Ingalls, and stated to them that I had been directed to prepare this order, and that I would be very much obliged to any of them if they would look it over and point out any faults in it then, rather than after it was put into execution; that I desired it scrutinized carefully, with a view of discovering anything in it which might be misunderstood. Some of these officers—I do not now remember which, I am very sure

General Gibbon was one; I think General Hancock was there, but whether he read it over or not I am not sure—some of these officers read it over, and said that they thought it was correctly prepared. The corps commanders were then sent for by General Meade to report to headquarters. The order which I had prepared was given to General Williams, and was copied by the clerks or was in process of being copied by them. As General Sickles rode up to headquarters, in pursuance of the request of General Meade, the battle broke out in front of General Sickles's corps, and there was no council held. General Sickles returned immediately, and every corps commander there rode immediately to his command. Without my memoranda I cannot fix the hour of this occurrence, but it was during the 2d day of July."

The testimony of General Williams, the adjutant general of General Meade, is as follows:

"Question. Do you know anything about an order on the 2d of July to withdraw the army?

"Answer. The orders for the movements of the army under the present arrangement are generally prepared by the chief of staff, and the manuscripts of the orders are turned over to me to have copies prepared for those to whom they are to be distributed; and I am held responsible that the orders are correctly copied, and that they are delivered to the persons for whom they are intended.

"In regard to the order of the 2d of July, to the best of my recollection and belief, the chief of staff either handed to me or to my clerk an order looking to a contingency which possibly might happen of the army being compelled to assume a new position. To the best of my belief such an order was prepared, and I presume it may have been signed by me, and possibly the copies may have been prepared for the corps and other commanders. Orders of such a character are usually made out in manifold, in order to save time. The particular [lxiii] order in question, however, was never distributed; no vestige of it is to be found among any of the records of my office; it must have been destroyed within a day or two after it was prepared. I have no reason to suppose, other than the fact that the order was given to me or my clerk by the chief of staff, that General Meade had any knowledge of it. It was not for me to look beyond the order of the chief of staff. Whether or not a copy of that order was given to Major General Butterfield, who was then acting as chief of staff, I am unable to say, and I cannot certainly state whether the rough draught was ever handed back to him. I only know that there is nothing in relation to that order to be found among the records in my charge. The order was never recorded or issued in any sense. I do not now remember the exact tenor of the order, but to the best of my belief it was an order which, if carried out, would have involved a retrograde movement of the army."

General Gibbon says:

"There is a matter connected with a report in regard to the retreat of the army from Gettysburg, which I think it proper to mention in my testimony. It is this: some time during the day of the 2d of July, but before this fight with General Sickles's corps had taken place, I was at General Meade's headquarters, as I frequently was during the day; I consequently knew a great deal of the dispositions made, and order given, for the troops to come up. I had been urged frequently in the morning of that day, by General Meade, to hurry up to the field, and I heard of the other corps that were coming up; I therefore had but one idea in regard to General Meade's intention, which was to concentrate the whole army there for the purpose of fighting a battle; when, therefore, on coming out of the little room in which he had his office, I met General Butterfield, his chief of staff, and he asked me to read over with him, and compare with a map he had there, a draught of an order which he had, and I asked him what it was, and he told me that it was an order for the army to retreat, I was struck with a great deal of astonishment, and I recollect very well my exclamation, 'Great God! General Meade does not intend to leave this position?' General Butterfield did not say that General Meade did intend to leave; he merely said something to the effect that it was necessary to be prepared, in case it should be necessary to leave, or some remark of that kind. He then showed me the order, and either he read it over and I pointed out the places on the map, or I read it over and he pointed out the places to which each corps was to go. When he got through, I remarked that it was all correctly drawn up.

"Until very recently I supposed that the order which General Butterfield showed me was an order in regard to the army falling back to a position which I heard General Meade had selected on Pipe Clay creek. But I am satisfied now that order must have been some different order from the one I had been thinking it was. Being firmly convinced, as I was at the time, that General Meade had no idea of falling back from the position there, it struck me as very remarkable that his chief of staff should be making out an order to retreat; and I still think so."

General Sickles says that he received some intimation that it was in contemplation to fall back from Gettysburg, and that the question was to be submitted to the corps commanders; that he was sent for to go to headquarters, but did not go until he received the second summons; and that just as he arrived there the battle began, and he returned to his corps without dismounting.

General Howe says in his testimony:

"I said to General Sedgwick, 'We ought to let our men have the best chance to rest that they can get right off; we are not likely to be called on to fight to-night; [lxiv] let us give the men a chance to get some coffee, and rest all they can, for there will be something done to-morrow undoubtedly.' He remarked to me, 'It is a little early yet; they are discussing whether we shall stay here, or move back to Westminster.' That is twenty-one or twenty-two miles. I said, 'It is some distance back there.' Said he, 'Can we move back?' I replied, 'Yes, if it is necessary; we have just come over the road, and we know it. The men are worn; but if it is necessary, the 6th corps can go back, after resting two or three hours.' General Sedgwick gave me to understand that our army would probably move back to Westminster.

"Question. This was the night after General Sickles was wounded?

"Answer. Yes, sir, this was the second day of the fight, the 2d of July.

"Question. Who was in that council discussing the question of retreating?

"Answer. I do not know. What I heard I had from General Sedgwick. He said, 'I think we are going to move back.' The impression he gave me was, that General Meade had the question under consideration. General Sedgwick said, 'The question of falling back was then being considered.' And the impression given to me was that we should move back to Westminster. Soon after, however, it seemed to be decided that we were to remain there."

It will be seen that General Meade is very emphatic in his statement that he never gave or contemplated the giving any such order. He says:

"I have understood that an idea has prevailed that I intended an order should be issued on the morning of the 2d of July requiring the withdrawal of the army or the retreat of the army from Gettysburg, which order was not issued, owing simply to the attack of the enemy having prevented it.

"In reply to that, I have only to say that I have no recollection of ever having directed such an order to be issued, or ever having contemplated the issuing of such an order; and that it does seem to me that to any intelligent mind who is made acquainted with the great exertions I made to mass my army at Gettysburg on the night of July the 1st, it must appear entirely incomprehensible that I should order it to retreat, after collecting all my army there, before the enemy had done anything to require me to make a movement of any kind."

Subsequently General Meade appeared and said:

"I desire to add a little to my testimony, with the permission of the committee.

"The chairman. Certainly; you are at liberty to make such additional statements as you please.

"The witness: I wanted to say a few words to the committee, in extension of the remarks which I made the last time I was here, in reference to a charge which I expected then would be made against me, and which I understand has since been made against me, to the effect that I intended that an order should be issued, on the morning of July 2, withdrawing the army from the position it then occupied at Gettysburg and retreating, before the enemy had done anything to require me to withdraw.

"It is proper that I should say that the fact of such a charge having been made here, or such a report given here, has reached me through outside sources, but in such a way that I can hardly disbelieve that such a statement has been made; and that it was made by an officer who occupied a very high and confidential position on my staff—the chief of staff, Major General Butterfield. Now, indulging in the utmost charity towards General Butterfield, and believing that he is sincere in what he says, I want to explain how it is possible that such an extraordinary idea could have got into his head.

"I utterly deny, under the full solemnity and sanctity of my oath, and in the firm conviction that the day will come when the secrets of all men shall be made [lxv] known—I utterly deny ever having intended or thought, for one instant, to withdraw that army, unless the military contingencies which the future should develop during the course of the day might render it a matter of necessity that the army should be withdrawn. I base this denial not only upon my own assertion and my own veracity, but I shall also show to the committee, from documentary evidence, the despatches and orders issued by me at different periods during that day, that if I did intend any such operation, I was at the same time doing things totally inconsistent with any such intention.

"I shall also ask the committee to call before them certain other officers of my staff, whose positions were as near and confidential to me as that of General Butterfield, who, if I had had any such intention, or had given any such orders as he said I gave, would have been parties to it, would have known it, and have made arrangements in consequence thereof; all of whom I am perfectly confident, will say they never heard of any such thing. I refer to General Hunt, chief of artillery, and who had artillery, occupying a space of from four to five miles, drawn out on the road, and who, if I had intended to have withdrawn that army, should have been told to get his trains out of the way the very first thing, because all the troops could not move until the artillery moved. I would also ask you to call upon General Ingalls, my chief quartermaster, who had charge of the trains; also General Warren, my chief engineer, who will tell you that he was with me the whole of the day, in constant intercourse and communication with me; and that instead of intending to withdraw my army, I was talking about other matters. All these officers will corroborate what I say, that I never mentioned any such purpose to any of them.

"General Butterfield remained at Taneytown on the night of the 1st of July, and did not join me on the field until about 9 or 10 o'clock in the morning of the 2d, I having arrived there at 1 o'clock. Soon after he arrived I did direct him to familiarize himself with the topography of the ground, and I directed him to send out staff officers to learn all the roads. As I have already mentioned in my previous testimony here, I had never before been at Gettysburg, and did not know how many roads ran from our position, or what directions they ran. My orders to General Butterfield were similar to this:

" 'General Butterfield, neither I nor any man can tell what the results of this day's operations may be. It is our duty to be prepared for every contingency, and I wish you to send out staff officers to learn all the roads that lead from this place, ascertain the positions of the corps—where their trains are; prepare to familiarize yourself with these details, so that in the event of any contingency, you can, without any order be ready to meet it.' "

"It was in anticipation of possible contingencies, and not at all that I had made up my mind to do anything of that kind.

"I would furthermore call the attention of the committee to the absurdity of such an idea. If I had directed the order to be issued, why was it not issued? With General Butterfield's capacity it would not have taken him more than ten or fifteen minutes to prepare such an order. We were furnished with what you call manifold letter-writers, so that after the frame work of an order is prepared, ten or a dozen copies may be made at once. Why was the order not issued, or if issued, why was it not executed? There was no obstacle to my withdrawing that army, if I had desired; the enemy presented none. There was not a moment from the time the first gun was fired at Gettysburg until we knew the enemy had retired that I could not have withdrawn my army. Therefore, if I had entertained such an idea, it seems to me extraordinary that I did not execute it."

* * * * * *

"That General Butterfield may have misapprehended what I said to him; that he may himself have deemed a retreat necessary, and thought we would be compelled to retreat in the course of the day, and in the excess of zeal, and [lxvi] desire to do more than he was called upon to do, may have drawn up an order of that kind, I do not deny; but I say he never showed me any such order, and it had not my sanction or authority."

General Hunt says in his testimony:

"Question. Had you any knowledge of any order being prepared during the battle of Gettysburg for the withdrawal of the army from the position it then occupied?

"Answer. No, sir. I know of no such order, and no such intention. I presume if any such intention had been entertained I should have known of it as soon as anybody, as the first thing to have been done was to get rid of the large reserve artillery and ammunition train under my charge, and which had been brought up on the morning of the 2d of July, under, or by the direction of, General Meade.

"Question. You say you had no knowledge or intimation of any such thing during the battle?

"Answer. None at all. The only time I ever had a thought such an idea might be entertained was on the night of the 2d of July. On that night I was down at the artillery reserve, refitting and reorganizing the batteries that had been cut up that day. I received a message from General Meade's headquarters—I do not now recollect whether it was from General Meade himself or from General Butterfield—stating that both General Tyler, who commanded the reserve artillery, and myself, were wanted at headquarters. I told General Tyler that it was impossible for me to go up just then, but that if the question came up about falling back, to cast my vote against it. He remained for some time, and I went up with him, perhaps a half an hour afterwards. On arriving at headquarters, I understood that the question had been spoken of as to what they should do, and there was no person at all in favor of leaving the ground we had then; that was just as the conversation closed."

General Sedgwick testifies as follows:

"Question. Have you any knowledge of the preparation of any order for the withdrawal of the army at any time during the battle of Gettysburg, or the retreat of the army from the position it then held?

"Answer. I never heard of any such order until within the last four weeks;

and when I first heard it I denied most positively that any such order could have been given. I was the second in command there, and reported to General Meade at a critical time; and if he contemplated so important a move, he would have informed me. Besides, his urging my corps forward shows that he intended to fight the battle there. General Meade undoubtedly was apprehensive that the enemy might turn his flank; and in that event he would have had to take up a new position; but I do not think he ever contemplated any retreat.

"Question. Had it been the intention of the commanding general to retreat the army, was not the order to you to come up in direct conflict with any such intended movement?

"Answer. Certainly it was. In the course of the night of the 1st and the morning of the 2d of July I received no less than three verbal messages from him to hurry up with all possible despatch."

From the outset, the committee attempted to show Meade in a bad light, asserting that there was evidence that he had wanted to abandon his position at Gettysburg. There was such testimony, to be sure, but only three officers—Sickles, Howe, and Butterfield—claimed that Meade had wanted to retreat, whereas six, including Meade, testified that he had not wanted to retreat. The rest of the witnesses either were not asked about the matter or answered that they did not know.

On the night of the 2d of July a council was held at General Meade's headquarters to determine upon the best action to be taken. General Meade testifies as follows, in reference to that council:

"The questions discussed by this council were: First, whether it was necessary for us to assume any different position from what we then held; and, secondly, whether, if we continued to maintain the position we then held, our [lxvii] operations of the next day should be offensive or defensive. The opinion of the council was unanimous, which agreed fully with my own views that we should maintain our lines as they were then held, and that we should wait the movements of the enemy, and see if he made any further attack before we assumed the offensive."

General Butterfield, in testimony, says:

"That evening, after the enemy were repulsed, a council of corps commanders was held. I kept minutes of that council, which I sent to General Williams, who informs me that they have been lost. The general question put to the corps commanders present at that council was, whether our army should remain on that field and continue the battle, or whether we should change to some other position. A vote of the corps commanders was taken in regard to that, and a majority were in favor of remaining on the field and fighting it out. General Slocum gave the first opinion; his answer was, 'Stay and fight it out.' I will not be positive as to what corps commanders differed with him; but the majority were for remaining on the line which the army then held, and fighting it out.

"Question. Can you give the opinion of each corps commander? Because, perhaps, in justice to them, that ought to be known.

"Answer. My impression is, that those generals can tell how they voted. I am clear in my memory that General Slocum voted to stay and fight it out, and that General Sykes so voted; that General Newton entered into a long discussion to show that that position was a disadvantageous one; that he was not prepared to vote to leave it, but he wanted the council to understand that he had objections to it. General Birney, I think, voted to stay and fight it out, as did General Hancock also. I do not remember what General Sedgwick's vote was, nor do I remember how General Howard voted; I think he had a great deal to say upon the subject. The reason I do not remember the votes exactly is, because I intrusted [*sic*] the matter to the memorandum which I sent General Williams. After the council had finished, General Meade arose from the table, and remarked that in his opinion, Gettysburg was no place to fight a battle; but it was settled to remain there, and the council dispersed."

General Birney also testifies that the council, on the night of the 2d of July, was divided on the question of retiring to another position; but that a majority were in favor of remaining at Gettysburg and awaiting the attack of the enemy.

Wade's bias is obvious. After citing Meade's testimony that the decision of the council to attack was unanimous, Wade undermined Meade's credibility by citing testimony to the contrary effect. Wade did not mention that Butterfield and Birney were the only ones to testify about a divided council. Nor did he cite other witnesses who testified to the unanimity of the decision.

On the 3d of July, no active operations took place until about noon, except on the extreme right, where the 12th corps drove the enemy from a position taken by them during the night, and which had been occupied by some of our troops that had been sent to the left during the fight of the 2d. Not long after midday the enemy opened a furious cannonade upon our line from a large number of guns, estimated at from 125 to 150 pieces. The cannonade is described by witnesses as exceeding anything that had occurred in any previous battle of the war. The cannonade and the assault that followed is thus described by General Hancock, who commanded that portion of the line against which it was directed:

"About 1 or 2 o'clock in the afternoon the enemy commenced a terrific cannonade, from probably 120 pieces of artillery, on the front of the line connecting Cemetery hill with Round Top, the left centre, commanded by me. That line consisted of the 1st, 2d, and 3d corps, of which I had the general command. I commanded that whole front. General Gibbon commanded the 2d corps in my [lxviii] absence, General Newton the 1st corps, and General Birney the 3d. That cannonade continued for probably an hour and a half. The enemy then made an assault at the end of that time; it was a very formidable assault, and made, I should judge, with about 18,000 infantry. When the columns of the enemy appeared it looked as if they were going to attack the centre of our line, but after marching straight out a little distance they seemed to incline a little to their left, as if their object was to march through my command and seize Cemetery hill, which I have no doubt was their intention. They attacked with wonderful spirit; nothing could have been more spirited. The shock of the assault fell upon the 2d and 3d divisions of the 2d corps, and those were the troops, assisted by a small brigade of Vermont troops, together with the artillery of our line, which fired from Round Top to Cemetery hill at the enemy all the way as they advanced whenever they had the opportunity. Those were the troops that really met the assault. No doubt there were other troops that fired a little, but those were the troops that really withstood the shock of the assault and repulsed. The attack of the enemy was met by about six small brigades of our troops, and was finally repulsed after a terrific contest at very close quarters, in which our troops took about thirty or forty colors and some 4,000 or 5,000 prisoners, with great loss to the enemy in killed and wounded. The repulse was a most signal one, and that decided the battle, and was practically the end of the fight. I was wounded at the close of the assault, and that ended my operations with the army for that campaign."

Other witnesses also testify to the terrific character of the cannonade, and the furious assault and its signal and complete repulse. The enemy fell back in great confusion behind their artillery line, leaving it insufficiently supported. General Hancock states that while wounded, and just before being carried off the field, he dictated a note to General Meade, urging that the 5th and 6th corps should be at once ordered to advance and pursue the retreating enemy. His testimony is as follows:

"I must ['may' in the transcript of his testimony] say one thing here: I think it was, probably, an unfortunate thing that I was wounded at the time I was, and equally unfortunate that General Gibbon was also wounded, because the absence of a prominent commander, who knew the circumstances thoroughly, at such a moment as that, was a great disadvantage. I think that our lines should have advanced immediately, and I believe we should have won a great victory. I was very confident that the advance would be made. General Meade told me before the fight that if the enemy attacked me he intended to put the 5th and 6th corps on the enemy's flank; I therefore, when I was wounded, and lying down in my ambulance and about leaving the field, dictated a note to General Meade, and told him if he would put in the 5th and 6th corps I believed he would win a great victory. I asked him afterwards, when I returned to the army, what he had done in the premises. He said he had ordered the movement, but the troops were slow in collecting, and moved so slowly that nothing was done before night, except that some of the Pennsylvania reserves went out and met Hood's division, it was understood, of the enemy, and actually overthrew it, assisted, no doubt, in some measure, by their knowledge of their failure in the assault. There were only two divisions of the enemy on our extreme left, opposite Round Top, and there was a gap in their line of one mile that their assault had left, and I believe if our whole line had advanced with spirit, it is not unlikely that we would have taken all their artillery at that point. I think that was a fault; that we should have pushed the enemy there, for we do not often catch them in that position; and the rule is, and it is natural, that when you repulse or defeat an enemy [lxix] you should pursue him; and I believe it is a rare thing that one party beats another and does not pursue him, and I think that on that occasion it only required an order and prompt execution."

Other witnesses concur in the opinion that if a prompt and vigorous advance had been made immediately after the repulse of the enemy, it would have resulted in a great victory, and the loss of the most, if not the whole, of the line of artillery from which the enemy had opened previous to their assault. Orders were given to General Sykes and General Sedgwick to advance with the 5th corps, but the movement was made so slowly that nothing practically resulted from it, except the capture of some prisoners on the left.

The alteration of the word "may" to "must" in Hancock's testimony is noteworthy. While it may have been a simple typographical error, it nonetheless alters the entire tone of Hancock's statement.

At the conclusion of the battle on Friday, our troops were in good condition, in the best of spirits, and anxious to be led against the enemy. The three days of the battle had been for the most of them comparatively days of rest, and though we lost heavily, our loss had not been so great as that of the enemy, while the morale of our troops was far better. General Howe speaks of the battle as the most orderly fight he had ever been in; that the position did the work for us; that there was no maneuvering, no combinations on our part, no great generalship displayed, for none was needed; and at the close of the fight our men were not much jaded or fatigued, but had plenty of fight in them, and were comparatively fresh.

Wade's summary of Howe's testimony is not correct. Following the words "no great generalship displayed," Wade has added "for none was needed."

The considerations which seemed to influence the general in command and the corps commanders, in relation to the pursuit of the enemy after their final repulse, are these: General Meade says that even on the 5th of July he was not satisfied that the enemy was in full retreat for the Potomac, or what his further movements would be, and was not aware of the injury he had inflicted upon the enemy in the battle that had just taken place.

Wade is incorrect. The words he attributed to Meade were in fact taken from Wadsworth's testimony, in reply to a question about why Meade had not counterattacked on July 3.

General Warren says, "there was a tone among most of the prominent officers that we had quite saved the country for a time, and that we had done enough; that we might jeopard all we had won by trying to do too much."

All the witnesses but General Meade state that it was very apparent, on the morning of the 4th of July, that the enemy were in full retreat, and Generals Pleasonton, Warren, Birney, and others state that they counseled an immediate pursuit. General Birney says that he asked and obtained permission to make an attack that morning on the enemy as they were crossing a point near him on the pike to Hagerstown; but just as he had commenced the movement to attack, a staff officer rode up with a written order from General Meade not to attack, but to let the enemy go, which was done. General Pleasonton states that when he urged General Meade to order an immediate advance of the army after the enemy, he replied that "he was not sure they might not make another attack on him, and to satisfy himself, he wanted to know first that they were in retreat, and for that reason I was to send the cavalry out to ascertain." He states that General Gregg, 22 miles on the Chambersburg road, reported at 8 o'clock on the morning of the 4th, "that the road was strewn with wounded and stragglers, ambulances and caissons, and that there was great demoralization and confusion." This was immediately reported to General Meade, but no pursuit was ordered.

Wade's summary addresses the criticism that Meade failed to follow up Lee in a timely manner. If everyone knew the enemy was in full retreat on July 4, Meade's failure to act was inexplicable except in terms of the charge that he did not want to fight Lee. Yet Wade's report is completely inaccurate. Of the twelve witnesses who were at Gettysburg on July 4, only two—Pleasonton and Howe—said Lee was in retreat on July 4. Of the remaining ten witnesses, two testified that they did not know Lee's movements, six were not even asked about Lee's retreat, and one (Wadsworth) was unclear about the issue. The tenth witness was Birney, and Wade recounted how Birney had asked for permission to fire on an enemy column near him. While the story itself is highly suspect, Birney testified that this occurred on July 5, not July 4.

[lxx] But little was done on the 4th of July. General Warren says:

"On the morning of the 4th General Meade ordered demonstrations in front of our line, but they were very feebly made. And when the officers met together that evening to report the state of things in their front, there was so little definitely known as to the position and designs of the enemy, that after some consultation they determined, I believe, to try and find out something before they did move."

That night a council of war was held. Its deliberations and results are thus described by General Butterfield, from memoranda taken at the time:

"I have here the minutes I kept of the council of the 4th of July. That council was held at the headquarters of General Neal. He gave up his headquarters to General Meade. The council was opened by General Meade explaining his instructions and asking the corps commanders for their advice as to what course he should pursue.

"Question. Can you state what General Meade said his instructions were?

"Answer. I think he said his instructions were to cover Washington and Baltimore. He said he had no knowledge of General Foster's movements. There was a rumor that General Foster was coming up from Washington with re-enforcements. General Meade said he desired the earnest assistance and advice of every corps commander. The corps commanders commenced giving their opinions, beginning with General Slocum, and followed by General Sedgwick and General Howard. Their advice, according to my memorandum here, was as follows:

"General Slocum would move on an interior line as far as Emmitsburg, and then, if the enemy had not gone from Gettysburg, hold on there, and push out a force at once with a view of preventing the enemy from crossing the Potomac.

"General Sedgwick would wait at Gettysburg until certain that the enemy were moving away.

"General Howard would like to remain at Gettysburg and ascertain what the enemy were doing, but thought it would do no harm to send a corps to Emmitsburg.

"General Meade then determined to change the manner of procedure in the council, and the following questions were written by his instructions. A portion of these questions are in his handwriting, and a portion in mine.

"The first question was, 'Shall this army remain here?' (That is, at Gettysburg.)

"Second. 'If we remain here, shall we assume the offensive?'

"Third. 'Do you deem it expedient to move towards Williamsport, through Emmitsburg?'

"Fourth. 'Shall we pursue the enemy if he is retreating on his direct line of retreat?'

"To the first question General Newton answered 'No'; to the second question, 'No'; and to the third question, 'Yes.'

"General Slocum answered to the first question, 'No'; the second question was involved in that answer; to the third question, 'Yes'; to the fourth question, 'To pursue on the direct line of retreat, with cavalry moving with the infantry, to cut him off'.

"General Sedgwick, to the first question, answered, 'Would remain here (at

Gettysburg) until positive information concerning their movement'; to the second question, 'No'; to the third question, 'Yes'; to the fourth question, 'Only cavalry.'

[lxxi] "General Howard, to the first question, did not exactly say yes, and did not exactly say no, but would commence a movement to-morrow; to the second question, 'No'; to the third question, 'Yes'; to the fourth question, By a show of force.

"General Sykes, to the first question, as to remaining at Gettysburg, answered, 'Until we know where the enemy is gone'; to the second question 'No'; to the third question he made no answer, his answer to the first question involving that; to the fourth question he answered, 'He would pursue with cavalry only.'

"General Birney, to the first question, answered, 'Yes, until we see'; to the second question, 'No'; to the fourth question, 'He thinks not.'

"General Pleasonton, to the first question, answered, 'No'; to the second question, 'No'; to the third question, 'Move by that route'; to the fourth question, 'Would pursue with infantry and cavalry.'

"General Hays answered to the first question, 'Yes, until we find out where the enemy are, and what they are doing'; to the second question, 'No'; to the third question, 'Yes, if we move'; to the fourth question, 'No, only with cavalry.'

"General Warren, as to the first question, whether we should remain there, answered, 'Yes, until we see what they are doing'; to the second question, about assuming the offensive, 'Not if the enemy remains.'

"Those are the questions to the corps commanders, and their answers. The summary which I made for General Meade in the council of the answers to the first question, whether we should remain at Gettysburg, was—

"Those in favor: Birney, Sedgwick, Sykes, Hays, and Warren.

"Opposed: Newton, Pleasonton, and Slocum.

"Doubtful: Howard."

On the 5th of July the 6th corps commenced to follow the enemy and on the 6th and 7th the rest of the army moved, going to Frederick rather than directly after the enemy, on account of some apprehensions of the difficulty of following the enemy through the mountain passes, which were reported to be strongly fortified. General Howe states that his division had the lead of the 6th corps, after passing Boonsboro, but he was directed to move carefully, and not to come in contact with the enemy, as a general engagement was not desired. He states that when near Funkstown General Buford reported to him that his cavalry held a strong position some distance to the front, which, in his opinion, the enemy should not be allowed to occupy, but that he was pretty hardly engaged there; his ammunition was nearly out, and that he was expected to go further to the right; and asked General Howe to send forward a brigade and hold the position. General Howe applied to General Sedgwick for permission to relieve General Buford, but received in reply the answer, "No; we do not want to bring on a general engagement." General Buford considered the position of such importance that General Howe applied a second time for permission to occupy it, representing that General Buford would soon be compelled to abandon it, as his ammunition was giving out. To this application he received the reply that he might occupy the position if General Buford left it. General Buford did leave it, and General Howe occupied and held the position. General Pleasonton states that on the morning of the 12th of July the cavalry in front of General Slocum's command drove the [lxxii] enemy from an important position, and could have held it, but General Slocum ordered it to halt, for fear of bringing on a general engagement, and the enemy afterwards brought a strong force there and held the point.

In reference to the movement of our army after the battle of Gettysburg, General Warren testifies:

"We commenced the pursuit with the 6th corps on the 5th of July, and on the 6th a large portion of the army moved towards Emmitsburg, and all that was left followed the next day. On July 7 the headquarters were at Frederick; on July 8 headquarters were at Middletown, and nearly all the army was concentrated in the neighborhood of that place and South mountain. On July 9 headquarters were at South Mountain house, and the advance of the army at Boonsboro and Rohrersville. On July 10 the headquarters were moved to Antietam creek; the left of the line crossed the creek, and the right of the line moved up near Funkstown. On the 11th of July the engineers put a new bridge over the Antietam creek; the left of the line advanced to Fairplay and Jones's crossroads, while the right remained nearly stationary. In my opinion we should have fought the enemy the next morning July 12."

No attack was ordered, but the question was submitted to a council of the corps commanders on the night of the 12th of July.

General Meade says:

"I represented to those generals, so far as I knew it, the situation of affairs. I told them that I had reason to believe, from all I could ascertain, that General Lee's position was a very strong one, and that he was prepared to give battle, and defend it if attacked; that it was not in my power, from a want of knowledge of the ground, and from not having had time to make reconnaissances, to indicate any precise mode of attack, or any precise point of attack; that, nevertheless, I was in favor of moving forward and attacking the enemy, and taking the consequences; but that I left it to their judgment, and would not do it unless it met with their approval."

Generals Howard, Pleasonton, and Wadsworth were in favor of attacking the enemy at once. General Warren, who was not then in command of a corps, says: "I do not think I ever saw the principal corps commanders so unanimous in favor of not fighting as on that occasion." The opinion of the council being strongly against attacking the enemy at that time, the 13th of July was passed in reconnoitering the enemy's position. But General Meade says that the day was rainy and misty, and not much information was obtained. General Meade, however, ordered an attack to be made at daylight of the 14th; but when the army moved forward it was ascertained that the whole rebel army had crossed the night of the 13th, and had escaped.

General Meade says:

"It is proper I should say that an examination of the enemy's lines, and of the defences which he had made, brings me clearly to the opinion that an attack under the circumstances in which I had proposed to make it would have resulted disastrously to our arms."

* * * * * *

"And my opinion is now that General Lee evacuated that position, not from any want of ammunition, or the fear that he would be dislodged by any active operations on my part, but that he was fearful that a force would be sent by Harpers [lxxiii] Ferry to cut off his communications—which I had intended to do, having brought up a bridge from Washington, and sent the cavalry down there—and that he could not have maintained that position probably a day if his communications had been cut. That was what caused him to retire."

Again we see skillful editing by Wade. Meade's testimony here appears as if it was in answer to a single question, with some nonessential parts left out. Yet the part of Meade's testimony after the asterisks was in answer to a later question.

Additionally, Wade omitted Meade's statement on Lee's defenses, "of which I now have a map from an accurate survey which can be laid before your com-

mittee." The map is included in the Military Atlas for the Official Records *but not in the committee papers and shows a rather formidable series of defenses.*[2]

This opinion of General Meade is not sustained by that of any other general who has appeared before the committee. Generals Pleasonton, Warren, Birney, Doubleday, and Howe all concur in the opinion that an attack upon the enemy before he recrossed the Potomac would have been most disastrous to him, and have resulted in the dispersion if not the capture of the greater portion of his army.

The section of Wade's report concerning the Bristoe and Mine Run campaigns is not included here.

It will thus be seen that no attack was made by the Army of the Potomac upon the rebel army, under Lee, from the time of the battle of Chancellorsville, under General Hooker, until Lieutenant General Grant assumed the active control of that army and commenced the campaign which has so lately resulted in the capture of the rebel capital and the annihilation of Lee's army, followed by the entire destruction of the rebel military power. The battle of Gettysburg, though important in its results, was purely a defensive battle on our part, and was not followed by such active measures as in the opinion of the majority of the witnesses were necessary and practicable to enable us to reap the full fruits of the victory there gained.

General Warren, who attributes the failure of the army of the Potomac, while under General Meade's command, to achieve and [*sic*] great and practical success over the enemy rather to the failure of the officers under him than to anything on the part of General Meade, gave the following testimony in March, 1864:

"Question. Is it not your opinion that we have lost a great many opportunities by hesitating and waiting at the decisive points?

[lxxvi] "Answer. Yes, sir. I will enumerate the points where, during the last year, I think we have lost opportunities.

"I think we should have advanced on the evening of the 3d of July, after the enemy were repulsed at Gettysburg, with all the force we had on our left.

2. Capt. Calvin D. Cowles, comp., *The Official Military Atlas of the Civil War* (1891–95; reprint, with an introduction by Richard Sommers, New York: Gramercy Books, 1983), plate 42, number 5.

"I think we should have attacked the enemy at Williamsport on the morning of the 12th of July. I think we were as ready then as we ever were, and the enemy was not ready at all.

"Then we lost another opportunity at Manassas gap, on the 23d of July, while the enemy was retreating.

"Then, again, we lost another opportunity when the enemy attacked me on the 14th of October at Bristow. Perhaps not at that point exactly, but during that movement, we missed an opportunity that we should be very glad to have again.

"Then, again, we lost a good opportunity after we recrossed the Rappahannock on the 8th of November.

"And another opportunity was lost in not making the junction we should have had at Robertson's tavern on the 27th of November.

"Nearly all these delays and failures, I think, are due not so much to General Meade as to his plans and expectations not being carried out.

"Question. And you think that, on the occasions you have enumerated, with promptness and energy of action serious injury might have been inflicted upon the enemy?

"Answer. Yes, sir; almost amounting to his destruction."

Your committee could not forbear asking the witnesses before them, if the army, after all these indecisive advances and retrograde movements, still retained confidence in its commanding general. Various answers were returned to this inquiry, all, however, tending to establish the fact that much discouragement had been felt by the army at these ineffective operations, and that but for the highly intelligent character of the rank and file it could never have retained even its then effective condition. General Pleasonton states that the cavalry under his command did not retain confidence in the military ability of General Meade. General Birney states the same about his corps, stating that while General Meade was rather liked as a man, he was not regarded as a man of resolution, or one who is willing to assume that responsibility required by the position he occupies. General Howe states that, in his opinion, the rank and file of the army do not regard General Meade as possessed of that zeal, activity, and energy necessary to carry on an offensive warfare generally, but he admits that the most of the corps commanders would probably say that General Meade was eminently qualified for the command he now holds. That opinion General Howe qualifies, however, by stating that so far as he has observed, the most of the principal officers of the army of the Potomac, including its commanding general, are governed by the same sympathies, feelings, and considerations which were infused into the army by its commander during the Peninsular campaign. General Birney says that many of the principal officers believed that General McClellan was the only general who should command this army; although there is not as much of that feeling now as formerly. General Doubleday bluntly says: "There has always been a great deal of favoritism in the army of the Potomac. No man who is an anti-slavery man or an anti-McClellan man can expect decent [lxxvii] treatment in that army as at present constituted." General Warren states that after the battle of Gettysburg the army was deprived of many of its best corps commanders, General Reynolds having been killed, Generals Sickles and Hancock wounded, and General Meade made commander of the army; that since that time the corps commanders have not been all equal to their position, and consequently the army had been less effective in its operations.

Respectfully submitted.

B. F. Wade,

Chairman.

For Benjamin Wade, committee reports were a powerful propaganda weapon. Yet the power of the Joint Committee on the Conduct of the War had begun to wane by early 1864, as two events demonstrated. First, neither Wade nor any other member of the committee had a voice in the appointment of Ulysses S. Grant to lieutenant general in command of the armies of the Union. The committee's lack of input about Grant clearly reveals a decline in power of a body that had forced McClellan out of command. The committee's weakening power was also evident on March 4, when Wade, Chandler, and Loan failed to have Meade summarily removed from command after the committee had heard from only three witnesses. Although members of the committee believed they had enough clout to make such a demand early in the hearings, Lincoln refused to be cowed by their threat to go public with their evidence. This demonstrates the continuing growth and maturity of Lincoln as a politician as well as the decline of the influence of the committee.

The reports marked the end of the Joint Committee on the Conduct of the War, but hardly settled the controversies that continue to surround the Gettysburg campaign.

21 Meade on Trial

AFTER AN INVESTIGATION that went on for nearly a year, the Joint Committee on the Conduct of the War closed the Meade hearings on February 1, 1865. The committee's report and transcripts, published at the end of the war, had no actual impact on anything. No changes were made in military personnel or policies. No careers, political or military, were substantially helped or hurt. Nor was there anything in the testimony that raised Meade to heroic heights or condemned him as a blundering failure. As the nation became lost in the Lincoln assassination and Reconstruction, the Meade hearings were quickly relegated to obscurity.

An account of the Meade hearings, then, may appear to be full of sound and fury, signifying . . . nothing. Intended to destroy the career of one man and to advance the career of another, the hearings failed to accomplish either goal. Meade continued as commander of the Army of the Potomac, serving in the shadow of Grant until the end of the war. Fighting Joe Hooker remained exiled in the West, where he achieved some degree of redemption in his so-called "Battle above the Clouds." In 1864 when his junior O. O. Howard was promoted over him to command of the Army of Tennessee, Hooker asked to be relieved. His request was promptly granted, and he spent the remainder of the war in administrative posts.[1]

Benjamin Wade, chairman of the Joint Committee on the Conduct of the War, became president of the Senate in 1867. Wade thus stood next in line for the presidency if Andrew Johnson, who had been impeached, was removed from office. Despite the conflict of interest, Wade voted for Johnson's impeachment; he had even begun to pick his own cabinet when Johnson was

1. Warner, *Generals in Blue,* 234–5.

narrowly acquitted. This was a heavy blow for Wade, and his political career never recovered. Failing in his bid for reelection to the Senate, Wade returned to his law practice in 1869 and died in 1878.[2]

Zachariah Chandler, the second most powerful member on the Joint Committee on the Conduct of the War, remained in the Senate until 1875, when he was defeated in his bid for another term. Chandler then served in the Grant administration as secretary of the interior. With the election of Rutherford B. Hayes, Chandler's presence on the national political scene seemed to be at an end, but he was to have one last fling in the Senate. In 1879 the man that had ousted Chandler from his long-held Senate seat resigned due to ill health. Appointed by the Michigan legislature to the vacant seat, Chandler returned to Washington. His service, however, was to be of short duration. During a speaking tour he died in Chicago on October 31, 1879.[3]

Of the witnesses involved in the hearings, three stand out. Meade revealed himself as a man imbued with a strong sense of honor and duty, although ill-equipped to deal with the political maneuvering of the hearings. Caught unawares by the committee's detailed questioning, he proved to be an adept extemporaneous speaker, reciting from memory a complicated series of events covering a two-week period some eight months earlier. That he made mistakes in recounting the sequence of events is not nearly so surprising as the fact that he made so few.

Meade's rationale behind the decisions he made at Gettysburg is still valid. While others, especially with the benefit of hindsight, might have done otherwise, Meade's actions were logical. Gettysburg probably could have been fought better, but in the end—and despite all later attempts to find fault—Meade had won the battle.

Meade was conservative by nature, training, and experience, and it seems entirely predictable that he would move slowly and cautiously while he acquainted himself with his new command. Lee understood his adversary quite well when he observed that Meade would "commit no blunder in my front, and if I make one he will make haste to take advantage of it." It should also be kept in mind that Meade had commanded the army for only three days before fighting one of the bloodiest battles of the war, winning an important victory and turning back Lee and the seemingly invincible Army of Northern Virginia.[4]

2. *DAB*, 10:305.

3. Walter Buell, "Zachariah Chandler: Part Three," 432–44.

4. Douglas Southall Freeman, *R. E. Lee: A Biography*, 4 vols. (New York: Charles Scribner's Sons, 1935), 3:64.

Meade's frequent use of councils during the Gettysburg campaign revealed considerable uncertainty on his part. Whether he called his councils as a means of gathering information and exchanging ideas (as he contended), or to escape or diffuse responsibility (as others have charged), these councils had a negative impact on the army. They gave the impression that no one was in charge and that the army was commanded by a committee, which lessened the confidence of the officers and men in their commander. At the same time, councils discouraged aggressive action by subordinates who participated in them. More conservative council members might change plans, making aggressive actions look poorly conceived or wasteful of lives. The assembling of a council and its ensuing discussions could also waste valuable time, as seen at Williamsport, delaying action and decisions. But the most damaging effect of councils of war was the one that Halleck had warned Meade about: "It is proverbial that councils of war never fight." Meade's councils of July 2, 3, and 13 proved Halleck's point.[5]

Yet Meade was an excellent general on the tactical defensive. His timely maneuvering of troops to plug holes in the Union line, his skill in adapting to unexpected developments or anticipating Lee's movements, and even his use of the full resources of his army, marked an improvement over previous commanders of the Army of the Potomac. But notwithstanding these attributes, Meade was not the man Lincoln sought to win the war. His brilliance on defense was offset by his conservative nature on offense. It is hard to imagine Meade engaging in the bloody war of attrition that Grant believed was the best and fastest way to beat the South. Lincoln judged that the war would not be won without a man like Grant, and he was summoned from the West.

Of the major witnesses against Meade, the one who appeared in the worst light in the hearings was Daniel Sickles. While he was a competent, even promising, general, the hearings demonstrated his flawed character. Vindictive, vain, and overly ambitious, he was often a stranger to the truth. In later years Sickles became a pathological liar when it came to Gettysburg, building, at least in his own mind, an irrefutable case that he was the hero of Gettysburg and that but for him the battle, even the war, would have been lost.

Daniel Butterfield came off only marginally better than Sickles. Equally loose with the truth, he lacked Sickles's lawyerly skills. Butterfield was at best a mediocre officer and an incompetent chief of staff. After Gettysburg he went

5. *OR*, vol. 27, pt. 1, p. 92.

west with Hooker and commanded a division in the Twentieth Corps for only six weeks before becoming ill; he never again served in the field. In his testimony before the committee, Butterfield presented himself as a staff officer just doing his job. But this bland persona is belied by his actions in going absent without leave from the army to testify against Meade, as well as by his testimony itself. His reciprocated dislike of Meade (who was not an easy man to befriend in any case) and his anger over being bumped from command of the Fifth Corps spurred the resentment that he vented during the hearings. Although his frustration was understandable, Butterfield's disloyalty to his commanding officer revealed his true character. In his testimony, he had no greater purpose in mind than striking back at Meade and helping his friends Joe Hooker and Dan Sickles.

DID THE COMMITTEE PROVE ITS CASE AGAINST MEADE?

As chairman of the committee, Wade's most potent weapon was his report summarizing the hearings, which gave him the opportunity to present the testimony in a manner most favorable to his own ends. Wade did not specifically state any of the charges against Meade, relying instead on a carefully worded narrative of events supported by selective quotes to make his points. From the outset, Wade gave short shrift to Meade's side of the story. In reviewing Wade's summary, testimony from the transcripts and other facts that were known to Wade will be presented in Meade's defense.

1) *Meade had no plans of his own, merely following the plans developed by Hooker. Meade did not choose the field at Gettysburg, letting others make that decision, and once there had wanted to retreat.*

Wade opened his report with an attempt to establish that Meade deserved no credit for the battle at Gettysburg. He did not plan the movements leading to Gettysburg and he did not choose the battlefield; in effect, he was merely along for the ride. Even worse, he had wanted to retreat once the fight had begun. The inference is that Meade's reputation as a successful general—and consequently his right to command the army—was in fact the result of the others' efforts, which Meade simply capitalized on. These charges had begun circulating within a few months of Gettysburg, doubtless with the energetic assistance of Dan Sickles. As early as December 1863, Meade heard such rumors, commenting wryly, "I suppose after awhile it will be discovered I was not at Gettysburg at all."[6]

In the opening sentence of his report, Wade wrote that Meade's assumption of command "seems to have been attended by no immediate changes" except for the addition of troops and powers of command not granted to Hooker. Wade also noted that Hooker's "plans and views" were fully disclosed to Meade by Butterfield, who continued to act as Meade's chief of staff. The only evidence Wade provided for these assertions was a quote from Warren's testimony that the "troops continued to move on just the same as if the command had not been changed."[7]

Wade presented these statements as generally agreed-upon facts that required no further discussion, but that was not the case. Meade did receive troops denied or not offered to Hooker—the garrison at Harpers Ferry—but Hooker's request for those troops had been decidedly impolitic. His first request for the Harpers Ferry garrison was couched as a demand, which was not likely to be viewed favorably by his superior, Halleck. When his request was denied, Hooker then tried to go over Halleck's head to Lincoln and Stanton. While a professional such as Halleck might not have allowed such petty annoyances to dictate his decisions, they would certainly have affected the degree of his cooperation.[8]

Meade, on the other hand, had command over the garrison at Harpers Ferry specifically included in his orders, but he was still unsure what he could do with it. On June 28 he was told that he could "diminish or increase it as you think the circumstances justify." The next morning Meade notified Halleck, "I have ordered the abandonment of Harpers Ferry." Two things differentiated the situations under Hooker and Meade. First, Meade was careful to explain why he abandoned the post and what he was going to do with the troops. Secondly, the administration was gradually unfettering its commanders from the chains of micromanagement with which it had previously bound them. Hooker had lost the confidence of the administration and would not benefit from the liberalization of oversight. In the culmination of this trend, Grant would receive virtual carte blanche.[9]

Wade made the point that Meade was fully aware of Hooker's plans, insin-

6. *LLM,* to his wife, December 7, 1863, 2:160.

7. *CCW,* lv.

8. *OR,* vol. 27, pt. 1, p. 60.

9. Ibid., 62–3, 66–7.

uating that Meade merely completed a campaign mapped out by Hooker. It is difficult to ascertain what specific plans, if any, Hooker may have had. On June 24 he wrote to Halleck of moving to sever Ewell's corps, north of the Potomac, from the rest of Lee's army. Not certain if Ewell's advance comprised a raid or an invasion, Hooker proposed that if it was merely a raid, he would strike south towards Lee's line of communication in the direction of Richmond. If it was an actual invasion, he would follow Lee's army north. While Hooker had the seed of an idea, it never blossomed into anything and had already been overtaken by events.[10]

If Hooker had a more concrete plan, Meade did not know it. As he testified before the committee, "I received from him [Hooker] no intimation of any plan, or any views that he may have had up to that moment. And I am not aware that he had any." Meade, however, quickly notified Halleck of his own intentions, providing him with a general plan at 7 A.M. on June 28 (after his meeting with Hooker). By 11 A.M. on June 29 Meade's plan had evolved to encompass specific troop movements.[11]

The charge that Meade did not pick the battlefield at Gettysburg was closely related to the accusation that he had no strategic plans of his own. As Wade pointed out, choosing one's ground was always an important consideration because it could play a major role in the outcome of a battle. Wade credited Pleasonton for choosing the field, although others (including Sickles) claimed the honor. Wade probably took Pleasonton at his word about his visits to the area, which was simply not true. Pleasonton also falsely claimed that in anticipation of the coming battle, he had sent his strongest division to Gettysburg. Yet Pleasonton's battle report listed Buford's assignment as "to cover and protect the line of march" of the army. It also revealed that only two brigades, the First and Second, were even sent in the general direction of Gettysburg—not, as Wade wrote in his report, the whole division.[12]

Wade could have easily checked Pleasonton's claim to have anticipated the fight at Gettysburg by reading his battle report. Apparently he did not. Throughout the hearings, Wade (and other members of the committee) failed to verify or follow up on even the most ridiculous claims by witnesses. This lackadaisical approach, while giving new meaning to the term "investigate," allowed the members of the committee to pick and choose what they wanted to believe, in effect creating their own facts.

10. *CCW,* lv; *OR,* vol. 27, pt. 1, pp. 55–6.

11. *CCW,* 329; *OR,* vol. 27, pt. 1, pp. 61–2, 66–7.

12. *CCW,* lv; *OR,* vol. 27, pt. 1, pp. 913–8.

The most damaging part of the charge against Meade was that he considered abandoning his position and retreating on the morning of July 2. Wade's summary of the first day's action suggested a drawn battle, ending with the Union forces' orderly withdrawal through the town to take up new positions on Cemetery Ridge. Under such circumstances any decision to withdraw from the field would have revealed an unwillingness to fight. The importance of the charge is suggested by the fact that five full pages of the twenty-two-page report were devoted to a discussion of it. As Wade pointed out in a classic understatement, however, "there is some controversy on that point."[13]

Citing the testimony of eight witnesses—four supporting Meade, four opposed to him—Wade devoted nearly two pages to a discussion of the alleged plan to retreat on July 2. Wade began with Butterfield's unequivocal statement that Meade had him prepare an order to withdraw. Butterfield related that he told Meade that if the order was to be carried out, others should review it for accuracy and clarity, to which Meade had no objection. After having the order read over by others, Butterfield testified, he had prepared copies of the order while the corps commanders were summoned. Before the last of them—Sickles—arrived, fighting broke out and the meeting was canceled. Butterfield plainly implied that the beginning of Longstreet's attack on July 2 interrupted Meade's plan to retreat.[14]

Butterfield's testimony was by far the most damaging to Meade. As chief of staff, Butterfield was in a better position than anyone to know exactly what was going on at headquarters. He established the existence, at least temporarily, of an order to retreat. Wade's summary of his testimony was designed to leave the impression that the retreat order would be issued during the meeting of the corps commanders (which is probably the impression that Butterfield wanted to leave as well). Yet Wade skipped over the next question in Butterfield's testimony: "Did this collision of General Sickle's corps with the enemy prevent the order [to retreat] being executed which you had prepared?" This question went straight to the heart of the matter and should have been included in the report, but it was not. Equally important, and equally ignored, was Butterfield's answer: "It is impossible for me to state that, because General Meade had not communicated to me his intention to execute that order regardless of the opinion of the corps commanders, or whether he intended to have the order submitted to them. . . . It is for him to say whether he intended

13. *CCW*, lxi–lxvi, lxi.

14. Ibid., lxi–lxii.

to execute it or not. *He may have desired it prepared for an emergency* [emphasis added], without any view of executing it then, or he may have had it prepared with a full view of its execution." In light of Meade's testimony that if such an order was prepared it was only to meet possible contingencies, this statement completely undermines the rest of Butterfield's testimony.[15]

Wade next turned to Seth Williams's testimony. Williams confirmed that a retreat order was prepared but described it as "looking to a contingency which possibly might happen." Furthermore, he had "no reason to suppose . . . General Meade had any knowledge of it." Nevertheless, Williams corroborated Butterfield's evidence that such an order existed at one time. Wade also mentioned Sickles in support of this charge, though his relevant testimony is distilled to only one sentence in the report. This is likely because Sickles had only vague knowledge on this point, and he contradicted Butterfield in various details.[16]

Howe, a division commander, was quoted more extensively. Up to this point, the report had concentrated on the specific retreat order that had been prepared on the morning of July 2. Howe's testimony changed the focus to that evening's council. Howe testified that Sedgwick—his Sixth Corps commander—had told him that "they" discussed whether to retreat or not, and that Sedgwick seemed to believe they would retreat.[17]

By citing Howe's testimony, Wade attempted to show that in addition to the retreat order that had been drafted in the morning, Meade's evening council had also discussed a withdrawal. But this assertion is problematic: Howe's testimony, like Sickles's, was nothing more than hearsay and should be judged accordingly. There are other problems with it as well. Howe placed the time of the conversation with Sedgwick at dusk, about 7:30 P.M. on July 2. Yet Meade did not summon his corps commanders to the council until after dark, when the fighting had died down. Given the distances involved and the pressing matters facing the corps commanders at the end of the day's fighting, it is doubtful that the council could have convened much before 9:00 P.M.[18]

The "they" Howe referred to presents another problem. If he meant to refer to the July 2 council, his conversation with Sedgwick must have been at a later time than he recalled. If so, the decision had already been made, and why

15. Ibid., 425, 436.

16. Ibid., lxii–lxiii.

17. Ibid., lxiv.

18. Nofi, *Gettysburg Campaign, June–July 1863*, 169; Gibbon, "The Council of War on the Second Day," *B&L*, 3:313.

would Sedgwick have reported that "they" were still discussing a retreat? If Howe correctly remembered the time of the conversation, the council had not yet convened and there would have been no way to know what would be discussed. Sedgwick was not asked about this conversation with Howe; such omissions were not unusual in the hearings. Given Sedgwick's testimony about the council, Wade's failure to include it in his report is not unexpected either. When asked about the council Sedgwick said that the "question submitted, I believe, was, whether we should attack the enemy, or wait in position and receive an attack. The decision was pretty much unanimous that we should receive the attack."[19]

A third possibility is that Sedgwick's "they"referred to Meade and members of his staff. According to Sedgwick's own testimony, he arrived on the field about 2:00 P.M. and went to Meade's headquarters for orders. Not finding Meade there—the general had gone to Sickles's Third Corps line—Sedgwick had waited for him. Upon Meade's return, they discussed Sickles's line, Sedgwick received his orders, and he left. In his testimony, Sedgwick made no mention of a contemplated retreat, and he had no other opportunity during the day to know what was being discussed at headquarters.[20]

In its presentation of Meade's side of the story, the report is as evenhanded as it ever gets. Wade cited the testimony of Meade, Gibbon, Hunt, and Sedgwick as representative of Meade's defense. Wade noted that Meade's denial of ever having given or even considered a retreat order was "very emphatic." ("Indignant" might have been closer to the mark; recall that Meade declared, "I utterly deny, under the full solemnity and sanctity of my oath, and in the firm conviction that the day will come when the secrets of all men shall be made known" that he ever considered such an order.) Of course, Meade did not have to rely on his reputation for honesty as his sole defense. As Meade pointed out in his first appearance before the committee, it made no sense to mass his army for battle, only to order a retreat without being forced to do so by the enemy.[21]

As Wade noted, Meade offered the committee the names of three men—Generals Hunt, Ingalls, and Warren—as officers "whose positions were as near and confidential to me as that of General Butterfield, who, if I had any such intention, or had given any such orders as he said I gave, would have been par-

19. *LLM,* 2:96; *CCW,* 460.

20. Ibid.

21. Ibid., lxiv, 349, 436.

ties to it, would have known it, and have made arrangements in consequence thereof." Ingalls, the quartermaster general of the Army of the Potomac, would have been a valuable witness on this point because his massive trains would have been one of the first things to move, but he was not called before the committee.[22]

Wade cited part of Gibbon's testimony to show a morning retreat order was prepared, but it shreds the notion that Meade intended to issue the order, even calling into question Meade's knowledge of its existence. As Gibbon testified, when shown the order at headquarters on the morning of July 2 he responded, "'Great God! General Meade does not intend to leave this position?' General Butterfield did not say General Meade did intend to leave; he merely said something to the effect that it was necessary to be prepared in case it should be necessary to leave, or some remark of that kind." Wade also cited another potshot at Butterfield from Gibbon's testimony, "Being firmly convinced, as I was at the time, that General Meade had no idea of falling back from the position there, it struck me as very remarkable that his chief of staff should be making such an order to retreat; and I still think so."[23]

The inclusion of Hunt's testimony about the morning retreat order seems a little surprising. Hunt was questioned by neither Wade nor Chandler, but by Daniel Gooch. Gooch was no friend of the administration or the military leadership, but his style of questioning lacked Wade's aggressiveness. It should be remembered here that Wade wanted not only to demonstrate the existence of the retreat order, but to prove that Meade had intended to issue it and would have done so but for Longstreet's attack.

Hunt replied emphatically to Gooch's question about the preparation of an order to retreat: "I know of no such order and no such intention." Pointedly Hunt noted that if a retreat had been considered, "I should have known of it as soon as anybody, as the first thing to have been done was to get rid of the large reserve artillery and ammunition train under my charge, and which had been brought up on the morning of the 2d of July, under, or by the direction of, General Meade." But if Gooch lacked Wade's inquisitorial skill, he nonetheless was able to elicit potentially damaging testimony. He rephrased and repeated the question: did Hunt have any knowledge or intimation of any retreat order during the battle? Here, Gooch made his point, eliciting from Hunt the testimony that Wade used in his report, "The only time I ever had a thought such

22. Ibid., lxv.
23. Ibid., lxiii.

an idea might be entertained was on the night of the 2d of July. . . . On arriving at headquarters I understood that the question had been spoken of as to what they should do, and there was no person at all in favor of leaving the ground we had taken; that was just as the conversation closed." (In the report, there are two transcription errors in this quotation. The last part of the sentence should read, "of leaving the ground we had *then;* that was just as the *consultation* closed.") Hunt thus corroborated Howe's testimony that a retreat had been considered. Although Hunt believed that the council was unanimous in its decision not to retreat, other witnesses saw no such solidarity of opinion.[24]

Wade skillfully edited Hunt's testimony at this point. Hunt went on to say, "Just about daylight on the 2d of July General Meade ordered the reserve artillery brought up. I sent my aid[e] for it, and it came up about 8 o'clock in the morning, I think; so that at that time there could have been no question of leaving." Had this portion of Hunt's testimony been included in the report, it would have substantially bolstered Meade's claim that he had had no plans or thoughts of a withdrawal.[25]

Wade also included a part of Sedgwick's testimony in Meade's defense. Gooch asked Sedgwick if he knew about the preparation of any order to retreat during the battle. Sedgwick replied positively that he had never heard of any such order during Gettysburg and that, as second in command, he would have been told if Meade had considered an order to retreat. It is somewhat surprising that Wade cited a second question and answer from Sedgwick's testimony, since it provided additional support to Meade's defense. In a follow-up to Gooch's question, Moses Odell asked whether, if it had been Meade's intention to retreat, his orders for Sedgwick's corps were in conflict with such a plan. "It certainly was," replied Sedgwick, adding that he had received at least three messages to hurry his corps up.[26]

Meade's suggestion of calling Warren to corroborate his testimony on the retreat question was of no value. Although Warren did testify, he was not asked about the morning retreat order, and he had slept through the July 2 council meeting.[27]

In his testimony, Meade alluded to dispatches and orders issued on July 2, but these documents did not appear in the report. Meade's first appearance

24. Ibid., lxvi, 452.
25. Ibid.
26. Ibid., lxvi.
27. Ibid., 379.

before the committee had caught him unprepared, and he had to speak without the benefit of reviewing his files or bringing any documents with him. His second appearance, however, came ten days later, after Butterfield testified. Meade was aware of the contents of Butterfield's testimony, and he came prepared with copies of dispatches and orders to lay before the committee. In an effort to quash the charge that he had intended to retreat on July 2, Meade offered as evidence two dispatches to Slocum, who commanded the Twelfth Corps. The first, timed 9:30 A.M., asked Slocum's opinion about launching an attack in his area. The second, signed by Butterfield, directed the attack to be carried out as soon as the Sixth Corps arrived to join the Twelfth. It is particularly noteworthy that Butterfield signed the second dispatch, since it proves that he knew that Meade planned to take offensive action. Meade could not attack and withdraw at the same time.[28]

The attack did not take place, however. Both Slocum and Warren (who had been sent to examine the area) felt that the ground was not favorable for an attack by either side, and, in fact, it was not. Did Meade change his mind and determine to retreat after learning this? The documentary evidence introduced by Meade showed that he did not. Longstreet's attack, which interrupted the meeting of the corps commanders (and when, according to Butterfield, the retreat order would be issued), did not occur until late afternoon. In a telegram to Halleck timed 3:00 P.M., Meade briefly reviewed the day's events and stated that he had delayed his attack in order to await the arrival of the Sixth Corps and others. He had also sent his trains to the rear of his main battle line, a necessary first step in preparing for battle, to get them safely out of the way. Sending the trains to the rear would have also been the first step in a retreat; but by holding them near at hand, it is plain that Meade had no intention of retreating, as his dispatches and other evidence reveal.[29]

Wade also quoted Meade's attempt to explain how Butterfield might have come up with the idea of a retreat. Meade said that he had told Butterfield to make himself familiar with the roads in the area and the locations of the various corps and their trains. "It was," testified Meade, "in anticipation of possible contingencies," not to prepare for a retreat. In support of this contention Meade produced another document, timed "supposed about 10 A.M.," assigning staff officers from the various corps to essentially the same task.[30]

28. Ibid., lxv, 437.

29. Ibid., 437–9.

30. Ibid., lxv, 438.

This was Wade's case concerning the July 2 retreat order. Did he prove the charge? Wade did demonstrate beyond a doubt that such an order was produced. But was it meant to be issued or was it merely a contingency plan? In fact, did Meade even know of its existence at the time? Though this charge originated with Sickles, his testimony was only lightly touched upon. Wade's only credible witness on this point was Butterfield. Yet, as Wade acknowledged in his report, Butterfield could not state with absolute certainty that Meade intended to issue the order.

This section of the charge is thus plainly refuted by both testimony and documents found in the transcripts. Butterfield undermined his own testimony by volunteering that he did not know whether or not the order was to be issued and acknowledging that it could have been part of a contingency plan. Wade's report was severely weakened by its reliance on hearsay and on the recollections of a disgruntled witness. Meade was able to produce more witnesses, as well as documentary evidence, in support of his position.

Wade still had one more chance to prove that Meade had wanted to retreat at Gettysburg. He hoped to show that the general had urged a withdrawal at the July 2 council, and would have done so except for the objections of his corps commanders. Once again, this accusation originated with Sickles; in his testimony, Sickles had claimed, "I have reason to know that his [Meade's] plan of operations was changed again on Thursday [July 2], and that he resumed, in substance, the plan that he had on Wednesday morning, which was to fall back to Pipe creek, or to some place in that neighborhood." Wade did not follow up on this statement during the hearings, and Sickles never produced any tangible evidence for his belief.[31]

Wade began this part of the report by citing Meade's testimony about the questions covered at the meeting. "First, whether it was necessary for us to assume any different position from what we then held; and, secondly, whether, if we continued to maintain the position we then held, our operations of the next day should be offensive or defensive. The opinion of the council was unanimous, which agreed fully with my own views that we should maintain our lines as they were then held, and that we should wait the movements of the enemy, and see if he made any further attack before we assumed the offensive," Meade testified. Meade himself had asked whether the army should abandon its position; it was the corps commanders who had decided to fight. Once the council's opinion was known, Meade could not or would not admit

31. Ibid., 299–300.

of any disagreement with it. Wade surely hoped that Meade's testimony would be read in such a light.[32]

Wade then cited the testimony of Butterfield, who had kept minutes of the meeting (although the minutes, Williams later testified, had unfortunately been lost). "The general question put to the corps commanders present at that council was, whether our army should remain on that field and continue the battle, or whether we should change to some other position. . . . a majority were in favor of remaining on the field and fighting it out. . . . After the council had finished, General Meade arose from the table, and remarked that, in his opinion, Gettysburg was no place to fight a battle; but it was settled to remain there."[33]

Wade also drew on the testimony of Birney, who said that the council was divided but that a majority favored staying. Birney had had more to say on the matter, but Wade oddly chose not to use it. According to Birney, Meade had stated that he did not want to fight unless he was certain of victory and that he would leave the decision up to the corps commanders.[34]

Butterfield's minutes could have supplied hard evidence—something notably missing in Wade's report—about the July 2 council; but, like the retreat order, the minutes were missing. The last person to have had both documents had been Seth Williams, Meade's assistant adjutant general. Was this more than just coincidence? Wade and Butterfield might well have thought so. In fact, the retreat order, never having been issued, would quickly have been discarded as a matter of course. The history of Butterfield's minutes is more curious. In 1881, nine years after Meade's death and eighteen years after the battle of Gettysburg, John Gibbon, who had commanded the Second Division, Second Corps in that battle, met with Meade's son George in Philadelphia. George Meade showed Gibbon the original minutes of the council on July 2, which had been found among Meade's personal effects after his death. Neither Gibbon nor George Meade ever revealed how the minutes came into Meade's possession, although Gibbon later published them.[35]

In his report Wade made no explicit defense of Meade, although he did cite Meade's testimony about the council. There certainly was a defense to be made. During the hearings four other officers were directly asked about the July 2 council: Gibbon, Hancock, Hunt, and Sedgwick. Gibbon testified, "I do

32. Ibid., lxvi–lxvii.

33. Ibid., lxvii.

34. Ibid., 368.

35. Gibbon, *Recollections,* 142.

not recollect that General Meade said much upon the subject during the council. He appeared to me to be waiting to listen to the reports and opinions of his corps commanders. I do not recollect having heard him express a decided opinion one way or the other. I certainly did not hear him express any preference for retreating." He also stated that Butterfield wrote down the questions to be considered by the council at the direction of Meade. Yet Gibbon later changed his story. In an article in *Battles and Leaders of the Civil War* and also in his memoirs, *Personal Recollections of the Civil War,* Gibbon asserted that the council questions were written out at Butterfield's suggestion. In light of Meade's belief that Butterfield had "from the time I assumed command, to treasure up incidents, remarks and papers to pervert and distort in the future to my injury," this is a change worthy of note.[36]

Of the three other officers who were asked specifically about the council on the night of July 2, Hancock testified that Butterfield had put the questions, and the decision to stay and fight had been unanimous. Hunt, who arrived after the meeting had ended, understood that the question of retreat had been discussed, but that "there was no person at all in favor of leaving the ground we had then." Sedgwick remembered the question as being whether they should attack or wait for the enemy's attack, but said that it was "pretty much unanimous that we should receive the attack." None of these officers nor Meade recalled a split over the decision to stay and fight, as Butterfield and Birney had testified.[37]

In his report Wade cited Butterfield's attribution to Meade the comment that Gettysburg was no place to fight a battle. But did Meade say this? Other than Butterfield's own testimony, no evidence exists to support it. There is, however, an interesting refutation. Gibbon testified that Meade had summed up the vote with, "That, then, is the decision." In his later writings Gibbon identified Major General John Newton, then commanding the First Corps, as saying, "this is no place to fight a battle" in reference to "some minor details of the line."[38]

Meade was aware of newspaper reports that he had favored a retreat from Gettysburg, and on March 10, 1864, he sent a circular letter to Generals Newton, Sedgwick, Slocum, Sykes, and Adolphus Williams, asking for a statement about that night's events and whether he had favored a retreat. Though Slo-

36. *CCW,* 442–3; *B&L,* 3:313, Gibbon, *Recollections,* 141; *LLM,* to his wife, March 20, 1864, 2:181.

37. *CCW,* 407, 452, 460.

38. Ibid., 442; Gibbon, *Recollections,* 313; *B&L,* 3:141.

cum claimed never to have gotten the letter, all others sent replies supporting Meade. Newton, Sedgwick, and Sykes were still with the Army of the Potomac, and Meade would have had their answers before he testified for the second time on April 4.[39]

Meade's March 10 circular reveals his lack of legal knowledge or advice of legal counsel. In it, he asked if at any time he had "insisted" on a withdrawal. However, that was not the point Wade would try to make. Wade wanted to demonstrate that Meade had wanted to retreat but was dissuaded from doing so by his corps commanders. Had Meade "insisted" on a retreat, it would have been an order; while his corps commanders might have argued with him, it is unlikely that they would have changed his mind. None of Meade's respondents remembered him "insisting" on a withdrawal, but had he introduced the letters into his testimony, Wade would have been able to rip them apart and perhaps even use them against Meade. Possibly someone pointed out this potential problem to Meade, which would explain why he did not use the letters.[40]

In sum, the weight of the evidence does not support the charge. Gibbon's post–Civil War writings on the July 2 council, which are generally accepted as the best account of it, add further support to Meade's defense. The first charge, except for a few minor and debatable points, is thoroughly refuted. In particular, there is no credible proof that Meade ever considered retreating from Gettysburg, except as a possible contingency.

2) *Meade failed to follow up the rebel army after its defeat at Gettysburg in a timely manner.*

The final three charges addressed Meade's ability as a general and questioned his willingness to fight. Was Meade's heart in the struggle to save the Union or was he, like McClellan and others, in favor of a reconciliation on terms more favorable to the South than the committee sought?

Wade established the background by reviewing the condition of the army at the close of the battle. The three days of the battle, he noted, had been "comparatively days of rest" for most of the troops involved. While the Army of the Potomac had suffered heavy casualties, the enemy had been even harder hit; moreover, Wade argued, the Union army had much higher morale. Division

39. *OR,* vol. 27, pt. 1, pp. 123–7, 139; *LLM,* 2: 414, 418–9.
40. *OR,* vol. 27, pt. 1, p. 123.

commander Albion Howe was the source of this dubious contention. Howe's division was relegated to minor operations of the battle; in comparison to other fights Howe had been in, Gettysburg might have seemed fairly easy duty. The Sixth Corps, to which Howe belonged, was the largest in the army and suffered the fewest casualties, only some 242 total. Howe's division, the smallest in the corps, reported the lowest casualty figure for the battle, sixteen.[41]

Wade continued with Howe's observations that the position did the fighting for them, that no great generalship was involved (or even needed), and that at the end of the battle "our men were not much jaded or fatigued, but had plenty of fight in them, and were comparatively fresh." Wade's report thus depicted a battle that practically any junior officer could have won and an army ready to march to Richmond on the heels of a defeated and demoralized enemy.[42]

Why did Wade rely on Howe's testimony? Four corps commanders and the commander of the army himself—all in a better position to summarize the battle than a division commander—had testified before the committee. The testimony of nine other troop commanders, the artillery chief, and the head of the cavalry was also available. Yet Wade turned to Howe's account. This was because Howe's testimony undermined Meade's reputation as the victor of Gettysburg, the greatest battle of the war. If it could be proved that Gettysburg had virtually fought itself and that Meade had no real impact on the battle, the task of removing him from command became easier. There is little question that Wade intentionally painted a false picture of Gettysburg, and Howe's testimony fit his agenda perfectly.

Wade's report next considered the Union pursuit from Gettysburg. In his discussion of the reasons for the slowness of the pursuit, Wade cited Meade's testimony to the effect that even on July 5, Meade was not certain whether or not the Army of Northern Virginia was headed for the Potomac and that he was unaware of the damage he had inflicted on the rebels. Wade also cited Warren's comment that the "prominent officers" felt that they had done enough just by winning the battle. In their view, to try for a more complete victory by following Lee could have jeopardized all that they had accomplished.[43]

Wade was playing very loose with the truth here. His summary of events

41. *CCW*, lxix; Busey and Martin, *Regimental Strengths and Losses*, 270, 272.

42. *CCW*, lxix.

43. Ibid.

was designed to give the impression that Lee had begun his retreat on July 4 and Meade should have begun his pursuit then. But that was not the case, as Meade—and Wade himself—knew. In his first appearance before the committee, Meade testified that on July 4 Ewell's Confederate Second Corps had disappeared from the Union right. Sending out reconnaissance, Meade had found that the rebels had not gone far and were in a position along Seminary Ridge, "parallel to my left and left center."[44]

Wade was right in that on July 5 Meade was not "satisfied that he [Lee] was in full retreat for the Potomac." The notion that Meade believed Lee might not be withdrawing completely from the Gettysburg area does not reflect the actual testimony. Meade was aware of Lee's withdrawal from his front, but this had created new concerns. Meade testified that he thought that Lee was withdrawing into the Cumberland Valley, across the mountains, but was uncertain what he would do after that. From Meade's perspective Lee had several options available to him: he could make a stand in the mountain passes; he could continue his move north using the mountains for a screen; he could move south along the mountains until appearing out of one of the numerous gaps to turn Meade's flank; or he could retreat back across the Potomac. On July 5 all of these options had seemed possible.[45]

Wade's report also accurately noted that Meade was unaware of the damage he had done to Lee's army. It seems somewhat odd that Wade ignored the rest of Meade's answer, in which he said, "although satisfied that I had punished him very severely." This was a natural opening for Wade to ask why, if Meade felt that he had inflicted very severe losses on the enemy, he was not more aggressive in his pursuit. The fact that on July 5 Meade was not aware of how badly he may have hurt the rebels is hardly surprising; he would not yet have known his own losses with certainty. Moreover, contemporary estimates had placed Lee's force at upwards of 100,000 men. Even the loss of 25,000 to 30,000 troops would have left Lee with an army approximately equal to Meade's available troops on July 5.[46]

Wade scored some points with Warren's comment on the attitudes of the senior officers. A sense of satisfaction with what they had accomplished so far was natural, but was a fear of jeopardizing their gains by further action justified? In hindsight it would seem not, but they had to make decisions based on available information. Their hesitancy under the circumstances is quite un-

44. Ibid., 333–4.
45. Ibid., 334.
46. Ibid.

derstandable. Intelligence reported that Lee's army at least equaled the Army of the Potomac in numbers. The rebels would now be fighting on the defensive, probably on a field of their own choosing and most likely from prepared positions. Meade's concern about a Pickett's charge in reverse was entirely justified, and the corps commanders saw this as easily as he did. Warren was a blunt man, and although his testimony generally favored Meade, it could and did cut both ways.

Wade commented that "all the witnesses but General Meade" testified that it was obvious that Lee was in full retreat on the morning of July 4. Yet that was not the case. Lee's trains, the first to withdraw, did not leave the Gettysburg area until around 4:00 P.M. under the command of Brigadier General John Imboden. The infantry, accompanied by most of the artillery, did not begin to leave until late that night. Throughout the day of July 4, the Army of Northern Virginia instead waited across the valley for Meade's expected attack. As yet more evidence of Meade's lack of aggressiveness, Wade's statement was damaging. Again, however, Wade's version of the evidence was at odds with the truth. Fifteen witnesses, excluding Meade, testified before the committee. Four—Sickles, Doubleday, Gibbon, and Hancock—either had not been present for the enemy's retreat or were not asked about it in the hearings. Butterfield and Warren both testified that they did not know when Lee's army retreated. Generals Birney, Hunt, Sedgwick, Williams, and Crawford correctly placed the time of the retreat as the night of July 4 or the day of July 5. Humphreys was asked if the rebels had retreated on July 3, and he answered in the negative. Only three witnesses—Howe, Pleasonton, and Wadsworth—thought the enemy was retreating on July 4.[47]

Wade quickly moved on to argue that some of Meade's generals had wanted to attack, even if Meade had not. The report cited Birney's testimony that he had wanted to attack an enemy column but had received a written order from Meade not to do so. Wade did not mention that this incident occurred on July 5. Birney's testimony has problems of its own. In his battle report Birney makes no mention of his desire to attack, and there are no copies of a written order telling him not to attack. In fact, Birney's report basically ends on July 2, when he returned to command of his division. Nor do any reports from his brigade or regimental commanders corroborate his testimony. In short, Birney's story is totally unsubstantiated.[48]

47. John D. Imboden, "The Confederate Retreat from Gettysburg," *B&L,* 3:423; *CCW,* 314, 360, 369, 379, 394, 408, 417, 433, 444, 454, 460, 466, 471.

48. *CCW,* 368; *OR,* vol. 27, pt. 1, pp. 482–8, 493–5, 514–6, 529–37.

Wade also cited the testimony of Pleasonton, who claimed that by 8:00 A.M. on July 4, Brigadier General David Gregg, commanding the Second Cavalry Division, reported that he had ridden twenty-two miles on the Chambersburg road and had found many signs of the enemy retreating in panic. Pleasonton testified that he had reported Gregg's findings to Meade. It should come as no surprise that Pleasonton's version of events is not accurate. Gregg's battle report states that on the morning of July 4, he moved a portion of his division (Colonel J. Irvin Gregg's brigade) out on a reconnaissance toward Hunterstown, which was east of Gettysburg, not west toward Lee. Gregg's brigade did not join the pursuit until July 5. Colonel John McIntosh's brigade, the only other brigade in the division, spent July 4 observing the enemy from a position on the extreme left of the army. He also reported joining the pursuit on July 5.[49]

Pleasonton's testimony allowed Wade to assert in his report that nothing was done with Gregg's information and "no pursuit was ordered." But Lee was not in retreat on July 4 and Gregg's division was not in pursuit. Meade's own testimony was that he sent the cavalry out on July 5, but this contradiction of Pleasonton's testimony was not reported by Wade.[50]

Wade's case regarding a timely pursuit was ultimately undercut by his own report when he stated that on the "5th of July the 6th corps commenced to follow the enemy." Though it is debatable whether the movement of the Sixth Corps was actually a pursuit or a reconnaissance, Meade could not have moved any faster.[51]

3) *With Lee and his army trapped against the Potomac, Meade failed to attack and destroy him.*

In the Meade hearings, Wade made a tactical error by concentrating on Lee's withdrawal from Gettysburg before addressing the issue of Lee's escape across the Potomac. Meade was particularly vulnerable to criticism about his pursuit of Lee and was roundly criticized by nearly everyone, in and out of the army, for his failure to bring Lee to battle before his arrival at Williamsport. Wade most likely realized, however, that this issue was not amenable to the committee's purposes. A tedious recital of the details of military logistics—the lack of shoes for soldiers, the lack of fodder for horses, the long, exhaust-

49. *CCW,* lxix; *OR,* vol. 27, pt. 1, pp. 957, 977.
50. *CCW,* lxix, 334.
51. Ibid, lxxi.

ing marches over muddy roads—lacked glamor, and had few political implications.[52]

Meade's slow pursuit of Lee's army after Gettysburg diminished the luster of his victory, but Lee's escape at Williamsport entirely overshadowed it. As the committee saw it, Lee's badly beaten and demoralized army was short of ammunition and trapped against a swollen, unfordable river, just waiting to be captured or destroyed. Meanwhile, the Army of the Potomac—flush with victory, well rested, and heavily reinforced—had strolled through the countryside, avoiding any major contact with the enemy, in an effort simply to herd them back across the Potomac. Presented with a golden opportunity to crush Lee and end the war, Meade had fumbled it away.

The charge seems almost to prove itself. Lee was trapped against the Potomac, Meade did not bring him to battle, and the Army of Northern Virginia safely recrossed the river. It is all so obvious, in fact, that Wade devoted little more than a page to it in his report. He began by citing Warren's testimony, which gave the movements of Meade's headquarters and Warren's opinion that "we should have fought the enemy the next morning, July 12," the day before Lee slipped back across the river. As Wade pointedly noted, "no attack was ordered." Instead, Meade held yet another council, asking his corps commanders what to do.[53]

In the report, Meade's testimony about the council, not surprisingly, did not show him in a particularly favorable light. He stated that the rebels held a very strong position and were ready to fight but declared his desire to attack. Meade also admitted that he did not know the ground, had not had time to make any reconnaissance, and did not know exactly how or where to attack. Nonetheless, he was ready to charge ahead.[54]

Was Meade, as Wade seemed to want to suggest, so stupid or bad a general that he would launch an ill-planned attack, only being saved from such a blunder by his corps commanders? No. Meade gave the committee his reasons for wanting to attack, despite the less than ideal circumstances. He was extremely aware of the importance of not letting Lee escape without another battle, and Williamsport was his last chance. At the same time he appreciated the fact that in case of a Union defeat, "the whole question would be reversed, the road to Washington and to the north open, and all the fruits of my victory at Gettysburg dissipated."[55]

52. For a detailed description of Meade's pursuit and the problems he faced, see *GC*, 544–65.

53. *CCW*, lxxii–lxxiii.

54. Ibid., lxxii.

55. Ibid., 336.

Was Meade so desperate to stop Lee that he would blunder forward unprepared? Again the answer is no. That Meade came off so poorly on this point was in large part his own fault. Meade did not remember, or at least he did not mention to the committee, a July 12 conversation with Humphreys, by this time his chief of staff, in which an attack was discussed in detail. Meade planned to advance the army, probing Lee's line and developing an attack at its weakest points. In other words, as Humphreys testified, Meade intended a "reconnaissance in force, as it is called, to be converted into an attack." Yet even had Meade mentioned this plan, it is doubtful that Wade would have included it in the report, just as he did not include Humphreys's testimony on this point. Although only Humphreys testified directly to Meade's plan, there were other indications that Meade planned an attack for July 13. In a telegram to Halleck timed 4:30 P.M. on July 12, preceding that night's council, Meade wrote that he intended to attack the next day. His telegram did not give any details of the impending assault, but his intention was clear.[56]

Wade's report next considered the council held on the night of July 12. In addition to Meade, only three generals—Howard, Pleasonton, and Wadsworth—favored an attack. With the council divided but with a majority adamant in opposition, Meade postponed an attack until July 14. Then, of course, it was discovered that Lee had slipped away the night before.[57]

In the report, Wade made little of the July 12 council, despite—or perhaps because—of the fact that some of the testimony contained valuable insights into the decision not to attack. For example, Warren testified that the attack was voted down because the corps commanders "considered the enemy's positions and intrenchments were too strong to carry, and they quoted such instances as the first battle of Fredericksburg, and our own repulse of the rebel forces at Malvern Hills and Gettysburg." In his testimony, Wadsworth pointed out, "It will be observed that four of the officers who opposed the attack were the ranking officers of the army, next to General Meade, and held, in every respect, the highest positions in the army." Sedgwick testified, "They occupied a very strong position there [at Williamsport]. I think they were at that time quite as strong as we were, for we had received no re-enforcements. . . . the enemy occupied too strong a position for General Meade to attack."[58]

Wade next used Meade's own words against him. In his first appearance before the committee, Meade had testified that an examination of Lee's aban-

56. Ibid., 396; *OR*, vol. 27, pt. 1, p. 91.

57. Newton, the corps commander, was ill. *CCW*, lxxii, 397.

58. Ibid., 381, 415, 462.

doned lines brought him "clearly to the opinion that an attack under the circumstances in which I had proposed to make it would have resulted disastrously to our arms." Using asterisks to indicate the omission of seemingly unimportant material, Wade gave the impression that Meade's statement continued with a comment on Lee's withdrawal. After considering the situation, Meade told the committee, he believed that the only reason Lee retreated was because he was afraid that his supply lines would be cut. It was this fear of isolation—not Meade and his army—that had caused Lee to retreat. Actually, the two statements were not related to each other at all. Meade's comment about Lee's withdrawal came three questions later in his testimony, in reply to an inquiry about rebel expenditure of small arms ammunition. Meade testified that Lee was not short of ammunition, as was generally supposed, because he was supplied from Winchester. Due to the strength of Lee's position, only the fear of being cut off from this base made him withdraw.[59]

Wade ended his discussion of this charge by noting that no other witness before the committee supported Meade's opinion that an attack would have resulted in disaster. He then listed five witnesses who believed that a Union attack would have captured or dispersed most of Lee's army: Pleasonton, whose cavalry troopers would not have been directly involved in the assault; Warren, who had no troop command; Birney, who was not at Williamsport; Doubleday, who also was not at Williamsport; and Howe, who from his testimony seemed to possess the vision of Napoleon. He had timed the rate of fire and duration of all the rebel barrages at Gettysburg and was sufficiently informed about Lee's transportation situation to know that the rebels' artillery ammunition was nearly exhausted. In Howe's opinion, with only a small fight the rebels would have been defeated and captured or killed. More significantly, Wade falsely claimed that Meade alone believed that an attack would not succeed. Sedgwick also thought that the "enemy occupied too strong a position for General Meade to attack."[60]

Did Wade prove this charge? The great weight of the evidence available to Wade, but not used, clearly shows that he did not. The damage that he was able to do was mostly attributable to his skillful editing techniques rather than facts.

59. Ibid., lxxii–lxxiii, 335–6; *LLM,* to his wife, March 6, 1864, 2:169. By March 8, 1864, Meade was convinced that members of the Committee on the Conduct of the War were conspiring with Doubleday and Sickles to have him removed from command. *LLM,* to his wife, March 8, 1864, 2:176.

60. *CCW,* 316, 462.

4) *Due to Meade's timidity and failures, he was not fit to command the Army of the Potomac.*

This was by far the most serious of the charges against Meade. The other three charges and their supporting arguments built to this one point: Meade was unfit to command the army. If proven, it was a direct call for Meade's removal from command. Wade did not shrink from strongly implying as much.

Following examinations of the Bristoe and Mine Run campaigns, Wade began his summation. He pointed out that the Army of the Potomac made no attacks during the time that Meade was in command. He also noted that once Grant was given control of the Army of the Potomac, he had begun a campaign that ultimately captured Richmond, destroyed Lee's army, and ended the war.[61]

Both the Bristoe and Mine Run campaigns had been ones of maneuvering for position; neither campaign saw a major battle, although contact with the enemy had been made during the Bristoe campaign. The Bristoe campaign had resulted in Lee withdrawing his army after a race for position which Meade had won. Unable to place the Federal forces in a position favorable for his attack, Lee had returned to his base. During the Mine Run campaign Meade had called off an attack that had been suggested by Warren. This had been done at Warren's own insistence when he discovered the enemy had strengthened his position and was waiting in great force for him.

Actually, in the roughly nine months of his command, Meade ordered three major attacks: July 3 at Gettysburg, July 14 at Williamsport, and December 1 during the Mine Run campaign. The attack at Gettysburg was called off after troops took too long to form up. At Williamsport, Lee had already slipped away before the attack could be made. The attack during the Mine Run campaign was canceled by Warren. While this hardly comprised a sterling record, it was not the utter passivity suggested by Wade.

Wade, while acknowledging that Gettysburg was "important in its results," seemed to belittle it as a purely defensive battle. Indeed, Gettysburg was an indication that Meade did not have the aggressiveness Wade and the committee thought necessary in an army commander. In addition, Wade's report indicated that the battle of Gettysburg was not followed up forcefully enough, and that Meade had failed to take the "necessary and practicable" steps "to reap the full fruits of the victory there gained." This echoed Hancock's testimony about

61. Ibid., lxxv.

the lack of a Union counterattack on July 3, "we shall never reap the just fruits of a victory until we do follow it up promptly." It is a justifiable criticism of Meade.[62]

Wade again drew on Warren's testimony to emphasize the "failure of the army of the Potomac, while under General Meade's command, to achieve and [*sic*] great and practical success over the enemy." While Warren included the caveat that Meade himself was not so much to blame as the officers under him for their failure to carry out his plans, he then listed various opportunities to attack that had been lost "by hesitating and waiting at the decisive points." In all, he detailed six missed opportunities; in the Gettysburg campaign, however, he mentioned only July 3 and July 12 at Williamsport. The events of July 3 and the absence of a counterattack have already been examined in detail. But could Meade have attacked at Williamsport? On the morning of July 12, much of the Army of the Potomac was still moving toward the Confederate lines around Williamsport. Contact was made with rebel skirmishers, units were deployed into battle lines, and the advance slowed even more. By late afternoon, the army was in line facing Lee's positions. At that time, Meade spoke to Humphreys about his plan for a reconnaissance in force the next morning. Given Meade's testimony of his willingness to attack without the benefit of a reconnaissance and his private admission to his wife that he hesitated, he probably could have attacked on July 13. At some point, however, he changed his mind, instead sending out reconnaissance to develop a picture of the enemy line. By 4:30 P.M. that day an attack had been put off until the next day. That was no doubt for the best. A hastily organized attack launched by only part of the army doubtless would have resulted in the disaster Meade had anticipated.[63]

Wade next turned to the notion that under Meade the army was discouraged and retained its effectiveness only because of the high intelligence of its rank and file. Wade cited Pleasonton's testimony that his cavalry did not have confidence in Meade's military ability. Birney felt the same about his corps, adding that Meade lacked resolve and avoided the responsibilities of his position. Howe thought the soldiers believed that Meade lacked the "zeal, activity, and energy necessary," although he allowed that the corps commanders probably thought Meade was "eminently qualified" for command of the army.[64]

62. Ibid., lxxv, 409.

63. Ibid., lxxii, lxxv, lxxvi, 396; Wainwright, *A Diary of Battle,* ed. Nevins, 259; *LLM,* to his wife, July 14, 1863, 2:134; *OR*, vol. 27, pt. 1, p. 91.

64. *CCW,* lxxvi.

Wade noted that several witnesses before the committee agreed that there was low morale in the army. This observation was largely correct, but Wade stopped a little short of a fair representation of the testimony. In addition to Howe, Pleasonton, and Birney, the committee heard from eight other officers who were with the Army of the Potomac during the Gettysburg campaign. One, Warren, believed that poor performances by the corps commanders—not Meade—lay behind the failures of the army and any resulting discouragement in it. None of the other seven officers were asked, and none volunteered, that the troops suffered from low morale.[65]

In his report, Wade saved the specter of McClellan for last. He cited Howe's testimony that most of the main officers in the Army of the Potomac, including Meade, were in sympathy with and influenced by McClellan. Birney testified that many officers still believed McClellan was the only man to command the army, though not as many as before. Doubleday was even more blunt, claiming that no man received decent treatment in the army who opposed slavery or who did not support McClellan. The evil visage of McClellan and his followers was resurrected as a symbol of much that was wrong with the army.[66]

Although McClellan still had many friends and political allies in the army, his popularity and influence had diminished greatly since the early years of the war and he was no longer the threat that Wade believed him to be. On November 8, 1864, McClellan had resigned his commission and left the army, at the same time losing the presidential election to Lincoln. His margin of defeat in the popular vote was about 10 percent (403,000 out of some four million votes cast). In the electoral college, McClellan's defeat was even more decisive; he carried only 3 states with 21 votes to Lincoln's 22 states and territories with 212 votes. The army vote was a runaway for the Republican ticket; 78 percent of the votes cast in the field went to Lincoln. In the Army of the Potomac, McClellan's old command and presumed power base, only 30 percent of the men voted for their former commander.[67]

Wade's use of witnesses' testimony is mixed. He presented Howe's testimony accurately. Howe seems to have seen conspiracies in the army's higher levels at every turn. With nothing concrete to support his suspicions, however,

65. Ibid., 388.

66. Ibid, lxxvi.

67. Stephen W. Sears, *George B. McClellan: The Young Napoleon* (New York: Da Capo Press, 1999), 485–6.

his impressions were based on what he called "certain sympathies, feelings, and considerations of action."[68]

Wade's treatment of Birney's testimony is more questionable. Birney's assertion that many of the principal officers in the Army of the Potomac thought McClellan was the "only general who should command this army" was taken out of context and did not accurately represent his testimony about McClellan's influence on the army under Meade. It came in reply to a question from Wade whether there was politics in the army and if the corps commanders supported each other enthusiastically. In a surprising assertion, Birney claimed not to believe there was "anything like politics" in the army. He then went on to say that several corps commanders, though not as many as Wade alleged, were very strong admirers of McClellan and felt that he should command the army. Even so, they supported each other and obeyed orders.[69]

Wade had no reason to misquote Doubleday, who was a bitter and disillusioned man when he appeared before the committee. Displaced from command of the First Corps, he had quit the army in the field and had served the rest of the war in Washington. Doubleday believed that the cause of all his troubles was George Meade.

Although Wade closed the report with a parting shot at the corps commanders, he had already completed his case against Meade. The hearings were not conducted as a trial and made no pretense of being one. Even given the lowered evidentiary standard of this sort of proceeding, and leaving aside information that has been uncovered by subsequent scholarship, an evaluation of all the testimony presented to the committee reveals the report for what it was—a highly biased effort by a man with his own agenda to destroy the career of another.

Why Wade chose to publish a report filled with innuendo, half-truths, and outright lies almost defies understanding. Was his hatred for West Point officers in general, and Democrats in particular, so intense that he would go to any lengths to root them out of the army? Such a base motivation seems unlikely, but it is not beyond the range of possibility.

Did Wade publish the report to help Daniel Sickles in his quest for vindication and recognition? This also seems unlikely. Sickles was not a particular friend of Wade and was already discredited in both the army and Congress.

68. *CCW*, 327–8.

69. Ibid., lxxvi, 375.

Wade used Sickles for his own ends insofar as their mutual interest coincided but otherwise had no reason to help him.

Did Wade believe that he was actually producing a fair and balanced report? Again, this is improbable. Wade had the full transcript available to him while drafting the report, and its inconsistencies, contradictions, and lies must have been just as obvious to him as to us.

In the end, Wade's motivation in publishing the report appears to have been essentially political. Wade knew that his final report was a powerful tool for putting himself and his views in the public eye, which was never a bad thing for a politician. (His previous report on the McClellan hearings had been published and sold as a pamphlet by the *New York Times.*) The Meade report could possibly enhance his chances for higher political office. Wade realized that a critical report on Meade would help to solidify his standing within the faction of radical Republicans. Although their influence was on the wane, they still represented a powerful segment in Congress, and their support would be valuable to him.[70]

Time, however, has passed its own judgment on Meade and on the hearings of the Joint Committee on the Conduct of the War. The once powerful and influential committee is now only an obscure blip on the changing screen of history, and the Meade hearings are not even that. George Gordon Meade, after a long military career, is remembered primarily for three days in July 1863, when he commanded the Union army in its pivotal victory at Gettysburg.

70. Trefousse, *Benjamin Wade,* 203.

Appendix

THROUGHOUT THE TESTIMONY various officers not appearing before the committee are referred to by the witnesses. Some of them are well known, while others are rather obscure. To assist both the novice and the student of Gettysburg, a list of those officers mentioned but not testifying, with a brief note on their command at the time of Gettysburg, is given below. All were with the Army of the Potomac unless otherwise noted.

MAJOR GENERAL RICHARD H. ANDERSON, CSA. Commander of Anderson's Division, A. P. Hill's Third Corps, Army of Northern Virginia.

BRIGADIER GENERAL JAMES JAY ARCHER, CSA. Commander of the Third Brigade, Heth's Division, A.P. Hill's Third Corps.

BRIGADIER GENERAL LEWIS ADDISON ARMISTEAD, CSA. Commander of Armistead's Brigade, Pickett's Division, Longstreet's First Corps. He was mortally wounded on Cemetery Ridge during Pickett's charge.

BRIGADIER GENERAL WILLIAM BARKSDALE, CSA. Commander of Barksdale's Brigade, McLaws's Division, Longstreet's First Corps. He was mortally wounded at the Peach Orchard on July 2.

BRIGADIER GENERAL JAMES BARNES. Commander of the First Division, Fifth Corps at Gettysburg, where he was wounded.

BRIGADIER GENERAL HENRY BAXTER. Commander of the Second Brigade, Second Division, First Corps.

Colonel Hiram Berdan. Commander of the First U.S. Sharpshooters. Nominally a part of the Second Brigade, First Division, Third Corps, Berdan operated independently and commanded both the First and Second Sharpshooters.

Colonel George H. Biddle. Commander of the Ninety-fifth New York, Second Brigade, First Division, First Corps.

Brigadier General John Buford. Commander of the First Division, Cavalry Corps. A truly outstanding cavalry leader, he died of typhoid fever on December 16, 1863, in Washington, D.C.

Major General Benjamin Franklin Butler. Best known for his actions as military governor of New Orleans, he was widely despised and derided as a criminal throughout the South. An incompetent general, he was so politically influential that Lincoln could not relieve him until 1865. He was not with the Army of the Potomac.

Brigadier General John Curtis Caldwell. Commander of the First Brigade, First Division, Second Corps.

Colonel Samuel S. Carroll. Commander of the First Brigade, Third Division, Second Corps.

Major General Darius Nash Couch. Commander of the Department of the Susquehanna and the Pennsylvania militia.

Brigadier General George Armstrong Custer. Commander of Second Brigade, Third Division, Cavalry Corps. An able cavalry commander, he was aggressive almost to a fault.

Brigadier General Lysander Cutler. Commander of the Second Brigade, First Division.

Brigadier General Joseph R. Davis, CSA. Commander of the Fourth Brigade, Heth's Division, Third Corps.

Lieutenant Colonel Rufus R. Dawes. Commander of the Sixth Wisconsin, First Brigade, First Division, First Corps.

Colonel Hannibal Day. Commander of the First Brigade, Second Division, Fifth Corps.

Major General John A. Dix. Commander of the Department of Virginia, with some 32,000 troops scattered along the coast. He was not with the Army of the Potomac.

Lieutenant General Richard Stoddert Ewell, CSA. Commander of the Second Corps of the Army of Northern Virginia.

Brigadier General Elon John Farnsworth. Commander of the First Brigade, Third Division, Cavalry Corps. He was goaded by Kilpatrick into a suicidal charge at Gettysburg, in which he was killed.

COLONEL JOSEPH W. FISHER. Commander of the Third Brigade, Third Division, Fifth Corps.

MAJOR GENERAL JOHN GRAY FOSTER. Commander of the Department of North Carolina. He also commanded a detachment of the Eighteenth Corps at St. Helena in the Department of the South. He was not with the Army of the Potomac.

COLONEL EDWARD B. FOWLER. Commander of the Eighty-fourth New York, also known as the Fourteenth Brooklyn, Second Brigade, First Division, First Corps.

MAJOR GENERAL WILLIAM HENRY FRENCH. Commander of the garrison at Harper's Ferry. He was placed in command of the Third Corps at Gettysburg after Sickles was wounded, replacing Major General David B. Birney.

BRIGADIER GENERAL JOHN WHITE GEARY. Commander of the Second Division, Twelfth Corps.

BRIGADIER GENERAL GEORGE HENRY GORDON. Commander of the First Division, Eleventh Corps for about three weeks during the pursuit of Lee's army.

BRIGADIER GENERAL CHARLES KINNAIRD GRAHAM. Commander of the First Brigade, First Division, Third Corps. At Gettysburg he was wounded in the head and captured at the Peach Orchard. He was exchanged in September 1863.

BRIGADIER GENERAL GEORGE SEARS GREENE. Commander of the Third Brigade, Second Division, Twelfth Corps.

BRIGADIER GENERAL DAVID MCMURTRIE GREGG. Commander of the Second Division, Cavalry Corps.

CAPTAIN JAMES A. HALL. Commander of the Second Maine Artillery Battery, First Corps Artillery Brigade.

MAJOR GENERAL HENRY WAGER HALLECK. General in chief of the army stationed in Washington.

COLONEL JAMES A. HARDIE. War Office staff.

LIEUTENANT FRANKLIN ARETAS HASKELL. Aide to General John Gibbon, commander of the Second Division, Second Corps.

BRIGADIER GENERAL WILLIAM HAYS. Commander of the Third Division, Second Corps. After Gettysburg he replaced the wounded Hancock in command of the Second Corps.

MAJOR GENERAL SAMUEL PETER HEINTZELMAN. Commander of the Twenty-second Corps and the Department of Washington, D.C. He was not with the Army of the Potomac.

Lieutenant General Ambrose Powell Hill, CSA. Commander of the Third Corps.

Major General Oliver Otis Howard. Commander of the Eleventh Corps.

Brigadier General Rufus Ingalls. Chief Quartermaster.

Brigadier General Hugh Judson Kilpatrick. Commander of the Third Division, Cavalry Corps.

Colonel David Lang, CSA. Commander of Perry's Florida Brigade, Anderson's Division, Third Corps.

Brigadier General Henry Hayes Lockwood. Commander of the Second Brigade, First Division, Twelfth Corps. One month shy of forty-nine, he was one of the oldest Federal general officers at Gettysburg.

Lieutenant General James Longstreet, CSA. Commander of the First Corps, Army of Northern Virginia.

Colonel William McCandless. Commander of the First Brigade, Third Division, Fifth Corps.

Brigadier General Solomon Meredith. Commander of the famous Iron Brigade, First Brigade, First Division, First Corps, at Gettysburg, where he was wounded.

Brigadier General Wesley Merritt. Commander of the Reserve Brigade, First Division, Cavalry Corps.

Major General Robert Huston Milroy. Commander of the Second Division, Eighth Corps, District of Winchester. In June 1863, Milroy was defeated by Ewell at Winchester, suffering heavy losses and abandoning many of his men, though a board of investigation cleared him of any blame. He was not with the Army of the Potomac.

Captain Alexander Moore. A member of Meade's staff.

Brigadier General Thomas Hewson Neill. Commander of the Third Brigade, Second Division, Sixth Corps.

Major General John Newton. Commander of the Third Division, Sixth Corps. He replaced Major General John Reynolds, taking command of the First Corps from Doubleday.

Major General John Pope. Commander of the Army of the James, predecessor of the Army of the Potomac.

Colonel Francis V. Randall. Commander of the Thirteenth Vermont, Third Brigade, Third Division, First Corps.

Captain George E. Randolph. Chief of Artillery, Third Corps.

MAJOR GENERAL JOHN FULTON REYNOLDS. Commander of the First Corps, he led the left wing of the Army of the Potomac. Killed on July 1, he was considered one of the best officers in the Union Army.

COLONEL JAMES C. RICE. Commander of the Forty-fourth New York, Third Brigade, First Division, Fifth Corps. He took command of the brigade from the mortally wounded Colonel Strong Vincent.

BRIGADIER GENERAL JOHN CLEVELAND ROBINSON. Commander of the Second Division, First Corps.

MAJOR GENERAL ROBERT C. SCHENCK. Commander of the Middle Department of Baltimore. He was elected to Congress while on sick leave and resigned from the army on December 5, 1863. At the time of the Meade hearings, Schenck was a member of Congress, where he became chairman of the committee on military affairs. Schenck was not with the Army of the Potomac.

MAJOR GENERAL CARL SCHURZ. Commander of the Third Division, Eleventh Corps.

MAJOR GENERAL HENRY WARNER SLOCUM. Commander of the Twelfth Corps, he led the right wing of the Army of the Potomac at Gettysburg.

BRIGADIER GENERAL JOHN POTTS SLOUGH. Military governor of Alexandria. He was not with the Army of the Potomac.

BRIGADIER GENERAL WILLIAM FARRAR "BALDY" SMITH. Commander of militia detachments in Couch's Department of the Susquehanna.

BRIGADIER GENERAL GEORGE JERRISON STANNARD. Commander of the Third Brigade, Third Division, First Corps, he was severely wounded at Gettysburg.

COLONEL ROY STONE. Commander of the Second Brigade, Third Division, First Corps.

MAJOR GENERAL GEORGE SYKES. Commander of the Fifth Corps.

BRIGADIER GENERAL HENRY DWIGHT TERRY. Terry replaced Major General John Newton when he was given command of the First Corps.

MAJOR HENRY TREMAIN. Aide-de-camp of Major General Daniel Sickles, commander of the Third Corps.

BRIGADIER GENERAL ISAAC RIDGEWAY TRIMBLE, CSA. Commander of Pender's Division. Wounded at Second Bull Run, upon his return to the army he was attached as an aide to Ewell. When Pender was wounded, Trimble was given command of Pender's division and led it in Pickett's charge, when he was again wounded and captured.

BRIGADIER GENERAL ROBERT O. TYLER. Commander of the Army of the Potomac's Artillery Reserve.

Colonel Strong Vincent. Commander of the Third Brigade, First Division, Fifth Corps until mortally wounded on July 2.

Brigadier General Alexander S. Webb. Commander of the Second Brigade, Second Corps.

Brigadier General Cadmus Marcellus Wilcox, CSA. Commander of a brigade in Anderson's Division, Third Corps.

Brigadier General Alpheus Starkey Williams. Commander of the First Division, Twelfth Corps.

Brigadier General Horatio Gouverneur Wright. Commander of the First Division, Sixth Corps.

Bibliography

Alexander, Edward Porter. *Military Memoirs of a Confederate: A Critical Narrative.* 1907. Reprint, New York: Da Capo Press, 1993.

Andrews, J. Cutler. *The North Reports the Civil War.* Pittsburgh: University of Pittsburgh Press, 1955.

Bache, Richard Meade. *Life of General George Gordon Meade: Commander of the Army of the Potomac.* Philadelphia: Henry T. Coates, 1897.

Bachelder, John D. *Map—Position of Troops—Third Day.* Boston: n.p., 1876.

Bauer, K. Jack. *The Mexican War, 1846–1848.* New York: Macmillan, 1974.

Benjamin, Charles F. "Hooker's Appointment and Removal." In *B&L.* 3:239–43.

Bigelow, John Jr. *Chancellorsville.* N.d. Reprint, New York: Konecky & Konecky, 1995.

Biographical Dictionary of the American Congress, 1774–1971. Washington, D.C.: GPO, 1971.

Boatner, Mark Mayo, III. *The Civil War Dictionary.* New York: Vintage, 1987.

Boritt, Gabor S. "Unfinished Work: Lincoln, Meade, and Gettysburg." In *Lincoln's Generals,* ed. Gabor S. Boritt. New York: Oxford University Press, 1994.

Brichford, Maynard. "Congress at the Outbreak of the War." *Civil War History* 3, no. 1 (March 1957).

Buell, Walter. "Zachariah Chandler." In three parts. *Magazine of Western History* 4, nos. 1, 3, and 4 (May, July, August 1886): 338–52, 432–44.

Busey, John W., and David G. Martin. *Regimental Strengths and Losses at Gettysburg.* Hightstown, N.J.: Longstreet House, 1994.

Butterfield, Julia Lorrilard. A *Biographical Memorial of General Daniel Butterfield.* New York: Grafton Press, 1904.

Byrne, Frank L., and Andrew T. Weaver, eds. *Haskell of Gettysburg.* Kent, Ohio: Kent State University Press, 1989.

Cleaves, Freeman. *Meade of Gettysburg.* Norman: University of Oklahoma Press, 1960.

Coddington, Edwin B. *The Gettysburg Campaign: A Study in Command.* New York: Charles Scribner's Sons, 1984.

Congressional Globe. 46 vols. Washington, D.C., 1834–1873.

Congressional Quarterly's Guide to Congress. 4th ed. Washington, D.C.: Congressional Quarterly, 1991.

Cowles, Captain Calvin D., comp. *The Official Military Atlas of the Civil War.* 1891–1895. Reprint, with an introduction by Richard Sommers. New York: Gramercy Books, 1983.

Craven, Avery. *The Coming of the Civil War.* Chicago: University of Chicago Press, 1957.

Dana, Charles. *Recollections of the Civil War.* 1898. Reprint, Lincoln: University of Nebraska Press, 1996.

Detroit Post and Tribune. *Zachariah Chandler: An Outline Sketch of His Life and Public Service.* Detroit: Detroit Post and Tribune Publishers, 1880.

Doubleday, Abner. *Chancellorsville and Gettysburg.* 1882. Reprint, with an introduction by Gary W. Gallagher, New York: Da Capo Press, 1994.

DuBois, James T., and Gertrude S. Mathews. *Galusha A. Grow: Father of the Homestead Law.* New York: Houghton Mifflin, 1917.

Fahrney, Ralph Ray. *Horace Greeley and the Tribune in the Civil War.* Cedar Rapids, Iowa: Torch Press, 1936.

Freeman, Douglas Southall. *R. E. Lee: A Biography.* 4 vols. New York: Charles Scribner's Sons, 1935.

Gallagher, Gary W., ed. *Two Eyewitnesses at Gettysburg: The Personal Accounts of Whitelaw Reid and A. J. L. Fremantle.* St. James, N.Y.: Brandywine Press, 1994.

George, Sister Mary Karl. *Zachariah Chandler: A Political Biography.* East Lansing: Michigan State University Press, 1969.

Gibbon, John. "The Council of War on the Second Day." In *B&L,* 3:313–4.

———. *Personal Recollections of the Civil War.* 1928. Reprint, Dayton, Ohio: Press of Morningside Bookshop, 1988.

Gorham, Charles C. *Life and Public Service of Edwin M. Stanton.* 2 vols. New York: Houghton Mifflin, 1899.

Grant, Ulysses S. *Personal Memoirs of U. S. Grant.* 1885. Reprint, New York: Konecky & Konecky, 1992.

Hancock, Almira R. *Reminiscences of Winfield Scott Hancock.* New York: Charles L. Webster, 1887.

Hebert, Walter H. *Fighting Joe Hooker.* Indianapolis: Bobbs-Merrill, 1944.

Higginson, Thomas Wentworth, "Regular and Volunteer Officers." *Atlantic Monthly* 14 (1864): 343–51.

Historicus. "The Battle of Gettysburg. Important Communication from an Eye Witness. How the Victory Was Won and How Its Advantages Were Lost. Generals Halleck's and Meade's Official Reports Refuted." *New York Herald,* March 12, 1864.

Holt, Michael F. "The Politician's War." In Kenneth M. Stampp, ed., *The Causes of the Civil War.* New York: Simon & Schuster, 1991.

Humphreys, Henry H. *Andrew Atkinson Humphreys: A Biography.* Philadelphia: John C. Winston, 1924.

Hunt, H. Draper. *Hannibal Hamlin of Maine: Lincoln's First Vice-President.* Syracuse, N.Y.: Syracuse University Press, 1969.

Hunt, Henry J. "The First Day at Gettysburg." In *B&L,* 3:255–84.

———. "The Second Day at Gettysburg." In *B&L,* 3:290–313.

———. "The Third Day at Gettysburg." In *B&L,* 3:369–85.

Hyman, Harold M. *A More Perfect Union: The Impact of the Civil War and Reconstruction on the Constitution.* New York: Alfred A. Knopf, 1978.

Ilisevich, Robert D. *Galusha A. Grow: The People's Candidate.* Pittsburgh: University of Pittsburgh Press, 1988.

Irwin, Richard B. "Ball's Bluff and the Arrest of General Stone." In *B&L,* 2:123–34.

Johnson, Robert U., and Clarence C. Buel, eds. *Battles and Leaders of the Civil War.* 4 vols. 1884–89. Reprint, New York: Thomas Yoseloff, 1956.

Jordan, David M. *Winfield Scott Hancock: A Soldier's Life.* Indianapolis: Indiana University Press, 1988.

Kennedy, J. C. G. *Population of the United States in 1860.* Washington, D.C.: GPO, 1864.

Ladd, David L., and Audrey J. Ladd, eds. *The Bachelder Papers.* Dayton, Ohio: Morningside House, 1994.

Lincoln, Abraham. *The Collected Works of Abraham Lincoln.* Ed. Roy P. Basler. 8 vols. New Brunswick, N.J.: Rutgers University Press, 1963.

Livermore, Thomas L. *Numbers and Losses in the Civil War in America, 1861–1865.* 1900. Reprint, Carlisle, Pa.: John Kallmann, 1996.

Longacre, Edward G. "Alfred Pleasonton: Knight of Romance." *Civil War Times Illustrated* 13 (1973): 12–23.

———. *The Cavalry at Gettysburg.* Lincoln: University of Nebraska Press, 1986.

Longstreet, James. "Lee in Pennsylvania." In *Annals of the War,* ed. Alexander K. McClure. 1879. Reprint, Edison, N.J.: Blue & Gray Press, 1996.

Lyman, Theodore, and George R. Agassiz, eds. *Meade's Headquarters, 1863–65: Letters of Colonel Theodore Lyman from the Wilderness to Appomattox.* Boston: Atlantic Monthly, 1922.

———, eds. *With Grant and Meade from the Wilderness to Appomattox.* Lincoln: University of Nebraska Press, 1994.

McClure, Alexander K., ed. *Annals of the War.* 1879. Reprint, Edison, N.J.: Blue & Gray Press, 1996.

McPherson, James M. *Battle Cry of Freedom: The Civil War Era.* New York: Oxford University Press, 1988.

———. *Ordeal by Fire: The Civil War and Reconstruction.* New York: Alfred A. Knopf, 1982.

Malone, Dumas, ed. *Dictionary of American Biography.* 11 vols. New York: Charles Scribner's Sons, 1936.

Marshall, Jeffery D., ed. *A War of the People: Vermont Civil War Letters.* Hanover, N.H.: University Press of New England, 1999.

Meade, George. The Battle of Gettysburg: From the *Life and Letters of George Gordon Meade,* ed. George Gordon Meade. 1924. Reprint, York, Pa.: First Capitol Antiquarian Book and Paper Market, 1988.

———. *Life and Letters of George Gordon Meade,* ed. George Gordon Meade. 2 vols. New York: Charles Scribner's Sons, 1913.

Morrison, James Lunsford Jr. "The United States Military Academy, 1833–1866: Years of Progress and Turmoil." Ph.D. diss., Columbia University, 1970.

Nofi, Albert A. *The Gettysburg Campaign, June–July 1863.* Conshohocken, Pa.: Combined Books, 1986.

Patterson, Gerard. "Daniel Butterfield." *Civil War Times Illustrated* 12 (1973): 13–9.

Pfanz, Harry W. *Gettysburg: The Second Day.* Chapel Hill: University of North Carolina Press, 1987.

Pierson, William Whatley, Jr. "The Committee on the Conduct of the War." *American Historical Review* 23 (1918): 550–76.

Pleasonton, Alfred. "The Successes and Failures of Chancellorsville." In *B&L,* 3:172–82.

Porter, Horace. *Campaigning with Grant.* 1897. Reprint, New York: Konecky & Konecky, 1992.

Presidential Elections 1789–1996. Washington, D.C.: Congressional Quarterly, 1997.

Register of the Officers and Cadets of the U.S. Military Academy. West Point, N.Y.: United States Military Academy, 1832–1835.

Reynolds, Donald E. *Editors Make War: Southern Newspapers in the Secession Crisis.* Nashville: Vanderbilt University Press, 1970.

Rhea, Gordon C. *The Battle of the Wilderness, May 5–6, 1864.* Baton Rouge: Louisiana State University Press, 1994.

Riddle, A. G. *The Life of Benjamin F. Wade.* Cleveland: William W. William, 1886.

Sandburg, Carl. *Abraham Lincoln: The Prairie Years and the War Years.* 1954. Reprint, New York: Harcourt Brace, 1982.

———. *Abraham Lincoln: The War Years.* 4 vols. New York: Harcourt Brace, 1939.

Sauers, Richard A. *A Caspian Sea of Ink: The Meade-Sickles Controversy.* Baltimore: Butternut and Blue Press, 1989.

Sears, Stephen W. *George B. McClellan: The Young Napoleon.* New York: Da Capo Press, 1999.

———, ed. *The Civil War Papers of George B. McClellan: Selected Correspondence, 1860–1865.* New York: Da Capo Press, 1992.

Sifakis, Stewart. *Who Was Who in the Civil War.* New York: Facts on File, 1988.

Stewart, George R. *Pickett's Charge: A Microhistory of the Final Attack at Gettysburg, July 3, 1863.* Boston: Houghton Mifflin, 1959.

Swanberg, W. A. *Sickles the Incredible.* 1956. Reprint, Gettysburg, Pa.: Stan Clark Military Books, 1991.

Tap, Bruce. *Over Lincoln's Shoulder: The Committee on the Conduct of the War.* Lawrence: University Press of Kansas, 1998.

Taylor, Emerson Gifford. *Gouverneur Kemble Warren: The Life and Letters of an American Soldier, 1830–1882.* New York: Houghton Mifflin, 1932.

Taylor, John M. *William Henry Seward: Lincoln's Right Hand.* Washington, D.C.: Brassey's, 1991.

Thomas, Benjamin P., and Harold M. Hyman. *Stanton: The Life and Times of Lincoln's Secretary of War.* New York: Alfred A. Knopf, 1962.

Trefousse, Hans L. *Benjamin Franklin Wade: Radical Republican from Ohio.* New York: Twayne, 1963.

———. "The Joint Committee on the Conduct of the War: A Reassessment." *Civil War History* 10 (1964), 5–19.

Tucker, Glenn. *Lee and Longstreet at Gettysburg.* Indianapolis: Bobbs-Merrill, 1968.

U.S. Congress. *Joint Committee on the Conduct of the War: Reports.* 3 vols. Washington, D.C.: Government Printing Office, 1865.

U.S. War Department. *The War of the Rebellion. A Compilation of the Official Records of the Union and Confederate Armies.* 128 vols. Washington, D.C.: Government Printing Office, 1880–1901.

Volpe, Vernon L. "Benjamin Wade's Strange Defeat." *Ohio History* 97 (1988): 122–32.

Wainwright, Charles S. *A Diary of Battle: The Personal Journals of Colonel Charles S. Wainwright, 1861–1865,* ed. Allan Nevins. Gettysburg, Pa.: Stan Clark Military Books, 1962.

Walther, Edward H. *The Fire Eaters.* Baton Rouge: Louisiana State University Press, 1992.

Warner, Ezra J. *Generals in Blue: The Lives of the Union Commanders.* Baton Rouge: Louisiana State University Press, 1964.

———. *Generals in Gray: The Lives of the Confederate Commanders.* Baton Rouge: Louisiana State University Press, 1959.

Williams, T. Harry. *Lincoln and the Radicals.* Madison: University of Wisconsin Press, 1941.

Winslow, Richard Elliot, III. *General John Sedgwick: The Story of a Union Corps Commander.* Novato, Calif.: Presidio Press, 1981.

Wise, Jennings Cropper. *The Long Arm of Lee.* 2 vols. 1915. Reprint, Lincoln: University of Nebraska Press, 1991.

Index